# Prescriptive Legal Positivism: Law, Rights and Democracy

Tom Campbell

UCL PRESS

# AUTHOR'S BIOGRAPHY

Tom Campbell is a graduate of the Universities of Glasgow and Oxford. He was Professor of Philosophy in the University of Stirling (1973–79), Professor of Jurisprudence at the University of Glasgow (1980–90) and Professor of Law at the Australian National University (1990–2001). He is currently Professorial Fellow in the Centre for Applied Philosophy and Public Ethics (CAPPE), an Australian Research Council Special Research Centre, at Charles Sturt University, Canberra. His principal books are *Adam Smith's Science of Morals*, (Allen & Unwin, 1970); *Seven Theories of Human Society* (OUP, 1981); *The Left and Rights* (Routledge and Kegan Paul, 1983); *Justice* (Macmillan, 1988/2001); and *The Legal Theory of Ethical Positivism* (Dartmouth, 1996). He is a Fellow of the Royal Society of Edinburgh and the Academy of the Social Sciences of Australia.

# Prescriptive Legal Positivism: Law, Rights and Democracy

**Tom Campbell**

UCL PRESS

First published in Great Britain 2004 by UCL Press
an imprint of Cavendish Publishing Limited, The Glass House,
Wharton Street, London WC1X 9PX, United Kingdom
Telephone: + 44 (0)20 7278 8000    Facsimile: + 44 (0)20 7278 8080
Email: info@uclpress.com
Website: www.uclpress.com

Published in the United States by Cavendish Publishing
c/o International Specialized Book Services,
5824 NE Hassalo Street, Portland,
Oregon 97213-3644, USA

Published in Australia by Cavendish Publishing (Australia) Pty Ltd
45 Beach Street, Coogee, NSW 2034, Australia
Telephone: + 61 (2)9664 0909    Facsimile: +61 (2)9664 5420



British Library Cataloguing in Publication Data

Campbell, Tom 1938–
Prescriptive legal positivism: law, rights and democracy
1 Legal positivism
1 Title
340.1'12

Library of Congress Cataloguing in Publication Data
Data available

Paperback ISBN 1-84472-022-5
Paperback ISBN 978-1-844-72022-4
Hardback ISBN 1-84472-023-4
Hardback ISBN 978-1-844-72023-1

1 3 5 7 9 10 8 6 4 2

Printed and bound in Great Britain

*To David Raphael,*
*mentor and friend*

# Acknowledgments

While these essays, published in various fora over the past 20 years, are almost entirely unchanged in content, an enormous amount of detailed work was required to prepare them for this publication. My warm thanks go to Mr Mike Bowern for his painstaking and thoughtful work on the text of this book. Any remaining errors are mine.

Grateful acknowledgment is given by this author and publisher to the editors, publishers and institutions of the material listed below, for their kind permission to reprint the articles included in this volume.

Chapter 2: 'The point of legal positivism', *King's College Law Journal,* Vol 9, 1998, 63–97, Oxford: Hart Publishing.

Chapter 3: 'The ethics of positivism', in *The Legal Theory of Ethical Positivism,* Aldershot: Ashgate/Dartmouth, 1996, 95–124.

Chapter 4: 'Legal positivism and political power', in A Vincent (ed), *Political Theory: Tradition and Diversity,* Cambridge: CUP, 1997, 172–92.

Chapter 5: 'Legislative intent and democratic decision making', in N Naffine, R Owens and J Williams (eds), *Intention in Law and Philosophy,* Aldershot: Ashgate/Dartmouth, 2001, 291–320.

Chapter 6: 'Judicial activism – justice or treason?', *Otago Law Review,* Vol 10, 2003, 307–26.

Chapter 7: 'The legalism of rights', in *The Left and Rights,* London: Routledge and Kegan Paul, 1983, 35–57.

Chapter 8: 'The individualism of rights', in *The Left and Rights,* London: Routledge and Kegan Paul, 1983, 83–102.

Chapter 9: 'Democracy, human rights and positive law', *Sydney Law Review,* Vol 16, 1994, 193–212, Sydney: The Law Book Company.

Chapter 10: 'Human rights: a culture of controversy', *Journal of Law and Society,* Vol 26, 1999, 6–22, Oxford: Blackwell.

Chapter 11: 'Incorporation through interpretation', in TD Campbell, KD Ewing and A Tomkins (eds), *Sceptical Essays on Human Rights,* Oxford: OUP, 2002, 79–101.

Chapter 12: 'Democracy in a world of global markets', in C Sampford and T Round (eds), *Beyond the Republic,* Sydney: Federation Press, 2001, 78–92.

Chapter 13: 'Legal positivism and deliberative democracy', *Current Legal Problems,* Vol 15, 1998, 68–92; Oxford: OUP.

Chapter 14: 'Democratic aspects of legal positivism', in TD Campbell and J Goldsworthy (eds), *Judicial Power, Democracy and Legal Positivism,* Aldershot: Ashgate/Dartmouth, 2000, 3–26.

Chapter 15: 'Legislating human rights', in L Wintgens, *Theory and Practice of Legislation: Essays in Legisprudence,* Aldershot: Ashgate/Dartmouth, 2004 (in press).

# Contents

# INTRODUCTION

1

# REPOSITIONING LEGAL POSITIVISM

This book brings together a selection of work dealing with theories of law, rights and democracy from a constitutional point of view. They seek a coming together of legal and political philosophy in a normative framework variously called 'the legal theory of ethical positivism', 'prescriptive legal positivism' or simply 'democratic positivism', depending on those aspects of the theory that are emphasised in the particular essay. The selection presents a (partial) political philosophy that focuses on how rights should be promoted through law in a democratic manner. It is hoped that the constitutional approach of prescriptive positivism will appeal to people with quite dissimilar political views on substantive issues. For this reason, it can be filled out in various ways to inform political philosophies ranging from radical individualism to highly communal versions of social democracy. Indeed, its central preoccupation is with mechanisms for resolving and living with conflict and disagreement in pluralistic and diverse societies. It is, however, uncompromising in its commitment to democracy and human rights and has its own particular slant on how these two ruling ideas of contemporary law and politics can be integrated in a mutually sustaining manner.

## DEVELOPING THE IDEAS

As anxieties about global terrorism, sporadic wars, increasing inequality, pervasive corruption and environmental degradation gather pace, our attention turns to basic questions of justice, rationality and good governance. In this context, a once unfashionable set of ideas about law and equality is re-emerging as a key ingredient of sustainable democracy and world peace. The linguistic vehicle for this set of ideas is the discourse surrounding the rule of law, the idea that governments ought to operate through and be subject to laws, and that other organisations and individuals must accept and obey these laws but are otherwise free to act as they think fit.

A particular version of the rule of law has to do with the governance of positive law or, more precisely, the governance of rules. According to legal positivism, the benefits of the rule of law require that the laws in question are existing general rules (that is, rules applying to particular classes of persons and actions) that are sufficiently clear and specific to enable members of a society to agree whether or not the rules have been followed or breached, even when they disagree about the desirability of the rules in question. It is this version of the rule of law that I call 'prescriptive legal positivism'.

The publishers of this book tried to dissuade me from having the words 'legal positivism' in the title. This is understandable. Legal positivism is generally identified as an arid, conservative theory of law that mistakenly presents the practice of law as the mechanical application of rules without thought to the consequences for human wellbeing and social justice in particular cases, focuses on the enforcement of these rules through the operations of sanctions, and postulates an unrealistic notion of sovereignty as the possession of unlimited power. Law, according to this negative stereotype of legal positivism, is variously a blunt instrument of open-ended social control, or a conservative device for stifling social progress.[1]

This is not an attractive picture, either morally or intellectually. Morally, legal positivism is seen as discouraging reliance on individual conscience and legitimating the ordering of society on the basis of threats and violence according to a master plan. Intellectually, legal positivism is held to misrepresent the principled discussions about justice that feature in the best legal reasoning, to overestimate the social efficacy of external sanctions, and to ignore the difficulty of making sense of sovereignty itself, let alone its attribution to 'the people'. Given this widely accepted negative image, it must be a good marketing strategy to banish 'legal positivism' from the title of any book and substitute some more benign term such as 'the rule of law' or, better still, 'human rights' or 'justice'.

Despite the fact that most of the essays in this book are about human rights and the rule of law, I resisted this advice because what is distinctive about these essays is the particular approach taken to these core concepts, an approach that stems in the main from the vision of law articulated in classical legal positivism, particularly in the work of Jeremy Bentham. What I take from this tradition is not the conceptual dogmatism of Bentham's disciple John Austin, for whom law is defined as the (general) commands of an (unlimited) sovereign power. Rather, I derive from classical legal positivism a prescriptive or normative model of a valuable type of law in which there is a coherent system of general rules that are clear, intelligible, specific, legitimated by the consent of those to whom they apply and enforced through a unitary hierarchy of impartial tribunals whose job it is to apply these rules to particular circumstances and review the consistency of government actions with the democratically enacted rules. Hence the title 'prescriptive legal positivism'.

In its Benthamite form, prescriptive legal positivism is a radical, indeed a revolutionary theory, both legally and politically. It provided, in the early 19th century, a powerful critique of the disorder, obscurity and conservatism of the common law and provided a key ingredient in the case for popular democracy as the legitimate source of a new legal order that would serve 'the greatest happiness of the greatest number'. Given this history, it is fascinating to note how, a century and a half later, legal positivism came to be widely regarded as a purely conceptual theory about the 'meaning' of law with highly conservative implications that prioritise 'black letter law' over issues of law reform and democratic progress.

---

1 For a recent discussion of this image, see AJ Sebok, 'Misunderstanding legal positivism', *Michigan Law Review*, Vol 93, 1995, 2054–132, reprinted in TD Campbell and A Stone, *Legal Positivism*, Aldershot: Ashgate/Dartmouth, 1999.

The explanations for such a turnaround in the image of legal positivism are complex. They include the emergence of appropriate moral concern for disadvantaged minorities in societies where 'the greatest number' are relatively well off, and the contingent association of legal positivism with extreme liberal conceptions of the role of the state that encourage and entrench social and economic inequality. Legal positivism has also come to be seen as a form of judicial false-consciousness, whereby the collective ideology of judiciaries is that courts 'discover' but do not 'make' law, which in practice serves to disguise and legitimate controversial and often oppressive judicial decisions that are in fact the exercise of judicial discretion.

Notwithstanding the plausibility of this analysis as applied to particular historical periods, the line of thought that has prompted most of the essays in this book is that a revised version of Benthamite positivism, which places the normative aspects of his approach above the conceptual and empirical elements, has considerable relevance to contemporary legal systems and democratic polities in ways that run counter to the perceived pernicious history of legal positivism and legal positivists.

The revisionary rehabilitation of legal positivism has to start with an awareness of the strong normative aspects running through the writings of Hobbes, Kant, Bentham, Austin and, more recently, Kelsen and Hart. Behind their conceptual preoccupations, each is strongly motivated by certain moral values and political concerns which is in no way at odds with the positivist mantra that we must always distinguish between law as it is and law as it ought to be. Without claiming that these paradigmatic positivists should be interpreted as full-blooded prescriptive positivists, there are sufficient normative ingredients in their theories on which to build a prescriptive legal positivism that takes conceptual analysis to be no more than a tool for moral argument and the empirical theses of classical positivism as establishing the possibility, rather than the actuality, of a truly positivist system of law.

There is a certain pleasure to be derived from re-presenting familiar theories in a new, and perhaps exciting, guise. Fascination with historical and philosophical reconfiguring of the ideological associations of social theories grew out of my doctoral studies on the moral theory of Adam Smith.[2] Smith, despite his massive influence on the development of market economics and the minimal state, expounded a social theory of morality whose egalitarian and interventionist implications were profound and far-reaching for his time. Smith's support for free basic education and strong controls over business practice are well known, but it is not, perhaps, appreciated that these apparent anomalies flow from his general theory of the social nature of human beings and the significance of rooting social institutions in what he called 'the moral sentiments' as derived from the experience of socialisation in human development.

Studying the gap between the reputation and the reality of Adam Smith's economic and social theory was interesting in itself. Even more interesting was the

2 TD Campbell, *Adam Smith's Science of Morals*, London: George Allen & Unwin, 1971.

realisation that, despite the natural law ambience of much of his work and his devotion to classical Greek philosophy, at base the normative aspects of Smith's theory are utilitarian, not so much with respect to its psychological egoism (of which Smith has a very socialised version), but in relation to its foundational moral premise. Smith's commitment to the general wellbeing is epistemologically grounded in our unshakeable preference, from an impartial position in which our own wellbeing is not at stake, for the happiness over the unhappiness of 'any sentient being'. Smith may not be a prescriptive or practicing utilitarian, for he questions our ability to act directly to maximise the general happiness when our own welfare is involved, but he is a 'contemplative utilitarian', in that his evaluations of social situations as desirable or undesirable are ultimately based on judgments of comparative human wellbeing.[3]

Further, it was through Smith's analysis of the emergence of conscience in the life of a socialised individual that I became interested in the multiple and essential role of rules in an orderly, prosperous and just human society. On Smith's analysis, moral rules are generated by generalisations as to what gains the approval and disapproval of disinterested spectators, a process in which we all participate in the course of our moral development and education. Humans learn to use these generalisations to predict how others will react to our conduct, so enabling us to avoid censure and punishment, and obtain praise and reward. In this process, we learn to view our own conduct from the point of view of the observers of our conduct – the impartial spectators – and so, through sympathy and imagination, come to blame or praise ourselves, hence the phenomenon of conscience or 'the man within'.[4] While this process produces self-directed or autonomous human beings, this does not mean that individuals can or should follow their own sentiments when deciding how to act. This is because, in the moment of action, we tend to self-partiality so that, as participants, we inevitably fail to adopt the impartial point of view. Therefore, rules are to be strictly followed in practice because they prevent us being misled by inevitable self-preference of the agent and enable us instead to act in ways that secure the approval of others and, in retrospect, the approval of our own conscience. For this reason, rules which are contingent in origin are necessary in practice. Moreover, these rules are not subject to market negotiation but are moral prerequisites of acceptable economic conduct that contributes to a system that works for the maximisation of human wellbeing.

The study of Adam Smith's moral and social theory fostered in me a sceptical attitude towards the ideological pigeon-holing of our inherited social and political theories. If the acknowledged founder of rationalist economics is at base a social welfare theorist, then it is well to be open-minded about the possibility of transcending the orthodox battle-lines of competing social and political philosophies.

---

3 See TD Campbell, 'Scientific explanation and ethical justification in *The Moral Sentiments*', in AS Skinner and T Wilson (eds), *Essays on Adam Smith*, Oxford: Clarendon Press, 1975, 68–82.

4 Adam Smith, *The Theory of Moral Sentiments*, 6th edn, London: A Strahan, 1790, Vol 1, 321: 'the supposed impartial and well-informed spectator … the man within the breast, the great judge and arbiter of their conduct.'

This scepticism extended to a recognition of the limited significance of the philosophical fashions of post-World War II analytical philosophy. I accepted, and still accept, the logical positivist critique of the *a priori* synthetic. There are no substantial truths that are conceptually necessary and it is a mistaken philosophical goal to seek to discover such *a priori* truths. Detached conceptual analysis is the articulation of (sometimes useful) tautologies, but not a source of knowledge in itself.

On the other hand, it seemed both under- and over-ambitious to concentrate exclusively on the Wittgensteinian strategy of analysing ordinary language in the context of its social operations. The reduction of analysis to explicating the subtleties of ordinary language in its workaday settings, while often illuminating and useful in dissolving some sorts of philosophical puzzles, is not the be-all and end-all of legitimate philosophical ambition. Further, the idea that philosophy is a purely 'meta' or 'second-order' activity that cannot be directly involved in 'first-order' or substantive moral and political issues is under-ambitious, as the subsequent re-emergence of applied philosophy has demonstrated.

However, it is a mistake to claim that such ordinary language analysis can set authoritative benchmarks for conceptual propriety or take us very far in understanding the social realities of which such discourses are a crucial part. Such extravagant claims for sociologically-oriented analytical techniques are clearly over-ambitious, although they can be suggestive and certainly contributed much to the persuasiveness of HLA Hart's *The Concept of Law*.[5] Conceptual analysis I take to be an important subordinate methodology within either descriptive, explanatory or normative discourses.

These methodological starting points opened the way for endorsing the sort of applied moral philosophy familiar to me through my 18th century studies and rekindled through the impact of John Rawls and his successors,[6] and provided further encouragement for sceptical critique of dogmatism in social and political theory together with an openness to creative reconstruction of traditional understandings of the conceptual packages on offer.

An early example of this approach is my critique of one of the key assumptions in Rawls's theory of justice. 'Justice', according to Rawls, 'is the first virtue of social institutions'.[7] It seemed to me that this does not accord with our moral intuitions, appeals to which feature centrally in Rawlsian methodology. It is not difficult to identify social situations in which we think that other virtues, such as kindness or truthfulness, should take precedence over the pursuit of justice, even when considering which foundational social institutions we wish to have. Nor does the automatic priority of justice accord with the discourse of justice in its standard

---

5 Such as his distinction between having an obligation and being obliged – *The Concept of Law*, Oxford: Clarendon Press, 1961.

6 And, of course, his predecessors, particularly DD Raphael, then Professor of Politics at the University of Glasgow, supervisor of my PhD.

7 J Rawls, *A Theory of Justice*, Oxford: OUP, 1971, 3: 'Justice is the first virtue of social institutions, as truth is of systems of thought.'

social contexts, where justice is routinely held in a balance with other considerations without raising questions of impropriety. Putting these two considerations together, we may ask what sort of family life or community it would be if the priority consideration were always to be achieving justice.

This would not matter if Rawls were simply indicating a postulate of his theory with no independent epistemological or philosophical significance. However, when he comes to formulate his (and by implication our) moral intuitions about justice, he uses the assumption to confront us with the question as to what considerations we would put first in order of priority when designing the basic institutions of our society. This is a fair question, but is it a question about justice? Or, to put it another way, can he assume that we would always put considerations of justice first in answering such a question as to our priorities?

Again, this would not matter as long as we keep clear in our minds the contingent conceptual assumption that is being made, but this is quickly lost sight of when it comes to such questions as whether justice can be analysed in terms of merit or desert. In fact, one of the most enduring beliefs about justice is that it has something to do with treating people according to their deserts. However, on the Rawlsian assumption about the priority of justice, it is difficult to analyse justice in terms of desert, for treating people according to their deserts is an implausible candidate for being an overriding social value. The effect of excluding desert from justice (for which Rawls himself has other arguments) is to cut the theory off from the discourse of justice as it actually operates in real (that is, practical and everyday) social and political arguments. While, of course, that discourse does not itself have probative value in relation to the scope of the concepts and values involved, it is unhelpful and confusing to develop a political theory of justice that is so far removed from the ordinary language of justice, especially if you are using an idiosyncratic conceptual assumption to generate the moral intuitions on which the theory is based.

Thinking laterally on the matter, it seemed better, pragmatically, intellectually and morally, to acknowledge a deeply rooted social assumption connecting justice with desert, but contest the thesis that people getting what they deserve is an overriding social or institutional value. Pragmatically, this fits better with the ordinary discourse of justice, thus facilitating effective communication. Intellectually, it avoids making a controversial assumption at the basis of a general theory of social values. Morally, it leaves open the possibility of articulating the morally preferable thesis that the virtue of humanity, conceived of as a compassionate concern for the alleviation of human suffering, ought in many circumstances to take priority over justice, justice being conceived of as the righting of wrongs done by some human beings to others.[8]

This meritorian theory of justice set a pattern of presenting apparently conservative theories (such as that justice is a matter of desert) as potentially

---

8 See TD Campbell, 'Humanity before justice', *British Journal of Political Science*, Vol 4, 1974, 51–63.

quite radical, both in what it can be used to affirm (that in certain areas, such as criminal law, it is a moral requirement not to punish innocent people or inflict punishment beyond that which is deserved), and what it can be used to deny (that we have no obligations to those whom we have not harmed). Moreover, in its attempt to define justice in a relatively precise manner, it manifests one of the virtues of prescriptive legal positivism, that we should attempt to reach agreement on the meaning of key terms at a level of specificity at which they have some useful meaning. In the case of justice, once detached from the concept of desert, the word becomes a free-floating term to which we can give such content as our moral commitments suggest, which weakens its usefulness in clarifying policy issues.

This extended example of the sometimes rather mischievous but happily liberating methodology at work in this collection of essays illustrates both the style and the purpose that characterises them. The objective is not conceptual innovation for its own sake, but a form of creative analytical re-ordering that enables the articulation of political views that serve a progressive purpose in contemporary contexts by drawing on traditional ideas and deploying them in novel ways to meet changing circumstances. Thus, legal positivism is represented as a prescriptive theory whose multiple justifications for the governance of rules offers partial solutions to many of the problems brought forth by our current social and political circumstances. This approach enables us to draw effectively on ideas and practices that are deeply rooted in our philosophical history while adapting them to meet our current circumstances. It is a technique I have sought to deploy in relation to justice, rights, democracy and law.

Cumulatively, the essays present the working out of a political philosophy grounded in an egalitarian form of humanitarianism that, contrary to the usual juxtaposition of utilitarianism and rights, actually requires instantiation in a system of rights. Rights are taken to combine an emphasis on the identification of prime human interests and a commitment to protecting and realising these interests through adopting and sustaining a system of positive rules on which public entitlements are based. In this system, rules – that is, general but specific prescriptions of conduct – have a form that is conducive to impartial decision-making and administration and a content that is democratically determined.

There is, therefore, a supportive relationship between rights, law and democracy that is theoretically mediated by a prescriptive form of legal positivism according to which a desirable system of law consists of specific rules that can be understood, followed and applied without recourse to controversial moral judgments. Such positive rules provide the basis for rights claims and remedies within that society. Some of the benefits of positivist legal systems (such as predictability and certainty) are not confined to democracies, but others (such as enhancing the impartiality of political debate and decision-making, and maximising democratic accountability) can arise only within democratic polities. For this reason, in its more developed forms, I use the term 'democratic positivism' to refer to the general theory of law and politics whose formulation is progressively outlined in these essays.

## LAW

At its strongest, my thesis is that the contemporary pariah image of legal positivism is an ideologically motivated caricature that neglects its role in democratic theory and seeks to undermine the democratic process by questioning the legitimacy of popular rule and setting up devices for thwarting the sovereignty of the people. Putting it more mildly, the misrepresentation of legal positivism cuts us off from some valuable lines of thought for the development of our legal and political goals by irrationally excluding certain alternatives.

The essays in Part I of the book seek to articulate and defend another, more favourable, interpretation of legal positivism as one ingredient of a theory that brings together the virtues of rules and the virtues of democracy. It opens with a relatively recent essay, 'The Point of Legal Positivism', that presents an overview of the theory presented at greater length as 'ethical positivism' in *The Legal Theory of Ethical Positivism,* a term that I chose in preference to the ambiguous 'normative positivism', which is applied to positivist theories – like that of HLA Hart – that take norms as the object of investigation, in contrast to those – like Scandinavian realism – that reduce norms to brute (or non-institutional) facts.[9]

Having identified ethical legal positivism in the technical terms of the day as a form of prescriptive hard legal positivism, that is, as asserting that a rule of recognition (HLA Hart's term for the rule that determines what is and what is not law), as well as other legal norms, ought not to contain moral terms, the essay goes on to distinguish legal positivism from logical positivism, particularly with respect to the logical positivist rejection of the objectivity – even the meaningfulness – of moral discourse.[10] Some legal positivists have been logical positivists in this respect, but most have adhered to the idea of moral truth, while making sure to distinguish between morality and fact, between what ought to be the case and what is the case – a distinction that some claim to be the very essence of legal positivism.

The essay then summarises the moral and practical reasons why we should adopt prescriptive hard positivism. These reasons are all types of rule rationale, covering the utility of socially recognised rules for behavioural control and co-ordination, the requirement of justice that like cases be treated alike, the ideal of liberty which requires that we know in advance the legal consequences of our action, and the role of rules in the limitation and monitoring of state action, through empowerment of those who have the right to govern and as a device for encouraging that power to be used in an equitable and transparent manner. All

---

9 In addition to the references to be found in the ensuing chapters, it is worth mentioning subsequent contributions of considerable importance in this area: GJ Postema, 'Jurisprudence as practical philosophy', *Legal Theory*, Vol 4, 1998, 328; SJ Shapiro, 'Law, morality and the guidance of conduct', *Legal Theory*, Vol 6, 2000, 127; J Waldron, *Law and Disagreement*, Oxford: OUP, 1999; L Alexander and E Sherwin, *The Rule of Rule: Morality, Rules and the Dilemmas of Law,* Durham, NC and London: Duke University Press, 2001.

10 As in AJ Ayer, *Language, Truth and Logic*, Harmondsworth: Penguin, 1936.

these considerations point to the need for precise rules, the independence of rule-making from rule application, and the existence of rule-governed democratic process. These arguments, developed from the work of Hobbes, Smith, Rousseau, Kant, Bentham, Hart, Fuller, Raz, Schauer and Waldron, are elaborated and defended in different ways throughout this book, as are the practical implications of adopting the theory, also surveyed in this opening chapter.

Although I now tend to use the term 'prescriptive legal positivism' (or sometimes, to distinguish it from the authoritarian Hobbesian tradition, 'democratic positivism') instead of 'ethical positivism', this is a loss in so far as the label 'ethical positivism' helps to bring out an important aspect of the theory, namely the thesis that a legal system conforming to the ideals of prescriptive legal positivism cannot operate without ethical practices governing the behaviour of those who administer and those who are subject to the system. The commitment to rule-governance cannot itself be completely rule-governed and, with respect to judicial authority in particular, cannot be itself legally enforced. The ethical preconditions of legal positivism is the theme of the second chapter, 'The Ethics of Positivism'. The term 'ethics' is particularly appropriate here as it relates to the moral rights, duties and virtues that relate to the roles that people fill as legislators, judges, lawyers, police and citizens within a legal system. Legislators must make genuine and sincere efforts to enact rules that are clear, precise, specific and prospective, judges must endeavour to apply these rules as expression of the intention of the legislators even when they disagree with their content, lawyers must not ignore or wilfully misinterpret the rules for their own or their clients' benefit, police must show the same good faith in their understanding and application of the rules that govern their conduct, and citizens have an ethical duty to abide by the laws and not seek to advantage themselves by self-serving misreadings of what is required of them.

In this chapter, the limits and force of these ethical obligations are explored, particularly in relation to lawyers, whose exalted self-image is contrasted to their sleazy reputation, and judges, whose integrity in excluding their personal and collective preferences for particular types of outcome is an unenforceable ethical duty on which the rule of positive law depends. Some attention is given to the right course of action where there is genuine doubt as to the meaning and application of (perhaps formally defective) rules, an issue that is taken up at more length in later chapters. The point is made, however, that the ethical commitments required by prescriptive positivism fall initially on the creators of law – the legislatures – and indirectly, therefore, on the voters, whose representatives are the legislators and all residents in the society to whom the laws apply. Prescriptive legal positivism is in the first instance a theory of legislation rather than a theory of adjudication. The temptation for legislators is to fudge the difficult choices that have to be made in order to enact clear rules rather than messy compromises. The more positive ethical duty of legislators is to enter in good faith into debate and decision about what rules there are to be, appreciating the significance of what I call the 'moral form argument' for rule-governance, namely that deciding on rules rather than particular circumstances confronts us directly with determining what distinctions are morally important.

The remaining chapters in Part I develop these themes in different ways. Chapter 3 addresses the concepts of judicial and political power. The sometimes rather technical argument rejects a distinction between judicial and political power that is based on the contrast of *de jure* (legal) and *de facto* (political) power, since authority is an essential ingredient of political as well as legal power, and accepts that judicial power often has both *de jure* and *de facto* political aspects. However, crucially, legal power need not have the autonomy to impose its will on unwilling others, a feature that is essential to political power. Without endorsing the conceptual thesis that the more circumscribed legal power, the more distinctively legal it is, it is contended that this conjunction represents an ideal form of the separation of 'powers'.

Applying this analysis to constitutional issues, it is accepted that supreme courts must have ultimate *de facto* power to determine constitutional cases but that this does not give them *de jure* power to determine, for instance, the mode of interpretation that they use in deciding such cases. For constitutions to work, courts must have *de facto* power to make such determinations without being subject to legislative override, but this does not mean that how they carry out this task cannot be an abuse of judicial power. The idea of constitutional law requires that courts have the last say on what the constitution is to mean and how it applies to particular circumstances, but this does not mean that how they carry out this task cannot be subjected to politically appropriate moral criticism of how they carry out a role whose correct performance is, in the end, a matter of trust.

These themes are developed in Chapter 4 in relation to the vexed concept of legislative intent and the theories of statutory interpretation that depend upon it. The bald contention is that legislatures have a duty to legislate, judiciaries have a duty to interpret legislation, and citizens have the right to act on the assumption that legal rights and obligations can be identified through the contextually plain meaning of the words enacted as law. In other words, the legislative intent that matters from the point of view of determining how legislation is to be interpreted is a normative conception to the effect that a legislature should be taken to intend the contextually plain meaning of the words adopted as law. Here, 'contextually' means the type of social circumstances to which the legislation is addressed. This thesis is located in the discourse of philosophical theories of meaning and competing theories of statutory interpretation, but is justified in terms of preferred functions of law and the need to trace the legitimacy of legal obligations to their democratic origins.

This discussion of legislative intent provides a concrete theory of statutory interpretation to explicate the implications of prescriptive legal positivism. It also illustrates the way in which conceptual analysis alone cannot solve problems that are essentially moral and political but does serve to make manifest the alternative conceptual schemes available to normative (or explanatory) theory. It also illustrates the way in which an apparently conservative conceptualisation – in this case the apparently originalist notion of legislative intent – can be justified on the basis of its radical potential, in this case through greater empowerment of democratically legitimated change. This approach may not seem radical to activist judges intent on using their position to bring about what they regard as desirable social changes, but conservatism with respect to the judicial role is not to be equated with political conservatism.

The final chapter in Part I is developed from a polemical lecture on 'judicial activism' that uses Australian examples to draw attention to the constitutional dangers arising not only out of the activities of maverick judges who seek to develop the law according to their own political ideals, but also those liberal theories of interpretation, most clearly expressed in Ronald Dworkin's enticing theory of making the law 'the best that it can be' that gives intellectual legitimation to the judicial activism which, however well-meaning, threatens the basis of political responsibility for the content of law.[11] This is a theme that is taken up again in Part III, which deals with the issue of how human rights ought to be protected and enhanced through law in a democracy.

## RIGHTS

Prior to developing the theory of prescriptive legal positivism, it was the concept of rights that featured centrally in my work.

Through the 1970s, with the Cold War still pervading international relations and socialist foundations for the welfare state still a credible political position in western democracies, the gathering strength of human rights discourse in association with the still weak but hopeful growth of the United Nations, the idea of human rights presented a difficult challenge to those who were in favour of the concept of a universal welfare state underpinned by a strong democratic process that had brought about impressive social reforms, such as the abolition of capital punishment, the decriminalisation of homosexual practices, anti-discrimination law, and a measure of racial and gender equality, as well as full employment, a national health service and universal free education in most western states. Were rights to be viewed as a revival of individualistic liberalism of the sort that had held back the development of collective organisation and the emergence of the welfare state, or were they a powerful means to bring about further racial and gender equality? Were rights to be seen as part of the ideology of rampant capitalism reasserting itself against social democracy or a means for ensuring that the horrors of the Holocaust would never be repeated?

In this context, my work on rights was part of the search for a 'third way' between liberal capitalism and welfare socialism. *The Left and Rights: A Conceptual Analysis of the Idea of Socialist Rights*, published in 1983, sought to detach the idea of rights from the sort of bourgeois ideology critiqued by Karl Marx and demonstrate its compatibility with an acceptable vision of a socialist utopia capable of expressing the goals of social democracy. This was accomplished by combining a quasi-legalistic conception of rights, in which assertions of moral rights were interpreted as implying demands for the implementation of rules that could legitimate and guarantee certain expectations regarding interpersonal

11 R Dworkin, *Law's Empire*, London: Fontana, 1986. Dworkin himself, rather idiosyncratically, defines 'judicial activism' as unprincipled judicial decision-making.

conduct, with a version of the 'interest theory' of rights to the effect that a right is, or ought to give rise to, a rule-protected interest. The individualistic associations of the interest theory were loosened by an analysis of 'interest' that detached it from a pure notion of self-interest to include what individuals are legitimately 'interested in', including their role in promoting the wellbeing of others.

*The Left and Rights* was widely read but has long been out of print. For this reason, two of its key chapters dealing with the analysis of rights are reproduced here. The first, Chapter 6 of this volume, deals at some length with the arguments for the rule of law, expressed there in terms of formal justice. It does not include the important associated discussion denying, in principle, the necessary connection between rule governance and coercion which was the basis of one of the central Marxist critiques of liberal law and rights. The second, Chapter 7 in this volume, is a discussion of the 'interest' as against the 'will' theory of rights, according to which a right exists when the right holder can require the performance of, or waive, the duty that is correlative to the right in question. Following HLA Hart's presentation of Bentham's interest theory of rights, and Neil MacCormick's work on children's rights,[12] I argue that the will theory fits only a sub-category of rights – 'option rights' – and thus inadmissibly blocks the articulation of important welfare rights. More generally, the will theory fallaciously generalises from a particular instrumental aspect of some rights (giving power to a right holder over the conduct of others) to the conclusion that all rights are to be justified in terms of expressing freedom of choice.

Later in that book and in the ensuing years I wrote on a number of specific rights and the difficulties involved in reaching agreement on their content at a level of specificity that determines the moral and political issues at stake when deciding what constitutes, for instance, the right to work,[13] or the right to freedom of expression.[14] It was the epistemological questions arising within such debates that led me to be convinced that constitutional provisions for protecting abstractly expressed rights through judicial review of legislation was an ineffective and ultimately damaging instrument from the point of view of human rights. In the two remaining chapters of Part II, this case is presented, first in relation to the period of the Mason Court in Australia, which utilised the concept of implied constitutional rights to read the right of political communication into a constitution whose creators had explicitly rejected the bill of rights approach to rights protection. This is an interesting example, as the constructed implied right was used to strike down a (not very radical) attempt to control the impact of money on the electoral process by restricting political advertising during election periods.

The second chapter deals with the compromise solution, introduced to the UK through the Human Rights Act 1998, whereby courts can issue 'Declarations of

---

12 DN MacCormick, 'Rights in legislation', in PMS Hacker and J Raz (eds), *Law, Morality and Society*, Oxford: Clarendon Press, 1977.

13 *The Left and Rights*, Chapter 9.

14 'Free speech rationales', in TD Campbell and W Sadurski (eds), *Freedom of Communication*, Aldershot: Dartmouth, 1994, 17–44.

Incompatibility' that do not invalidate legislation but enable Parliament to fast-track appropriate amendments to the legislation that the court deemed incompatible with the European Convention on Human Rights. More importantly, in practice, courts are required to interpret legislation to render it compatible, 'if possible', with the Convention Rights. The chapter explains how courts, when they wish, are able to use this 'interpretation clause' to rewrite legislation in a way that goes far beyond any conception of statutory interpretation that seeks to determine the intention of Parliament. This explains why it is sometimes thought that the Human Rights Act incorporates the European Convention on Human Rights, as if UK courts have been empowered to directly apply the Convention rather than merely use it as a basis for 'interpretation' and Declarations of Incompatibility.

## DEMOCRACY

The issue of court-centred bills of rights is central to the discussions of democracy that constitute Part III. One of the most difficult connections to break in the minds of human rights supporters is between the goal of promotion of human rights and the particular means of using judicial power to invalidate legislation of the basis of their perceived violations of constitutionally entrenched bills of rights. This particular instrument for promoting human rights has come to be seen as a litmus test for commitment to human rights as such. This has happened despite the well known fact that such judicial review of legislation is a direct violation of the human right to share equally in the choice of government and hence the choice of laws. The incredulity expressed in legal academia at the combination of a commitment to furthering human rights and a rejection of court-administered bills of rights is prevalent enough to warrant explanation. It may well have something to do with the attraction that enhancing the power of courts holds for those who aspire to study and advise courts on how they should handle such powers.

When reasons are given in favour of court-administered bills of rights, central amongst these is the thesis that electoral democracy is in practice deficient and needs a countervailing judicial power to protect minorities against the majority of voters and to protect us all against untrustworthy politicians. It is this argument that takes us to the third main topic of this book, theories of democracy. My general position is sketched in Chapter 12, which tackles democratic theory in the context of globalisation.

The theory of democracy offered is an amalgam of the Benthamite justification that citizens have a measure of self-protection through using representative democracy to produce an artificial harmony of interests between representatives desiring to be re-elected and voters electing those who are to represent them. This is the simplistic market model of democracy that supporters of court-administered bills of rights attribute to their opponents. It is the model that most evidently raises the problem of how the interests of those who lose out in the electoral process are to be protected. This is where the idea of entrenched rights administered by courts is introduced as the counter-majoritarian device.

There are, however, other approaches to minority rights. One of these approaches is the deliberative theory of democracy that places reliance on the development of consensus through public debate as to what constitutes the public good, a debate in which all affected have an equal right to participate. I argue that such an idealistic approach to democracy can never take the place of the raw power of majority voting, but that it can serve to mitigate the problem of selfish majorities, particularly if the public debate is centred on the general rules that are to be authoritative in that society. This analysis brings together deliberative democracy and the moral form rationale for the governance of rules outlined above.

This association of legal positivism and deliberative democracy is developed in the subsequent chapter, going into more detail with respect to the work of Jurgen Habermas and examining his ambivalent attitude towards the role of judiciaries in democratic polities that embody his ideals. The concept of 'democratic positivism' is explicitly formulated in the next chapter ('Democratic Aspects of Legal Positivism'), which presents the by now familiar rationales for rule governance in the light of their role in constituting an acceptable model of democracy. This is explored in response to a number of critiques of the legal theory of prescriptive positivism. One such critique is that the theory wrongly assumes the existence of a sufficiently homogeneous common language and way of life to make effective communication possible. In the absence of such communality, it is argued, we cannot hope to create and administer positivistically good legislation or distinguish judicial activism from judicial fidelity to law. Similar problems relate to the threshold of conformity required for the governance of rules to produce its promised benefits.

Such difficulties are treated as an occasion for exploring further devices for improving democratic systems. One of these is accepting a degree of court-centred judicial review with respect to legislative principles such as the formal characteristics of generality, clarity and specificity, perhaps extended to a requirement for effective deliberation, consultation and disclosure, despite the evident dangers of judicial abuse of any delaying power that they might wield in such a process.

In a final chapter another tack is explored, whereby quasi-constitutional status is given to 'human rights legislation', such as racial discrimination laws, that is enacted specifically to promote human rights. Such legislation could be protected from implied amendment through the interpretation of subsequent legislation, and special majorities or procedures might be required for its amendment. Another device proposed to place human rights more centrally on the democratic agenda is a democratically endorsed bill of rights that is not directly justiciable but has a constitutional role through entrenched parliamentary procedures that enable a human rights committee of a Parliament to delay legislation that they deem to be a potential violation of the 'democratic bill of rights'. Such a bill of rights could provide the educational and nation-building role sometimes ascribed to court-administered bills of rights, and serve to legitimise giving enhanced powers to special constituted human rights committees.

## WORK IN PROGRESS

Several elements of democratic legal positivism require further development and refinement. There is a need to demonstrate that abstract statements of human rights are capable of being systematically translated into specific rules of a sort that would make positivistically good human rights legislation. There is also an enormous challenge in considering how to achieve more broadly based participation in public dialogue concerning the rules that we have to have to realise a formally good positivist system. Then there is the problem of attaining, through education, persuasion and no doubt a good deal of institutional manipulation, an effective positivist ethic amongst those who make, apply and are subject to law. Beyond this, the empirical assumptions made as to the consequences of rule-governance require testing and adaptation in the light of available evidence, although it has to be remembered that the potential benefits of rule-governance are not vitiated by evidence drawn from systems where there is a lack of ethical commitment to this form of the rule of law.

Some of this work I have in hand, in so far as if it is successful, may help to provide alternative models for human rights implementation. When disillusionment at the failures of court-centred bills of rights and the misuse of human rights discourse in the power politics of international relations reasserts itself, it is important that there are other and more credible visions of how human rights can be protected and enhanced in ways that render them mainstream to a democratic process in which individuals and communities feel themselves to be truly participant.

# PART 1:
# LAW

2

# THE POINT OF LEGAL POSITIVISM

The theory of legal positivism is usually taken to be analytical, descriptive and explanatory.[1] The point of legal positivism, on this view, is to provide an accurate account of law as it actually is rather than as it ought to be. This, it is assumed, follows from the positivist insistence that natural law theory neglects the logical distinction between description and prescription, and in particular confuses the analysis of law with its critique. This view can be challenged if we distinguish prescriptions relating to the content of law from those relating to its form. Using this distinction, I argue that it is illuminating and fruitful to regard legal positivism as a normative theory which seeks to determine what law ought to be, not with respect to its content but with respect to its form.[2]

The normative interpretation of legal positivism avoids purely semantic arguments about the definition of law and places descriptive disagreements about law in a meaningful context in which these competing analyses and descriptions are seen to have some bearing on alternative legal ideals, thus escaping the twin traps of purely definitional disagreements about legal concepts on the one hand and inconclusive exchanges of information about different legal systems on the other. In addition to furthering the better understanding of the varieties of legal positivism, the normative reading of positivism enables us to bypass unrewarding discussions as to the defining features of legal positivism itself.[3]

For most contemporary legal theorists, legal positivism is little more than a backcloth which serves to highlight the superiority of their own more sophisticated and more enlightened approaches to law. Positivism, it is claimed, misdescribes law as a set of discrete rules which are identified, understood and applied through the technical expertise of legal officials whose work is detached from the moral and political disagreements of everyday life.[4] More specifically, legal positivism is said to have failed to come to terms with the interpretative turn in legal philosophy which has brought to light the crucial role of judges and judicial culture in the ascription of meaning and significance to rules which in themselves are compatible with an infinite number of different interpretations.

---

1 See, for instance, WJ Waluchow, *Inclusive Legal Positivism*, Oxford: Clarendon Press, 1994, Chapter 2.

2 For variations on this view of legal positivism, see TD Campbell, *The Legal Theory of Ethical Positivism*, Aldershot: Ashgate/Dartmouth, 1996; DN MacCormick, 'The ethics of legalism', *Ratio Juris*, Vol 2, 1989, 184; J Raz, *The Authority of Law: Essays on Law and Morality*, Oxford: OUP, 1979, 50; and J Waldron, 'The rule of law in contemporary liberal theory', *Ratio Juris*, Vol 2, 1989, 79.

3 Useful working definitions of legal positivism may be found in HLA Hart, *Essays in Jurisprudence and Philosophy*, Oxford: Clarendon Press, 1983, 57–59; and J Coleman, 'Negative and positive positivism', *Journal of Legal Studies*, Vol 11, 1982, 139.

4 'This is broadly the criticism of the legal realists, particularly the "rule-skeptics"': see J Frank, *Law and the Modern Mind*, New York: Brentano's, 1930, vii.

The demise of 'plain meaning' goes hand in hand with the reported death of legal positivism.[5]

Since any account of law as an entirely autonomous system of rules is demonstrably defective as a descriptive exercise, it is easy to see why it is considered that legal positivism must be a discredited theory. Every lawyer knows that legal decisions depend on a multitude of factors not given in the relevant legal rules. The descriptive goals of legal positivism are doubly questionable if they are associated with the narrow empiricism of scientific positivism according to which only empirical generalisations that can be falsified by sensory observations are candidates for scientific truth.[6] This would mean that all meaningful statements about law, other than definitions, would have to refer to observable phenomena, such as physical sanctions, thus distorting the understanding of law from the viewpoint of participants. Any account of law which ignores its intelligibility and meaning from the point of view of those who operate and are affected by its normative structures cannot provide a satisfactory account of such a complex social institution, as HLA Hart so lucidly demonstrated.[7]

The misdescriptions of legal process said to be perpetrated by legal positivists involve unwarranted conceptual dogmas which define law in terms of social facts, such as the commands of the powerful, to the exclusion of those moral and democratic factors which impact routinely on the actual practice of law. An ideological twist is given to this critique of legal positivism by pointing out that this systematic misdescription of law as a set of determinate rules has the ideological function of disguising the political power of judiciaries, which are thereby better able to impose their own values by passing off their decisions as the morally neutral application of pre-existing rules and encouraging the belief that citizens and judges alike are duty bound to manifest total obedience to the requirements of an objectively determined 'law'. On this view, the point of legal positivism is to be found in a hidden ideological agenda, namely the legitimation of a system that disguises the political power of lawyers and the class interests they represent.[8]

These criticisms have considerable force and their constant repetition has led to a situation in which legal positivism is widely held to be an obviously false and perhaps dangerous legal theory, a historical curiosity which is unhelpful in relation to the development of law and legal systems, a theory which is expounded only to pave the way for other theoretical approaches by identifying the mistakes that it embodies. One consequence of the eclipse of legal positivism

---

5 See S Kripke, *Wittgenstein on Rules and Private Language*, Cambridge, MA: Harvard University Press, 1982; C Yablon, 'The indeterminacy of law: critical legal studies and the problem of legal explanation', *Cardozo Law Review*, Vol 6, 1985, 917; and C Norris, 'Law deconstruction and the resistance of theory', *Journal of Law and Society*, Vol 15, 1988, 165.

6 As in K Lee, *The Positivist Science of Law*, Aldershot: Gower, 1989.

7 HLA Hart, *The Concept of Law*, Oxford: Clarendon Press, 1961, Chapter 2.

8 See AC Hutchinson and P Monahan, *The Rule of Law: Ideal or Ideology?*, Toronto: Carswell Legal Publications, 1986; and V Kerruish, *Jurisprudence as Ideology*, London: Routledge, 1991.

is that it no longer readily fills the role of an official theory which can be used to justify the reality and importance of legal knowledge and the centrality of black letter law in legal education. Senior judges openly repudiate the 'fairy tales', associated with legal positivism, that judges do not make law and that courts do not have to make difficult decisions on which authoritative guidance is not to be found in existing texts. More generally, the demise of legal positivism is welcomed by those who see the theory as having had a negative effect on the development of law by obscuring the realities of legal process in which, while relatively little is actually circumscribed by substantive and procedural rules, the pretence or illusion that legal rules do determine legal outcomes is an effective bar to the open consideration of relevant arguments and the progressive development of the law. Legal positivism is not only false, it is also said to be pernicious as a theory which protects entrenched interests and renders courts less than responsive to changing social needs and the wellbeing of oppressed groups within society.[9]

The scenario changes markedly if we take the view that the point of legal positivism is not to provide primarily analytical and descriptive tools but relates directly to an account of what laws and legal systems ought to be like. If legal positivism is a normative theory, then its descriptive inadequacies are not necessarily fatal and its alleged ideological biases may be openly confronted, assessed and responded to. Descriptive failure does not negate prescriptive endeavour unless the former demonstrates the impracticality of the latter. Indeed, pointing out such failures – in this case by demonstrating that actual legal process is routinely affected by extraneous social values, political pressures and judicial prejudices – may turn out to be a catalyst for the reaffirmation of its prescriptive aspirations. In particular, the demonstration that courts are often class, gender and race biased may be the occasion for the reaffirmation of the role of rules in helping to combat arbitrary and prejudiced decision-making by authorities.

The point of legal positivism – understood as an ethical theory concerning the legally relevant conduct of citizens, legislators and judges – can be seen as the provision of a model and a justification for the construct of a legal system which approaches as far as is practicable the realisation of an autonomous system of rules as a necessary part of any acceptable political system. The autonomy in question relates not to the inputs to legal systems which, on the democratic model of legal positivism at least, are the rules emanating from legislatures, but to the court-centred processes whose function is to apply legal rules to particular circumstances and resolve the questions of law and fact which are brought to their attention.[10] The point of legal positivism, so understood, is to commend that legal systems be developed in such a way as to maximise the social and political benefits of having a system of readily identifiable mandatory rules of such clarity,

---

9 See RW Gordon, 'New developments in legal theory', in D Kairys (ed), *The Politics of Law*, New York: Pantheon, 1982.

10 See G Postema, 'Law's autonomy and public practical reason', in RP George (ed), *The Autonomy of Law: Essays in Legal Positivism*, Oxford: OUP, 1996, Chapter 4.

precision and scope that they can be routinely understood and applied without recourse to contentious moral and political judgments.[11]

It is no easy task to rehabilitate legal positivism when the theory is so widely regarded as both intellectually flawed and also retrograde in its social and political implications. However, legal positivism is not without its defenders and even amongst its critics there is increasing recognition that the theory has had an undeservedly bad press in recent years. In his introduction to a recent collection of essays on legal positivism, Stephen Guest notes that much criticism of the approach with respect to the distinction between morality and law is superficial, and overlooks obvious dissimilarities between them:

> Because of these characteristic differences between legal and moral rules we can ask questions about legal positivism which search the point of thinking about the law in this way. This is where it becomes exciting. If we ask the question of point we move away from a descriptive account of law in terms (say) of empirical sources of legal authority to an account based on the practical human value in making some actions dependent upon legal determination rather than upon moral determination. We should ask directly: What is served by perpetuating the idea that human determinations are higher in some sense than moral – perhaps God-given – determinations? Taking a line like this easily ends up in a value-laden account, perhaps in the conclusion that positivism is a good or bad moral theory, a sub-theory of a general theory of political morality.[12]

Taking up Guest's invitation,[13] this essay reflects on the point of legal positivism by exploring some of the political and moral objectives underlying and directing the development of the theory. It seeks to exemplify the belief that it is an illuminating and exciting (because liberating) exercise to put into focus the moral and political aspects of the positivist enterprise and, in particular, to see legal positivism as a theory which recommends that we create and sustain legal systems in which laws are identified, followed and applied without recourse to the moral opinions of those involved in these processes. I call this approach the legal theory of ethical positivism.[14]

## CLEARING THE WAY FOR ETHICAL POSITIVISM

It has long been acknowledged that legal positivists do have moral and political views. The classical legal positivists, Jeremy Bentham and John Austin, are moral as well as psychological utilitarians. Even Hobbes, to whose theory of absolute political sovereignty legal positivism may be traced, can be argued to have

---

11 Thus, J Raz, *op cit* fn 2, 47: 'A law has a source if its contents and existence can be determined without using moral arguments.'

12 S Guest (ed), *Positivism Today*, Aldershot: Dartmouth, 1996, x.

13 See R Dworkin, *Taking Rights Seriously*, London: Duckworth, 1977, 347. Dworkin suggests that we see legal positivism as 'a political theory about the point or function of the law' along the lines that 'law provides a settled, public and dependable set of standards whose force cannot be called into question by some official's conception of policy and morality'. See also R Dworkin, *Law's Empire*, London: Fontana, 1986, 45–113.

14 See TD Campbell, *The Legal Theory of Ethical Positivism*, Aldershot: Dartmouth, 1996.

subscribed to foundational values of life and obedience to God which go beyond mere prudentialism. What distinguishes the founding fathers as legal positivists, it is agreed, is not their lack of moral beliefs, but their separation of these beliefs from their definitions and descriptions of law, the most famous of all defining positivist quotations being Austin's declaration that 'the existence of law is one thing; its merit or demerit another'.[15]

The distinction between the existence and the merit of law has been taken to imply that the theory of legal positivism is itself confined to the study of the existence as opposed to the merit of law. This is a fallacious assumption. A theory of how law ought to be can, consistently with its own premises, commend a legal system in which scrupulous attention is paid to the distinction between 'is' and 'ought' in relation to such matters as the identification and application of laws. Indeed, drawing the is/ought distinction is a precondition of the contention that legal officers ought to refrain from making value judgments in the course of their work and that law-makers ought to provide laws that can be handled in such a value-free manner. If no such distinction can be made, then it makes no sense to require that it should be implemented in practice, and once such a distinction is made it is possible to present moral reasons for supporting non-moral practices. Thus, the point of legal positivism could, consistently with the logical distinction between is and ought, be a moral point, the presentation of a distinctive approach to law that identifies the social and political benefits of a system of rules which are followed and administered in ways that do not depend on the moral evaluation of their content by those who follow and administer them.

The multiple relationships between law and morality are a tangled web which must be explored and analysed if we are to appreciate the nature of ethical positivism. It is helpful to distinguish the empirical, conceptual and prescriptive forms of the relationships between law and morality.

Legal positivism is associated with the thesis that there is no necessary (that is, conceptual) relationship between law and morals. This has become known as the 'separability thesis', according to which law and morality can be both identified and analysed in their own terms without reference to the other.[16] In Hart's words, 'there is no necessary connection between law and morals or law as it is and ought to be'.[17] On a more precise and stronger view of the conceptual relationship between law and morals, called 'hard' or 'exclusive' positivism, it is held to be conceptually incoherent for a legal system to incorporate any reference to morality in its rule of recognition, that is, in the list of the sources of law which are recognised by its courts.[18] Hard positivism is often articulated only to establish the analytical superiority of 'soft' or 'inclusive' positivism, the thesis that a rule of

---

15 J Austin, *The Province of Jurisprudence Determined,* London: Weidenfeld & Nicolson, 1955, 184.

16 J Coleman, 'Negative and positive positivism', *Journal of Legal Studies,* Vol 11, 1982, 139.

17 HLA Hart, 'Positivism and the separation of law and morals', *Harvard Law Review,* Vol 71, 1958, 593 at 601. See also HLA Hart, *op cit* fn 7, 253.

18 For positions along these lines, see J Raz, *op cit* fn 2, 50; and R Dworkin, *Taking Rights Seriously, op cit* fn 13, 2nd edn, 1978, 347–48.

recognition may include moral criteria but need not do so. In contrast, the thesis that law must incorporate a reference to morality in the rule of recognition is rejected as a form of natural law theory which falls altogether outside the range of positivist theories.

Ethical positivism presupposes soft positivism, holding that a legal system, with conceptual propriety, may or may not incorporate morality within its rule of recognition, but this claim is ancillary to its main contention that a legal system *ought* not to include moral criteria in the authoritative list of the sources of law. This is a prescriptive, not an analytical nor descriptive, form of hard or exclusive legal positivism.[19]

The conceptual analysis of law and morality should not be mistaken for empirical claims about the factual relationships involved between moral and legal phenomena. The conceptual separability thesis is not a 'separation thesis', as we may call the view that morality and law are empirically distinct phenomena. In fact, no positivist denies that morality and law interact, and that there is a contingent overlap between the content and functions of a society's morality and its laws. Indeed, the separability thesis is a required presupposition of statements about the interaction between the two systems and the extent of their actual separation. Moreover, as we have seen, on the soft positivist view adopted by most positivists, it is explicitly envisaged that legal systems may incorporate moral content in a formal way. It is not part of ethical positivism to make empirical claims about the actual separation of law and morality, with respect either to the contents of ordinary law and the rule of recognition or the social functions of law and morals; other than that it is feasible in practice to achieve a degree of separation between the moral and legal activities of those charged with the implementation of legal rules.

Indeed, legal positivism generally has been deeply engaged in demonstrating the similarities of law and morals as social sub-systems, both in content and form. Austin's account of positive morality and Hart's analysis of legal obligation as a sub-set of social obligations affirm the significant empirical connections between law and morality as social phenomena.[20] Both theorists, however, go on to describe the mechanisms whereby positive morality and positive law may be distinguished and separated when it is desirable to do so.

Some confusion is generated over these empirical issues by the failure to distinguish between the methods and the objectives of positivist theory. Many legal positivists do see themselves as engaging in a scientific and therefore value-neutral study of law (and indeed of morality), but this methodological positivism

---

19 Being able to select its preferred reading of the separability thesis in accordance with its theoretical objectives, ethical positivism is not affected by a 'farewell to legal positivism' which points to the fact that there are multiple possible formulations of the separability thesis. See K Fuber, 'Farewell to legal positivism', in RP George (ed), *op cit* fn 10, Chapter 5. One of the many versions of the separability thesis proffered by Fuber fits with ethical positivism: 'The Neutral-Content Thesis (NCT)' that '[t]he content of the definition of basic juridical expressions should be value-free', 134.

20 HLA Hart, *Law Liberty and Morality*, Stanford: Stanford University Press, 1963, 20; and *op cit* fn 7, 79–88.

does not state that the conclusions they come up with are bound to be that morality is not involved in the identification of law by those actually involved in the systems in question, or even that there is no necessary connection between law and morality.[21] That would be to confuse the scientific method of the observing persons with the scientific (or non-scientific) conduct of the observed persons. Positivists as scientists may discover that lawyers are anything but scientific in their approach to law. However, it must be said that some positivists have made such an assumption themselves and imputed their own scientific positivism to the legal officers of the system in question. The ethical positivist does not make this mistake. Indeed, the complaint of ethical positivism is precisely that many legal participants do not in fact take on the value-neutral attitude towards the law which it would be appropriate for them to adopt.

This takes us to the third mode of relationship between law and morals – the prescriptive mode – from which point of view we can identify ethical positivism as a theory which goes beyond the separability thesis to make the claim that there not only can be but ought to be a clear separation between law and morals in the practice of law. The claim is not that there should be no overlap in the content of law and morality, a matter on which the theory, given its restricted scope, is basically neutral, but rather that the rule of recognition ought not to contain terms that invite moral judgment. This is the prescriptive separation thesis or, more specifically, prescriptive hard positivism.[22]

It is important to note that excluding moral terms from the rule of recognition does not mean that no reference whatsoever may be made to the moral beliefs of all or certain members of the society in question, or to the moral doctrines of a holy book or other source of moral authority, provided that these can be identified in an empirical way. It is possible in principle to discover meaning without endorsing the moral views prevalent in a society or contained in a particular text whose meaning can be established by the use of agreed linguistic conventions. What ought to be excluded from a rule of recognition, according to ethical positivism, is language which requires a moral judgment to be made before the rule in question can be given sufficient content to guide actual conduct. References to positive morality or religious sources can still be included in a rule of recognition as long as these can be identified as social sources. Such possible sources of law are unlikely to serve the purposes of law if the criteria of identification are such as to provide no clear guidance as to the content of the law arising from them. Reference to accepted standards, particularly in situations where no such agreed standards exist, will not make for good law, but there is no in principle objection to a rule of recognition making reference to a society's morality, provided there is a homogeneous set of moral customs in the society in

---

21 See SR Perry, 'The varieties of legal positivism', *Canadian Journal of Law and Jurisprudence*, Vol IX, 1996, 361.

22 'Prescriptive hard positivism' is to be preferred as it relates ethical positivism specifically to the rule of recognition as distinct from law-making activity. 'Prescriptive separation' is a label which may be better applied to Neil MacCormick's moral disestablishmentarianism whereby it is contended that laws should incorporate as little as possible of a society's morality. See N MacCormick, 'A moralistic case for amoralistic law?', *Valparaiso University Law Review*, Vol 20, 1985, 1.

question and the content of this morality can be established in an empirical and uncontroversial way.

As these conditions are not met in contemporary pluralistic societies, effective rules of recognition in such societies must provide ways of determining which, if any, elements of positive morality are to be recognised as legally binding. In this respect the prescriptive separation of law and morals is of particular significance in the diverse pluralities of postmodern societies.

It is one thing to specify the nature of ethical positivism as prescriptive hard positivism, but why should we be moved to adopt the thesis that moral criteria should not feature in the sources of the law utilised by citizens as subjects, bureaucracies as administrators and courts as adjudicators? Ethical positivism is not a conceptual claim as to the meaning of 'law', although it can be contended that it fits well enough with the different feel of legal and moral discourse to which Guest refers. Nor is it an empirical claim as to the actual separation of law and morality in legal process. Ethical positivism is more of a critique than an account of what courts do or do not do, so that the ethical positivist is spurred on rather than deflated by the evidence of systematic political bias in courts. It therefore requires justification in moral and political terms. Before exploring these justifications of legal positivism as a prescriptive theory it is helpful to deal with some preliminary obstacles to this reading of legal positivism.

One hurdle to be overcome in the presentation of ethical positivism is the association of legal positivism with logical positivism, the philosophical doctrine popular from the 1930s to the 1950s, which permitted only two categories of meaningful assertion, empirical or falsifiable assertions on the one hand, and analytical statements about the meaning of words on the other.[23] It follows, on the theory, that moral language is excluded from the realm of meaningful discourse and its apparent objectivity must be explained away by, for instance, arguing that it is no more than disguised expressions of emotion. If legal positivism is construed as an application of logical positivism, then it is difficult to regard it as primarily an ethical theory and easy to see why it is regarded as a form of empirical reductivism which, by taking the morality out of law, rescues law from the realm of mere subjectivity.

Some theorists who may, perhaps controversially, be identified as legal positivists do espouse the tenets of logical positivism and seek to provide an analysis of law that dispenses with moral categories altogether, on the grounds that moral statements are nothing more than expressions of emotion. Alf Ross and the Scandinavian legal realists generally fit readily into that category.[24] However, subjectivist theories of morality have never been a defining characteristic of legal positivism. We only need to think of the firmly objective moral theory of Jeremy Bentham and John Austin, whose utilitarian ethical theory underpinned all their other work, to see that there is no general incongruity in attributing deep moral

---

23 The classic formulation is in AJ Ayer, *Language, Truth and Logic*, London: Victor Gollancz Ltd, 1936.

24 A Ross, *On Law and Justice*, London: Stevens & Sons, 1958.

purpose to positivist theories. Nor can it be assumed that all those who adopt subjectivist theories of ethics thereby take morality less seriously.

It is, however, correct to say that many legal positivists are concerned with the diversity of moral opinions and the intractable nature of moral disagreement. This is often given as one reason for adopting a positivist line on the separation of law and morality with respect to their content, so that law can be used to promote social cohesion and serve as a basis for adjudication of disputes between persons with contrary moral views. However, there is no basis for the association of emotivism in ethics with either extreme moral diversity or incorrigible moral disagreement. The existence of objective truths does not guarantee agreement as to what these truths might be, and disagreement amongst those whose convictions are bolstered by a belief in the objective rightness of their views may prove even less tractable than the disputes of emotivists.[25]

It may be concluded that legal positivism neither presupposes nor requires the logical positivist view of morality but there may be a much closer association with the second prong of logical positivism – scientific empiricism – according to which experience is the sole source of knowledge beyond the meanings of the words we use to describe it. The association with scientific positivism is a more formidable hurdle to overcome in the representation of legal positivism as an ethical theory. The classical positivists, Bentham and Austin, are strongly influenced by the empiricist epistemology that underlies their efforts to rid the law of vague and insubstantial language which, in their view, pervades the common law. It is plausible to see Austin's entire scheme of definitions dealing with commands, sanctions, sovereigns and habits, as an attempt to analyse law purely in terms of empirically observable categories. Even Hart, who eschews crude empiricism for a more hermeneutical approach to law that concentrates on the meaningfulness of the phenomenal to the participants, sees himself as engaged in a sociological enterprise which is intended to give us a readily intelligible descriptive account of an apparently mysterious aspect of human society.[26]

Of course there are counter-examples of canonical legal positivists who are by no means scientific empiricists. Hobbes sought geometric rather than empirical foundations. Kelsen has a Kantian methodology independent of separating law from empiricist science,[27] and Kant himself, arguably also a legal positivist, is evidently no empiricist.[28] Nevertheless, there are close ties between legal positivism and the empiricist strand of logical positivism in so far as, in distinguishing law and morality, it opens the way for the assertion that law should lend itself to explanation by empirical methods. Indeed, it is clear that there is a strong anti-metaphysical point to much legal positivism.

However, ethical positivism is not imperialistic in its reading of legal positivism. Actual positivists' theories have a number of distinct objectives. It is

---

25 The best general treatment of these issues is JL Mackie, *Ethics: Inventing Right and Wrong*, Harmondsworth: Penguin, 1977.

26 HLA Hart, *op cit* fn 7, preface.

27 H Kelsen, *The Pure Theory of Law*, Berkeley: University of California Press, 1967.

28 See J Waldron, 'Kant's legal positivism', *Harvard Law Review*, Vol 109, 1996, 1535.

not contended that all positivisms have the same point, or that any positivism has only one objective. Positivists are individually more or less concerned with analysis, with description and with prescription in different blends and with different emphases. What is claimed is that we cannot exclude prescriptive concerns from the core of positivist theory, that this aspect of positivism is compatible with its other characteristic features, and that this strand of positivist theory has been unduly neglected and may usefully be emphasised as a tool of understanding and a cue to the potential relevance of the positivist tradition to current debates within constitutional and political philosophy.

Explicating ethical positivism as an element within political philosophy is not a historical exercise, although it can be most illuminating as a way of understanding the works of the classical positivists. Nor is it a 'best that it can be' interpretation that tries to give a coherent yet morally appealing picture of a whole tradition. Ethical positivism is a living and developing form of positivism rather than an interpretative tool. It is not tied to making sense, moral or otherwise, of the history of positivism, but seeks to enunciate a satisfactory contemporary theory of law. Accepting that law is an interpretative activity in the broad sense in which interpretation is a matter of adopting meanings which suit specific evaluative ends, ethical positivism is not undermined by the fact that many legal positivists have major ontological and scientific objectives which are not directly related to the moral goals which also feature in the history of legal positivism.

A further obstacle to the acceptance of ethical positivism is the assumption that legal positivism cannot allow any valuations about law to enter into the substance of the theory without contradicting its distinctive premise as to the distinction between law and morality and lapsing into a form of natural law.[29] This is, however, a psychological rather than a philosophical block, for, as we have seen, there is no inconsistency, once having distinguished the two forms of discourse, from indulging in both modes separately. Nevertheless, it can be argued that the whole point of making the distinction in the context of classical legal positivism was to found a separate discipline of jurisprudence, or the science of law, which has no room for arguments about the proper content or form of law. The science of law is not to be contaminated with the science of legislation.

There are two significant responses to be made to this historical truth. The first is that the moral judgments which the founding fathers of legal positivism eschewed were judgments about the proper content of law, and not about the reasons for engaging in the value-free scientific study of law. There may be moral reasons for engaging in a discipline which is not itself moral. Clearly Bentham, Austin and, less arguably, Kelsen had just such moral bases for embarking on and pursuing their enterprises. It has to be acknowledged that the evaluations of ethical positivism are not primarily directed to the intrinsic worth of purely

---

29 Such arguments occur in D Beyleveld and R Brownsword, *Law as a Moral Judgment*, London: Sweet & Maxwell, 1986; M Detmold, *The Unity of Law and Morality: A Refutation of Legal Positivism*, London: Routledge, 1984; and J Finnis, *Natural Law and Natural Rights*, Oxford: Clarendon Press, 1980.

descriptive and explanatory ventures, but neither are they directed at the proper content of law. Their concern is to argue that law should consist of fixed and clear rules applicable and applied without recourse to value judgments.

The second response is that it is possible to view the scientific elements of the classical positivists as directed more to establishing the possibility of a value-free legal system rather than demonstrating its actual existence, even within the confines of developed cultures. Value-free here means value-neutrality only in relation to the thought processes and decisions required of participants to operate such systems in so far as they relate to the recognition and application, rather than the making, of law. At the same time, it is clear that legal positivists have not in practice refrained from value judgments in relation to the form of law. This may or may not be an inconsistency on their part, but we do not need to go further into textual analysis and historical interpretation to make the claim that ethical positivism does not run counter to the tradition from which it has emerged.

It would be unhelpful, however, to speak of ethical positivism if the theory turned out to be more intelligibly classified as a form of soft natural law, which argues for a necessary connection between morality and the form rather than the content of law.[30] This would save legal positivism from moral vacuity only to have it captured by natural law, a very Pyrrhic victory. The simple answer to this line of analysis is that ethical positivism makes no claim that law, to be law, must fulfil certain moral goals, in either its content or its form. It is not the case that the concept of law is necessarily linked to morality simply because law requires moral justification. Not everything which requires moral justification is itself a moral enterprise. There is no backtracking in ethical positivism from the positivist position that there are bad laws which are still laws and bad concepts of law that are still concepts of law. Nor is there any claim that law has any objective purposes beyond those determined by human beings. We are therefore a long way from embracing the key concepts of natural law, despite the fact that natural law theory itself has plenty of argument for the utility and moral potential of positive law.

There are multiple similarities between ethical positivism and Lon Fuller's theory of procedural natural law, since both see law as a purposive enterprise which calls for a bundle of certain techniques typically referred to as the rule of law.[31] If human beings are going to be subject to the governance of law, then that law must consist of rules which are clear, prospective, practicable, promulgated and stable. Ethical positivism adds to but does not demur about this. However, ethical positivism does not follow Fuller down the path of asserting that these techniques, as the moral content of the law, satisfy these conditions of legality. Ethical positivism is not, therefore, even a procedural form of natural law, if natural law is taken to involve an assumption of an internal and necessary connection between good form and good substance. And, it may be added, natural law theory has no monopoly over objectivism in moral theory. Natural

---

30 For different versions of this type of approach, see D Beyleveld and R Brownsword, *ibid*; M Detmold, *ibid*; and P Soper, *A Theory of Law*, Cambridge, MA: Harvard University Press, 1984.

31 L Fuller, *The Morality of Law*, New Haven, CT: Yale University Press, 1969.

law represents those forms of objectivist morality that rest on a style of teleological reasoning about the goodness of nature which are alien to the more utilitarian tradition from which ethical positivism emerges.

Less reputable explanations for resistance to ethical positivism arise from its role as the scapegoat theory of law on which is blamed much of the current disillusionment with law and lawyers. This scapegoating has encouraged caricatures of legal positivism which make it the ideal type of a villainous theory – morally blind, intellectually backward and politically oppressive caricatures that die slowly in the face of counter-arguments and instances. The particular matters in these caricatures that require more considered analysis relate particularly to the alleged amoralism, or even the immorality, of positivism in requiring absolute obedience from citizens and judges alike, whatever the moral content of the laws in question, a position which fits ill with the increasingly accepted practice of later prosecuting at law those who fail in their moral duty to disobey evil laws.[32]

Ethical positivism does, as we will see, commend general submission to laws which we have no moral reason to obey other than the fact that they are laws, and does suggest that there are important moral reasons why we should not resort to our own moral opinions simply because the law is in conflict with them. Ethical positivism cannot, therefore, entirely go along with the response which is open to descriptive positivism that legal positivism, by encouraging us to distinguish between law as it is and law as it ought to be, encourages us to be more critical of laws and therefore to follow our conscience when it conflicts with an evil law. While ethical positivism is not committed to absolute and unthinking obedience to law, it does point out that allowing action on a moral right of disobedience to laws which are believed to be unjust would, if widely approved, undermine law as a system which, by ensuring conformity, promotes co-operation and order and resolves conflict. Ethical positivism offers many convincing reasons why it is routinely right to subordinate personal moral opinions to legal duties except in the most exceptional circumstances. This is not an amoral position but a second-order moral case for departing from our own first-order moral judgments when these run counter to the established laws of our jurisdiction. What these second-order reasons are is considered in the next section.

A second significant riposte to the scapegoat caricature of legal positivism is to point out the confusion of assuming that actual ethical positivists must behave as if they were in a positivistically perfect system when in fact they are having to operate in situations where the laws lack many of the prime qualities of good positive law. A positivist judge, for instance, cannot and should not make 'mechanical' judgments when confronted with vague and ambiguous laws or situations for which there is no law at all. All positivists have allowed for

32 This ongoing debate follows the exchange in HLA Hart, 'The separation of law and morals', *Harvard Law Review*, Vol 71, 1958, 597; and L Fuller, 'The separation of morality and law: a reply to Professor Hart', *Harvard Law Review*, Vol 71, 1958, 595. See D Dyzenhaus, *Hard Cases in Wicked Legal Systems: South African Law in the Perspective of Legal Philosophy*, Oxford: Clarendon Press, 1991.

discretionary judgments, at least as second-best solutions which may be best practice when confronted with formally bad law. Often, rather arbitrary rules of statutory interpretation can be seen as artificial devices for limiting such discretion in ways that least compromise the ideals, such as certainty and decisiveness, on which legal positivism rests.

Nevertheless, acknowledgment that the success of the positivist scheme depends on the degree to which there is conformity to the positivist model does make it clear that ethical positivism cannot be a purely prescriptive theory. The prescriptions presuppose not only that a society could approximate to the positivist ideal of law but that to a significant degree this conformity is achieved in practice. Ethical positivism, in arguing that following rules has social advantages, does presuppose more than the mere distinction between 'is' and 'ought' and the preference for formally good law over formally bad law. Many of the arguments outlined below presuppose such general conformity to positive law as is required to produce the predicted patterns of conduct which are said to be advantageous. If, for instance, there is only patchy conformity to the rule of the road there is likely to be little benefit in any particular person abiding by it. This is why efficacy, in the sense of general compliance or habitual obedience to law, is often regarded as a precondition of legal validity in the positivist scheme of things.[33] There must be a threshold of conformity which in turn presupposes a certain threshold of formal virtue in the law with respect to its clarity and precision before the arguments of ethical positivism for rule governance have any real purchase.

Some reasons for adopting rule governance presuppose more conformity than others. Co-ordination of large numbers of people in potentially dangerous situations is more vulnerable to the non-observance or the non-availability of law than more private and less dangerous interactions. But the general point may be conceded that, while it is not primarily a descriptive theory of law, ethical positivism does presuppose a degree of empirical realism which may be lacking in some societies most of the time and in all societies some of the time. This in itself may help to explain why the view of positivism as an empirical theory is so firmly entrenched. This is an understandable mistake, for the normative goals of ethical positivism rest on the empirical possibility of implementing the positivist models of law which have been taken as descriptions of actual systems.

## JUSTIFYING ETHICAL POSITIVISM

Outlining the moral reasons that ethical positivists give to support their view that the functions of rule creation and rule application ought to be kept separate and that the latter ought to be conducted in as value-free a manner as possible is a daunting task. It does not require a complete political philosophy, for ethical positivism is not directly concerned with the choice of specific legal content.

---

33 See TD Campbell, 'Obligation: societal, political and legal', in P Harris (ed), *Political Obligation*, London: Routledge, 1990.

Indeed, one of its claims is that it is a theory which can accommodate a very wide range of different political philosophies. But the task of justifying ethical positivism does require the provision of rationales for having a type of political system which is both expressed and contained in the use of rules as the dominant mode of government.

Fortunately, this extensive task can tap into some familiar arguments and positions relating to the rule of law as part of a democratic system, which point to the many advantages of utilising rules both as instruments of and constraints on government. To appreciate the force of these arguments we must first have an analysis of the idea of a rule as it features in the contention that rules are essential ingredients of legitimate governance and gain some insight into the role of rules both in society generally and with respect to the ways in which states govern. We may start with John Austin's classic positivistic account of law in terms of the commands of the sovereign. This is in essence a rule-based picture of law since the Austinian commands are general commands, both with respect to their addressees and their content.[34] Hart has no difficulty in detaching these general commands from the image of a commander, offering his famous analysis of rules in terms of social regularity supported by an internal attitude on the part of social participants, which manifests itself in strong critical responses to deviations from the patterns of conduct in question.[35] It is a feature of such social rules that they are mandatory, in that they feature as requirements to which the individual must conform to avoid either sanctions or social and perhaps self criticism.

To this analysis of social rules as regularities in conduct supported by internal attitudes of praise and blame must be added an important distinction between 'rules of thumb', which offer guidance but may be departed from if and when their recommendations do not appear to serve their purported ends,[36] and 'real' or 'mandatory' rules, which call for conformity irrespective of their immediate perceived utility. Mandatory rules, which specify the considerations that must be taken account of in specified circumstances and exclude all other consideration, are the sort of rules which feature in the rationales of ethical positivism.[37]

Rule rationales start from the assumption that all mandatory rules require justification if only in the sense that reasons must be given as to why we should take those and only those considerations specified in the rule into account when making practical decisions. Indeed, there seems something perverse in not taking all relevant considerations into account on every occasion. In other words, there is a strong *prima facie* case against rules as a form of irrationalism. Rules of thumb are

---

34 J Austin, *The Province of Jurisprudence Determined*, London: Weidenfeld & Nicolson, 1955, Lecture I.

35 HLA Hart, *op cit* fn 7, 79–81.

36 F Schauer, *Playing by the Rules: A Philosophical Analysis of Rule-Based Decision-Making*, Cambridge: CUP, 1991, ll.

37 Thus, G Warnock, *The Object of Morality*, London: Methuen, 1971, 65: '[Rules] exclude from practical consideration the particular merits of particular cases by specifying in advance what is to be done whatever the circumstance of particular cases may be.' See also J Raz, *op cit* fn 2, 35–45, 73–76.

easy enough to justify since they facilitate quick decisions that draw on the cumulative experience derived from trial and error but can be departed from if those using them decide that they are not helpful in particular circumstances. However, mandatory rules, which add the deprivation of freedom of choice to the irrationality of excluding relevant reasons, are not so readily justified.

The task of justifying the governance of mandatory rules is particularly challenging because we are not dealing here with the justification of particular rules by reference to their content but with the justification of having rules of any content, the justifications for which must, therefore, be largely content-free. It may be easy enough to give reasons why we should or should not adopt and follow this or that particular rule; it is less easy to see why we should adopt and conform to rules in general and do so without making an independent assessment of their content, hence the appeal of anarchism in political philosophy and the plausibility of situation or contextual ethics in moral philosophy.

However, once we embark on a search for rule rationales they are found to be in ready supply. In the main, rule rationales may be divided into those whose object is control and those whose objective is co-ordination. Control rules are seen as mechanisms for preventing harmful and ensuring beneficial conduct, and are closely tied into mechanisms of sanction and education. The strategy of removing certain matters from the choice of individuals is justified as the only effective way to achieve the behavioural control required. If left to their own devices, individuals, either through stupidity or selfishness, will cause needless and unacceptable harm to themselves and others. Ideally, such rules should make it absolutely clear what is required of persons in a way which is not open to rationalisations of a sort that enable individuals to escape their often burdensome requirements, hence the alleged need to exclude moral terms from social control rules, for moral terms invite subjective judgments which provide scope for self-serving exceptions.[38]

Co-ordination rules may usefully be divided into the facilitative rules, such as the rules of contract, which enable agreements to be made and enforced; convenience rules, which enable efficient co-operation in areas of no moral significance in themselves, such as the rules of the road; distributive rules, which are designed to enable large groups of people to achieve an overall pattern in the distribution of benefits and burden; and output rules, which are designed to co-ordinate the economic activities of large groups for the production of material goods and other social benefits.[39] All these have in common the idea that co-ordinated action is a more effective way of achieving any goals which require the involvement of large numbers of people who are often unknown to each other. In all these cases, allowing people to make up their own minds about whether or not to follow the rules and whether or not to modify them in this way or that is to

---

38 Thus, J Raz, *op cit* fn 2, 51, argues that it is a function of law to 'provide publicly ascertainable standards by which members of the society are held to be bound so that they cannot excuse nonconformity by challenging the justification of the standard'.

39 See G Postema, 'Co-ordination and convention at the foundations of law', *Journal of Legal Studies*, Vol XI, 1982, 165.

invite confusion and breakdown in the co-ordination of the activities in question. Similarly, confusion as to the content of such rules is as destructive of their objectives as it is in the case of control rules.

There are other rule rationales that cut across these general categories of rule-rationale. Therefore, there are psychological advantages of reassurance and self-confidence in orderliness which are distinct from its instrumental benefits for other purposes.[40] Peace of mind is promoted, particularly in complex societies, by widespread conformity to clear and precise rules. Considerations of justice and fairness are also closely related in part to the existence of rules that capture the differences and similarities which are determinative of how people do and ought to treat each other, and in particular how individuals and groups are and ought to be treated by the state. Systematically treating like cases alike and unlike cases differently is inconceivable without the routinisation of rules.[41]

These diverse rationales illustrate the wide scope of the considerations that legal positivists can bring to bear on what may appear to be the difficult task of justifying having mandatory rules. The rationales are all independent of a judgment as to what particular rules are justified, although they make reference to the sort of activities to which rules are directed and the general nature of the objectives that rules may be used to achieve. All the rationales apply to social rules in general as well as to legal rules; the added ingredient that is required to justify legal rules is contentious but not dissimilar to the rationales for having rules in general. The factors that turn rationales for having rules into rationales for having laws relate mainly to the seriousness of the purposes the rules serve and the extent to which general conformity to precise and agreed rules is a precondition of their effectiveness. These matters are at the core of legal and political philosophy but they do not bear directly on the general rationales for having some rules of the types outlined above.

However, there are particular considerations which come to the fore when rules are adopted officially, not only with respect to their meaning but also in relation to the use of coercion and sanctions to enforce them. We have covered some of the positive reasons for rule enforcement already and these may readily be translated into considerations which support the creation and sustenance of states as a means whereby such enforcement is achieved. Of course, there are other arguments which also point to the moral value of states, defined as co-ordinated centres of decision-making and social co-operation. These justifications of states may in themselves make no reference to rules. Particular commands in the pursuit of military, economic and social ends are evident means for the attainment of many of the goals set for states by all political philosophies. However, the power which states acquire over their citizens gives rise to yet another rule rationale that relates to the ways in which that power is used and monitored. Here we come to the familiar arguments that states – justified states – must govern in accordance with publicly known rules and control and co-ordinate their citizens through the

---

40 See V Aubert, 'Some social functions of legislation', *Acta Sociologica*, Vol 10, 1966, 99.

41 See TD Campbell, *Justice*, London: Macmillan, 1988, Chapter 2.

medium of rules which guarantee them a certain predictability and freedom in their lives.[42]

It is in this context that the constitutional relevance of ethical positivism comes into play. Thus, there is the requirement that the rules which governments must obey have to be clear and precise, otherwise they put no real limitations on governments. There is also the argument that the power of the state over the citizen is so great and the danger of arbitrary conduct to benefit the interests of members of a government and the associated apparatus so threatening, that only a requirement of precise and clear rule governance can provide any protection to the citizens and provide a guaranteed sphere of individual freedom.[43]

Both considerations require a separation of powers in which the makers of the rules, whose conduct is intended to be channelled and controlled by the rules in question, cannot themselves make judgments about how they apply to particular circumstances. Without this separation of legislative and adjudicative functions, it is argued, there is no effective defence against the selective and inconsistent application of laws to suit the interests of those who both make and apply the law. All these rationales are part of familiar and basic rule of law arguments which point to the rule of clear and precise positive law as a precondition of the practical distinction between law-making and law-application. Vague and ambiguous rules effectively transfer political authority to courts, who enjoy the freedom to shape the law themselves according to their own values and preferences.

At this point, ethical positivism must be seen as part of wider political philosophies, some of which incorporate a theory of democratic positivism which asserts that political legitimacy depends on having mandatory rules that relate to the democratic process from which they emerge. This is in itself a large subject and constitutes a major source of arguments that support the force and relevance of ethical positivism to contemporary politics. Thus, it can be argued that focusing electoral politics on the choice of rules rather than simply on the choice of rulers is an important aspect of making the choices of large electorates accord with the political ideal of equal political power. Further, debate about and choice of rules can have an important part to play in turning mere majority decision-making into the sort of democratic decision-making which produces approximation to a consensus about what constitutes justice and the common good.

This bare outline of the case for ethical positivism illustrates the barrage of arguments that can be mustered in favour of positive rule-governance.[44] These rationales do not all take us in exactly the same direction with respect to the sort of rule-governance that they require, but all point to the central role of mandatory rules expressed in clear and precise terms and applied without recourse to the moral opinions of those involved, including citizens, administrators and judges.

---

42 See J Waldron, 'The rule of law in contemporary liberal theory', *Ratio Juris*, Vol 2, 1989, 79.

43 P Pettit, *Republicanism*, Oxford: OUP, 1996.

44 For a more extended treatment, see TD Campbell, *The Legal Theory of Ethical Positivism*, Aldershot: Dartmouth, 1996.

So cumulatively powerful are the arguments for positive rules that only a demonstration of overwhelmingly powerful counter-arguments could prevent ethical positivism establishing its credentials as an ingredient of any acceptable political philosophy. Only the scope of the rules and the spheres in which they should operate remain at issue. While there are such counter-arguments which relate to other political ideas, particularly the values of spontaneity and freedom, these can be accommodated by rolling back the range and scope of the rules we adopt. It is government, not the totality of social and economic life, that ethical positivism wishes to further and confine through rule-governance.

Much more difficult for the ethical positivist are those arguments which purport to demonstrate that positivism sets up an irrelevant ideal because no actual society approaches anywhere near the level of actual instantiation that is required to achieve its objectives. Some of these arguments are empirical ones which point to the gap between the ideals of good positive law and the actuality of patchy implementation, rule-bending, rule-ignoring and rule-absence. Other arguments are more epistemological and *a priori* in that they seek to demonstrate that rules, due to their necessary indeterminacy, cannot possibly fulfil the functions allotted to them even if judges, contra-factually, were always committed to interpreting and enforcing rules in a value-neutral way.[45]

Both the empirical and the epistemological counterattacks represent major challenges to ethical positivism. At one level they can be dealt with in a fairly summary manner. Given the general effectiveness of much administration based on specific legislation and the general utility of, for instance, road traffic law, it is difficult for critics of ethical positivism to demonstrate conclusively the total impracticality of the positivist model. It then becomes a question of the degree to which it is feasible to approximate to this ideal and the areas of social life in which conformity is most readily achieved and is most important.

Similarly, no philosophical argument can convincingly deny, without falling into self-contradiction, that a considerable measure of successful communication does actually take place, particularly amongst persons sharing the same language and social experience. If a philosophical theory of language cannot account for cases of evident communicative success, then it is clearly defective as a theory. The communicative problem for law lies in sustaining successful communication where some participants in the process have vested interests in undermining that communication to avoid unwelcome consequences.

Much more fruitful in this context are studies which seek to identify the conditions of rule-conformity and in particular the conditions of successful communication of norms within linguistic communities. Once it is accepted that legal positivism is an aspirational ideal rather than a repository of descriptive and explanatory truths about all legal systems, issues of conformity and communication can be viewed as offering evidence of the gaps between the aspiration and the reality which can be addressed by efforts to reduce these gaps,

---

45 For treatments of these issues, see B Bix, *Law, Language and Legal Determinacy*, Oxford: Clarendon Press, 1993; and A Marmor (ed), *Interpretation and Legal Theory*, Oxford: Clarendon Press, 1992.

particularly where they are resulting in injustice and inefficiency. Thus, evidence of systematic bias in the interpretation and application of rules in relation to class or gender can be met by efforts to provide rules which are more explicit with respect to these unwelcome social consequences and to provide education and information to those involved which makes them more aware of the insidious impact of class and gender prejudices and so improve the quality of impartial rule-application.

More abstract arguments about the indeterminacy of all rules on the grounds, for instance, that any sequence of numbers can potentially be developed in an infinite number of ways, can be met by evidence of the impact of shared expectations in producing stability in practice and the institutional devices that can be put in place to correct unexpected departures from familiar patterns. In general, linguistic studies that demonstrate the conventional nature of language and the relativity of the possibility of understanding symbols to particular cultures and periods may be accepted as showing that shared meanings and successful communication are unstable cultural achievements which require constant renewal and repair. In other words, plain and 'natural' meaning is a socially dependent and variable cultural phenomenon whose shifting parameters are a constant challenge not only to legislators and judges but to all members of a linguistic community seeking to share a common framework for their different ways of life.

This grand programme of widespread communicative success will seem naïve to those whose familiarity with actual legal process leads them to expect that lawyers and judges are frequently engaged in efforts to destabilise agreed meanings and disrupt patterns of interpretation which aid communication by the introduction of unsuspected ambiguities and novel readings which favour their clients' interests or their views as to how the law might be suitably developed. Further, given the palpable (if overstated) truth of the legal realist contention that the law is what the courts declare it to be through their particular decisions, the chances of attaining the positivist model within an adversarial common law system that expects courts to be involved in legal development are slim indeed.

It is undoubtedly the case that a favourable legal culture adhered to in good faith by legal officials is one of the preconditions of the instantiation of the positivist model. Only courts committed to positivist ideals and provided with rules which have satisfactory levels of clarity, precision and comprehensiveness will come up with a positivist system of law. Everyone agrees that rules do not administer themselves and only have meanings in terms of the linguistic conventions of specific groups. No individual can be forced to adopt those meanings which are clearest within the terms of the linguistic conventions of their community. Legal realism is correct in saying that, beyond the finite system of appeals, there is no way of enforcing positivist legality, but that is not to say that a system which is administered by persons conversant with the communicative conventions of the relevant community, who are provided with good positivist laws and are committed to the positivist legal ideal, cannot achieve what actual courts often do not provide. The 'ethics' of ethical positivism refers not simply to the justificatory arguments in favour of the creation of positivistically good laws but also to the conduct and method of those who are required to administer such a system. Without courts committed to the ideals of ethical positivism, the benefits of positivist law are not available. On the theory of ethical positivism, lawyers' ethics ought to be as much about a good faith commitment to positivist law as about the more familiar issues of honesty, loyalty, diligence and confidentiality.[46]

## THE IMPLICATIONS OF ETHICAL POSITIVISM

If the point of legal positivism is to set out the ideal form of a legal system, it is to be expected that it is partisan with respect to legal reforms which bear on the style and process of law while remaining neutral as to the desirable content of particular laws. Ethical positivism helps, therefore, to make sense of the fact that supposedly purely scientific positivist accounts of law are put forward by theorists with evident reformist agendas. Of no one is this more true than Jeremy Bentham, whose hostility towards the obscurities and mystifications of common law, sarcastic repudiation of the pretensions of universal and inalienable non-legal rights, and enthusiasm for radical codification of law are as well known as his commitment to utilitarian social and political reform. I conclude, therefore, with some indications of the sort of prescriptions that flow from the adoption of the positivist model in contemporary circumstances. Some of these indications relate, as in the case of Bentham, to issues which apply generally to the rule of law, and others, also following Bentham, have more directly to do with the role of law within a democratic system.

The implications of ethical positivism go far beyond the conduct of courts. Indeed, it is a theory which is primarily addressed to the nature and form of legislation as the preferred source of new law. If the statutes are not clear, precise and intelligible in terms of the linguistic practices of the community to which they are addressed, then courts can do relatively little towards the instantiation of the positivist ideal.

In many ways, the preference of ethical positivism for statute law as the prime source of new law rides on the back of considerations of democratic legitimacy, but there are more general grounds for reaching the same preference, one of which can be seen in the emphasis given to the priority of the words of the statutory text as against the lesser significance given to the actual words of common law judgments. Despite all the difficulties that arise in the interpretation of texts, they proffer at least the prospect of agreement on what law requires. Towards this end, ethical positivism is bound to focus on the capacity of the legal system to identify the authoritative text of the law and to develop a mode of interpreting that text which justifies the significance given to it in the process of legislation. Courts, on the positivist view, must show respect for the words which have been debated and voted on in accordance with the formal procedures of legislatures without having

46 For a radically different view, which implicated legal positivism in the disarray of current professional legal ethics, see W Simon, *The Practice of Justice: A Theory of Lawyers' Ethics*, Cambridge, MA: Harvard University Press, 1998.

to embark on the hopeless process of seeking to discover hidden intentions and legislative motives lying behind the choices which make the law. Working this through imposes on the ethical positivist a duty to enunciate a normative theory of legislation which identifies the authority-creating moments of legislation in the light of the positivist ideal of formally 'good' law. This is a task which requires attention in equal measure to the court-centred jurisprudential debate on the interpretation of law.

A similar combination of democratic and more general rule of law considerations features in the implications of ethical positivism with respect to bills of rights. Concentrating, again, on the non-democratic rationales for rule-governance, the distrust of ethical positivism for bills of rights relates principally to the vague and indeterminate meanings of broadly drawn statements of rights and open-ended exception clauses which place the full weight of legislative responsibility on the 'interpretations' of courts. While this may be manageable in relation to some basic human rights which it is generally agreed that government ought to but do not always respect, the scope of fundamental rights now include some of the most contentious and intractable political disputes characteristic of modern societies. The examples of abortion in relation to the right to life, campaign expenditure in relation to freedom of expression and the right to strike in relation to freedom of association serve to indicate that contemporary human rights discourse is not confined to policing the performance of government in relation to self-evidently illegitimate conduct. The claim that precision is given to these rights by reference to the case law of human rights courts only highlights the fact that precision is achieved in an *ad hoc* manner by those same bodies whose role it is to apply and enforce the rights in question.[47]

Legal positivism in its normative form does not in itself exclude fundamental laws which are taken as lexically prior in the case of conflict with other sources of law and is generally neutral with respect to the democracy-based arguments for and against entrenched laws, but the theory does throw up a range of considerations which militate against giving such status to unspecific and boundless assertions of rights that generate controversy as soon as attempts are made to concretise them in a form that bears on actual circumstances.[48] Paradoxically, it is the absence of mechanisms for translating such abstractions into determinative decisions – something which positivists are routinely accused of pretending they are in possession of – that gives legal positivists such qualms about loosely phrased legal rights. Judicial confidence in Kantian methods of universalisation, or Rawlsian techniques of impartial decision-making, or Dworkinian exhortations to interpret a legal tradition as the 'best that it can be',

---

47 For a critical overview of these issues, see TD Campbell, 'Democracy, human rights and positive law', *Sydney Law Review*, Vol 16, 1994, 195.

48 WJ Waluchow, *op cit* fn 1, Chapter 5, argues that exclusive legal positivism cannot explain the law of 'charter states' where moral meaning is part of the law. Prescriptive hard legal positivism accepts his account but takes his evidence as a ground for rejecting 'charters' which invite moral readings. R Dworkin, *Freedom's Law: The Moral Reading of the American Constitution*, Cambridge, MA: Harvard University Press, 1996, argues that such moral readings of the American Constitution, while not generally accepted explicitly, are normal and should be commended.

do little to reassure the ethical positivist that there is no need for a great deal more precision in the statement of rights before they are placed in the hands of the uncertain jurisprudence of courts whose determinations are legally sovereign in the case of constitutionally entrenched bills of rights.

These examples of the practical implications of ethical positivism could be augmented in relation to such matters as alternative dispute resolution, anti-discrimination law and judicial review of administrative action. However, the examples given are sufficient to illustrate the way in which regarding legal positivism as a political ideal generates debate in a focused manner around what are amongst the most contentious and significant issues arising in contemporary constitutional law. These debates show that ethical positivism has something to offer that is very different from generalised abstractions. It does not, lie these abstractions, seek to capture the general features of all actual systems of law and definitions of fundamental legal concepts in order to circumscribe imaginative debate on the reform of legal systems.

The liberating and focused debates which are brought to the fore by interpreting legal positivism, along with other major jurisprudential theories, as competing political ideals are not confined to specific political and constitutional matters, but also have bearing on some of the most persistent abstract debates in legal theory, such as the nature of legal obligation. For instance, if we add to the analysis of mandatory rules given above reasons of the sort that have been referred to in providing rationales for rule-governance, then we are likely to come as near as is possible to a meaningful notion of legal obligation, and one which is quite distinct from the prudential rationales relating to the sanctions which may follow disregard for the law, with which legal positivism is normally associated. In giving us a multiplicity of reasons why we should conform to laws in relative abstraction from our approval or disapproval of their content, ethical positivism renders more intelligible the idea that there is an obligation to obey the law which is not contingent on our approval of its specific content. That, however, is another story and a different point.

# 3

# THE ETHICS OF POSITIVISM

Positivist ideals relate directly to the political justification of prescriptive positivism. The ethics of positivism have to do with the conduct of those who fill the various roles within a system of government through rules – principally legislators, citizens, lawyers and judges. Questions of ethics cannot be resolved without reference to the ideals of the institution within which these roles have meaning and the justifications which support that system. The objective of this chapter is to explore the ethics of the legal theory of ethical positivism (LEP) in this context.

Ethics is a matter both of the moral standards of conduct which ought to govern the performance of the various legal roles and of the required commitment and conformity to these standards, typically where there are no legal sanctions involved.[1] This is partly a matter of devising and seeking conformity to appropriate rules of conduct, but also involves the choice of alternative performances when the rules do not or cannot adequately cover the situations in question.

'Ethics' is the appropriate term here, not simply because much of the normative substance relates to role performance rather than personal behaviour, but also because the rules and standards are not in themselves laws, although some of them may be administered in a quasi-legal manner by the professional groups involved and their determinations may be challenged and adjudicated as law.[2] If ethics is reduced to a legal-style enforcement of professional rules then it becomes in effect a matter of regulation rather than morality and, given that the professional sanctions are enforceable at law, is in many ways indistinguishable from law itself. In such circumstances the 'ethical' tag is justified, if at all, by the fact that the moral standards required by the official rules of the role are 'higher' than those which are expected of other people. In fact, much of the content of what is taken to be a matter of 'professional ethics' involves standards which merely put some limits to the apparent immoralities that are licensed by the role of lawyers in protecting the interests of clients. In general, lawyers' ethics may be perceived as rather 'lower' than average on the scale of morally admirable

---

1 In a broader sense, 'ethics' is used for the philosophy of morals: see AC Ewing, *Ethics*, New York: Free Press, 1953; B Williams, *Ethics and the Limits of Philosophy*, Glasgow: Collins, 1985; and O Brink, *Moral Realism and the Foundations of Ethics*, Cambridge: CUP, 1989.

2 Examples of professional codes of conduct include the American Bar Association's Model Rules of Professional Conduct (1983) and the Solicitors' Professional Conduct and Practice Rules (1994) promulgated by the Council of the Law Society of New South Wales.

conduct. Moreover, there are aspects of professional codes which are directed towards protecting the interests of the profession and regulating internal competition between lawyers. To the extent that such matters are central to codes of professional 'ethics', there is little that is ethical about them.[3]

It is part of the paradox of politics that no legal system can adequately deal with the problem of controlling the controllers. Whatever the division of powers involved in a polity, one or more parts of the constitutionally defined political system has to be trusted to act appropriately with respect to the foundational rules and goals of the constitution. Thus, for constitutional government to exist, it is arguable that some body other than the legislature must decide whether or not the legislature is acting within its powers. There is no evident constitutional manner in which the power to make such decisions can be reviewed by the legislature without rendering them vacuous. In this case, courts, in their constitutional rulings with respect to the validity of legislation, must simply be trusted. Alternatively, the legislature may be left to act within its constitutional powers with no external legal controls. It then has to be trusted to remain within the conventions which govern the propriety of its proceedings. Whichever body is given the final decision on such matters has an ethical choice, in that there can be no immediate sanction involved and no legal remedy readily available. This trust is diluted rather than avoided by a Madisonian system which takes the separation of powers to the point where the effectiveness of government is in doubt.[4] This means that some role occupants, individually or jointly, can get away with whatever they decide, short of unconstitutional political moves being made against them. This does not mean that there are no rules involved. The ethics of roles are governed by social or political conventions as well as by explicitly enacted constitutions. However, it is characteristic of such situations that they are under-determined by the rules and conventions involved, which, in the absence of readily available mechanisms for overt change, are subject to flexible interpretations and gradual changes to accommodate the political pressures of the time.

These factors arise most evidently in the case of high constitutional roles such as those occupied by Supreme Court justices, presidents and Parliaments, but they also have application to lesser roles within a legal system even though the rules may be more available and far more readily changed at hierarchically lower levels. Here also problems of enforcement often mean that it is not easy to police and assure conformity with the proprieties of role performance. Indeed, it is a sociological truism that legal systems require most citizens to obey the law other than from a fear of legal sanctions. Similarly, no legal system can operate without a degree of conscientious conformity to the role standards by lawyers and judges.[5]

---

3 TL Shaffer, 'The legal ethics of radical individualism', *Texas Law Review,* Vol 65, 1987, 297: 'Most of what American lawyers and law teachers call legal ethics is not ethics. Most of what is called legal ethics is similar to rules made by administrative agencies. It is regulatory. Its appeal is not to conscience, but to sanction. It seeks mandate rather than insight.'

4 The *locus classicus* is James Madison, *The Federalist Papers,* num 51.

5 For a helpful introductory discussion, see J Waldron, *The Law,* London: Routledge, 1990, Chapter 4.

In addition, there is another ethical aspect of all role fulfilment in relation to rules which is particularly relevant to LEP. However sound the rules may be from a positivist viewpoint, it is possible to adopt attitudes towards rules which represent a good faith attempt to understand the rules and follow them conscientiously, a bad faith avoidance of this objective or, somewhere in between, an endeavour to read the *rules* in the way which best suits the individual concerned and follow them only to the extent that is necessary to avoid sanctions. It is trite to say that it is morally preferable to follow the spirit rather than the letter of the law. If by the 'spirit' of the law we mean the purposes of the rule-makers rather than the meaning – or 'letter' – of the law, then this is not part of the ideal of LEP, which subscribes to the view that rules exclude such considerations. But following the spirit of the law can also be taken to imply that rules should be read and followed in good faith, that is, by taking an impartial view of their meaning and conscientiously endeavouring to follow the rule so read. 'Impartiality' here means no more than bracketing off the consequences for the individual concerned from the factors which are allowed to influence the decisions made, except in so far as these consequences have a moral relevance which can be appreciated from the point of view of those not directly involved. In other words, impartiality involves viewing the situation as you would if you were not one of those principally affected: the point of view which is suggested by the principle of universalisability.[6]

It is contended that the ideals of LEP are not realisable unless the majority of participants in a legal system take such an 'ethical' attitude towards their role enactment, whether as legislator, citizen, lawyer or judge. We shall see that this runs counter to the idea that it is the duty of a lawyer to do whatever serves the interests of a client even if this means suppressing evidence, intentionally distorting the otherwise clear meanings of rules and seeking to frustrate and delay the legal process, to mention a cross-section of the practices which give lawyers and lawyering a bad name.

First, we need to review the general argument that law as an institution is amoral, an argument which would destroy the foundation of the whole idea that positivism has a legal ethic.

## LEGAL POSITIVISM AND THE ALLEGED AMORALITY OF LAW

The separability thesis, according to which law and morality are conceptually distinct, often gives rise to the mistaken view that legal positivism cannot be based on an affirmative moral or ethical view of law and politics. It is also necessary to distinguish LEP from the more specific thesis of moral disestablishmentarianism, according to which the extent to which the morality of a society is reflected in the content of law ought to be minimised. Moreover, LEP

6 This limited sociological conception of impartiality is central to the moral and legal theory of Adam Smith. See A Smith, DD Raphael and AL Macfie (eds), *The Theory of Moral Sentiments*, Oxford: Clarendon Press, 1976.

does not take the view that laws can be neutral with respect to the morality of different ways of life, but only that they be identifiable and applicable without the exercise of autonomous first-order moral judgments.

On the other hand, it has been acknowledged that there is basis for the contention that some positivists are amoral (that is, non-moral rather than immoral), in that legal positivism has historical connections with 'positivism' as a hard-nosed empiricist theory of science which has no place for questions which involve critical moral evaluation. Versions of such amoral legal positivism have been espoused by logical positivists and others who hold that moral judgments are non-cognitivist, in that they are ultimately a matter of personal preference rather than intellectually or empirically testable belief. Logical positivists, and some legal positivists, are dismissive of any objectivity or epistemology that is not based either in empirically falsifiable propositions or in analytical truths derived from morally contingent definitions.

These philosophical views with respect to the subjectivity of moral opinion are often associated with legal positivism and linked in with the fact that many classical legal positivists have tended to come out firmly for unconditional obedience to law, whether substantively good or bad. Before commenting on these associations, we should note that while positivists, like everyone else, cannot without contradiction deny that there is a *legal* obligation to obey or respect all positive laws, modern positivists take it to be a virtue of their theory that the sharp distinction between what law is and what law ought to be makes it a visibly open question whether citizens are morally bound to carry out their legal obligations. The classic positivists tend to Bentham's view that the citizen is under a moral duty to obey punctually, but to censure freely,[7] but modem positivists are keen to emphasise that the censure may involve recommending legal nonconformity. Certainly Austin, amongst others, invokes the spectre of anarchy as grounds for condemning the use of individual judgment in the making of decisions about whether or not to obey law,[8] although he does so on the basis of a cognitivist epistemology. Further, these positivists argue that natural law has the disadvantage with respect to social order that those who accept the theory will tend to make up their own mind about the morality and hence – in accordance with natural law theory – the legality of what is required of them by courts or statutes. This argument has little force unless it is assumed that, under positivism, disobedience on the grounds that the law is believed to be immoral is not a moral option. In this case, it might appear that the positivist is renouncing a moral approach to law and this may be the basis for the view that positivism is an amoral theory.

This conclusion fails to take account of the fact that an absolutist theory of political obligation must be based on moral reasons for the suspension of

7 See GJ Postema, *Bentham and the Common Law*, Oxford: Clarendon Press, 1986, 318–19; J Bentham, *An Introduction to the Principles of Morals and Legislation*, R Burns and HLA Hart (eds), Oxford: Clarendon Press, 1970, Chapter 2.

8 J Austin, *The Province of Jurisprudence Determined*, London: Weidenfeld & Nicolson, 1955, Lecture VI.

individual judgment concerning the morality of a law when it comes to the point of deciding whether to abide by it. These moral reasons are second-order ones in that they do not engage directly with the morality or immorality of particular laws and focus instead on the reasons for having laws. Such second-order moral reasons are aptly called 'ethical' as distinct from moral. At this point, LEP feeds on all the varied arguments that have been presented for the utility and morality of government through rules.[9] Convenience conventions and organisational institutional arrangements do not work without general conformity; deterrence requires that we in general disallow individuals' conscientious objections, while democracy and justice require the general acceptance of those majority decisions which are expressed in the form of rules. All these considerations morally ground arguments for conformity without immediate regard to substance. However, we have seen that none of these rule rationales justify total suspension of individual moral judgment. Not only do most of them involve some assessment of the efficacy and benefits of conformity to rules in accordance with some view of their type and purpose, but all of them require us to accept the possibility that, in particular instances, the harm done by conformity so clearly outweighs the possible benefits as to make the conformity morally unacceptable. While there is a danger of self-partiality in anyone acting from such assessments of their own conduct where this enables them to avoid a burden which would otherwise fall on them, positivists may accept that it is sometimes morally correct to act in accordance with such assessments despite the danger of self-interested delusion and the prospect of undermining the generally beneficial habits of obedience on which social order depends.

A great deal in the debate about the moral defeasibility of legal obedience depends on the extent to which there is moral disagreement in a society, particularly moral disagreement on this very topic – namely, how far the individuals should follow their own conscience in practical reasoning about the force of specific legal obligations. Where it is known that a significant number of citizens have strong moral reservations about enacted laws and hold to the belief that conformity to such laws is either not morally required or actually morally unacceptable, then those rule rationales which depend upon the assumption of general conformity are potentially undermined. Conformity may, of course, be obtained by deterrence and incentive means, but this may not be effective and has moral costs in its impact on the significant liberties and moral dignity of the disaffected citizens.

In such situations, the moral question to be addressed is whether the cost in terms of liberty and moral dignity which results from requiring people to act against their first-order moral convictions is worth paying for the (perhaps reduced) benefits obtainable through the set of rules in question. It is hard to come to a position on such matters without paying attention to the moral views of the dissenters. Where their views have some plausibility, moral or empirical, this would appear to weaken the case for enforcing conformity, something which may cause few moral qualms where the dissenters hold what are regarded as

---

9 TD Campbell, *The Legal Theory of Ethical Positivism*, Aldershot: Dartmouth, 1996.

outrageous beliefs about, for instance, a fundamental human right. There can ultimately be no defensible line-drawing with respect to morally permissible or required disobedience without reference to the moral substance of the laws in question.

However, to give weight to the differential acceptability of the divergent moral opinions which threaten legal conformity does seem to presuppose a cognitivist meta-ethic, for we require some confidence in the universalisability of our own moral judgment if we are to treat the views of others as unreasonable or outrageous.[10] Here we do come to a logical connection between the issue of political obligation and at least some forms of legal positivism, for many positivists adopt a non-cognitivist view of ethics which would appear to preclude their taking the sort of moral stand that is required to justify disobedience to valid law. Conversely, denying that there is such a thing as moral truth gives them one reason for rejecting the natural lawyer's commitment to disobeying unjust laws, namely that we have no way of knowing what is substantively just. Since LEP involves a cognitive moral epistemology, it looks as if it cannot rely on this particular argument against individual moral discretion in the face of morally questionable law, but, if the version of cognitivism held by the legal positivist is such that it is very difficult to arrive at moral truth, at least on certain matters, and if it is allowed that the selfishness and ignorance of human beings means that there is a weak correlation between such knowledge of moral truth as they possess and their actual conduct, then the implications for moral discretion of the admission of an objectivist meta-ethics is greatly reduced; but then so is the scope for condemning particular laws as outrageously immoral.

It is clear, then, that LEP does not take an amoral view towards the question of our moral obligation to obey or disobey laws, although other legal positivists may do so. In general, LEP presents an array of ethical reasons for legal conformity: significant liberty, fairness, the efficient pursuit of public goods and the general happiness and, where applicable, respect for democratic power. What LEP does is to point up a number of arguments in favour of adherence to positivistic rules which provide defeasible rationales for conformity to positive law which are sufficiently specific for us to work out a moral position in relation to our response to grossly immoral rules and regimes. This is not an amoral position, although it is one which morally requires that we, as citizen, lawyer or judge, routinely subordinate our own first-order moral views as to the substance of a piece of legislation to our second-order or ethical views about the legitimacy and value of the system as a whole. If it is the case that subordination to valid law is not always morally overriding, it must be the case that a moral judgment has to be made in each case, not about the validity of the law, but about whether to conform with it. If the decision is taken simply in terms of the content of the rule then that is never compatible with the role of a citizen or judge, but it is always a moral option to override the moral reasons in favour of rule conformity because of the gross

10 This is a controversial philosophical view which may be said to mix up ethics and meta-ethics; however, I would argue strongly that meta-ethics does have implications for the degree of seriousness it is rational to invest in moral judgment. For the opposing view, see JL Mackie, *Ethics: Inventing Right and Wrong*, Harmondsworth: Penguin, 1977.

immorality of the rule in question. The choice of whether or not to conform in these cases is not a legal judgment but an ethical one, and it is an ethical one which is compatible with the moral foundations of LEP. This means that, potentially, any judgment as to role performance is a matter of ethics. It follows that the way such a decision should be reached must conform to the requirements of impartiality and good faith that were outlined in the introduction to this chapter. This is a long way from regarding legal systems from an amoral point of view.

## LAWYERS' ETHICS

Defending positivism against amoralism is to confront only the lesser charge, for it is often argued that positivism is an ideology which seeks to legitimise not only the amorality of law but the immorality of lawyers.[11] We shall consider shortly the plausibility of associating positivism, the dominant theory of many civil law jurisdictions, with the alleged shortcomings of the adversarial method, which is a feature of common law systems, but first we must examine the substance of the charge that lawyering is no job for a morally good person.[12]

In accordance with the popular jibe, the difference between lawyers and rats is that there are some things that rats just will not do.[13] In contrast to rats, lawyers are perceived, no doubt unfairly, as being willing to lie, conceal, manipulate and do down anyone other than their client. In their more defensible forms, these actions are regarded as a matter of the lawyers' duty to their clients within an adversarial system. In their less palatable form they are regarded as part and parcel of the purely pragmatic conduct of lawyers in the pay of the wealthy and unprincipled clients on whom they depend for their livelihood. Such criticisms, particularly the latter, draw indignant repudiations from a profession which regards itself as having a high calling and a position in society which is justified by professional standards of integrity and trustworthiness: it is simply a matter of public misunderstanding that single-mindedness in the protection of a client's interest is anything but a particular commitment to seeing that justice is done. Here we seem to have uncovered another paradox, to the effect that the self-image of the lawyer as having higher than average ethical standards, and thus being especially worthy of public trust, is grounded in much the same conduct as gives rise to the public perception of lawyers as unworthy of respect.

Something in this mismatch between the internal and external views of the legal professional is due to difficulty in appreciating the nature of role morality, that is, the rights and duties which attach to a position within a social institution rather than as ordinary persons.[14] These difficulties in understanding role

---

11 WH Simon, 'The ideology of advocacy: procedural justice and professional ethics', *Wisconsin Law Review*, Vol 29, 1978, 30–144.

12 For the provocative phraseology, see C Fried, 'The lawyer as friend: the moral foundations of the lawyer–client relation', *Yale Law Journal*, Vol 85, 1976, 1060–89.

13 For this and other quips, see D Luban (ed), *The Ethics of Lawyers*, Aldershot: Dartmouth, 1994, xiff.

14 Thus R Wasserstrom, 'Lawyers as professionals: some moral issues', *Human Rights*, Vol 5, 1975, 1–24.

morality as instrumental within larger social organisations are exacerbated by the nature of the lawyers' task in advising and representing clients in a legal system which culminates in an adversarial process in which the just outcome is held to depend on two conflicting parties doing their best to discredit the contentions of the other side. The gladiatorial contest, moreover, is being adjudicated by an impartial umpire, perhaps with the assistance of a jury that takes no active part in the proceedings. Once the subtleties of role morality in general and the adversarial legal role in particular are appreciated, then, it is argued, it will be seen that good lawyers are indeed good persons because they are striving to do their best for someone else in a situation where that person's important interests are under attack and vulnerable to coercive and detrimental intervention. Lawyers' duty is to subordinate their own views and interests to those of the clients in whose service they must deploy their legal and other skills and knowledge, hence the twin ideas of neutrality with respect to the moral goals and character of the client and zealous partisanship in furthering the interests identified to him or her.[15]

As we will see when we come to the role of the judge, it is easy to appreciate that persons with special responsibilities must have higher standards of ethical conduct than others. Thus, judges, like most officials, have a duty to impartiality which does not apply to the individual citizen. However, the example of soldiers in war notwithstanding, it is not so easy as to assimilate the idea that special responsibilities may require exemptions from the ordinary standards of moral conduct. We therefore find it hard to accept that lawyers are entitled to lie for their clients or withhold evidence that would clearly establish that their client is guilty, or legally liable. While an element of partisanship may be admirable, especially in defence of an accused or an underprivileged civil litigant, we are less likely to warm to the delaying tactics, manipulations and try-ons that lawyers may adopt in the service of wealthy corporate clients.

Despite an extensive literature on these matters, there is little agreement on the precise parameters of the lawyers' role. There are certainly difficult lines to draw in such matters. Even if lawyers should subordinate their own interests to those of the client, may they sacrifice the interests of others by withholding evidence, or destroying the credibility of witnesses they know to be telling the truth? Is permitting the presentation of perjured evidence simply the price to be paid for the assurances of confidentiality which encourage the disclosure by clients of information that may be necessary for lawyers to carry out their appointed task or representative role? The challenge is to discover a principled way in which lines can be drawn between acceptable partiality and unacceptable partisanship. It is uncontroversial that the lawyer may do only that which is within the law, but that does not help us answer questions about what the law should be in these matters. In any case, we are concerned with professional standards which go beyond the legal minimum. Nor can we settle for the neat thesis that the lawyer may do only what the client may do for himself, for the client's morality may diverge from that of the lawyer, and this formulation does not enable us to arrive at a specific service

---

15 See SL Pepper, 'The lawyer's amoral ethical role: a defense, some problems and some possibilities', *American Bar Foundation Research Journal*, 1986, 613–35.

role which involves doing things for clients that the clients cannot do for themselves.

Unavoidably, therefore, we have to confront the nature of court process in relation to its functions and the ways in which it carries out those functions. The standard thesis put forward by practitioners is that justice is served if court proceedings are adversarial, with each party's legal representative putting forward the best legal and evidential arguments on each side with a judge whose duty is to enforce rules of procedure and choose between the two cases as presented, perhaps with the assistance of a jury for the determination of matters of fact. Thus, it is often asserted that the prime purpose of a trial is to arrive at the truth regarding disputed claims or accusations, and to apply the relevant legal rules to the court's view of what actually occurred. It is in the determination of factual disputes that courts are mainly concerned and to which the adversarial system seems particularly germane. If, it is argued, there is an open debate between parties who are striving to establish or to disprove a particular allegation of fact then we are most likely to have before the tribunal all the evidence which is relevant to its determinations. The specialist role of looking for evidence either for or against a factual contention is said to be particularly effective in establishing the truth, hence also the importance of eyewitnesses and the need to test their recollections by vigorous questioning.[16]

In relation to the purposes of law, all this would be highly persuasive if it were true that unfettered adversarialism produces factual accuracy better than any practical alternative. In particular, it would fit neatly with a positivist model according to which the idea is to apply rules accurately, which must require reliable fact-finding above all else. It is less persuasive on a realist view in terms of which we can look for favourable or predictable decisions but not of accurate or correct ones.

The effectiveness of the adversarial system with respect to fact-finding cannot be explored here, although we may note that there is little evidence to support its effectiveness as against civil law methods.[17] But the argument does have the merit of making the question of professional ethics dependent on empirical claims about the workings and outcomes of alternative legal systems. The principle we are looking for in relation to ethical line drawing in professional practice becomes, at least in part, a matter of testing alternative court procedures in the light of desired results. It then becomes a matter of empirical investigation to discover what role conduct is best adapted to the system's objectives. This immediately frees us from a dogmatic commitment to serving a client's interests come what may, for the professional role becomes that of doing for the client only that which maximises the effectiveness of the system. Given this approach, it is likely that we will be able to come to some conclusions about such matters as the ethics of destroying the credibility of a witness whom the lawyer knows to be telling the

---

16 See MH Freedman, 'Personal responsibility in professional systems', *Catholic University Law Review*, Vol 27, 1978, 191–205.

17 For critiques of the accuracy of the adversarial method in relation to the assessment of evidence, see WH Simon, *op cit* fn 11, 119–30.

truth, failing to reveal relevant evidence to the other side or telling and supporting lies.[18]

The prospects of agreement on lawyers' advocacy roles may be disputed as resting on naïve beliefs about the possibility of knowing what is in fact true or false, as distinct from seeking to prove one or the other.[19] It may be that the lawyers' zealous partisanship is justified by the fact that consensual factual beliefs rest on common prejudices rather than sound evidence, prejudices which are shared by the individuals who act as lawyers. The role of lawyers is to appreciate that such consensus is an inadequate empirical basis for important determinations of truth or falsity and to force themselves to try and see the alleged facts from a different perspective, and in particular to see the events in question from the perspective of the client. Thus, whatever the lawyer believes to the contrary, the client may in fact be innocent; therefore it is right for lawyers to pretend that they believe this so as to give that client's point of view proper representation. This may even apply where the defendant shares the common prejudices and so has what might be regarded as a distorted view of his own conduct. In such cases, the lawyer's duty is to challenge even the client's perceptions if it is in that client's interests to do so.

Similar points may be made about the lawyer's role in arguing questions of law. The positivist's ideal of respecting the plain meaning of legal rules is countered by the lawyer's duty to argue for that reading of the rules which most favours her client's case, hence the motivation, perhaps the duty, to undermine the positivist goal of achieving rules which can command consensus as to their meaning as well as their content. It might seem odd that a lawyer's duty is to render plain meanings obscure, but audience understandings of the same words and sentences can vary enormously within a given society. Some such processes may be seen as the best way of arriving at an agreed meaning for a rule in social situations where communication is a problem and rules are not plain in relation to the diverse criteria of meaning actually in operation. Certainly, this approach is appropriate when we are seeking to improve legislation by removing obscurities

---

18 The standard examples of so called 'moral dilemmas' whose mere formulation can be seen as the basis for moral criticism are those discussed in MH Freedman, 'Professional responsibility of the criminal defense lawyer: the three hardest questions', *Minnesota Law Review*, Vol 64, 1966, 1989. They all relate the criminal defence advocacy: attempting to discredit an adverse witness whom the lawyer knows to be telling the truth, putting a witness on the stand whom the lawyer knows will commit perjury, and counselling a client in a way which will encourage him to commit perjury. Examples which may be thought to be nearer to real dilemmas often relate to the duty of client confidentiality in situations where innocent persons will suffer unless that confidence is breached.

19 'Sir, you do not know [a cause] to be good or bad until the Judge determines it … An argument which does not convince yourself, may convince the Judge to whom you urge it: [A]nd if it does convince him, why then, Sir, you are wrong and he is right' (Boswell, *The Life of Johnson*, 1987, 47f). DL Rhode, 'The ethical perspectives on legal practice', *Stanford Law Review*, Vol 37, 1985, 619, takes this to be a positivist view, although it smacks more of legal realism.

and ambiguities. It may be thought to be equally helpful in arriving at an authoritative sense of relevant law.[20]

This is difficult terrain, but solutions can be sought by examining how court lawyers' roles contribute to the role that the judge is expected to play. If, in brief, judges are enjoined to exercise considerable imagination as to putative fact situations and considerable open-mindedness as to how rules may have been understood by those to whom they are addressed, then we believe that their role performance would not be assisted by suppression of relevant evidence or deliberate deceit, or by placing witnesses and litigants in situations where they are pressured in a way which makes it less likely that they will give honest and accurate accounts. But it does allow for a considerable effort on behalf of lawyer and judge to see the matters in dispute from the points of view of both parties.

We may argue that the parameters of the court lawyers' duties are set by the ideal of the accurate application of law in situations of dispute and the particular way in which the system in question seeks to attain that objective. Commitment to clients' interests thereby becomes secondary in theory but may be all but paramount in practice. Much the same can be said about other lawyer functions, such as advising and mediating, but not all lawyering has to be seen in the context of possible litigation, and not all litigation is motivated by narrow self-interest. Law is for the good man as well as the bad man, and legal advice may be sought, and perhaps should be routinely assumed to be sought, with a view to determining legal rights and duties for the purpose of enabling the enquirer to conform to the requirements of the law. Indeed, we can say that, from the point of view of LEP, while it is the lawyer's duty to advise the client in terms of what he may and may not do legally, this does not mean concentrating on how closely a person can get to breaking the law in the pursuit of his personal objectives without actually violating or going beyond the law.[21]

In an influential article on the failure of legal positivism and other theories of law to justify the adversarial system, William H Simon both castigates legal positivism for endorsing what he calls the ideology of advocacy and argues that it in fact fails to provide an adequate defence of the system.[22] Simon's analysis is unhelpful in its caricature of positivism as an extreme manifestation of egoistic liberalism which has not developed since the time of Hobbes, except to take on board a measure of American legal realism.[23] He fails to notice that most legal positivists have not supported the adversarial system. Simon does treat legal positivism prescriptively, although he assumes that social order in the interests of

---

20 The recognition of the distinction between a possible interpretation and a manipulative try-on may, of course, be difficult to institutionalise, but it is a characteristic of many moral distinctions that they fail to be made by the agent in question.

21 WH Simon, *op cit* fn 11, 30, argues that positivists assume their clients to be egoistic individualists when in fact they may not be so at all. While it is true that this strand is an element within the utilitarian individualism of Hobbes and some later utilitarian positivists, it is unclear why this legal viewpoint is particularly tied to contemporary legal positivism.

22 WH Simon, *op cit* fn 11.

23 WH Simon, *op cit* fn 11, 39–42.

individual autonomy is its sole supporting value, ignoring altogether such matters as Hart's focus on facilitative rules. The substance of his argument is to the effect that the existing legal system does not produce the certainty and predictability that is the positivist's *raison dêtre* for law. This is because legal positivists, having introduced procedural rules to control the power of the state, take justice to be a matter of sticking to these adjectival rules rather than seeing to the accurate application of first-order law. Further, lawyers are said to fail to treat their clients as autonomous beings by erroneously attributing to them the egoistic rationalism of the theory itself.[24]

Simon marshals a great deal of evidence which demonstrates that, in the United States at least, procedural rules are used to thwart the discovery of truth, litigation is undertaken for reasons other than enforcing the arbitrary will of the sovereign and settlements are routinely made which ignore substantive law. His persuasive conclusion is that the procedural discretion given by the common law in civil cases to litigants (and so in effect their lawyers) means that the law is in the hands of private power and is used by the wealthy as a form of legalised blackmail so that 'the threat to the citizen from the sovereign has been alleviated only at the cost of aggravating the threat from his fellow citizens'.[25] Simon argues that positivism can offer no help in restoring the credibility of the adversarial model because it lacks any notion of shared values on which to reassert substantive justice or render accessible the non-egoistic ends of clients.

In fact, however, there are plenty of positivist sources beyond Simon's simplistic caricature on which we can draw for these tasks. In particular, the approach to the procedural complexities of the common law adopted by Bentham coincides with Simon's own critique of the fetishism of process. It is precisely in the attempt to reform procedure in a way which makes it serve the end of accurate rule application that positivism can make a contribution to clarifying the issues of legal ethics. Bentham's argument is that the system should be flexible in the admission of evidence so that the court can make its own evaluations of its worth.[26] This goes with a move to debunk the mythological complexities in the law of evidence, a matter in which Simon echoes Bentham by identifying it as a source of the commercial value. Indeed, Bentham's recommendation that each person be his own lawyer is remarkably similar to Simon's own idea of non-professional advocacy.[27]

Simon's empirical evidence cannot be put lightly to one side when contemplating the prospects for realising a positivist system of adjudication. In particular, there is an enormous problem in the incompatibility of lawyering as a private business designed to generate income for the lawyer by serving the interests of the consumer and the role of lawyer as a servant of the court with a public function which has to do with ensuring justice for all. While this problem

---

24 WH Simon, *op cit* fn 11, 58: 'The Positivist lawyer is not an advisor, but a lobbyist for a peculiar theory of human nature.'

25 WH Simon, *op cit* fn 11, 48.

26 GJ Postema, *op cit* fn 7, 347–50.

27 WH Simon, *op cit* fn 7, 130–44.

may be less acute in those jurisdictions where the lawyer is more of a civil servant than a business person, this has its own disadvantages in so far as government through rules is intended to distance the government from the implementation of its enactments. Here we are up against another dilemma arising out of the paradox of politics: whether to view the role of lawyers and judges as part of or independent of government.[28] If it is accepted that an independent bar is the better option as a system of defending accused persons and enforcing legal obligations, then we have to put great weight on the private monopoly of legal services being entrusted to a group of specialists with a powerful public morality which puts the interests of formal justice above those of their clients. This must apply particularly within an adversarial system that enjoins strict confidentiality and specialist partisanship. If these values are not combined with a real commitment to honesty, and a total repudiation of misusing protective procedures to manipulate legal process in the service of illegalities, then the justification for the privileged access of the lawyer to clients and court is without foundation.

There is much else that can be said about the ethics of lawyering, and a great deal of it concerns nothing peculiar to role morality except that it is heightened by the monopoly privileges of lawyers that render them open to temptations with respect to overcharging and other abuses of privilege. These matters are secondary to the overall picture that is rooted in the instrumental role of the lawyer as the mediator between the citizen and the legal process. In relation to the court-centred matters on which we have concentrated, this means seeing the lawyer as contributing to a process of accurate first-order rule implementation in a way which takes into account the difficulties of establishing truth and meanings and the need to do this in a way which is not biased against the parties involved. In other words, lawyers' ethics are subordinate to the adjudicative process which, as we shall now see, is dependent for its functioning on respect for its ethical rationales.

## THE ETHICS OF ADJUDICATION

It is the arguments for government through rules which serve to explain the need to separate rule application from rule-making. If rules are to fulfil their functions, they must be applied as well as promulgated. Legal systems presume that most initial rule application is done by the persons to whom they are addressed, the rule followers, whose conformity is the prerequisite of government via rules. However, a measure of nonconformity and inevitable disputes about conformity or nonconformity render self-application insufficient, hence the need for systems of rule enforcement, principally (a) in the detection, proof and punishment/rectification of nonconformity and (b) in the settlement of disputes between individuals as to their mutual conduct in relation to the rules.

In both aspects, disagreement about the meaning and scope of the rules may require resolution in the light of circumstances which are not clearly defined by

28 For the contrast between civil and common lawyers in this respect, see RL Abel and PSC Lewis, *Lawyers in Society*, Berkeley: University of California Press, 1988–89.

the applicable rules. In principle, such determinations or clarifications might be done by those who create the rules in the first place. This would at least have the advantage that rule-makers would be required to provide the necessary specification and interpretation of the rules which have been legitimated by their enactments. However, there are many powerful arguments for making the enforcement of rules and the settlement of disputes in relation to rules a specialist and distinct activity of a specially trained set of officials:[29]

(a) the advantages of requiring governments to govern via rules is dissipated if governments have power over the application of rules. The interpretative element in rule application gives scope for varying the application of rules in ways which violate their purported universalisation, to the detriment of both fairness and efficiency;

(b) the processes of accurate fact-finding in relation to rules is a complex and time-consuming activity requiring specialist application and skills and removed from the political pressures which would lead to differential rule application according to the political affiliations and significance of those involved;

(c) the task of selecting and interpreting rules as expressions of political choice, while holding to the generality of their form, is a complex process requiring a distinctive professional skill and ethic. This is the central topic of the rest of this chapter.

In sum, such arguments present an overwhelming case for a distinct judicial role which institutionalises the conceptual distinction between rule creation and rule application. Exactly how the judicial role should be carried out is a central preoccupation of LEP. The models adopted follow in large measure from the reasons given for having separate adjudication, particularly the avoidance of political bias in the application of rules to concrete circumstances.

The analysis here centres on the fact, agreed by all legal theorists, that rules do not apply themselves. There is always a fallible human activity involved in taking a general rule and applying it to particular circumstances. There is the problem of identifying which rules to apply in the first place. Then there is the task of seeing whether the situation defined in the rule as required or permissible has occurred in the case in point. This requires knowledge of the meaning of the rule and evidence about the historical event in question. The first is rendered problematic by the fact that rules are always general, referring to types of situation, whereas fact situations are particular and involve an infinite specificity of existences, only some of which are to be selected as relevant to the issue. The fact situation will include many facets not covered by the rule that may have relevance to the specification of what has occurred. The second is rendered problematic by the difficulty of reconstructing the past on the basis of second-hand evidence rather than direct inspection.

---

29 For a more detailed summary, see J Wroblewski, *The Judicial Application of Law*, Dordrecht: Kluwer, 1992.

Given that it will often be a very difficult task to apply rules with any accuracy to past events, it is easy to see how those who apply the rules could be influenced by their personal preferences for a certain type of outcome. This would mean, however, that power is then being exercised by the person applying the rule rather than by the rule creator, thus defeating the objectives for which rule governance is established. For its completion, LEP needs, therefore, to provide an account of how judges ought to go about their task, a technique and an ethic of judging. The professional ethic of judging involves a number of elements which are summarised here:

(a) reading the rules in some appropriate register of the ordinary natural language of the society in which they are adopted and to which they apply;

(b) understanding the rules as expressions of political choices selected from amongst the alternatives known to be available in that culture at that time; but

(c) limiting that understanding to the rule-formulated versions of such political choices rather than the further objectives of the legislature; thus, while it is proper to see the rule as a purposive attempt to control or facilitate human activities so as to achieve certain objectives, it is improper to vary the rule in ways not specified or evidently implied in the rule on the grounds that this might better promote these background purposes;

(d) minimising bias by reducing as far as is possible the effects on the processes of fact-finding and rule interpretation of the personal value assumptions of the judges;

(e) maximising impartiality in judgment by disqualifying judges with a personal interest in the outcome of the case and utilising techniques to give scope for the appreciation of the disparate points of view of those who are directly involved;

(f) giving priority to the recent decisions of legislative authority over the implications of previous legislation or past judicial decisions; but

(g) subordinate to (f), having regard to the rationales for adopting the ideal of government through rules, especially the liberty advantage and moral form advantage, and being sensitive to the distinction between types of rules, particularly co-operative and control rules, in the extent to which they may be modified in the light of particular circumstances; and

(h) accepting the duty to make exceptions in the application of rules when the results are unexpected and clearly contrary to uncontroversial consensual values.

Such objectives and maxims must be multiplied and extended in the form of techniques of interpretation and precise rules of procedural and natural justice, but, however well formed, they will always be manipulable by those who have the interest and *de facto* power to do so. Ultimately, therefore, the attainment of rule through law depends greatly on the integrity of the judiciary in its commitment to positivism and its awareness of the insistent and insidious effects of social prejudices and powerful self-interests.

Central to this sketch of judicial ethics are the concepts of impartiality and bias.[30] Both can be explicated in terms of instrumental values which contribute to accurate rule selection and application. In its weaker form, impartiality is a formal matter which requires that no one is a judge in their own case or, more widely, in a case the outcome of which has direct relevance to their own material interests. The marginal problems with such a principle relate to cases where the judge is a member of a social group that may benefit differentially from a precedent-establishing decision. In its stronger form, impartiality is a matter of giving equal weight to the same considerations without regard to the individuals or classes of person involved, unless the latter is specified in the rule. This is axiomatic where the considerations are identified in the rules themselves, but there are always many factors which have to be taken as understood or implied and which therefore give scope for arbitrariness. The techniques applicable here involve a combination utilising assumed background rules, which are designed to deal with partiality, and psychological devices related to imagination and sympathy, which help to bring to bear the interests of all parties, even those socially and economically distant from that of the judge.

Bias, on the other hand, has more to do with tendencies to view situations and meanings from a social and cultural viewpoint which favours one party above others. This may be regarded as a source of strong partiality which is less visible and explicit. Since all perceptions and readings are affected by background cultural assumptions, there is a sense in which bias is ineliminable, but the effect of bias can be reduced by paying attention to the cultural positions of the parties involved so as to bring to the fore perceptions of social circumstances which are particularly relevant to the parties involved.

The idea of continuing judicial education is not therefore necessarily a product of realist assumptions according to which it is the judges who are the actual law-makers, that is, those whose particular decisions actually determine the legal outcome in any particular case. In accordance with the tenets of legal realism, it is evident that good judges must be schooled in all aspects of the impact of their decisions on the interests and values of those involved and the wider society. They must be economists, psychologists and sociologists, to say nothing of moral and political 'experts'. Something of these requirements may also hold within LEP in so far as it is accepted that often judges must make decisions where there is insufficient guidance from existing law, but a decision cannot or should not wait on a political determination. In such circumstances, judges must be as able and informed as the best law-makers but, even when adequate legislation is available, it cannot be argued that judicial skill is as simple as purely legal expertise in terms of knowledge as to which are the relevant rules and how they relate to each other. The processes of interpretation in hard cases involve an extensive knowledge of the social and political context of the creation and continued use of the rule. And even in relatively easy cases judges have to be sufficiently aware of the social sources of moral and political bias and the ways in which these can affect the way

30 For helpful analyses of impartiality and bias, see Leader, 'Impartiality, bias and the judiciary', in A Hunt, *Reading Dworkin Critically*, New York: Berg, 1992, 241–68.

that rules are read and understood in order to avoid the danger of being affected by the values and assumptions of their own particular socio-economic group.

At the core of the judicial ethic is the unenforceable ideal of self-restraint in relation to the use of the *de facto* power to influence the outcome in a way which is pleasing to the judge's personal predelictions. The temptations here are hard to resist for many reasons, including the fact that many theories of adjudication actually encourage the exercise of moral judgment in the course of legal reasoning. Indeed, the whole tradition of common law reasoning is so loose as to invite moral reflection in terms of the similarities and differences between fact situations on which the analogical development of the common law is said to take place.

There are two further debates which are particularly relevant to these matters. The first is the argument we have already touched on as to the ultimate moral responsibility of everyone, lawyer and judge included, for their actions. The second is the particular difficulties which arise for judges in relation to the rule of recognition. Both may be illustrated by reference to Hart's difficulty in distinguishing between an internal attitude that is required to understand a rule and an internal attitude that involves endorsement of the rule. Hart appears to argue that for a legal system to exist, the judges and other officials must endorse its substance.[31] In fact, all he requires to claim is that officials are sufficiently inside the system to understand the rules in question. However, others have filled this theme out by saying that, as a moral agent, a judge must approve of what she is doing, that this involves approving of the substance of her decision and that this in turn involves making moral judgments about the correctness of the valid law she is applying.

It is surely correct as an analytical truth that a moral agent must make all significant practical choices as moral choices, for which she can be praised or blamed. It does not follow, however, that the proper criterion for every choice must be moral, only that the activity in question must pass moral scrutiny. Thus, as a moral agent, I must morally justify my action of playing golf every week when I might be working, but this does not mean that my choice of club is a moral choice. The same reasoning applies, according to positivism, in relation to judging, which calls for legal reasoning, not moral reasoning. Of course, participating in moral reasoning needs justification in moral terms, and taking on paid employment as a judge or lawyer is particularly in need of moral justification. This does not mean, however, that judgments within the activities of judging or presenting cases are themselves moral judgments.[32]

Somehow it is thought that law must be different. Must judges not morally endorse the decisions they make? Law is not simply a technical matter because its outcomes have impact on people's interests. This ignores the possibility that it is not the duty of judges to apply what they think to be right, but to apply the law. If

---

31 HLA Hart, *The Concept of Law*, OUP, 1961 (2nd edn, 1994), 56.

32 D Beyleveld and R Brownsword, *Law as a Moral Judgment*, London: Sweet & Maxwell, 1986.

judges consider this is an immoral activity, they ought to resign from their position. Here the judge is not in any position different in principle from the citizen of a democratic country who accepts the moral obligation to abide by the outcome of the democratic process.

Perhaps there is a particular problem with the rule of recognition. Thus, Postema notes how Hart responds when confronted with the fact that judges may be challenged about the rule of recognition they use.[33] Postema is unhappy with Hart saying they just note current practice in the judiciary with respect to the acceptance and rejection of possible sources of law. Surely judges must justify the rule or recognition they use, either individually or collectively? Perhaps the assumption is that judges are free to choose the rule of recognition in a way that they are not free to adopt other rules. But this is clearly not the case, for such rules are the result of political determination over who has the power to make law. The question of who has this power is something which calls for moral justification, but not by judges in particular.

Postema's line is to argue that, by pointing to the conventional rules, judges are offering a form of normative justification based on the same grounds as any other convention: 'At bottom his [Hart's] claim is that the authority of criteria of validity ultimately rest not on the justice, correctness, or truth of the criteria as a matter of critical morality but, rather, on convention.'[34] His argument is that conventions are grounded in the social benefits of practices which embody some generally recognised ways of securing mutually beneficial co-ordination:

> The rule of recognition, then, is best understood as involving a convention, that is, a regularity in the behaviour of law-applying officials and citizens in situations calling for the identification of valid legal standards, such that part of the reason why most officials conform to the regularity is that it is common knowledge that most officials and citizens conform to the regularity and that most officials and citizens expect most other officials and citizens to conform.[35]

In other words, the co-ordination benefits that we have noted apply to rules in general are particularly appropriate to the rule of recognition. This is understandable, given that the whole system of law cannot function in a predictable way without a mutually agreed rule of recognition. This is clearly pivotal in providing the benefits of co-ordination and order generally.

It seems to follow that, *qua* judge, a judge should adopt the rule of recognition in common use, but this is only in default of a higher political determination as to the foundation of the constitution. The convention argument is sound from a positivist point of view if judges have to make up their own minds which rule to use, but this does not mean that they have the right to make such a choice, otherwise we would have to concede that judges are the creators of constitutions, whereas, within any democratic ideology, the origin of valid law is a matter for political determination. The fact that it is difficult to control judges who usurp this

---

33 GJ Postema, *op cit* fn 7.
34 GJ Postema, *op cit* fn 7, 171.
35 GJ Postema, *op cit* fn 7, 198.

power is one of the main reasons for insisting upon the need for a powerful judicial ethic.

The general argument here is similar to that which must be deployed to interpret the undoubted fact that the day-to-day legal reality is that it is the judiciary which decides what is or is not a good or acceptable legal argument.[36] What counts as an acceptable argument depends on what is acceptable to 'a particular group, the legal audience'.[37] If this is correct then there is considerable responsibility on this group to maintain the approach legitimated in their system for the sort of reasons that Postema gives in relation to the rule of recognition. Realists such as Llewellyn see the importance of the judicial traditions and have their own recommendations to make as to which method is desirable.[38] Most realists prefer the grand style of flexibility in the light of perceived purpose and social utility, for they see the opportunity for judges to solve social problems by enlightened decision-making. Positivists clearly provide a more rule-governed approach. Given that such decision-making can never be tightly deductive, there is always the capacity of the individual and the group to move towards a partiality of power. Here there is some tension in LEP between those who would advocate a rational reconstruction of decided law in order to enhance coherence and consistency, and those who see this as a way of diluting or thwarting the contemporary political decisions which should be given authority over and above their compatibility with the outcomes of prior political process.

Looking ahead to the discussion of interpretation, there is a convergence of those who take legal reasoning to be a broad matter of practical reason merging with general moral reasoning and those who wish to keep a separation between the two, but accept that in some circumstances recourse must be had to second-best approaches where the law is unclear or in some other way inadequate for the circumstances in hand. These second-best approaches can be similar to the preferred methods of others in ideal conditions.

Traditionally, the central common law method of legal reasoning centres on precedent and analogy. Precedent uses decided cases as a flexible basis for deriving, through a formulation of the ratio of a case by examining the facts which were crucial in the reported decision, a rule or principle to apply to the case in hand.[39] Analogy comes in when comparing decided cases with other sets of facts

---

36 See J Bell, 'The acceptability of legal arguments', in DN MacCormick and P Birks (eds), *The Legal Mind*, Oxford: Clarendon Press, 1986, 45–65.

37 J Bell, *ibid*, 46. See also A Aarnio, 'The foundations of legal reasoning', *Rechtstheorie*, Vol 12, 1981, 131; A Peczenick, *The Basis of Legal Justification*, Lund: Lund University Press, 1983; and R Alexy, *A Theory of Legal Argumentation*, Oxford: Clarendon Press, 1989, for legal argument as a form of social activity which is part of a way of life, with specific rules and practices and important conventions and understandings. Note also AWB Simpson, 'The common law and legal theory', in RS Summers, *Oxford Essays in Jurisprudence*, 2nd series, Oxford: OUP, 1973, who speaks of law as a set of social practices observed and ideas received by a caste of lawyers.

38 Principally, KN Llewellyn, *The Common Law Tradition*, Chicago: University of Chicago Press, 1960.

39 See J Harris, *Legal Philosophies*, London: Butterworths, 1980, Chapter 13; and AWB Simpson, *op cit* fn 37.

to determine whether the situations are relevantly similar.[40] This approach has the feature of merging reasoning about whether an existing rule of law covers a particular set of facts (are the facts of the situations from which the ratios that contribute to the formulation of a legal rule derive sufficiently similar to the case in point?) with reasoning about the formulation of the content of the legal rules which emerge from common law reasoning (what are the relevant similarities between the decided cases that contribute to the formulation of the legal rule?), and involves the variation of existing legal rules to take in situations which have not hitherto been regarded as relevantly similar but are now held to be so. In other words, common law precedent and analogy merges rule application, rule formulation and rule change. This is starkly clear in those many cases that determine the scope and generality of ratios and rules which are a matter of how broadly the rule or principle behind a series of decisions is to be formulated.[41]

At the same time, this form of reasoning can be placed in a wider context by looking on it as part of a more general process of establishing a set of coherent rules and principles. Thus, where a novel fact situation is confronted, a number of precedents and analogies can be brought to bear with the constraint that the process of reasoning should seek to render their application to the novel situation consistent with maintaining and developing the compatibility between the diverse pieces of the mosaic of accepted law. The coherence goal can, of course, be used both to guide decision in the case in point and to affect the interpretation of a decided case or rule of statute law to render it more consistent with decided cases.

Positivism has problems with the way in which traditional method merges the task of rule creation and rule application, and seeks to make a distinction between the analogies that are involved in the application of rules (what are the relevant similarities in terms of the rule?) and the analogies which are involved in varying a rule (for instance by extending it to cover fact situations not originally encompassed by the rule as at present formulated). LEP in particular has at least three worries about the confusion that this generates. One is the ease with which statutory rules can be altered by the judiciary. A second is the tendency to dilute legal changes by ironing out their novelties in the process of seeking coherence with existing law. A third is that, as the method of adapting existing law to deal with such problems as gaps in the law, it is unduly restrictive. Where rule creation or significant rule variation is involved, some loose analogical similarities which may further the coherence of laws may be helpful, but it is important that what is in effect a legislative decision should be undertaken, if it has to be, in the light of a wider range of factors, such as social policy, political morality and economic consequences. For such reasons, LEP seeks a sharper distinction between legislative and adjudicative modes of judicial activity, the latter being the prime purpose of the courts and the former being more in the nature of a regrettable second-best process designed to deal with defects in the form and coverage of existing positive law.

---

40 See B Cardozo, *The Nature of the Legal Process*, New Haven, CT: Yale University Press, 1921.

41 As in *Donoghue v Stevenson* [1932] AC 562.

The relevance of this discussion to judicial ethics is that judges ought in general to refrain from variation and creation of statute law and, where they do cross the boundary from application to creation of law, they should do so overtly and in the light of the full range of factors relevant to the legislative task. Making these distinctions clearly not only improves the manner in which the innovations deriving from judicial discretion are determined but clearly signals to the political process what is going on so that the uses of judicial discretion which, through the impact of precedent, have legislative force can be reviewed and, if necessary, amended by the prime legislative process.[42]

If we entrust to the judiciary for one reason or another the task of filling out the laws as a matter, perhaps, of delegated legislative power, then this does provide scope for opening up this aspect of judicial activity to the full impact of preferred methods of political and legislative reasoning. In this context, it makes sense and is ethically proper to call in the methods of Rawlsian equilibrium,[43] the discourse ethics of Habermas[44] or the empirical application of utilitarian or economic principles.[45] In general, these are to be preferred to methods which purport to restrict judicial legislation to methods which circumscribe its scope by insisting on a peculiarly legal dimension, such as Alexy's theory of legal argumentation[46] or Dworkin's Herculean method, which allows us to draw on principles but not on policy.[47] Such approaches not only are unduly limited in the scope of judicial reasoning in legislative mode but blur the distinction with the prime applicatory function of courts, thus encouraging every case to be approached in terms of what is a legislative challenge, albeit one that has to be met with an apparently and perhaps actually limited range of factors. Particularly when such methods are deployed in relation to bills of rights or fundamental principles of common law, they provide courts with the opportunity to revisit every legislative enactment to see whether or not they agree with the political judgments involved.[48]

For some legal theorists this is a welcome tendency. This may be openly argued by saying that courts are above some of the immediate political pressures to which politicians are subject and are therefore in a better position to argue clearly as a matter of principle and long-term policy, taking in the interests of the citizenry as a whole. Court-centred legislation is in this way preferable, particularly on matters with which legislatures have difficulty in coping, because, for instance, intense minorities are blocking important legislation and indifferent majorities are denying the significance of minority interests. Courts, in their

---

42 See J Waldron, *op cit* fn 5, 147. Contrast R Dworkin, *Law's Empire*, London: Fontana, 1986.

43 J Rawls, *A Theory of Justice*, Oxford: Clarendon Press, 1972; and J Rawls, *Political Liberalism*, New York: Columbia University Press, 1994.

44 J Habermas, *The Philosophical Discourse of Modernity*, Cambridge: Polity Press, 1987; and J Habermas, 'Toward a communication-concept of rational collective will-formation', *Ratio Juris*, Vol 2, 1989, 144–54.

45 For instance, R Posner, *Economic Analysis of Law*, Boston: Little, Brown, 1977.

46 R Alexy, *op cit* fn 37.

47 R Dworkin, *Taking Rights Seriously*, London: Duckworth, 1977.

48 See TD Campbell, 'Democracy, human rights, and positive law', *Sydney Law Review*, Vol 16, 1994, 195–212.

impartial role freed from the morally irrelevant pressures of electoral considerations, are the morally preferred legislators, at least on certain matters.[49]

This approach greatly exaggerates the significance of the impartiality of courts, impartiality which is suited more to the adjudicating of particular fact situations than to the choice of legislative alternatives. The impartiality of non-involvement does not enable decisions to be made between competing political values and the capacities of courts for arriving at well formulated policies are meagre compared with the policy-making resources available to the modern state. These claims cannot be substantiated adequately here. The former in particular would require us to offer a full critique of the limitations of the methods of Rawls[50] and Habermas[51] if they are claimed to be anything more than pointers towards how political discourse should be guided. The gist of the critique must be that no methods of this sort can be used to generate a consensus, for none of them can avoid the selection and prioritising of fundamental values, and all of them underestimate the intractable nature of the moral choices that have to be made to arrive at just and efficient legislation in relation to morally justified goals. It is perhaps easier to be brisk on the matter of the policy competence of courts, in that it is evident that, if courts are to be legislators in competition with the legislative branch of government with the backing of the administrative resources of modern government departments, then they will in large measure have to become indistinguishable in resources and accountability from the executive and legislative branches of government combined. This serves as a vivid reminder as to what is involved in collapsing the boundary between legal and political argumentation.

## THE LEGISLATIVE ETHIC AND THE ROLE OF THE CITIZEN

The ideal of the judicial professional ethic which requires that its prime mode and area of expertise is strictly adjudicative is dependent for its realisation on the raw material with which it is provided. This means that prior to judicial ethics there are legislative ethics, particularly the requirement that laws be enacted which are capable of being interpreted in positivist terms.[52] Other legislative norms (which are often erroneously taken to be primarily adjudicative norms) are consistency and comprehensiveness in legislation, prospectivity in relation to conduct and practicability in requiring only conduct with which citizens are able to comply.

These familiar aspects of the governance of rules can be fleshed out in a number of ways. One important dimension is the degree of specificity which a rule should embody. In the interests of clarifying a clear exclusionary force, rules should be as specific as possible, congruent with their objective. This is necessary also for maximising the liberty advantage and refining effectively the means for

---

49 This is argued lucidly in R Dworkin, *A Bill of Rights for Britain*, London: Chatto, 1990.

50 N Daniels, *Reading Rawls*, Oxford: Blackwell, 1975.

51 J Raz, *The Authority of Law: Essays on Law and Morality*, Oxford: OUP, 1979, 212.

52 One aspect of this demand is manifest in the 'plain language' movement.

reaching the goal of legislation. However, the moral-form advantage requires that such generalisations as are involved do not involve unfairness, with morally irrelevant distinctions being drawn in a way which makes some groups bear inequitable burden or enjoy unfair advantages. There is therefore some tension between the need for precision and the need for fairness.

There is a continuing argument about whether it is in the nature of rules to be precise, as distinct from principles, which are general. Some theorists take 'rule' to be a generic term to cover all norms specifying conduct, approved and permitted. Others see them as having a specific role, which differentiates them from principles and standards, for instance.[53] Principles may be simply more general than rules, or they may be rules (whether general or not) that embody an evidently moral or normative rationale (such as reasonableness). These may also be referred to as standards.

Initially, the positivist contention that law is, or ought to be, a system of rules may be taken as utilising a purely general concept of a rule to cover all behaviour-stipulating norms, but within more specific analyses of the functions of rules it becomes clear that some norms are better than others in securing these functions. Controlling conduct, co-ordinating activities and distributing fairly may be done more effectively by way of clear, concise, unambiguous, intelligible rules which are within the capacities of those addressed than by way of general principles or standards, even if these do point to certain background values.

In the context of this discussion, a 'good' rule is a rule which is good not in substance but in the characteristics which enable it to do its job. Of course these characteristics will vary with the job in question. Symbolic functions may often be served by vague and obscure but fine-sounding rules. Power allocative functions may be served by general rules or rules with moral terms, for these enhance the power of those who administer them. However, if we take the dominant social and political function of rules to be action guiding, conduct co-ordinating and power controlling, then good rules will tend to fall into the categories of clear and specific.

This is not uncontentious. There is a problem over highly specific rules that they approximate to particular commands. Some generality is required for efficacy and moral form, and yet generality which takes in substantial groups of individuals breeds vagueness. Nevertheless, rules may retain sufficient generality to be useful, and still be clear enough, if they do not use terms whose application is controversial or not open to public verification, and if they are pitched at a level of generality which takes in classes of conduct that are readily recognisable, either natural kinds or uncontroversial socially recognised categories.[54] It is also important, of course, that the level of the categorisation fits the nature of the objective of the rule. Thus, if it is dangerous animals that are in question, then that

---

53 For a discussion of rules and principles, see TD Campbell, 'Ethical positivism', in S Panou, G Bozonis, D Scorgas and P Trappe (eds), *Theory and Systems of Legal Philosophy*, Stuttgart: Steiner, 1988, 45–55.

54 For the concept of 'natural kinds' in a different context, see MS Moore, 'The semantics of judging', *Southern California Law Review*, Vol 54, 1981, 151–294.

is the best categorisation, provided we can give empirical content to the concept of 'dangerous'. Simply specifying a list of dangerous animals has the drawback that some dangerous animals may be missed out. On the other hand, a list of readily identifiable animals is more precise and more capable of generating agreement.

There are problems in the inclusion of vague moral judgment-inviting terms like 'just' and 'reasonable', which encourage extensive judicial discretion. But while it may not be possible to exclude these altogether, they can usually be interpreted as disguised references to accepted standards of conduct in the rules of society at the time, thus incorporating current practice into the law. This may be seen as acceptable if there is no significant controversy about these practices. Alternatively, such terminology may be read as an invitation to a judge and jury to express an opinion which is then taken as a sample of positive morality, but this is a doubtful procedure in a pluralistic or inegalitarian society. Or it may be taken as an invitation to investigate the state of public opinion or some section of it at the time.[55] However, in general, such legislation is undesirably vague and ambiguous in purpose and insufficiently restrictive of judicial legislation. It represents an understandable but regrettable passing of the legislative burden from governments to courts.

Considerations of this sort also apply to such matters as the promulgation and availability of rules, as there is little possibility of a conduct-guiding rule doing its job if the rules are not known and discoverable by those to whom they are addressed. Lon Fuller created a procedural version of natural law theory out of such ingredients, inferring the desirability of such qualities as clarity, prospectivity and publicity from the idea of law as 'the enterprise of subjecting human conduct to the governance of rules'.[56] The force of these points is dissipated by his concurrent insistence that such qualities not only are means of efficiently ensuring that rules serve their purposes but also have some validity as moral criteria in that a system which respects his eight ways of failing to make law will tend also to manifest respect for its subjects as moral agents. He concluded, rather too hastily, that law is in this sense an essentially moral enterprise. Nevertheless, Fuller seems to be on the verge of explicating the moral-form advantage which makes rule governance a necessary but not a sufficient condition of moral acceptability.

Hart decisively criticised this aspect of Fuller's move from the sound premise that government by rules protects a measure of liberty for the subjects by enabling them to avoid the consequences of violating such rules to the exaggerated conclusion that, in such a system, the content of the rules will tend to produce both justice and efficiency. Unfortunately for Fuller's scheme, 'good' rules can

---

55 As proposed in H Collins, 'Democracy and adjudication', in DN MacCormick and P Birks (eds), *The Legal Mind*, Oxford: Clarendon Press, 1986, 71: 'given that the legislature lacks credibility as a pure system of democratic control, it becomes acceptable to recognise that other institutions of government, like the courts, may equally claim authority derived from a democratic input even though that input is weak and incomplete.'

56 L Fuller, *The Morality of Law*, New Haven, CT: Yale University Press, 1969, Chapter 2.

very effectively serve awful purposes.[57] However, this wayward claim, which constitutes the natural law aspect of Fuller's theory, is not essential to its enduring contribution, namely to trace the significance of law to human purpose and in particular to the purpose of morally acceptable forms of governing. This is, of course, a characteristically positivist theme.

## CONCLUSION

In an ideal positivist world there would be no such thing as judicial legislation, although there would always be a legislative element in rendering general terms more precise in relation to the complexities of concrete situations. In the non-ideal world we actually inhabit, judicial legislation may be the lesser of the two evils. Particular aspects of the judicial ethic apply to situations where judicial legislation is required: for instance, where there are gaps in legislation and we have nothing but highly general principles to go by and some decision is required to avoid injustice or waste. Most positivists urge courts, in these second-best circumstances, to draw on the positive morality of existing social opinion. Where there is no clear positive morality or convention, it might be expected that LEP should commend devices to discourage judges from drawing on their own moral views. Indeed, in some cases even lottery methods may be preferred to moral adjudication, for randomness is preferable to systematic bias.[58] Indeed, some common law techniques, charitably interpreted, can be viewed as lotteries in relation to the competing interests at stake.

However, it is congruent with positivism to argue that, provided judicial legislation is subject to legislative overruling, as it normally is, what matters is that judicial legislation be conducted in accordance with ideal legislative method. This means going beyond consistency with existing law, although this certainly has merits where the outcome is non-controversial and decisive. It means going beyond arguments of principle in Dworkin's sense to include utilitarian aspects of the morality of legislation, provided that this is done overtly and after informed discussion and relevant expert evidence. One reason for taking this approach is that there are aspects of the judicial role that overlap with reasonable moral methodology. In particular, the impartiality of the judiciary may be thought to be an advantage, provided that matters of social class and intellectual elitism are not at issue. At this point, the methods of Rawls and Habermas may perhaps be followed through in courts to advantage, on the grounds that they approximate to an approach which is compatible with judicial neutrality. However, impartiality of form and effort, while it may iron out certain partialities and unfairnesses, is no substitute for making the moral choices which do not follow from adopting an impartial viewpoint alone. On the other hand, it is admitted that there may be good reason to eschew this as inviting this second-best approach to encroach into judicial practice in situations where it is not absolutely necessary.

---

57 HLA Hart, 'The separation of law and morals', *Harvard Law Review,* Vol 71, 1957–58, 593–629.

58 B Goodwin, *Justice by Lottery,* Hemel Hempstead: Simon & Schuster, 1992.

We thus have a framework for deriving an ethics of LEP according to which it is the duty of the legislature to enact formally good law that makes it possible for the citizen to understand and obey or fairly utilise enacted law, and for judges to confine themselves to its interpretation and application in an adjudicative manner when there is dispute about legally relevant conduct, either between private legal persons or between such persons and the state. In this context, we can work out the ethics of lawyers as deriving largely from their roles in processes of adjudication that are appropriately used to determine disputes and in advising and assisting clients with their affairs in the light of the ideal of the governance of rules.

4

# LEGAL POSITIVISM AND POLITICAL POWER

This chapter presents a thesis about legal positivism and political power, to the effect that positivism is a defensible theory which is addressed to both the facilitation and the proper limitation of power in society. More particularly, it is argued that ethical positivism, identified as an ethically normative mode of legal positivism,[1] is required to give point and purpose to the constitutional doctrine of the separation of powers. To articulate this broad thesis, some analytical work concerning varieties of power is undertaken which is of general relevance to the heartland of political theory. The object of this analysis is to identify the sort of power that judges can exercise, and to work out how we might distinguish between legitimate and illegitimate uses of judicial power. The chapter concludes that, in an adequately functioning democratic system, acceptable rationales for the doctrine of the separation of powers imply that judges should not exercise political power.

The current critical orthodoxy is that legal positivism is a doctrine which latently supports the mythological autonomy of law and hence, it is argued, underpins the often hidden political power of judges and lawyers.[2] The consensus is that legal positivism is a lawyers' theory which falsely legitimises the role of judges and enables them to exercise extensive political power without appearing to do so.[3] Magisterially above the political fracas, judges pronounce on what the law is. In fact, what they are doing is deciding cases in accordance with their own individual or group political judgment. This deception enhances judges' political power by making their decisions unchallengeable outside the legal sphere. Secure from political criticism or electoral pressure, the higher echelons of judicial establishments wield substantial political power without any accountability beyond the acquiescence of their peers.

This scenario does not require us to impute conspiratorial designs or calculated agenda to a group of persons who may be naïve politically and generally lacking in political *mens rea.* The assumed common sense is that judges are a narrow and internally socialised collective largely unaware of the political contestability of their social and economic assumptions. This is quite enough to fit the system which legal realists and critical legal scholars seek to render visible. On the other hand, the critical analysis is compatible with the situation where politically aware and calculating judicial officers make decisions that serve their

---

1 TD Campbell, *The Legal Theory of Ethical Positivism*, Aldershot: Dartmouth, 1996.

2 R Cotterrell, *The Politics of Jurisprudence*, London and Edinburgh: Butterworths, 1989, 216–35.

3 AC Hutchinson and P Monahan, *The Rule of Law: Ideal or Ideology?*, Toronto: Toronto University Press, 1986.

own ends or their own view of the public interest, while prudently disguising their objectives behind the citation of precedent and fulsome verbal deference to legal principle.

Legal positivism is standardly implicated in this charade, despite the fact that the manifest function of the theory is to provide a basis for sharply distinguishing law-making and law application, a distinction which positivists use to underpin the separation of legislative and judicial power. The critical thesis is that the distinction between making and applying law collapses, both in philosophical theory and in legal practice, but that the public appearance of independence in judicial reasoning gives it a political acceptability which it would not otherwise enjoy. Countering the critical analysis of judicial reasoning as an ideology of judicial power, which amounts to little more than *post hoc* rationalisation of decisions taken on other grounds, this chapter argues that legal positivism, in its prescriptive forms at least, is a doctrine which can help to limit the political power of courts and lawyers. The thesis is that legal positivism can be a theoretical basis for effectively curbing the power of courts and enhancing that of elected legislatures and democratic politics in general, as well as protecting the liberty and equality of citizens as individuals or groups. This type of legal positivism does not exclude the historical realities which critical realism exposes. It is clearly a superb basis for the exercise of political power when those affected do not realise that it is being exercised. Legal positivism has indeed often served to cloak judicial skulduggery and maintain entrenched class dominance. Nevertheless, positivism can still be utilised in good faith to provide the wise and virtuous judge with a theory that maximises democratic accountability and gives substance to the ideal of the rule of law.

In debating the proprieties of the exercise of judicial power, legal positivism confronts not only the empirical critiques of legal realism and critical legal studies, but also its historical rival – natural law theory. The current resurgence of natural law is in part a counter to the realist contention that judges are not bound either by existing law or external morality, and that whatever courts decide has the authority of law. A question left largely unanswered by legal realism relates to the way in which judges ought to make their decisions. This doctrinal void may be filled by many different political approaches. Thus, the economic analysis of law, in its normative forms, urges judges to decide cases on the basis of some model of economic rationality.[4] Legal realists themselves suggest a form of economic pragmatism. Other theorists provide a framework for judicial decision-making from some form of natural law that posits basic and universal moral imperatives for the general guidance of judicial determinations as well as citizen conduct.[5] Ethical positivism, in contrast, seeks to locate the required substantial moral choice in the realm of the political process in so far as it is directed towards legislative outcomes; the ethics of legal process are confined to the manner in which the politically determined law is to be interpreted and applied.

---

4 R Posner, *The Economic Analysis of Law*, Boston: Little, Brown, 1977.

5 J Finnis, *Natural Law and Natural Rights*, Oxford: Clarendon Press, 1980.

As a general analytical and descriptive theory, legal positivism has lost much of its credibility, and hence its ideological force. Many contemporary judges and most commentators take it to be evident that judges make law, rather than simply interpret and apply it; they assume this as a premise with which to justify quite radical judicial amendments of current law and increasingly bold political uses of broad constitutional provisions. Creative law-making used to be regarded as a *prima facie* abuse of judicial power. Now it no longer needs to be hidden behind lip service to a judicial ethic that confines legal judgment to the application of legal criteria, with legislatures as the sole ultimate legitimate source of new law. Politicised judicial practice has been deftly unmasked by legal realists and critical legal theorists. It is now the unashamed basis for asserting the inevitability, and hence (fallaciously) the acceptability, of judicial legislation. The constitutional consequence is a noticeable shift of political power from legislatures to courts.

The effectiveness of the ideological role of legal positivism, as identified by the critics, is contingent upon its descriptive credibility. If the political neutrality of judges is not given credence, then the exercise of political power behind the mask of that neutrality is weakened. Legal positivism is now verging on the threshold of losing that credibility as a descriptive theory of judicial practice. Moreover, by default and association with its discredited descriptive variant, legal positivism is also underrated as a constitutional ideal that can and should be cultivated. The confidence trick is collapsing, hence judicial loyalties are moving from orthodoxies of legal positivism to the pragmatics of legal realism or the moralism of natural law. Neither alternative is, however, a stable rationale for the exercise of judicial political power. Legal realism, as the theory that the law simply is what courts tend to decide, lacks both a sense of direction and the means to block the demand for political accountability. Natural law, as the theory that judges have a duty to apply universal moral principles, accords ill with the pluralism of current moral outlooks. Moreover, the overt politicising of judicial roles that is involved in both tactics brings corollaries: the right of others to make political criticism of judicial decisions; the demand for elected judges; the pressure on judges to follow accepted social and political norms, to be educated, to be questioned, to be pilloried and reduced to the status of mere politicians. If to resort to law is simply to engage in politics by other means, the protected status of the legally skilled but politically neutral judge is undermined.

All this has some way to run, as yet. In Europe and Australasia, judiciaries are flexing their constitutional muscles, resuscitating 19th century versions of the common law[6] or importing globalised rights rhetoric for selective implementation, often on the model of US constitutional jurisprudence. This makes it an exciting time to be involved with legal philosophy and constitutional law, disciplines that are heading for amalgamated intellectual dominance as the rout of black letter law continues. New forms of constitutional interpretation are gaining ground; they offer suggestions as to how judiciaries might go about selecting an interpretative approach on which to ground their now accepted

---

6 TRS Allan, *Law, Liberty and Justice: Legal Foundations of British Constitutionalism*, Oxford: Clarendon Press, 1993.

political role. Only rarely do we come across a contemporary political philosophy which seeks to depoliticise judiciaries in the cause of effective democratic government.

If we are to counter these trends, the first task is not one of normative political philosophy but of analytical political theory, the discipline which is directed to the analysis and understanding of politics rather than its reform. To arrive at any norms and strategies for the deployment and control of political power, we require an initial analysis of judicial power in contrast to political power. This analysis may then be used in the formulation of a normative philosophy concerning the proper methods and functions of judicial office.

## POWERS

When lawyers talk of judicial powers, they mean the legal capacities of the judicial organs of government in accordance with adjectival or 'power-conferring' (that is, facilitative) rules. In particular, judicial power is the legal capacity to hear and decide cases and make determinations that are binding on the parties concerned. Thus, when judicial power is vested by the Constitution in the High Court of Australia, the court has the legal capacity to adjudicate such particular disputes as are brought before it within its allotted jurisdiction, that is, the geographical area and type of law for which it has the legal capacity to hear and decide cases.[7] As legal powers, these are *de jure* and by definition legitimate within the legal system. In so far as they are viewed externally to the legal system, judicial powers may be viewed also as political rights requiring moral justification.

Whether or not constitutions may be said to give judiciaries *de jure* political power, however, is dependent on their content. Any *de facto* political power deriving therefrom depends on the extent to which their decisions are complied with. Thus, a *de jure* adjudicative 'power', if its content is such as to permit or require judges to decide cases as they please, gives judges *de jure* political power; if respected, it gives them *de facto* political power as well. On the other hand, a *de jure* power, or legal right, to decide a case in accordance with a specific set of consistent comprehensive and specific rules supplied to the judiciary, even if respected, does not give *de jure* or *de facto* political power.

To explicate this analysis, it is necessary to relate lawyers' talk of powers to the language of power in the discourse of political theory. Lawyers are interested in the legal capacity to alter the legal status of particular others. Political theorists are concerned with the autonomous or independent intentional control of the conduct of others in ways which may be contrary to the wishes and/or the interests of those others. Power, in the social sciences, is something that enables

---

7 L Zines, *The High Court and the Constitution*, 3rd edn, Sydney: Butterworths, 1992, 151–84.

the holder to make a difference in other people's lives whether they like it or not,[8] and to do so autonomously – on their own account, as it were – rather than as mere instruments of yet other people.

The dimension of autonomy is a necessary feature of political, but not of legal, power. However, if we enquire a little closer and ask what makes political power *political,* as distinct from economic or religious, then political and legal powers are less readily distinguishable in other respects. The concepts of 'power' and 'political power' are both strongly contested. A large part of what is meant by political power – where it is contrasted with, for instance, bribery or brute force – is control exercised through the possession of authority, that is, the ability to be accepted as having the right to command or permit within a non-native system, political or legal. The struggle for political power is in part the quest for such authoritative control over others as is exercised through the medium of the mutual recognition of the right to rule by rulers and ruled. The right to legislate is a formidable and important form of political – as distinct from, say, economic – power. It can be argued that authority of this sort is continuous with the capacity to communicate and persuade with respect to social behaviour.[9]

Evidently, the exercise of political power also involves an element of coercion, as one means of controlling others without obtaining their consent. Indeed, the right to use force in such a way is characteristic, and perhaps definitive, of political authority.[10] However, since political power has a necessary ingredient of *authority* to command (perhaps coercively), it cannot be said that legal powers are *de jure* and political powers *de facto.* There is some truth in this contrast: political power that is not *de facto,* in the sense of being effective, ceases to be regarded as political power because it lacks the property of actually controlling others. However, only that *de facto* control of (perhaps unwilling) others that involves the possession of *de jure* power is actually *political* power. This analysis also has application to legal powers. When theorists explicate legal validity, they deal in norms that enable people, especially judges, to recognise the rules that are authoritative in that jurisdiction, but they must do so in relation to effective systems, that is, systems in which the rules identified by judiciaries are acknowledged and adhered to in practice. In HLA Hart's terms, validity presupposes efficacy, that is, there cannot be a valid law unless a given population, and particularly legal officials, generally adhere to the system of which they are a part.[11] The connection is maybe stronger to the point of conceptual necessity in the case of political power, but the contrast with legal power is only a matter of degree.

The significant difference between political and legal power is, therefore, with respect to autonomy, a necessary feature of political, but not legal, power. The

---

8 R Dahl, 'The concept of power', *Behavioural Science,* Vol 1, 1957, 203; and S Lukes, *Power: A Radical View,* London: Macmillan, 1974, 26.

9 J Habermas, *The Theory of Communicative Action,* Boston: Beacon Press, 1984; and M Foucault, *Power-Knowledge,* New York: Pantheon, 1980.

10 M Weber, *The Theory of Social and Economic Organisation,* Glencoe, IL: Free Press, 1947, 132.

11 HLA Hart, *The Concept of Law,* Oxford: Clarendon Press, 1961, 100–01.

relative independence that is a necessary feature of political power, its identification with the source of control, is not a necessary feature of legal power. Decision-making within a legal system may be circumscribed in ways that lead us to say that the actors involved do not exercise the autonomous *de jure* capacity to impose their will on others, but still exercise legal power. On the other hand, the legal power to legislate does have such *de jure* power and normally a measure of *de facto* power as well (unless a legislature is entirely controlled externally). The same *may* hold of adjudication, if this is defined broadly as deciding particular cases, for this can be an open-ended *de jure* power allowing immense *de facto* power in relation to particular cases. However, in contrast to political power, adjudication can be circumscribed to the point where it lacks any significant autonomy and consequently is not, in that case, an instance of political power. Indeed, it may be said that the more circumscribed the power, the more distinctively legal it is.

This approach does not conceptualise power in an old-fashioned positivist model as a commodity or substance which can be hoarded and spent, or even located in one supreme sovereign.[12] It is understood that political power is a set of psychological and sociological, as well as physical, relationships; these relationships produce certain patterns of the distribution of benefits and burdens, in part through the normatively accepted hierarchy of command. Moreover, political power, so conceived, is not confined to the self-conscious attainment of such distributions. Political power could be attributed to those who get their way in competition with others even if it is not their intention to do so.

However, getting your own way may be regarded as twofold: intentional, in so far as the conduct of the power-holders is directed at achieving their own objectives; and, at the same time, non-intentional, with respect to overriding the wills and interests of others who may be adversely affected by the manner in which the power-holders obtain their objectives. The adverse impact on others is, in the latter case, something that just happens, an unintended side effect. Much social power is of this nature, and it is to be distinguished from political power in a narrower sense, which is the direct intention to exercise and control. Majority or elite attitudes often prevail without in any way being overtly directed at overriding the attitudes of minorities or majorities. We may speak of societal power as this capacity to obtain desired benefits, irrespective of the opposition or the lack of acquiescence of others, without seeking authority to command others. Societal power constitutes the background social reality that more self-conscious politics seeks to redirect. It is a significant part of the context of intentional political power. Most of what happens in a society is not in any strong sense intended, and may be ascribed to the operation of unchosen social, economic and material factors. Politics, as popularly conceived, operates as an overt struggle for position and influence; its effects are greatly exaggerated, and it operates in a relatively non-malleable social field in the causal interstices of human conduct. Conceptually, it is helpful to be stipulative here and take politics to be the

---

12 J Austin, *The Province of Jurisprudence Determined,* London: Weidenfeld & Nicolson, 1955.

conscious struggle for control over others; we speak of 'societal power' when referring to the capacity unwittingly to affect others to their detriment.

To attribute political power to judges is to imply that their role in the legal process is such that their values and outlooks produce coercive outcomes for the lives of others, even although their intention may be no more than to apply the rules previously determined by legislatures. In this case, we have an illustration of societal as distinct from (intentional) political power. It is generally agreed that, in a democratic society incorporating the idea of the rule of law, judges should not be involved in overt and intentional political activity and should not exercise political power as I have defined it. The deeper issue is whether the societal power exercised by judges through the legal process, by virtue of the fact that their values and outlooks have a significant effect on adjudicative outcomes, can and should be controlled by overtly political process.

Where we go to from this point is dependent on the issues that are in contention. The notion of political power, with its ingredients of authority and force, points us to fundamental normative questions relating to the justification of its existence, its distribution and its control. Even if we regard all force as *prima facie* undesirable or wrong, given its multiple uses in relation to evidently laudable goals, we may not wish to argue that the exercise of power is necessarily an evil phenomenon. As a means it may be tainted. It may be regarded as at best inferior to harmonious agreement and at worst entirely unacceptable.[13] These are matters which give us reason for resisting power, or at least reason for allocating power only to those whom we can hold accountable. We may require that such allocations be justified in relation to their outcomes, in terms of efficiency in the attainment of the objects that justify the political organisation in question. Much political philosophy has to do with the task of identifying those purposes which legitimate the exercise of force, and the proper limits to impose on its use.

No political philosophy has come up with a satisfactory answer to the problem of how to utilise and control political power within acceptable perimeters. The tragic paradox of politics is that societies need organised political power for many legitimate purposes, but the very existence of organised and centralised power is an inherent danger to social wellbeing due to its inherent potential to be used for purposes other than those which justify its existence. This unhappy conjunction of the need for, and vulnerability to, political power enables us to appreciate the nature of ethical positivism as a theory: it articulates how and why we can ameliorate the evil effects of political power and at the same time direct its legitimate functions in a humane and effective manner, hence the tensions between political and legal powers.

Where legal powers are seen as contributing to political power, this may be as part of an attempt to create channels for the effective exercise of political power originating outside the legal system, or the legal powers themselves may be an exercise of autonomous political power. Ethical positivism takes the former

13 TD Campbell, 'Power and resistance: a legal perspective', *Societas Ethica Jahresbericht*, 1986, 29–51.

approach, favouring an analysis of legal power which commends it as a channel for the political power of others, including political power directed to the control of the societal power of judges, thus judicial power is not an independent source of authoritative coercion. At the same time, however, the request that political power be exercised via the medium of general yet specific rules is seen as a potentially significant check on political power. It is in this context of the ambiguous interconnections of law and politics that this chapter proposes an analysis of political power which makes a degree of autonomy, in conjunction with effective claims to exercise binding authority, one of its defining features. Thus, it clears the way for the discussion of politics-free legal process as a feasible ideal.

## ETHICAL POSITIVISM

The legal theory of ethical positivism (LEP) sets out the importance of precise, clear rules as the medium for the implementation of political power.[14] LEP is in the tradition of legal positivism in two areas: its identification of valid law as the outcome of empirically identifiable actions; and its insistence that legal rules be empirically applicable, in that it is possible to see whether or not actual conduct is in accordance with such rules without at the same time making value judgments about the conduct or situation in question. One ethical aspect of LEP is that the orthodox positivist image of law is to be taken not as an attempt to describe actual legal systems but as a picture of an ideal towards which actual systems may approximate. As a model, it calls for an ethical rationale to justify the practices that constitute a positivist legal system. Moreover, according to the theory, the model of positivist law is ethical for another reason: this ideal picture cannot be realised unless the legal establishment is sufficiently committed to adhere to procedural and methodological requirements without being legally obliged to do so.

Current readings of legal positivism often assume that positivism goes along with the liberal assumption that there can be a set of substantive legal rules that are politically neutral, but this is not a tenet either of traditional positivism or of LEP. On the contrary, laws are taken to be the expressions of a particular political will, whose justification lies not in its inherent neutrality as between different social groups, but in the (usually democratic) credentials of its origins. However, given the empirical basis for the understanding and application of laws that meet positivist standards, formally good laws can be known and administered by officials who understand but do not accept their substance; this does involve a degree of procedural neutrality as a positivist objective. Such a procedural neutrality does not extend to the substance of law.

While traditional legal positivism has its own (usually utilitarian) specific value commitments, the theory itself is normally presented as a mixture of abstract analysis of legal concepts and empirical claims about the operation of actual legal systems. LEP, on the other hand, stresses the significance of the ideal

---

14 TD Campbell, *op cit* fn 1.

over the actual in the positivist model. Government through empirically applicable rules is justified by its provision of the possibility of the effective, fair, limited and predictable use of political power.[15] It is also claimed that the positivist model facilitates meaningful democratic decision-making. This aspirational ideal of a political system focused on the choice and impartial implementation of empirically applicable rules is the backcloth against which we can identify certain types of bias and oppression.

The core concept within LEP is the notion of general rules.[16] Rules lay down what must or may be done or not done. They are prescriptive and mandatory, removing or opening up certain choices for the individuals and groups to whom they apply.[17] Rules carry the intrinsic prescriptive notion that what they require must or may be done without any calculation of the consequences of so doing other than those provided for in the rule or accepted overriding rules. Rules, at least as they feature in legal positivism, are hard-and-fast requirements or permissions, rather than simply guidelines or rules of thumb. LEP defines and defends the moral and practical priority of such rules within a polity.

The most common liberal defence of government through rules is that rules enable individuals to protect their liberty, or freedom of action. Empirically applicable substantive rules, promulgated in advance of the application, may limit freedom in the sense of a person's right to act as they please. It follows that liberals, in general, support the minimalisation of law. Just as important for liberty is the fact that prescriptive rules, when they are known in advance, enable individuals to avoid breaking them and thus incurring the sanctions which follow from the contravention of these rules. We may call this the *liberty advantage* of rule governance.[18] An associated factor, also valued by liberalism, is that the prior enactment of clear and empirically applicable rules makes it reasonable to blame individuals for the harmful consequences of violating those rules.

Legal positivism does not favour the enforcement of moral rules as such but, equally, it does not seek conduct which is thought to be immoral. While particular rules may be morally either good or bad, the fact that they are rules – that is, are general in form with respect to types of conduct – makes them candidates for moral approval. They are suited to realising the ideal that rules ought to require conduct which is morally acceptable. This *moral-form advantage* of rules does not provide moral justification for any particular rule, but it does mean that the power exercised through such rules is in a form which renders it open to moral assessment. Morality has to do with the qualities of acts as a type of conduct in specified types of situation. Laws are formulated in similarly general terms and can therefore be readily assessed in moral terms.

Further, when government is conducted through the adoption and enforcement of rules, there are efficiency gains: the same questions do not have to

---

15 TD Campbell, *op cit* fn 1, 49–58.

16 F Schauer, *Playing by the Rules: A Philosophical Examination of Rule-Based Decision-Making*, Oxford: Clarendon Press, 1991.

17 J Raz, *Practical Reason and Norms*, London: Hutchinson, 1975, 35–45.

18 TD Campbell, *op cit* fn 1, 52.

be revisited on each occasion of choice, and the mutual interaction of decisions binding on groups can be foreseen and assessed in the light of their objectives. This *efficacious choice advantage* of rule governance directs our attention to the benefits, rather than the dangers, of political power, and serves as a pragmatic justification for the rule of law.[19]

A bureaucratic element of efficacious choice is the use of rules to set down the legal powers of public officials. This can limit as well as empower since, by implication, officials may act only within their powers. Additional political advantages accrue from government-through-rules when the government is democratic in form, for majorities have more power when they can establish general ongoing rules rather than seeking to make a long series of *ad hoc* decisions. Moreover, it is evident that majorities can exercise more extensive power through enacting general rules than they can merely through electing officials.

This brief survey of some of the alleged advantages of adopting a system of government via general rules illustrates the sorts of argument which are relevant to the justification of LEP. Some of these considerations relate to the facilitation of political power, others to its limitation. All require some separation of law-making from the implementation of law, for rules must have a relatively permanent existence and effect if any of the advantages outlined above are to apply. On this basis, the power we might want to give to judges is the power required for the implementation of rules, not the power to determine the content of these rules, nor the power to decide cases on their perceived merits in relation to background economic or moral goals. In summary, the division of functions (law-making and law application) is not simply a matter of expertise: it is a necessary feature of the rule governance on which the claimed benefits depend. Government-through-rules has structural frameworks in place which prevent legislatures from making *ad hoc* political decisions in unprincipled ways, and which limit justiciaries in the exercise of their societal powers in relation to individual cases.

## THE LIMITS OF LEGAL POWERS

The legal theory of ethical positivism works well for ordinary law. It is more flaky in relation to constitutional matters, if only because a legislature's *de jure* capacity as law-maker is dependent on constitutional rules that are not themselves the creation of that legislature. Legislatures cannot be constitutionally self-regulating without threatening the demise of constitutional government, or so it is standardly asserted, for instance in *R v Kirby ex p The Boilermakers' Society of Australia*.[20] Constitutional courts, it is said, must be ultimately responsible for determining the constitutionality of the activities of law-making bodies. Basic principles of rule governance exclude any body from assessing the propriety of its own conduct in relation to its constitutive rules.

---

19 TD Campbell, *op cit* fn 1, 60.

20 *R v Kirby ex p The Boilermakers' Society of Australia* (1956) 1–5 CLR 254, 268.

Unfortunately for this thesis, the same principles appear to prevent courts from assessing the constitutionality of their own activities. This takes us to a constitutional form of the tragic paradox of politics. An ultimate adjudicative authority is necessary for a political system, but no individual or body ought to be a judge in its own cause. The conundrum is how to give courts such ultimate constitutional judicial power, without at the same time handing to them unwarranted *de facto* political power. Systems to minimise and provide remedies for the abuse of judicial office are inherently problematic, for such systems themselves lack accountability.

There are difficulties in gaining even a theoretical foothold in the determination of what amounts to misuse of judicial power. While the idea of the abuse of judicial office is constitutionally indispensable, there is no neutral site from which to identify what does and what does not count as such abuse. The idea of judicial abuse cannot without circularity be captured in law, for it is the source of law that is contested. Ultimately, judicial legitimacy must be a matter of political, philosophical or judicial ethics. Further, the content of judicial ethics with respect to such matters as interpretive method or interstitial discretionary powers is also extensively contested. One theorist's idea of abuse is another theorist's ideal, and we are all theorists on such matters. Reasonable people may reasonably disagree about the proper role and methodology of judicial powers within a polity, and therefore on the propriety of the different ways in which judicial power may be exercised. There can be no constitutionally decisive way of determining these issues as a matter of theory.

One way in which we may seek such objectivity as is attainable in such matters is by drawing out the implications of the separation of powers doctrine as explicated and as justified by LEP. LEP does not embrace the sort of conceptualism that deduces interpretive methods from such notions as representative government or the concept of discursive democracy, or from judicial power itself. Choosing a method for the interpretation of a constitution is similar in character to choosing a system of government. Who should properly make that choice is practically insoluble as a matter of legal and political process, but it is possible to construct an ethic which has application to the conduct of those who are charged with the task of administering whatever governmental system is adopted. Thus, while courts may have to have, in any federal system, the ultimate say as to the interpretation of constitutional provisions that are authoritative in their society, they should not therefore have ethically free rein with respect to their interpretive methods. The impossibility of solving the classic riddle of guarding the guardians may entail that judges have the *de facto* as well as the *de jure* power to decide such matters in any way that they can get away with, but we need not accept that they have the moral right to rewrite constitutions through expansive interpretive methodologies. Judicial conduct in this regard cannot be legally, and perhaps also politically, overridden; nor is it, *ex hypothesi*, justiciable in some higher court. However, it does not follow that the judicial *de jure* powers of constitutional interpretation cannot be described as being abused. A constitutional court with the final say on constitutional matters has real opportunities to wield constitutionally unwarranted political power. Nevertheless, because of its constitutional ultimacy, the only legitimate checks on its activities are self-administered ethical ones.

In this manifestation of the paradox of politics, we are denied the benefits of a legal system without incurring the disadvantages of constant vulnerability to judicial impropriety. In the necessary absence of legitimate remedies for judicial abuse of *de jure* interpretive power, constitutional courts are bound to have considerable *de facto* political power, which is a measure of the gravity of their ethical responsibilities. That said, it is not entirely clear that courts cannot in principle be, with propriety, controlled by other branches of government when they step outside their judicial functions. Thus, the Australian Constitution confines the exercise of Commonwealth judicial power to the High Court and other federal courts. Uncontroversially, this means that the Parliament cannot act as a court and cannot tell courts how they must go about their business in a particular case: 'Commonwealth legislation proposing to direct a court exercising federal jurisdiction as to the manner in which it should decide a particular case would be invalid as an interference with the judicial power of the Commonwealth.'[21] Certainly, legislatures cannot usurp judicial power, but can courts usurp legislative power? The other side of the constitutional warrant of exclusive judicial power could be that this power is limited to judicial matters, as indeed was determined in the *Boilermakers'* case.[22]

This judgment leaves unresolved the issue of what constitutes a judicial matter. The principle that 'the legislature makes, the executive executes, and the judiciary construes the law'[23] is used to prevent the legislature construing laws.[24] It could as easily be used to exclude the judiciary from legislating. Indeed, it has been held that 'section I [of the Constitution], which vests legislative power in a Federal Parliament at the same time negates such power being vested in any other body'.[25]

Further, it is possible to give positivist substance to the traditional view that judges are bound to decide the cases that come before them in accordance with existing law. Thus Deane, Dawson, Gaudron and McHugh JJ:[26] 'Another important element which distinguishes a judicial decision is that it determines existing rights and duties and does so according to law. That is to say, it does so in relation to pre-existing standards rather than by the formulation of policy or the exercise of an administrative discretion.' On these lines, LEP asks that judicial development of law be tightly restricted; we should not, for instance, be content with laws that utilise very general standards, such as 'oppressive' and 'unjust', whose application requires political judgment. Thus, Windeyer[27] contends that

---

21 G Winterton, 'The separation of judicial power as an implied bill of rights', in G Lindell (ed), *Future Directions in Australian Constitutional Law,* Sydney: Federation Press, 1994, 198.

22 *Attorney-General (Cth) v The Queen ex p The Boilermakers' Society of Australia* (1957) 95 CLR 529.

23 *Wayman v Southard,* 23 US, 10 Wheaton I at 46, 1825, 1.

24 *New South Wales v The Commonwealth* (Wheat Case) (1915) 20 CLR 54.

25 *Attorney-General (Cth) v The Queen ex p The Boilermakers' Society of Australia* (1957) 95 CLR 529.

26 *Brandy v Human Rights and Equal Opportunity Commission* (1995) 127 ALR 1, 16.

27 *R v Trade Practices Tribunal ex p Tasmanian Breweries Pty Ltd* (1970) 123 CLR 361.

'the public interest is a concept which attracts indefinite considerations of policy that are more appropriate to law-making than to adjudication according to existing law ... an exercise of the legislative or administrative function of government rather than of judicial power'.

The orthodox position on the separation of legislative and judicial power is that, while the Australian Constitution clearly reserves Commonwealth judicial power exclusively for the appropriate courts, this does not exclude courts from exercising legislative or 'law-making' power. This is unsurprising within a common law jurisdiction, yet there are strong arguments against this position where it goes beyond filling in gaps in existing law pending legislative action. First, legislative power is explicitly given to the Parliament and, as a matter of constitutional interpretation, it could be taken as understood that this is an exclusive right. If not explicitly provided for in the written Constitution itself, it is a convention of the Constitution derived from its British sources that the Parliament is the legislative sovereign, and this can be taken to involve all law-making. Historically, this may be countered by citing the continuing role of the common law as a subordinate but judicially developing source of new law but, even if this tradition is not rejected as outmoded in a democratic society, it evidently does not apply in the sphere of constitutional law. Here we can draw on Brennan CJ's distinction[28] between the power to make common law and the power to make constitutional law. The former, but not the latter, is a valid exercise of judicial power, although it can be overridden.

The implicit denial of law-making power to courts, particularly with respect to constitutional matters, is not a fanciful constitutional doctrine in a field where the practice of drawing implications is common. A developing list of Australian cases imply that judicial power must be exercised in line with proper judicial process, as delineated in the rules of natural justice or due process; we might extrapolate from this and draw the conclusion that the substantive legal rules relevant to this process are the pre-existing authoritative rules emanating from the legislature. It can be further argued that it is an abuse of due process for courts to make up the substantive rules as they go along. If federal judicial power must be exercised 'in accordance with the judicial process', as Brennan, Deane and Dawson JJ all insist,[29] then, on this implication, it must be exercised in accordance with existing substantive law.

Currently, legal argument rages around whether *substantive* due process is implied in judicial power. *Leeth v The Commonwealth*[30] toys with the prospect, enunciated by Gaudron J, that courts may decide that substantive inequality is a basis for legal invalidity whenever the challenged law does not involve what the court believes to be relevant distinctions. Also, Deane and Toohey JJ hold that it is 'the duty of the court to extend to the parties before it equal justice, that is to say, to treat them fairly and impartially as equals before the law and to refrain from

---

28 *Theophanous v The Herald Weekly Times Ltd* (1994) 68 ALJR 104, 124–26.

29 *Chu Kheng Lim v Minister for Immigration, Local Government and Ethnic Affairs* (1992) 176 CLR 1.

30 *Leeth v The Commonwealth* (1992) 174 CLR 455, 493.

discrimination on irrelevant or irrational grounds'. This appears to come close to the assertion of substantive due process by Gaudron. Such *dicta* open up the remarkable prospect that judicial opinion – as to substantive equality or as to the relevance of distinctions embodied in legislation – could be used as the basis for judicial review of enacted legislation.

Equally, however, these opinions may themselves be regarded as unconstitutional, on the grounds that they are incompatible with the separation of powers in so far as this involves the exclusive or superior right of the Parliament to make law. In that case, we can argue from implied due process to a conclusion different from that enunciated by Gaudron, Deane and Toohey JJ, namely that the courts must apply existing law. This means that there could be an implied constitutional right to ethical positivism.

Against this conclusion stands the judgment of Mason CJ.[31] Here, Mason CJ argues that the presumption against retrospective legislation 'does not require that the rule or standard should have been ascertained precisely before the determination is made in the exercise of judicial power'. However, a measure of precision in law-making is required for the prohibition on retrospectivity to have any bite, for otherwise unspecific laws can be used to create unforeseeable legal obligations. It can also be argued that considerable precision is desirable, particularly in criminal matters, for reasons that bear on the liberty advantage and other values that justify the ideal of rule governance. Similar arguments can be deployed to prevent courts using interpretive methods that free them from adherence to the rules in question by enabling them to rewrite existing law when it seems contrary to their view of current social values.

These considerations may be regarded as a retreat from a discussion within political theory to an analysis of the constitutional law of a particular jurisdiction, thereby evading appropriate philosophical argument for establishing a satisfactory view of judicial power. One philosophical issue at stake here is the shaky distinction between law-making and law interpretation. To deploy the language of abuse in relation to judicial practice, and to make sense of claims to an implied constitutional right to ethical positivism, we need an agreed working distinction between the interpretation of existing rules and the creation of different or new rules. LEP argues that the first activity – rule interpretation, and the way in which it is carried out – is part of judicial legal power, and need not be exercised politically, whereas the second activity – rule change – is a matter of legislative power and is necessarily political.

To sketch a positivist position on this issue, we may distinguish between three possible species of 'interpretation': interpretation as comprehension, interpretation as bounded selection, and creative interpretation.[32] Interpretation as understanding is part of the capacity for meaningful language use,[33] but this

---

31 *Polynkovich v The Queen* (1991) 172 CLR 501, 532.

32 J Wroblewski, *The Judicial Application of Law*, Dordrecht: Kluwer, 1992.

33 D Davidson, *Inquiries into Truth and Interpretation*, Oxford: Clarendon Press, 1984, 141.

does not equate grasping meaning with interpretation in its other senses.[34] Indeed, the idea of interpretation as comprehension is an enlarged and misleading conception of interpretation: it confuses and diffuses the standard discourse so that it unhelpfully denotes all language-based understanding. Interpretation as bounded selection, on the other hand, is a conception that encapsulates the familiar practice of choosing between alternative meanings of a text, both or all of which are feasible within the linguistic community in question. This may be regarded, perhaps stipulatively in this context, as genuine interpretation.[35] Finally, creative interpretation is a conception which denotes more expansive developments of texts, such as filling in gaps in the coverage of the text, altering contextually evident meanings to give more desirable outcomes, and in other ways going beyond textual understanding and clarification to develop the text for some further purpose beyond understanding and the resolution of ambiguity.[36] While creative interpretation is often appropriate in such fields as artistic performance and literary criticism, in the legal sphere it can be regarded as an unwarranted and confusing extension of judicial method.

Following this scheme of interpretation types, we can articulate a position: courts may go beyond interpretation as understanding (which is not really interpretation at all), and use such methods as are approved to settle matters requiring bounded interpretation (their indispensable role), while stopping short of changing contextually evident, plain meanings for ulterior purposes (which may be classified as a *prima facie* abuse of judicial power). However, even if we can make sense of this ideal of judicial practice, this does not show it to be the preferable theory. These are matters on which we can all have views and on which there is little agreement. The choices between so called literalism and purposive styles, or between formalism and teleology, or between rights-directed and utilitarian tests, are all controversial, yet a great deal of the distribution of political power in a society depends on the outcome of the struggle for theoretical supremacy on these matters in so far as this affects the practice of courts. The *de jure* power to determine the interpretive style of courts, limited as it may be in legal doctrine and open as it may be in general to political criticism, cannot be restricted by institutions; in practice, it confers potentially substantial political power.

Legal realists stress the truism that the rules that matter to those involved are the rules applied by courts, and therefore the understanding of the rules arrived at by courts is what counts. Those whose understandings of the rules are adopted by courts are those who determine much of the outcome of the case and therefore the distribution of the contested resources. More broadly, the capacity to determine what interpretive method is deployed by courts affects the distributive pattern of disputed resources. Thus, a strict adherence by courts to contextually clear meanings of a written constitution may ensure a measure of political power

---

34 MAE Dummett, 'A nice derangement of epitaphs: some comments on Davidson and Hacking', in E LePore (ed), *Truth and Interpretation*, Oxford: Blackwell, 1986, 484.

35 C Perelman, *Justice, Law and Argument*, Dordrecht: Kluwer, 1980, 143–44.

36 HLA Hart, *op cit* fn 11, 138–44; and RM Dworkin, *Law's Empire*, London: Fontana, 1986, 52.

in a legislature, while an open-ended, purposive approach to a constitution gives extensive power to judiciaries who are able to come to their own ideas as to what purposes are at stake and how they are best realised.

In the context of the thesis that non-rule-based theories of legal interpretation are unacceptable, legally or politically, it is interesting to explore the role of legislatures in relation to the interpretation of their own laws. Constitutional experts might argue that a Parliament must be able to determine how, in general, its laws are to be interpreted. The Australian Parliament, in the Acts Interpretation Act 1901, lays down certain principles of interpretation, including provisions that permit or enjoin courts to have regard to the stated purposes of an Act when they have a problem of interpretation. This Act in fact says that judges should depart from the clear meaning of a rule if this will further the purposes of the Act (s 15AA).

The specific exhortation to follow purposes rather than rules is not, of course, compatible with LEP, for it enables courts to unmake law by reducing the rules to mere guidelines. As we have seen, it is part of the idea of a real rule, as distinct from a rule of thumb, that it cannot be departed from because of consequences not allowed for in the rule; otherwise we have not a rule, but simply an injunction to do what is best to reach a particular goal. It follows that any parliamentary right there may be to determine interpretive method cannot be permitted to undermine the rule-based nature of legitimate governance. And yet we may accept a legislature's right to decide how its own rules are to be interpreted, without agreeing that this power can extend to requiring that its rules be ignored if they do not have the desired outcomes in particular cases.

In practice, Australian courts have generally avoided paying explicit notice to this provision of the Acts Interpretation Act 1901. It may be that they think it a constitutional impropriety for the Parliament to interfere in the exercise of judicial legal power to this extent. It may be that the purposive requirement is judged to be in conflict with judicial process as set out by LEP, but if the High Court is able to adopt whatever interpretive method it pleases, however 'liberal' or policy-oriented it may be, then the Constitution's position on the separation of powers has been effectively amended in a way that is not provided for in the Constitution.

Who, then, should decide what is to be the authoritative interpretive method of courts? The answer is not self-evident. If courts must determine constitutionality, it might seem that courts must choose their method of constitutional interpretation. On the other hand, Parliaments have the right to make the rules; if the rules are not applied as the Parliament intended because of some unforeseen or unpredictable styles of 'interpretation', then the Parliament must have the right to change the rules in the light of what the courts make of them, so that they are more likely to have the outcomes the Parliament desires. In this case, legislatures should be able to establish how their rules are to be understood and interpreted as a necessary part of their legislative power. Legislating is a means of communication as to what must or may be done or not done, and the purposes of the communicators can claim priority in relation to how law ought to be understood.

It may only be in the case of constitutions that we have serious doubts about the interpretive sovereignty of legislatures within their sphere of competence, for Constitutions are not usually the creatures of the Parliaments they legitimate. The role of a Constitution is, *inter alia,* to keep parliamentarians in line with the model of government established in the Constitution, and yet this power of constitutional interpretation could be used to undermine the Parliament's right to legislate generally, by making it a matter of constitutional right for judiciaries to adopt whatever interpretive method they please. Ethical positivism, stressing as it does that government must be via specific general rules, acknowledges that there are problems in giving the power of determining constitutional interpretive method to legislatures. On the other hand, giving the courts an unrestricted capacity in this respect licenses an unbounded and unlimitable acquisition of power by courts at the expense of legislatures.

The LEP solution to this standoff is to give the choice of interpretive theory to courts, but to seek to establish political guidelines for the exercise of that choice, adherence to which is a matter of judicial ethics. That ethical system may be derived from a political philosophy, including particular views of democracy, the separation of powers and the rule of law. The substantive proposal of LEP with respect to the ethic of judicial power over interpretive method is this: interpretation should be guided by the disinterested search for clear contextual meanings that resolve ambiguities and obscurities by transparent devices that promote predictable selection between the alternative contextual meanings of a text. It follows that legal change in general, and constitutional amendment in particular, should be pursued through the avenues established within that constitution. The argument that constitutions must be adapted to changing circumstances, and that such changes may be read into existing text by judges, sounds plausible, but it undermines the normative control of constitutions in the same way as broad purposive interpretations undermine the intentions of ordinary legislation.

Back in the real world, we know, of course, that courts are not presented with good positive law: clear, unambiguous, comprehensive and consistent. Legal positivists have always recognised that we need some delegated legislation by judges to fill these gaps, to resolve these inconsistencies, and perhaps to make needed developments in areas where legislatures have not the time, inclination nor political will to venture.

Resort to the notion of delegated legislation is a neat way of preserving the integrity of democracy, but in political terms it is suspect. Delegated legislative power in the hands of courts undermines those arguments for the separation of powers that rest on their perceived and actual independence. Further, it brings with it the danger of abuse of such delegated power, as when clear and consistent law is ignored because in the opinion of the court it is substantively ineffective or unjust. Also, delegated legislation provides a new legal status quo, whose alteration requires effort and the exercise of political power that may not be available at any given time; therefore it may be, in effect, impossible to override it. Delegated legislative powers bestow a substantial measure of societal power, because it is usually more difficult to undo legislation than not to do it in the first place. The burden of inertia and the potential unpopularity of any change in the law give political advantage to judicial innovations. Delegated legislation changes the political scene. It not only sets a new agenda: it captures the high ground of established law, which is particularly powerful when popular opinion is against major legislative amendment of recent judicially developed law.

Nevertheless, in both constitutional and ordinary law, there is no evident mechanism for dealing with the paradox of creating, while controlling, ultimate decision-making power in a society; if this is the case, we have little choice but to acknowledge explicitly the necessity for a powerful judicial ethic, involving self-restraint and interpretive integrity. In practice, there is little that can legitimately be done, except public criticism, when judicial office is abused and subverted in terms of the norms of LEP. Perhaps only the desperate rely on the ethics of others, but democratic rule governance is a desperate business, and we may have no choice but to trust judiciaries with respect to the model of judicial power they adopt.

The legal theory of ethical positivism sets out to circumscribe the power of both politicians and judges, and to locate this circumscribed political power in the hands of the former, but theories carry no clout unless they are accepted as models and guides by political participants, including judicial ones. The *de facto* political power of judiciaries lies in the legally unrestrictable, and in this sense legally legitimate opportunities that judges have to adopt creative interpretations in and of their roles. However, LEP holds to the political view that the interpretive methods adopted should minimise the elements of political power that, in the normal course of events, accrue to those who exercise judicial power.

# 5

# LEGISLATIVE INTENT AND DEMOCRATIC DECISION-MAKING

The concept of intention is crucial in the interpretation of law by judges and by citizens. It is also fundamental with respect to the theory of legislation in a democracy and to the understanding of the authority and functions of law in general. Bringing these aspects together, I argue in this chapter that legislative intent should be analysed first in relation to the idea of a democratic political system and only secondarily, and derivatively, in relation to issues concerning statutory and constitutional construction. The substantive thesis I defend refines an institutional conception of legislative intent to propose that it is the duty of a democratic legislature to enact statutes which make formally good law, that is, law that is clear, unambiguous, readily applicable and unproblematic in that it can be understood and followed without difficulty. This means that citizens have a right to expect that statutes mean what they say, that legislatures have a duty to enact laws which can be understood, followed and applied on the basis of the contextually evident meaning of the words, and that courts have as their prime, if defeasible, duty the responsibility of applying the text, so understood.[1] In other words, in a democratic context, legislatures ought to be taken to intend the contextually evident meaning of their enactments. This is part of what I call 'democratic positivism'.[2]

This thesis takes legislative intent to be a normative concept that relates to the responsibility of legislatures, the members of which can be held politically accountable for, amongst other things, their formal enactments. It does not require interpreters and subjects to discover the actual or subjective intent or purpose shared by a majority of individuals within a legislative assembly. However, it retains the link between the legitimacy of law and the originating political will – in this case the will of the people – which is crucial to democratic forms of legal positivism and, indeed, to any form of democracy that incorporates the rule of positive law (that is, law which can be understood, followed and applied without recourse to speculation, controversial evaluation and political calculation).[3]

The proposed conception of legislative intent in a democracy is that the legislating assembly must be taken to intend that its enacted words be law and that those words be understood in terms of their public meaning as captured by

---

1 This position is partially articulated in TD Campbell, *The Legal Theory of Ethical Positivism*, Aldershot: Dartmouth, 1996, Chapter 6.

2 See TD Campbell, 'Democratic aspects of ethical positivism', in TD Campbell and J Goldsworthy (eds), *Judicial Power, Democracy and Legal Positivism*, Aldershot: Dartmouth, 2000, 3.

3 See TD Campbell, 'Legal positivism and deliberative democracy', in M Freeman (ed), *Current Legal Problems*, Vol 15, 1998, 65.

the conventions of language and legislation in that society at the time they are made, unless the legislators make it clear, through the text itself, that this is not the case. This may be achieved through the provision of stipulative definitions or some other way of making known what it is that the legislators intend to enact, provided this is consistent with the making of good positivist law. And so, while the intention of the legislature is the source and the basis for the authority of law, it is not the actual intent of the members of the legislature that directly determines the meaning of the words used in the enactment. The justification for this normative theory of legislative intent derives from the right of legislatures to make law, law being a set of publicly available rules for the control and facilitation of interpersonal conduct. Because the public nature of law is necessary to its operations, it is the legislature's right to choose the words and sentences of the law but not to dictate what they mean. This ultimately empirical justification is, as we shall see, reinforced by other considerations relating to moral form and political accountability.

The view that democratic legislatures should be taken to intend the contextual plain meaning of their enactments is not what is called in the literature an 'intentionalist' theory. Intentionalists regard the text as merely evidence of a subjective intent that is the real source of, and authority for, an enactment.[4] I argue that legislators are responsible for the public, not the private, meaning of their enactments. My view may be called 'textualist', although, as we will see, it is a contextual form of textualism and one which is governed by appropriate conventions for reading legislative texts. Further, it is a textualism which traces its authority to legislative intent as a political construct necessary for the institutional operation of what I call democratic positivism. It might, therefore, be labelled 'textual intentionalism'. My position is 'originalist' in so far as it takes the text in its public meaning at the time of enactment. However, it would be confusing to give it this label since 'originalism' is tied in the literature to original intention in a sense which goes beyond that which is to be found through the text and contemporary understanding of it and draws on the denotations originally present to the minds of legislators.[5] This diverges from the traditional idea of orthodox originalism, that is, that the meaning of legislation is the specific intention of the legislators as it is revealed in the text plus our knowledge of their beliefs and assumptions. Orthodox originalism suggests that the relevant intention is a meaning the legislature tries, but may fail, adequately to express in words, thus licensing us to use evidence of what the legislators actually meant, and in so doing to put aside the contextually plain meaning of the text. I am not, therefore, even a 'moderate intentionalist', to use Jeffrey Goldsworthy's useful label for a theory which accepts that the meaning of a statute is its 'original intended meaning'[6] but restricts evidence as to what legislators' intentions

---

4 L Alexander, 'All or nothing at all? The intentions of authorities and the authority of intentions', in A Marmor (ed), *Law and Interpretation*, Oxford: OUP, 1995, 357, 361.

5 P Brest, 'The misconceived quest for original understanding', *Boston University Law Review*, Vol 60, 1980, 204.

6 J Goldsworthy, 'Originalism in constitutional interpretation', *Federal Law Review*, Vol 25, 1997, 1, 12.

actually were to that which 'was readily available to their intended audience'.[7] Goldsworthy confines evidence of legislators' intent to what their audience can 'reasonably be expected to know' about those intentions, whereas I hold that citizens have a right and a duty to read the text in terms of the contextually evident meaning at the time of enactment, irrespective of evidence that legislators failed to get their actual meaning across through the text.[8]

The thesis is that the political will is expressed through the conscious and overt choice of language in a particular context, a choice made under the above assumptions. We can thereby relate the authority of legislation to the political authority of the representatives of the adult voting population which elects them to make law and governments to rule via positive law. This does not require us to undertake a usually fruitless search for the subjective intentions of a selected individual or groups of legislators. Legislative intent does not relate to private meanings or to any purposes, public or private, that are not stated or evidently implied in the text, but to the intentions which citizens and courts of the jurisdiction, conversant with the relevant linguistic conventions and implications of the process of making and transmitting laws, are entitled to find in the enacted text. This thesis does not derive from an abstract analysis of 'intention' or from an apolitical theory of interpretation, but from a combination of the ideal of governance through law and the democratic thesis that the right to determine the content of that law derives from the decisions of the populace as a whole. In brief, democratic governments are elected to govern through laws and are accountable in terms of the laws they make. Given the functions of law, on the positivist analysis I adopt, this is not a feasible system unless they are accountable for the contextually evident plain meaning of the legislation enacted.

In summary, this notion of legislative intent brings together commitments to:

(a) the democratic sources of legislation;

(b) the ideal of governance through positive law;

and, as is implicit in the combination of (a) and (b) above,

(c) priority for the adjudicative, rather than discretionary or law-making, role for courts.

The purposes of this thesis are to promote the utility and justice of law in societies marked by individual and group disagreement, to bolster the legitimacy of democratic process in dealing with disagreement by arriving at a working compromise as to legal rights and duties, and providing a framework within which courts can aspire to carry out functions which are part of, and yet routinely subordinate to, this political process. The political assumption here is that law is the creation of authoritative determinations of mandatory conduct through the

---

7 *Ibid*, 20.

8 For the terminology of intentionalism, textualism and originalism see Marmor, *op cit* fn 4; G Bassham, *Original Intent and the Constitution: A Philosophical Study*, Lanham, MD: Rowman and Littlefield, 1992; and S Levinson and S Mailloux (eds), *Interpreting Law and Literature: A Hermeneutic Reader*, Evanston, IL: Northwestern University Press, 1988.

selection and specification of moral and instrumental rules from the range of alternatives available in society.[9]

Some theorists will doubt the wisdom of running together three apparently distinct concerns: a theory of politics (the sources of legitimacy), a theory of law (particularly a theory of legal authority) and a theory of adjudication. I take the contrary view. These three areas of theorising are inextricably intertwined and must be dealt with coherently and comprehensively. We cannot know what judges ought to do until we have a view on the role of law in a justifiable political system. The compartmentalisation of discourses in legal philosophy is implicated in the current ideological shift to legitimating free-ranging judicial control of legal content. The concept of legislative intent is a crucial meeting place of theoretical concerns. A clear and coherent notion of legislative intent is required to give expression to the distinct concepts of democratic sovereignty, the rule of (positive) law and the methodology of legal adjudication. We have to make sense of the idea of the sovereign will of the people in connection with the making of rules which can be accurately and consistently applied by independent judicial officers, without recourse to controversial moral and political judgments. In enabling us to make these connections, the concept of legislative intent has the potential to unite the central strands of legally oriented political philosophy.

## THE THESIS

I have argued that a theory of legal interpretation which offers any guidance for practice requires a normative theory of legislative intent, that is, a prescriptive conception which lays down the sort of intent that should be adopted as the source of law, indicates what citizens have a right and a duty to assume about legislative intent, and establishes what sort of legislative intent judges have a duty to respect.

A normative theory cannot be derived from conceptual analysis alone. It follows that there is no prospect of deducing any useful conception of legislative intent from the concept of intention as such. Indeed, 'intention' covers a multiplicity of complex notions relating to action. The discourse of 'intention' may be used to identify, for example, (a) the objectives of conduct, (b) ulterior purposes, (c) commitments to future action, (d) decisions between alternative conduct, (e) motives for these commitments and decisions, (f) attempts to do something and (g) agents' knowledge of the consequences of their actions.[10] There is nothing in the concept of intention that requires us to adopt one of these multifarious conceptions, let alone give it a specific content, when we seek to identify what is to count as 'legislative intent'. The clarification of legislative intent requires that we make an articulate and overt choice between the range of

---

9 In this I follow J Raz, 'Authority, law and morality', *The Monist*, Vol 62, 1985, 295; and L Alexander, *op cit* fn 4, 359–60.

10 For useful explorations of these alternatives, see G MacCallum, 'Legislative intent', in R Summers (ed), *Essays in Jurisprudence*, 1970, 237; and G Bassham, *op cit* fn 8.

meanings available, limited only by the contexts with which we are dealing and the evaluative stance we decide to adopt.

Because we are dealing with a normative theory of legislative intent, what legislators and legislatures actually intend does not in itself qualify as legislative intent. Normative legislative intent may be regarded as a fiction, or a counterfactual assumption. It is not about what individual legislators would have intended if they had thought about the matter, but about what citizens and judges have a right to assume legislators intended, the meanings for which they can be held responsible, even if they had no such actual intentions.[11]

Nevertheless, a prescriptive conception of legislative intent must be capable of instantiation, otherwise it would not be reasonable to hold someone or any body of persons accountable in its terms. Moreover, it need not be a fiction. Indeed, the theory is that it ought not to be. With respect to my particular normative thesis, contextually evident plain meaning is what legislators both can and ought to intend. Contextually evident plain meaning is what citizens and courts have a duty to accept and a right to assume, just as, in making their wedding vows, a bride and groom have a reciprocal duty to mean what they say and a correlative right to assume that their about-to-be spouse means it when they say 'I do'.

The thesis is that legislators should be taken to intend the contextual plain meaning of words and sentences they enact as rules. However, legislators may make it clear (in plain language) in the text of the legislation in question that they are departing from, or seeking to give more clarity and definition to, what the words and sentences in the legislation mean in terms of the linguistic rules and conventions currently used to understand the communicative discourse of the people concerned. Further, contextual plain meaning takes into account the conventions assumed to hold with respect to legislative communication in general, as well as the shared assumptions of those who operate in the area of social life to which the legislation is addressed. This involves a defeasible commitment to plain meaning, any departure from which must be brought about through the use of further plain meanings.

The contextually evident plain meaning thesis has three types of advantage: (a) democratic; (b) rule of law; and (c) adjudicative.

(a) A core democratic advantage of legislative intention as contextual plain meaning is that plain meaning can serve as the shared intention of all members of the legislature. This applies equally to those who support and those who oppose the legislation in question, in that they accept it or reject it in these same terms. Agreement on meaning precedes acceptance and rejection of a text. Those who accept or reject a piece of legislation can be held accountable for their action with respect to an agreed public meaning of the enactment in question. Contextually evident meaning provides the common ground on which choice and responsibility may be based.

---

11 For a discussion of counterfactual intentions see N Stoljar, 'Counterfactuals in interpretation: the case against intentionalism' (1998) 20 ALR 29.

One advantage of this approach is that we do not have the problem of aggregating individual wills by settling on the coincidence of subjective intentions, be they linguistic intentions about how the individual legislators understand the words in question, purposive intentions about what the individual legislators hope to achieve by the legislation, or motive intentions about why the individual legislators support (or oppose) the legislation in question. No assumption is required that the individuals comprising the majority supporting the enactment have the same motives or the same reasons or the same further intentions, only that they share the intention to adopt (or in the case of the minority who oppose it, reject) the text in question on the assumption that it 'means what it says'.[12]

It may be argued that this notion of legislative intent undermines the democratic authority of legislation if that is thought to depend on legislation being the embodiment of the political purposes of the people's representatives, or a majority thereof.[13] However, that is not so in a democracy that incorporates the rule of law. In such a system, what matters is that the people, or their representatives, get to choose what the *law* is to be and that cannot be done except through a choice of text which can be understood and utilised without recourse to the very controversies which give rise to the need for a process for the resolution of political disagreement. Democratic process may, of course, either decrease or increase policy disagreements. Legislative enactment does not remove such disagreement as remains, but it does provide a decision in the form of an authoritative text by a majority, the members of which may continue to disagree with respect to objectives and motives.

In short, legislative intent as contextually evident meaning gives intelligible and realisable meaning to the concept of the will of 'the people' or their representatives, and provides a basis for assuming the democratic legitimacy of legislation adopted where the controlling assumption in the logic of the process is that the words mean not what the legislators think they mean or would like them to mean, but what they do mean in terms of the social and political community concerned. This meaning forms the content of the citizen's duty of conformity to law and the basis on which they may hold their representatives accountable.

(b) A core legal theory advantage of seeing legislative intention as contextual plain meaning with respect to, for instance, the idea of legal authority, is that contextual plain meaning has to be assumed in the formulation of many of the reasons which can be given for having mandatory rules applying to a given population – for instance, as a means to establishing a framework for co-operation, reaching agreement on what constitutes unacceptable conduct, setting up procedures for dispute, and administering a system for ordering the distribution of benefits and burdens in a society. All these functions require, I have

12 J Waldron makes a similar and perhaps stronger point in J Waldron, *Law and Disagreement*, Oxford: OUP, 1999, 142–46.

13 See D Lyons 'Constitutional interpretation and original meaning', *Social Philosophy and Policy*, Vol 4, 1986, 75, 81–82.

argued elsewhere,[14] a shared understanding of authoritative rules in common. In crude early positivist terms, legislative intent as contextual plain meaning can make sense of the idea of law as the command of the sovereign in a way which gives us a basis for understanding why we might wish to have a sovereign: namely, to achieve the decisive ordering of social relationships for the improvement of the lives of all subjects.

All this does not entail that only the text and the conventions of the language in question are relevant to our reading of it. The context in which the legislation occurs is an indispensable part of our understanding of it. Even linguistic conventions are often context-relative. However, law-making is an endeavour to arrive at relatively decontextualised general norms. More generally, the semantics and syntax of a language must be used in a context and take into account the social setting of the type of discourse involved, the general circumstances of the type of utterances in question (sometimes referred to as the pragmatics of discourse), and something of the particular circumstances of the enactment in question. In the case of legislation, these contexts include not only the pragmatics of the conventional understanding of what it is to legislate, but also the political and social situations from which the particular legislative proposals emerge and to which the legislation in question is addressed. Such contextual understandings of legislation exclude the personal or subjective intentions of legislators in the sense of their beliefs about the meaning of the words enacted as well as their motives and ulterior objectives, but it is inclusive of a shared understanding of the area of social life which is being regulated and the perceived problems and prospects which give rise to the legislative innovation.

Contextual understanding is constrained by the normative structures of institutional intention I have outlined, which require that when we look at context we do so selectively. We are not, for instance, interested in the motives of the legislators, which may be no more than keeping their jobs. Nor are we interested in grand statements of legislators' objectives which may bear little relationship to the enacted text. In seeking to understand context, we do so in order to determine what the text means as law, not to override the text in order to serve some other assumed or identified goal, such as the alleged or assumed objectives of legislators.

With formally good legislation, there can be 'contextually evident meanings' that are prior to any interpretation. By interpretation I mean here the processes to which we have recourse when we fail to find such plain meanings in an actual text and have to find some way of resolving ambiguities and vaguenesses. Interpretation in this sense is far removed from the creative so called 'interpretation' that takes place when it goes beyond the choice between alternative contestants for the category of plain meaning and becomes a more or less unbounded re-authorship of the text in the light of the values and beliefs of the so called interpreters. It is this contextually evident meaning that the legislators may be assumed to intend and that may therefore be said to be law. It

14 TD Campbell, *op cit* fn 1, Chapter 3.

suffices to give content to the ideal of legislative intent in a way that makes sense of the sovereignty of an assembly, that is, its right to make law. It provides a basis for developing ways of understanding the substance of law that makes it useable by citizens and sets the judiciary a manageable and appropriate task within a democratic polity.

The contextual plain meaning approach fits in with the rule of law thesis that sovereign authority must be exercised under and through the medium of rules, on the grounds that this provides advantages of predictability in the use of centralised power which enhances negative liberty, makes possible formal equality of opportunity, enables efficient administration and presents itself in a form which makes it amenable to moral and technical criticism. In other words, legislative intention as contextual plain meaning makes it possible for us to conceive of legislation as law in a sense which connects with standard and acceptable normative theories of the purpose and functions of law in a pluralist society.

(c) Finally, there is a core adjudicative advantage in the contextual plain meaning approach in that legislative intention as contextual plain meaning enables us to conceive of a feasible judicial duty to apply the laws the legislators intended to enact. We can use it to frame a description of the judicial role which is compatible with an initial presumption as to the propriety of excluding judges from law-making. It can also form the basis for developing a theory of how courts ought to tackle problems of interpretation, that is, problems that arise when it is not clear if there is a contextual plain meaning to be applied.

The thesis assumes that interpretation is required not to understand clear legislation, but to deal with the uncertainties that arise from the elusiveness of plain meaning. When interpretation does feature in judicial process, it is not a matter of delving into the subjective intentions – be they linguistic, political or personal – of individual legislators or selected legislators or drafters. The initial orientation of courts must be, however, an earnest endeavour to give significance to the choice of terms in the light of the alternatives that were available at the time of enactment and an appreciation of the assumptions at work in the area of life to which the legislation pertains. This makes clear that problems of adjudication are inseparable from ideals of legislation. More specifically, if legislators do not enact legislation which has contextually plain meaning, then judges cannot carry out their allotted function. To make this theory of legislative intent persuasive and acceptable we have to show that there is a clear idea of contextual plain meaning which:

(a) accords with a philosophically defensible theory of meaning; and

(b) fits with the rationales of democratic legitimacy that cohere with an acceptable prescriptive theory of the rule of law; and

(c) can be the basis for an acceptable judicial method and ethic.

I deal with each in turn.

## CONTEXTUAL PLAIN MEANING

Stipulating that legislative intent should be understood as the intention to enact laws in accordance with the public meaning of the terms used in the adopted text is initially simply that: a stipulation. The technical terminology of the philosophy of language can facilitate the clear articulation of the thesis, but it cannot itself justify the theory.

Thus, in general, the contextual plain meaning approach emphasises 'sentence meaning' rather than 'speaker's meaning'. Sentence meaning depends on semantics and syntax and is often spoken of as semantic or dictionary meaning, although this does not exclude shared assumptions in the contexts in which the discourse normally takes place, which are more readily understood as social or contextual. Even dictionary definitions standardly point to contexts. The contextual plain meaning approach is to say that words and sentences have meanings in terms of the linguistic rules and conventions of the community within which they have a communicative role.[15] This means that, in theory, words or other signs can have meanings even if they originate from an inanimate source, such as a random natural (ie, non-human) process. At any rate, we can understand a text without knowing anything about the psychological states or social situation of those uttering those sentences.

But is this enough to take us to an understanding of meanings in a specific enough manifestation to be of use in legal contexts? Goldsworthy points out that semantic meaning is a relatively thin conception of meaning which leaves out a great deal of what we need to understand a sentence in practical contexts. In ordinary conversation we rely on what is called 'utterance meaning', which takes into account those pragmatics of discourse that cannot be expressed in semantic rules. Goldsworthy's example is 'the cat is on the mat'. We cannot know, for instance, which cat and which mat is meant until we know the context of the utterance on a specific occasion. However, in asking what the sentence means, we need not take into account any private meanings the speaker may be utilising. Goldsworthy's utterance meaning, as part of his theory of moderate intentionalism,[16] involves only conventions and facts known to the audience by means of which they are able to understand such matters as the specific reference of a sentence.

This would suggest that the meaning of a law depends in part on the pragmatics connected with legal utterances in specific contexts. However, legislative utterances do not aim to identify particular cats and particular mats, but require conformity to general rules, such as 'cats shall not sit on mats'. In other words, the functions of legislation routinely require excluding a lot of what Goldsworthy takes in under the heading of everyday utterance meaning.[17] On the

---

15 Thus, A Marmor, *op cit* fn 4, esp 16–19.

16 J Goldsworthy, *op cit* fn 6, 19–21.

17 See J Goldsworthy's 'utterance meaning' which combines semantics, syntax and the pragmatics of the contexts in which language is used: 'Implications in language, law and the Constitution', in G Lindell (ed), *Future Directions in Australian Constitutional Law: Essays in Honour of Professor Leslie Zines*, Sydney: Federation Press, 1994, 150, 151.

other hand, there is room for a theory of 'legislative utterance' that provides the institutional context in which are embedded many assumptions, such as the conventions of statutory interpretation, as to what it is to enact and apply legislation. A narrow view of semantic meaning is clearly insufficient for legislative as well as everyday communication. Indeed, the understanding of what legislation involves, and what a particular piece of legislation is about – which may be termed 'legislative utterance' – is important to, and part of, what I mean by contextual plain meaning, for it brings in that part of the context which marks the communication not only as an enactment, with all the social, political and legal understandings that go with this, but also as an enactment addressed to relatively specific types of situation.

What can be resisted in this context is the reduction of legislative meaning to 'speaker's meaning', a concept which takes us back from semantics and syntax to the intentions involved in particular speech acts. Speaker's meaning puts the emphasis on what the speaker intended to say or do in the saying rather than on what she did say, and allows for the fact that a speaker may have an idiosyncratic understanding of the meaning of certain words and phrases or an incapacity to frame sentences with which she is satisfied as expressing her views and may have all sorts of further purposes in expressing the words in question. This is not the case with legislative meaning, which is, at the very least, closer to semantic meaning than to speaker's meaning.

It is worth noting that the classic theory of speaker's meaning developed by HP Grice is a rather more objective matter than such subjective intentionality.[18] Grice's theory is that meaning is, or involves, speaker's intention: 'a speaker S means that *p* by a declarative utterance of *x* to an audience A if and only if (a) S intends that A should come to believe that *p*; (b) S intends that A should recognise that S uttered *x* with intention (a); and (c) S intends that this recognition (b) should be among A's reasons for coming to believe that *p*.' (In more accessible formulation: S means something if she uses words intending that the audience believe that something, intending that the audience recognise this intention and intending that her use of these words in this way will be taken by the audience as a reason for believing that something.)

If this is what is meant by 'speaker's intention', then there is no difficulty in incorporating it into the conception of contextual plain meaning, as long as the speaker is taken as a legislator or legislators. For our purposes, we might want to have a version of Grice's speaker's meaning which relates to imperatives rather than propositions. The equivalent analysis might be: 'a commander C means to do *s* by a declarative utterance of *x* to an audience of subjects A if and only if (a) C intends that A should come to do *s*; (b) C intends that A should recognise that C uttered *x* with intention (a); and (c) C intends that this recognition (b) should be amongst A's reasons for doing *s*.' (In simpler language: a commander means to do something when she uses words intending that the audience do that thing, that the audience realise that she so intends, and that her uttering the words will be taken by the audience as a reason for so doing.)

---

18 HP Grice, 'Meaning', *Philosophical Review,* Vol 66, 1957, 377.

This is helpful in so far as legislation is viewed as an act of communication.[19] All communication involves some such intentions, as Grice outlines, as well as an understanding of the conventions that make successful communication feasible, but it tells us nothing about how audiences are to begin to know what it is that is meant by the utterances in question. All that we have is that communication requires audiences to be aware that utterances are made for purposes – for instance, in order to alter their beliefs or actions. Audiences must recognise that speakers are making utterances in order that they (audiences) come to believe what they (speakers) say, but this does not help us understand how audiences know what it is that is being said. In other words, Grice's account of speaker's meaning presumes semantic or sentence meaning. This takes us back to accounts of mutual understanding via conventions of language and communication that are shared by those concerned. And this involves understanding a text by deploying the shared conventions of the communicators, an understanding that can readily be conjoined to the thesis that an act is an act of legislation if and only if the legislators intend that their utterances be taken as rules to be followed and that this is understood by those to whom they are addressed. That is the intent of legislation and that intent may even be regarded as a constitutive element of legislation.

Grice's scheme of ideas is thus helpful in expressing my thesis of legislative intent more precisely, but this does not, of course, make the thesis correct. It may be argued, for instance, that legislators are doing all sorts of different things when they legislate. Thus, symbolic legislation may be enacted to affirm values rather than effect conduct, and a great deal of legislation may have more to do with gaining voter approval than altering citizen behaviour. This is an objection which can be made to Grice's analysis of speaker's meaning. Speakers may have all sorts of intentions other than changing other people's beliefs; for instance, speakers may intend to deceive or dissemble. Why then should we adopt Grice's assumptions? His analysis may be correct if we are out to answer the question 'did she really mean that?', but it will not help with the question 'what is she up to this time?' One answer is that it is possible to argue for some sort of fundamental commitments on which other intentions are parasitic. Perhaps we cannot have the intention to deceive unless we routinely have the intention to convey propositions accurately, thus making the intention to convey propositions more basic than the intention to deceive. This approach is reminiscent of the natural law argument for the priority of truth telling over deceit.[20] It may also be read into the Habermasian assumption of sincerity in dialogue.[21] And similarly, we may argue, symbolic legislation presumes, or is parasitic upon, the norm of ordinary legislation and ordinary legislation is command intentional.

---

19 Serious doubts can be raised about viewing legislation as communication. Although legislation must be communicated, it may be misleading to think of it simply in terms of legislators communicating with citizens, sometimes via judges, for legislation sets up rules to be followed by all (legislators included) rather than conveying a message about what some people want other people to do or be permitted to do. See H Hurd, 'Sovereignty in silence', *Yale Law Journal*, Vol 99, 1990, 945; and J Waldron, 'Legislators' intentions and unintentional legislation', in A Marmor, *op cit* fn 4, Chapter 9.

20 Thus, Thomas Aquinas, *Summa Theologica*, TC O'Brien (trans), Vol 41, 1972, q 110, art 1.

21 J Habermas, *The Theory of Communicative Action*, Cambridge: Polity Press, 1984–87.

Here it is helpful to introduce the terminology of speech act theory: the locution, the illocution, and the perlocution.[22] Locutions, according to JL Austin's scheme, are utterances with a certain sense and reference. Illocutions are what a person is doing in making an utterance (like giving an order or issuing a warning), including utterances whose performance are doing things (like getting married or enacting a law), which are sometimes called speech acts. Perlocutions are utterances whose performance has certain effects, such as changing people's beliefs or conduct, or are utterances seen from the point of view of their effects. Legislation, we may say, is a paradigmatic performative speech act, the act of making words into laws. And legislation may, and usually does, have all sorts of effects, many of them intended, such as to change behaviour, to bring about social justice, and so on. There may be a whole range of perlocutions that are not part of the locution, the sense and reference of the words whose illocutionary enactment makes them into legislation and has certain effects on action.

In this scheme, we may hold that locutions are primary. They are the basic data whose utterance may also become an illocution or a perlocution. Therefore, the assumptions that belong to locutions, or utterances *per se*, are basic. And then, it may be argued when we consider locutions, we can see that they are fundamental to all discourse. If this is correct, then we may say that speaker's meaning must presuppose locutions, which thus have philosophical priority. Only because locutions have meaning *per se* can we use locutions to tell lies, by turning them into perlocution.

However, we do not require recourse to such quasi-sophistries, which are suspect because of the way in which they draw on an essentialist conception of discourse. Instead, we can simply accept that the idea of speaker's meaning is normative. It is a prescriptive model about what we have a right to expect that speakers are intending to do in what they say. It sets up acceptable terms of conversation, which aid successful communication. Not only is it speaker's meaning rather than poet's meaning or mad person's meaning, it is a certain type of speaker's meaning: a communicator speaker's meaning perhaps, or maybe a 'good speaker's meaning', an idea which might put us on the scent of a conception of 'good legislative intent', a norm or standard which sets out what it is that ought to be intended in enactment. Good legislative intent involves such matters as choosing texts which, when read in terms of standard linguistic conventions, have the formal characteristics of clarity, consistency, precision and generality. These derive from a theory of the nature of the function of law as an instrument of, and limitation on, legitimate political power.

There are advantages, therefore, to a Gricean variation in terms of legislative meaning being tied to the intention to make law (which we can understand through Austin's conception of illocutionary acts) and to the idea of utterance meaning as a broader view than pure semantic or dictionary meaning, but not, I think, so broad as Goldsworthy's notion of discourse pragmatics in general. This enables us to have a conception of contextual plain meaning that does not go down the subjectivist path of postulating a meaning which legislators have in

22 See JL Austin, *How to do Things with Words*, London: OUP, 1962.

their minds, which they then put into words when trying to express their meaning and thereby communicate it to their audience. On that view, we read the words in order to get at the subjective speaker's meaning, that is, what is in the speaker's mind, if anything. In other words, texts are taken to be attempts to communicate the prior meanings or determinations of their authors.

This I take to be Larry Alexander's analysis when he writes: 'It [a text] is whatever that author intended to communicate through the marks or sounds.' Legislators make determinations which they then seek to communicate through texts, so 'we must look at their texts with an eye to discovering authorial intentions'.[23] However, while this is a possible view, it is not one that we 'must' accept as following from the very idea of what it is to have a text. It may be that we want to leave room for legislatures to indicate that they are using something different from dictionary meaning, provided they do this with stipulations which can be understood in terms of plain meanings. And I can accept that it is contingently feasible that legislators have a sense of knowing what they mean but fail in the attempt to communicate their beliefs. However, if it is a requirement of understanding of legislation that we grasp the subjective intentions, even just the individual semantic intentions of the legislators who vote for the enactment in question, then I suggest that most legislation does not have a meaning. This prospect seems to be admitted by Alexander in his category of 'failed legislation', which refers to legislation that has, for instance, been passed by a majority whose members have in mind very different instantiations of the terms adopted.

The issue here comes to a head when appeal is made to the beliefs of legislators regarding the legal changes made by an enactment, particularly with regard to whether the legislation would, for instance, make this or that specific and concrete example of conduct illegal. Are we to read a general term like 'cat' in the light of the images that the legislators have of cats (which may include tigers) or the plain meaning (which, we may hazard, excludes tigers, unless the context makes it clear that the legislation is dealing with zoos). In other words, should we seek to discover and follow the specific or concrete intentions of legislators with respect to what they would (perhaps counterfactually) accept as instantiations of a classificatory term?

Alexander argues that the assumptions of legislative authority require us to take evidence of such specific intentions seriously. I argue that we should not. My approach has the pragmatic advantage that it saves us from hopeless inquiries into subjective intent, and from even more hopeless inquiries into counterfactual specific intent. Would the legislators have considered leopards as cats if they had thought of the matter? On the other hand, it does not exclude the right of legislators to make it plain that they do indeed include or exclude tigers and leopards.

Does that make me a 'moderate intentionalist' in Bassham's sense,[24] in that I accept the legislators' semantic intentions relating to the definitions of the

23 L Alexander, *op cit* fn 4, 363.
24 G Bassham, *op cit* fn 8, 28–34.

classificatory terms but not their exemplars, or list of instantiations of the classification? I think not, for, unless the legislators give a stipulative definition of the term, it is to be understood as the audience understands it in terms of the public meaning of the language. This does not make me an immoderate intentionalist but rather not an intentionalist at all. In particular, I deny the right of legislators either to give authority to private meanings of general terms or to give authority to anything that the audience may care to make of the general terms chosen.

In trying to make clearer what I mean by contextually plain meaning, I may be thought to have drifted from identifying legislative intention into placing normative constraints on what is to count as legislative intention. I plead not guilty to drifting, as normative constraints are in the driving seat all the way, right to the core of identifying a particular notion of legislative intent. My conception of legislative intent is a notion of responsibility intention. What the legislators can be held accountable for is the public meaning of the words they enact and, to tie up with what I have just said, they are responsible for the foreseeable meaning which will be given to their legislation.

However, this seems to make the content of the legislators' responsibility relative to the expectations and practices of their audience, and perhaps the audience do not accept that legislators ought to be responsible only for contextual plain meaning. Perhaps audiences take the view that they can read the text in any way they like and that is what legislators ought to have foreseen they would do. Perhaps many do, but they ought not to. Audiences also have duties, and the duties of both legislators and audiences have to be read against a theory of law and a theory of democracy.

## DEMOCRATIC LEGITIMACY

My account of contextual plain meaning may seem quite removed from reality in a number of ways.[25] Thus, it may be argued that a prescriptive conception of legislative intent is unhelpful because a norm can offer no way of settling interpretive disputes in law, whereas there is at least the prospect of an inquiry into the actual intentions of legislators producing an objective grounds for settling interpretive disputes. However, this objection neglects to note that the norm in question seeks to establish the authority of what is ultimately a matter of fact, namely contextually evident meaning understood in terms of actual social conventions and practices. Moreover, it may be argued that evidence as to meaning in this sense is more readily available than knowledge of speakers' intentions since each competent speaker of a language has competence in determining plain meaning.

In support of this thesis, it can be argued that the whole logic of the legislative exercise is directed towards the adoption of certain words as the text of a statute.

---

25 See DN MacCormick, 'Ethical positivism and the practical force of rules', in TD Campbell and J Goldsworthy, *op cit* fn 2, 51–53.

Why do legislators argue over the words? Why do they bother over how these words will be understood? Why do they worry over what they believe the results of conformity to or use of those texts will be? All this only makes sense if we see a certain logic in the legislative process, a logic which assumes that the choice of words matters, that the intelligibility of those words is significant and that the consequences of their adoption as rules of action will have certain consequences.

This logic may not match the reality of what goes through the mind of the individual legislator. The text is drafted by bureaucrats on the instructions of members of the executive. Many members of a legislative assembly either do not read most legislation or do not understand what the text says, but they know that they have the right to suggest changes to the text of a bill; they know that the choice of words in the enactment matter. They know that they will be held accountable by electorates for what happens as a result of the application of the text of the enactment unless it can be shown that the rules were not enforced as enacted. There is, therefore, a powerful democratic argument in favour of plain meaning.

It is important to note that there is no sense of empirical impossibility or even unlikelihood of such a legislative intent being a reality within an operative democracy. The traditional idea of sovereign intent, it may reasonably be claimed, is a ridiculous fiction. It never has had much application to any particular system of law. Certainly it has no bearing at all on modern legal systems in which the sources of law are various, and the legislative process – the paradigmatic locus of the sovereignty fiction – is the outcome of many factors. Some of these factors are intentional acts of a large number of human beings, but these rarely add up to a will or an intention in the sense of an agreed objective. The idea of a sovereign will has no significant place in any remotely postmodern view of law as a diffuse network of social relationships, mediated by multiple shifting discourses, none of which have any foundational basis in a shared objective reality. However, the same difficulties do not apply to the notion of an agreement that enacted texts be read in terms of contextual plain meaning. It can be concluded that this theory may help us to make sense of the actual politico-legal process and is central to any democratically acceptable legal philosophy.

It could, however, be argued that electorates hold governments responsible for the results of their legislation whether or not these results are the outcome of conformity to their plain meaning. It could also be argued that courts have a duty to promote the outcomes intended by an elected government rather than apply the legislation in its contextually evident meaning, yet, in a system of government subject to the rule of law, it is necessary for governments to pursue their objectives in a law-like manner. Obtaining desired objectives in a manner that bypasses governance by rules is not legitimate within a democratic system that incorporates an ideal of the rule of law. It is certain, therefore, that courts do not have a duty to directly foster government objectives rather than apply democratically authorised rules. It is also arguable that citizens have a duty to reject governments that pursue their policies by non-legal means.

This position presupposes a theory along the lines of what I call democratic positivism.[26] Positive law, in the hard prescriptive sense in which I use the term, is law which is identifiable and intelligible without reference to contentious moral and political values. Democratic positivism is an ideal which advocates a system of government in which institutions are designed to give effect to the idea of equality of political power, that power being confined as much as possible to the choice of positive laws, that is, mandatory rules which can be identified and understood, followed and applied without recourse to contentious moral and political values. It is a system in which all adult persons as citizens share equally in the making of law and in the liabilities and capacities which arise from the law that they have made. It is a system that depends on the sustenance of institutions that give effect to equality in law-making, and to law application and utilisation that are an accurate reflection of the laws which have been made. Democracy is thus a matter of democratic will formation in the form of clear mandatory rules which are to be accurately and consistently operationalised.

It follows from these starting points that legislative intent is central to the understanding of law in a democracy, for legitimate law-making must be seen as an expression of democratic (that is, the people's) will. Conversely, determinative political intentions in a democracy must be primarily concerned with law-making, that is, the will that is expressed in the form of law in the positivist sense of general standing commands which have force until such time as the sovereign withdraws or amends them.

It is this thread of will-in-the-formation-of-law that gives force to the role of intention in such a politico-legal system. Personifying this, we say that the people's will rules through the medium of positive law. Positive law must, therefore, in some sense embody that popular will, or else the rationale for the system collapses. If laws do not embody the popular will then they lack legitimacy. Legislative intent is central to democratic positivism because valid law must be an expression of the will of the people. Law-making must not only be an intentional or purposive activity, it must embody the intentionality of the people. If this is unsustainable then democracy is unsustainable.

Collaterally, it may be thought, the idea of legislative intent may serve to provide a source of authoritative guidance in the case of laws whose meaning is in doubt in the process of application. After all, if, in a democracy, law is the expression of the will of the people, what better place to seek guidance as to the interpretation of muddy law than the intention of the Parliament which is constituted by the people's representatives? Hence the growing practice of looking to extra-legal sources, such as *Hansard*, or white papers, or political manifestos, as bases for clarifying and extending the text of enacted legislation.[27]

This is a mistake, or, at least, largely a mistake. Indeed, the primacy of the decision-making of the people as the proper source of law argues in precisely the

---

26 See TD Campbell, *op cit* fn 3, 75.

27 *Pepper v Hart* [1992] 3 WLR 1032. See E Campbell, L Poh-York and J Tooher, *Legal Research*, 4th edn, Sydney: Wm Gaunt & Sons, 1996, Chapter 15.

opposite direction. Only if we distinguish what is enacted from why it is enacted, that is, what legislators intend when they make law and what motivates them to make law, can we make sense of the idea of the will of the people in a way that coheres with an intelligible conception of legal legitimacy. Democratic will formation of law proscribes going behind those laws to subjective intentions of legislators to alter that law. Indeed, even if we make the strange assumption that parliamentary debates are themselves part of the text of the legislation, these debates must then be read in accordance with their contextual plain meaning and not as evidence of the subjective intentions of the proponents of the legislation.[28]

In support of such formalism, there are at least two rationales that relate to democratic positivism, that is, the idea that 'the people' are entitled to rule, but only via law-making.

In the first place, the legislative process is a matter of making a decisive choice of authoritative words whose positivistic purpose is to reach a decision that binds until that decision is legitimately changed, thus attracting all the familiar positivist benefits of certainty, predictability and authoritativeness that enable communities to enjoy the benefits of co-ordination, conflict resolution and conduct control. These benefits are not associated with hunting subjective intentions.

Second, what legislators ultimately agree upon through the process of voting is not reasons, or objectives, or motives, but words: agreed formulations in the language of the community to which the law is addressed. The binding decisions of the people are their choice of rules or laws, not decisions or views about particularities, which may well feature as the motives for their law-making activities. This is essential to the rule of law that requires publicly identifiable rules with publicly identifiable meanings. The notion of intention here is unashamedly normative: it expresses what legislative intention ought to be in a democratic polity that embraces the rule of positive law. At the same time, it attempts to encapsulate a realistic psychology and represents an almost necessary logic of legislative process.

However, we may reasonably ask 'why do we require democracies to be subject to the rule of law?' That is a gigantic question and here I provide only one, illustrative, answer. The rule of law makes democratic decision-making more democratic by minimising a standing shame of democracies, namely their tendency to neglect the interests of minorities.[29] By making democratic assemblies enact general rules, we make it more difficult for government coercion to be selectively applied to minority groups, and there is pressure to debate and to choose in terms of general principles which conform to the necessary logic of moral acceptability, the test of universalisability. Majorities may want to feather their own nests at the expense of minorities but they have to do so by means of

---

28 See J Waldron, *op cit* fn 12, 146.

29 Much of this analysis flows from Jean Jacques Rousseau, *The Social Contract* (first published 1762, 1963 edn, London: Dent). See also CR Sunstein, *The Partial Constitution*, Cambridge, MA: Harvard University Press, 1993; and J Rawls, *Political Liberalism*, New York: Columbia University Press, 1993.

general rules which at the very least help to make their self-preference explicit and, given the pressure of democratic debate, may modify their predations. In brief, if members of the majority wish to promote their self-interest in disproportionate and morally unacceptable ways, the requirement that they can choose only general laws and not particulars makes this more difficult to achieve. If so, this means that, in the interpretation of law, should we fall back on the intentions of the assembled legislators, we are undoing the moral disciplining effects of this aspect of the rule of law.

Thus, Senator X presses her fellow senators to support the bean growers of her state because she wants to save the jobs of her friends, relatives and constituents, but has to do so by proposing a law which provides benefits for all bean growers, thus ensuring that her buddies and supporters are not the only ones to benefit, and raising the issue of why it is bean growers rather than pea cultivators or vegetable gardeners generally that should benefit. If that legislation is passed, and becomes a matter of interpretative debate in court proceedings, we would not want to go back to Senator X's desire to benefit her own people as the basis for settling ambiguities or gaps in the enacted law. Rather, it is the words for which Senator X received majority support that have the authority. If they are unclear or incomplete we should not go back to the partial interests that promoted the legislation in the first place for authoritative guidance.

It is often argued that when we seek clarification of legislation through consulting the legislative debate we are not seeking to draw on the, no doubt often unworthy, motives of the individual legislators but the reasons that were given and accepted in the debate. It is not the fact that Senator Y voted one way on an amendment so as to get home early, but the explanation of that amendment professed by its proposers that gives us guidance as to the meaning of the clause in question. However, legislation is not even in part constituted by the reasons given in favour of it by members of a legislative assembly or their promoters or those who vote for the legislation. I may accept an amendment for my own reasons while rejecting the reasons given by its proposer. There may be as many reasons prompting support for a piece of legislation as there are members of the majority that vote for it, indeed many more, given that individuals may have more than one reason for their support.

Those evident facts of legislative psychology are often taken as a *reductio ad absurdum* of the view that legislative intent is relevant to anything: there is no one legislative intent to which appeal can be made for any purpose. Indeed, this is clearly the case if by legislative intent we mean the reasons the legislators have for supporting the enacted text. The whole point of legislation is to respond to the diversity of views as to what should be done and why it should be done, by establishing procedures through which we can make determinative decisions about what is to be done, but not why it is to be done.

Similar conclusions follow even if we adopt more restrictive understandings of legislative intent which exclude motives but include reasons or at least reasons of an acceptable type, such as the public purpose that the legislation is intended to serve, the problems it is intended to solve, or the goals that it is intended to promote. These may, of course, feature in the ulterior purposes legislators have for supporting the legislation, but they are a type of reason, and a type which may be thought more acceptable, particularly if the objectives in question can be described as some conception of the common good or public interest. Indeed, this is precisely the sort of thing that is meant by intention in statutory interpretation of the purposive sort, which has led to purposive preambles and the acceptability of purposive legal arguments in not only understanding but stretching a text so that the law better serves the desired objective.

This 'public reason' approach may appear to have democratic credentials if the purposes involved are those shared by the majority supporting the legislation,[30] and this can certainly be validated by having purposive preambles, or even by incorporating ministerial statements into the law by modifying the rule of recognition to include such currently extra-legal material. However, this is not compatible with democratic *positivism,* for such an approach undermines the point of law, which is intended to prevent the sovereign issuing commands of the form 'Do whatever promotes goal X or objective Y', and which requires that the sovereign commands be expressed in terms of specific general rules.

A mildly purposive approach may be considered acceptable if it is not used to create or develop or put aside legal rules but rather to gain a better understanding of them. There is a role for subjective intention as part of the context that helps us to establish the meaning of rules as distinct from their purpose. The investigation of legislative intention here is undertaken in relation to what meaning is intended by the use of the words embodied in the text. The idea is not to vary the rule in the light of legislative purpose, but to consult legislative purpose to get a better hold on the meaning of the rule. This may be done without extrapolating from exemplars or even the classificatory criteria which were in the minds of legislators but with the objective of comprehending the social situation to which the legislation is addressed and the role which legislation might have in that context.

## JUDICIAL METHOD

The perceived Achilles heel of legal positivism and the textual theory of legislative intent is the problem of interpretation. What does the theory of contextual plain meaning have to say to us when there is no clear contextual plain meaning? Are we in the whirlpool of judicial discretion, which draws in all vague and ambiguous rules, and thus ultimately all law, deep into the sea of arbitrary will?

The problems of interpretation arise when conventional meanings seem elusive and ambiguous. The assumption that legislators intend plain meaning as it will be perceived by the audience to which the legislation is addressed does not settle what that meaning is, in many cases, hence the democratic impulse is to look to the legislators to determine an authoritative meaning. We have said that this path is not open to us because of the difficulty of identifying any such

30 See Rawls, *ibid*, 225–27.

authoritative intention behind the words. Indeed, vague and ambiguous words are often chosen to obtain a majority for a text where no political agreement exists. An assembly is a group of individuals and does not normally have an intention as distinct from a number of intentions equal to the number of the members involved. It follows that appeal to legislative intent as the state of mind of those supporting or opposing the legislation will not settle matters of interpretation even if we could know what these legislators intended independently of what they said. They may say one thing but intend another.

Indeed, if legislators know that what they say in the assembly can be used to interpret the legislation, they may say things in the assembly in order to influence that interpretation, and these things may be contrary to what others in the assembly intend citizens and courts to accept as their intentions. Moreover, going into legislative history brings to light all sorts of reasons why members of the assembly support or oppose the legislation in question, and what their further intentions or ulterior motives are in so supporting or opposing. These often relate to the results they think will follow from the law and why they believe these to be beneficial or detrimental. Considering legislative intent, then, may confuse what the legislation says with the reasons why it has been enacted, and thereby undermine the social and moral functions of law by returning us to the morass of disparate opinions.

Where does this leave legal positivists in their search for the implementation of democratic positivism? We should note that this issue is not simply a matter of adjudication. The initial injunctions for formally good law are addressed to legislatures rather than courts. Secondly, we should note that, under the positivist regime, courts do have an adjudicative prescription to read the text in its plain and stipulated meaning, and it has to be assumed that this injunction does have considerable bite, given good legislative intent and drafting expertise. Thirdly, we may note that the approach is suspicious of perlocutionary meanings, however worthy, for varying the plain and stipulated meanings. Moreover, we have seen that it can allow use of extra-enactment data, such as *Hansard*, either to help with understanding rather than changing the rules, or, more realistically, to give meaning where there is no clear conventional meaning, or to choose between meanings where there is ambiguity and indeterminacy by exhibiting the context, but not by privileging the subjective intentions of individual legislators.

Here we have to look again at the conventions of discourse. These arise out of, and make most sense in, relatively restricted dialogic communities in standard situations.

All communication needs to be seen in context. I have referred to contextually plain meaning to bring this out. However, legislation is not a standard situation. It aims at both generality and precision. It has wide communicative ambition. It is supported by the system of separate adjudicative courts that can utilise conventions to help us grapple with meaning out of its primary contexts. This is part of the general objective of institutionalising government through rules. In this respect, legislation is not well conceived as a matter of communication at all. It is more a matter of setting up an authoritative text.

The practical implication of this thesis is that citizens and courts ought to be aware of the social situations to which the legislation applies and the sources of concern that led to the legislation in question. That does not mean identifying the precise reference that legislators would give to their general terms if asked, as an original intentionalist would require. The originalist approach assumes that the meaning of a general term is an extrapolation from paradigm exemplars, that sense is a generalisation of reference, so that we can extrapolate, but we cannot detach, the general terms from the specific examples that legislators had in mind. There is some attraction in this, since it turns interpretation into a factual inquiry, but legislators are making laws and laws are general and identify the features which any paradigm examples may be believed to possess. In this, laws identify the criteria of relevance that the assembly is prepared to see enforced. Legislators are not entitled to legislate on particulars: it would not be legislation if they did. It is possible for them to be mistaken as to whether the paradigm examples did have the characteristics attributed to them. And they certainly cannot require that we consider only *their* exemplars or standard examples. What we are bound by is the text, the general terms and not the examples that give that generalisation meaning. So there is logical space here for accepting the generalisation but rejecting the examples, and so taking the sense without the reference.

This still leaves us with the problem of how to deal with positivistically poor legislation. What of the interpretive problems that remain after plain meaning has run out? What is to be done with the imprecision, the gaps, the penumbral cases that remain? Legal positivists are castigated for having recourse to judicial discretion here, but they are right to speak of discretion because it draws attention to the fact that there are in these cases alternatives open to judges that are not determined by the content of the law. Further, legal positivists are as free as anyone to suggest interpretative rules and need not argue that it is a matter for individual judges to decide which rules to adopt. One such rule may be individual judicial discretion. Another is to dismiss any charge or suit where the law is not clear. No clear law can be taken to mean no remedy, or no conviction. Another, not very practical, rule for routine use is to refer the matter to the legislature. A further approach is to draw on positive morality, if there is any consensus on the matter. Others include arguing from the nearest perceived analogies with settled law, drawing on basic legal principles, or considering what enhances the internal consistency of the legal system. All of these are regrettable, in that it would be better to do without them altogether, and some are worse than others because of the scope they allow for the operation of unlegitimated values, but in second-best situations they may be acceptable stopgaps pending further legislative clarification.

A general problem with such default conventions is that they may be misused to overturn plain meanings. However, any interpretive method may be misused. The legal philosopher's task is to make clear that there is a distinction between use and misuse. Indeed, we can hope that an efficient system will have a legislative intent here, that is, an intent about what to do when the legislators make formally poor legislation. These then become part of the contextual legislative assumptions. They, too, may be misused, this time by legislatures, as excuses for fudging the difficult political choices.

In summary, the implications for interpretation of textual intentionalism are:

- we have no need to assume that the theory requires a counterfactual claim about a legislative assembly having a psychological unitary state of mind;
- we should not be intimidated by theories of language to say that indeterminacy is a necessary feature of a text-based system of law;
- such indeterminacy as there is, and there is a great deal, presents a problem for which we can reasonably seek solutions more or less compatible with democratic principles and the preferred functions of law;
- these solutions are partly in the conventions of interpretation we commend for mutual adoption by legislatures, courts and citizens;
- the problems of interpretation can be minimised by adoption and adherence to shared and recognised standards as to what counts as good legislative intent;
- minimising the need for interpretation is first a job for legislatures and only secondarily a job for courts;
- courts and citizens should not be expected to find the meaning of legislation in the subjective understandings of members of the legislature, whose legislative intention should be to express their subjective intentions in the public discourse which enables the words of the enactment to become law.

## CONCLUSION

Anxieties about, and denunciations of, legal positivism take a number of forms, one of which is that it serves as a theory to cloak the exercise of power by vested interests to the exclusion of the oppressed outsider groups within a hierarchical society.[31] We may note, in conclusion, that the thesis of contextual plain meaning provides one avenue of response to what is undoubtedly a danger that arises in the application of all legal philosophies and judicial methods.

First, the capacity for democratic change through political process requires that officials are limited by laws enacted by representative assemblies. Given that in a hierarchical society there is a tension between democratic will and elite power, the democratic output must be formed in such a way as to minimise the capacity of the power elites to ignore and evade the democratic will. I suggest that this is helped rather than hindered by precise, clear laws free of contestable terms.

Secondly, if we assume that administrative and judicial officials share the prejudices or rationality of the powerful, then it is appropriate to limit their

---

31 See M Davies, 'Legal separation and the concept of the person', in TD Campbell and J Goldsworthy, *op cit* fn 2, 115.

discretion and to enact rules that explicitly exclude what are perceived as legal contributions towards oppression and discrimination. The alternative strategy of replacing existing officials with more enlightened ones and giving them power unrestricted by anything but vague purpose-oriented guidelines is unrealistic. The best that we can hope for from enlightened adjudicators, I suspect, is the capacity to see the potential for abuse through the neglect of plain meaning, through the pretence that plain meaning exists when in fact it does not, and because of general human incapacity to envisage factual situations with which they are unfamiliar.

Thirdly, attention must be paid to the discrimination-defying potential of rules that exclude official action on the basis of offending categories such as race, religion and social class and the significance of requiring political decisions to be made in accordance with a general form that makes the nature of the political moral choices that are at stake more transparent.

That said, we may be worried by the apparent conservatism of the use of conceptual plain meaning, a conservatism that will be unwelcome to those who see many existing social relationships as unacceptable. I would suggest that conceptual plain meaning, when conjoined with the specificity and concreteness embraced by ethical positivism, is anything but conservative. The requirement that we formulate laws in the conventions of existing language gives us the capacity to formulate, for instance, rules forbidding common but unacceptable conduct. Plain meaning itself does not restrict, indeed it enhances, the range of alternatives open to us. Only where plain meaning is associated with vague terminology about 'reasonableness', 'honesty', 'fairness' etc does plain meaning tend to produce conservative results – hence the goal of precision of language, minimisation of official discretion and effectiveness of legislative review of judicial discretion.

There are undoubted limits to the utility of plain meaning in addressing profound social change. For many reasons, law must generally follow social and educational processes in which the discourse of a society is developed to express new insights and address new problems. In this respect, law can rarely be in the vanguard of social progress, but it can be a vital part of institutionalising and sustaining such progress as is built on other and deeper foundations.

# 6

# JUDICIAL ACTIVISM – JUSTICE OR TREASON?

Judicial ethics is about more than sustaining public confidence in the courts. It is, or should be, primarily about fidelity to law. However, law-abidingness in judicial method is not the standard fare of judicial ethics codes and handbooks, which tend to concentrate on pointing out that judicial officers should not publicly support political causes, just as they should not frequent hotel bars, or fall asleep on the bench. These matters are of some importance, but this is largely because they relate to more fundamental judicial matters, in particular, to the judicial duty to 'do justice according to law'.[1] This is the basal judicial duty that requires analysis and justification if we are to explore adequately the foundations of legal ethics.

While the ringing phrase 'justice according to law' gets little more than passing attention in judicial ethics handbooks, it is the linchpin of any system of judicial ethics. All the things that judges should *not* do in their lives have to be seen against assumptions about what they *should* do in court. Whatever your job, you should not turn up drunk or fall asleep at work. More specifically, judicial sins, such as showing bias, partiality or favouritism, derive their force from normative paradigms of the judicial task. It is because of our ideas about the role of courts in society, such as settling disputes or enforcing legal obligations, that we require judges to be impartial, unbiased, listen to both parties and, yes, perhaps justices do, therefore, have a particularly strong duty not to fall asleep on the job. However, is 'doing justice according to law' any more than a grand phrase that can be put to one side as a motherhood statement from which nothing specific follows?

We can certainly construe the term 'justice' here in many different ways. 'Justice' may mean anything from (a) the accurate application of authoritative rules of positive law (formal justice), through (b) treating the parties fairly according to some process model (procedural justice), to (c) dealing with people according to their deserts, or their needs, or their moral rights (or however we care to define substantive justice).[2] Interestingly, the phrase 'according to law' can be construed in almost exactly the same variety of ways as can the word 'justice'.

---

1 Thus, Chief Justice Gerard Brennan in his introduction to Justice JB Thomas, *Judicial Ethics in Australia*, 2nd edn, Sydney: LBC, 1997, v: 'Judging serves the community in two ways: by doing justice according to law in each case and by maintaining the rule of law in the community at large.' The judicial oath for the High Court of Australia starts with a pledge of allegiance to the Crown and continues: 'will do right to all manner of people according to law without fear or favour, affection or ill-will' (High Court of Australia Act 1979 (Cth)). The recent *Guide to Judicial Conduct*, Australian Institute of Judicial Administration 2002, 1, states explicitly that its prime concern is to uphold public confidence in the judiciary and only refers to the judicial duty to uphold the law in the context of indicating how to defend the judiciary against misinformed attacks.

2 For an overview of these distinctions see TD Campbell, *Justice*, 2nd edn, Basingstoke: Macmillan, 2001, Chapters 1 and 2.

'According to law' might mean (a) 'according to the authoritative rules', or (b) 'following procedural rules', or (c) 'acting in accordance with the substantive fundamental moral principles embedded in the very idea of law'.[3]

Because the terms 'justice' and 'according to law' can be interpreted to mean exactly the same thing and in a variety of different ways, it is easy to dismiss the phrase 'doing justice according to law' as a grand sounding pleonasm with whatever content we care to give it. This is hardly a promising basis for a system of judicial ethics.

Such vacuous pluralism may, however, be resisted. We can reasonably assume that 'according to law' is a way of limiting how judges may go about doing justice (whatever that is), at least to the point of saying that judges must make decisions that are in accordance with recognised legal principles and rules and do so in accordance with procedures that are similarly defined. That is, 'according to law' points at least to the justice of judges being formal, and procedural justice – not substantive justice – accessed independently of the content of positive law. A judge should not ignore 'the law' in the positivist sense of the rules and principles generally accepted as legally binding in the system in question, on the grounds that they were simply attempting to be 'just' in some undefined moral sense.

To say more about this, we need a theory to articulate and justify this scheme of things. This is to enter the controversial ground of philosophical jurisprudence. How ought judges to determine cases that come before them? What is the nature of judicial power? This in turn is meshed into the wider discipline of legal and political philosophy which deals with what sort of legal system we want to have and how this relates to our preferred political system.[4]

Over the past few decades there have been major shifts in the dominant paradigms of judicial reasoning. Amongst the judiciary (at least according to their public statements) we have moved from the standard espousal of a pretty strict commitment to following the rules and precedents, to a much more open-ended interpretive method in which the inevitability of judicial law-making is celebrated rather than minimised. The so called 'fairy tale' of the declaratory theory and the 'noble lie' that judges do not make law,[5] undermined by the teachings of legal realism and later on by various postmodernists,[6] has been replaced by a plethora

---

3 A position approached in TRS Allan, *Constitutional Justice,* Oxford: OUP, 2001, 21: 'Implicit in the requirement of equality before the law, therefore, when viewed as a constitutional safeguard, is a demand for the protection of *equal laws*.'

4 See TD Campbell, 'Grounding theories of legal interpretation', in J Goldsworthy and TD Campbell (eds), *Legal Interpretation in Democratic States,* Aldershot: Dartmouth, 2002, 29–45.

5 The moment that Anglo-Antipodean judges openly espoused law-making is often attributed to Lord Reid when, in 1972, he noted that 'There was a time when it was thought almost indecent to suggest that judges make law – they only declare it. Those with a taste for fairy tales seem to have thought that in some Aladdin's cave there is hidden the common law in all its splendour and that on a judge's appointment there descends on him knowledge of the magic words "open sesame"'. ('The judge as lawmaker', *Journal of the Society of Public Teachers of Law,* Vol 12, 1972, 22–29.) The new orthodoxy is manifest in Australia in Michael McHugh J, 'The law-making function of the judicial process', *The Australian Law Journal,* Vol 62, 1988, 15–31 and 116–27.

6 See, for instance, G Warnke, *Justice and Interpretation,* Cambridge: Polity Press, 1992.

of positions, from American pragmatism, through economic analysis, to inspirational moralism in which judges are allotted the task of protecting vulnerable minorities from the twin evils of majoritarian democracy and minority wealth.

Some of these changes are personified in the eclipse of the work of the Oxford philosopher Herbert Hart by that of his American successor Ronald Dworkin. Hart's position in *The Concept of Law*[7] is that law is a system of ordinary conduct guiding and facilitating rules identified and applied in accordance with a higher order but nevertheless actual social rule, called the rule of recognition, that enables us to identify the authorised first order rules that citizens are meant to follow and judges are meant to apply. For Hart, the routine application of these first order rules works pretty well most of the time, but they are sometimes unclear (since language is open textured), sometimes incomplete and sometimes absent, leaving room for a limited element of judicial discretion that gives scope for some common sense flexibility.

Hart confronted and headed off the legal realists, but was less able to deal with Ronald Dworkin who argued that this 'model of rules' is simply not how things work in the law.[8] Law, as all practitioners know, Dworkin argues, is full of principles, with basically moral content. These principles, such as equality before the law, or that no one should benefit from his or her own wrongdoing, can override rules in the service of rights and therefore justice, and these principles cannot be understood and applied, Dworkin argues, without the exercise of moral judgment.

With this sort of analysis, Dworkinians have convinced several cohorts of students and hence generations of present and future judges that it is the adjudicative duty of judges to make the law 'the best that it can be' and, by 'the best that it can be', he means, ultimately, the way that most nearly accords with the moral views of the individual judge, in practice with the concurrence of sufficient of his or her colleagues to carry the day in court. True, he applies this in the main to constitutional cases, and presents this as a way of interpreting existing legal materials, not creating law from scratch. Nevertheless, at bottom his theory is that 'the law' (and not just constitutional law) contains fundamental moral principles whose application involves the exercise of the first-order moral judgments of the judge, that is, moral judgments about substantive right and wrong, moral justice and injustice.[9]

---

7 HLA Hart, *The Concept of Law*, Oxford: Clarendon Press, 1962.

8 First in 'The model of rules', in *Taking Rights Seriously*, London: Duckworth, 1977, and later in *Law's Empire*, London: Fontana, 1986.

9 This position was implicit in his earlier work but is now openly espoused in *Freedom's Law: The Moral Reading of the American Constitution*, Oxford: OUP, 1997. Since this approach permits putting to one side precedents that do not accord with the moral outlook of the judge, and giving prominence to those that do, Dworkin's position is compatible with 'doing justice according to law' only in the very limited sense (a) that judicial decisions must be principled, that is, based on reasons – in his case primarily reasons that are grounded in individual rights and not consequentialist reasons that look to future wellbeing – and (b) that they aim to make the law coherent (that is, a consistent manifestation of the judge's first-order moral viewpoint). On the idiosyncratic grounds that his method is 'principled', Dworkin rejects the label 'judicial activism', which he confines to purely *ad hoc* decision-making.

This model of law as an extrapolation from judicial morals does meet with some resistance, principally on the grounds that Dworkin overestimates the judicial capacity to know what is morally right or wrong, and that the diversity of reasonable moral views that individual judges may hold is incompatible with producing an actual legal system that manifests the qualities of being both principled and coherent. There are just too many judicial cooks with a hand in this particular law-making broth.[10]

One locus of this resistance emanates from Australasia. Jeffrey Goldsworthy, Professor of Law at Monash; James Allan, a Canadian who has taught at Otago for many years; Jeremy Waldron, a New Zealander currently at Columbia University, New York; and I have all been dubbed by a not unfriendly critic 'the Antipodean Positivists'.[11] The critic is David Dyzenhaus, a South African working in Canada, who has condemned legal positivism for perpetuating the apartheid regime in his home country,[12] in much the same way as Gustav Radbruch and Lon Fuller argued that the Nazis could have been more effectively resisted had the judges of the Weimar Republic espoused the jurisprudence of natural law rather than legal positivism.

Putting aside the historical basis of such emotive claims,[13] the crucial thing to note about antipodean positivism is that it is not an old style analytical theory that seeks to define law as, for instance, the commands of the sovereign, but a normative or ethical theory that expresses a preference for a certain type of legal system, where, according to my own version at any rate, there is a set of fairly specific general rules that can be identified and applied without recourse to contentious moral or other speculative matters, a system that it is possible for citizens to understand and follow (no doubt with legal advice in complex areas) and judges to apply without recourse to controversial first-order moral judgments.[14]

I call this theory 'ethical positivism', partly because the positivism in question is justified by a political morality and not by pure conceptual analysis, but also because the theory requires ethical practitioners, particularly ethical judges and lawyers, to make it work. Waldron tends to use the term 'normative positivism' (despite the fact that this label is used for the rather different view that law is a system of norms not facts).[15] It is also, for reasons that will become clearer, sometimes called 'democratic positivism'. In this essay, I explore how ethical or

---

10 See A Hunt (ed), *Reading Dworkin Critically*, New York: Berg, 1992. Dworkin's own metaphor is that of the chain novel in which each chapter is seen as an attempt to develop and improve the literary quality of the work while retaining coherence with what has already been written by others. Legal systems are rather messier than that.

11 D Dyzenhaus, 'The justice of the common law: judges, democracy and the limits of the rule of law', unpublished lecture, Melbourne, 8 November 2000, 4.

12 D Dyzenhaus, *Hard Cases in Wicked Legal Systems: South African Law in the Perspective of Legal Philosophy*, Oxford: Clarendon Press, 1991.

13 But, arguing against this natural law position, see I Muller, *Hitler's Justice: The Courts of the Third Reich*, DL Schnieder (trans), Cambridge, MA: Harvard University Press, 1991.

14 TD Campbell, *The Legal Theory of Ethical Positivism*, Aldershot: Dartmouth, 1996.

15 But see J Waldron, 'Normative (or ethical) positivism', in J Coleman (ed), *Hart's Postscript*, Oxford: Hart, 2001, 410–34.

democratic positivism can be used to develop and justify a working definition of judicial activism that enables us to bring into focus significant types of unethical judicial conduct and give substance to the idea of doing justice according to law.

## JUDICIAL ACTIVISM

'Judicial activism' is a term not much liked by judges. Used pejoratively it suggests that the ethical judge is a passive, mechanical creature, a rather unflattering picture of judicial work. Used eulogistically it seems to imply that bold and creative judges are akin to political activists, a not very reputable bunch and another unwelcome judicial image. And if all 'judicial activism' refers to is the interstitial law-making aspect of judging, then it is no big deal these days. Everybody agrees, we are told, that judges make law to some extent, albeit in a particular incremental way, largely within the confines of those aspects of the common law that are their special provenance, and where it is necessary in the process of statutory interpretation. If none of these is what 'judicial activism' means then we have a hopelessly imprecise, ambiguous and unhelpfully emotive term that smacks of journalism rather than dispassionate analysis. 'Judicial activism', it is suggested, is a term to be discarded.[16]

I am not so sure about this. 'Judicial activism' is a term of political criticism and all terms of political criticism are fluid and contested. If we were to give up our political vocabulary on the grounds of indeterminacy, there would be precious little political discourse left. In these situations, we need to refine and articulate the points that are being made in the discourse, so that something more precise can be articulated and evaluated.[17] To do that, we need a theory of adjudication.

My suggestion is that we approach judicial activism not narrowly as having to do simply with the proper scope of judicial law-making, but through the broader notion of its contrary, judicial law-abidingness. On this approach, a judicial activist is essentially (a) a judge who does not apply all and only such relevant, existing, clear, positive law as is available, and (b) a judge who makes such decisions by drawing on his or her moral, political or religious views as to what the content of the law should be. I put in this second criterion because we have to distinguish the judicial activist from both the judicial sloth and the judicial ignoramus. The judicial activist has an overt or operative agenda for law reform in identifiable directions that require moral and political rather than legal

16 See J Sackville, 'Activism', in M Coper, A Blackshield and G Williams (eds), *Oxford Companion to the High Court*, Oxford: OUP, 2001, 6–7.

17 An interesting attempt to do this may be found in the introduction to KM Holland (ed), *Judicial Activism in Comparative Perspective*, London: Macmillan, 1991, 1: 'Judicial activism comes into existence when courts do not confine themselves to adjudication of legal conflicts but venture to make social policies, affecting thereby many more people and interests than if they had confined themselves to the resolution of narrow disputes. The activism of a court, thus, can be measured by the degree of power that it exercises over citizens, the legislature and the administration.'

legitimation. This is often described as making policy decisions, if only because it involves, or should involve, reasoned argument as to desirable social objectives and the means to their attainment.

In so far as judicial activism is a failure to apply existing law, it may be called 'negative judicial activism', and in so far as it replaces existing clear and relevant law with new rules, something which appellate courts have the capacity to do, it may be called 'positive judicial activism'. To this we must add adjudication which, when positive law is either *not* clear or *not* available, goes beyond what is necessary to achieve clarity and consistency in law in a minimalist way. I call this 'opportunistic activism'. By a 'minimalist way' I have in mind that which is necessary to deal with the case in hand, or in the case of appellate courts, to clarify a relatively confined area of law.[18]

In this wider context, the prime reason why judges should not be making law is that they should be applying it. Judicial law-abidingness rather than judicial inactivity is the virtue that contrasts with the sin of judicial activism. Judicial activism, as I have defined it (and as, I believe, it operates as a term of criticism outside the sphere of US Constitutional law), is not to be contrasted with judicial restraint, if this is characterised as a failure to apply existing law because it conflicts with government policy or, in the case of judicial review, with legislation that is being challenged as *ultra vires* or unconstitutional. Indeed, failure to apply clear constitutional rules is a classic example of negative judicial activism.[19]

As a matter of judicial ethics I do not argue that judicial activism is always wrong, but I do hold that, outside the confines of a fairly conservative common law methodology, it can sometimes be so wrong as to be treasonable, because it is a breach of trust and an abuse of judicial power that undermines the foundations of constitutional democracy. The fact that most activist judges are only trying to be just may be relevant to a plea in mitigation, but not an acceptable defence. Certain legal philosophers and many constitutional and international lawyers, including Ronald Dworkin, are thoroughly implicated in this treachery. So are all those judges, legislators and academic commentators who promote and condone the progressive expansion of vague moral standards into the corpus of the law, such as unconscionability, good faith and open-ended standards such as reasonableness. The theory behind the critique of judicial activism provides a basis for the criticism of enlarged judicial discretion in general.

---

18 Minimalism is sometimes referred to under the broad term of 'judicial restraint' which features in many of the 16 meanings of judicial restraint listed by HJ Abraham, *The Judicial Process*, 7th edn, New York: OUP, 1998, 385–410.

19 The US concept of judicial restraint is derived from JB Thayer, 'The origin and scope of the American doctrine of constitutional law', *Harvard Law Review*, Vol 7, 1893, 129; and AM Bickel, *The Least Dangerous Branch: The Supreme Court at the Bar of Politics*, 2nd edn, New Haven, CT: Yale University Press, 1965. For an analysis of judicial restraint that could be used as a contrary to my analysis of judicial activism, see J Daley, 'Defining judicial restraint', in TD Campbell and J Goldsworthy (eds), *Judicial Power, Democracy and Legal Positivism*, Aldershot: Dartmouth, 2000, 279–314 at 308: 'I have identified two principles of restraint as follows: (1) judges should make decisions on the basis of posited rules; and (2) judges should avoid exercising functions other than deciding on their own role and enforcing posited rules.'

More dispassionate scholars may agree with my conclusions but nevertheless deplore the language: surely treason is too strong a word for what is only after all a matter of jurisprudential opinion about how judges should decide cases, a matter of reasonable disagreement between reasonable people. Maybe, but such a tolerant approach underestimates the potential damage both to law and democracy that anything beyond spasmodic judicial activism can do.

In using the term treason I am not imputing evil intent to judges or others whose conduct undermines the democratic rule of positive law. Often, judicial activism is quite the reverse: a misguided attempt to do what is right, sometimes on a naïve assumption that their moral views are shared by all reasonable people. This can make the culture of judicial activism dangerously self-confident, arrogant and self-righteous.[20]

However, in case the language of treason still seems too strong, it should be emphasised that I am also not suggesting that judicial activism should be deemed a form of judicial misconduct justifying discipline and removal. My reticence here is not because judicial activism is not an abuse of office – it usually is – but rather on account of the fragility of constitutional government. We need to be absolutely sure that judges cannot be dismissed for making decisions unpopular with government or the press. We cannot therefore afford to make judicial activism a disciplinary offence leading to dismissal, for this would have an unacceptable chilling effect on judicial independence.

The problem here goes back to the unfortunate fact that we both need governments and have reason to fear the concentration of power that they involve. The tragic paradox of politics is the fact that in order to achieve the preconditions of an orderly and secure society we need to create a potential instrument of oppression. While democracy is an attempt to deal with this paradox by making government a revocable trust, a temporary grant of power to be exercised only under a system of law, no system can formally solve the problem of who guards the guardians, in this case the persons whose job it is to say, within the rule of positive law, when that law has been broken.

That government be a government of rules, that there be separation of powers between law-makers and law appliers, and that governments be vulnerable to the votes of the populace and that judges be *not* vulnerable in this way are amongst the greatest political achievements of human civilisations, but they cannot do away with the need to entrust someone with making final answers in such matters as the lawfulness of political conduct. In this situation, allowing Parliaments, or the governments that control them, to remove judges for judicial activism is likely to be a greater danger to constitutional democracy than permitting such activism to continue.

The need to protect judges in this way enhances rather than diminishes the sinfulness of judicial activism. Given that judges require immunity from external

---

20 To reverse the epigram in TS Eliot's *Murder in the Cathedral:* 'The last temptation is the greatest treason: To do the wrong deed for the right reason.' For the original word order, see TS Eliot, *Murder in the Cathedral,* London: Faber, 1935, pt 1: 'The last temptation is the greatest treason, To do the right deed for the wrong reason.'

control, judicial activists can rely on the fact that there is no acceptable way of institutionalising an effective counter to such abuse of judicial power. Because they are protected by the constitutional norms of judicial independence, judges are immune from the formal consequences of their misconduct. Judicial activism is not a risky path for judges. The cost is paid by the community through the damage that is done to our system of government. So I stick to my strong ethical terminology: judicial activism is, or may be, treason.

## DEMOCRATIC POSITIVISM

To explain and defend this position, I outline why we might want to adopt democratic positivism as a theory of how a legal system ought to operate. Why would we wish to adopt a theory that appears to advise not only citizens but judges to put aside their own ideas of substantive justice and replace them with apparently amoral rules that we follow simply because they are the law? This looks like the abnegation of responsibility all round.

There are two sorts of reasons for supporting the ideal of the rule of positive law. The first, the weaker of the two reasons, is that adopting legal positivism makes for having a formally good legal system, with all the social and economic benefits that flow from it. And the second, much stronger reason, is that legal positivism is necessary for the realisation of a democratic system of government, that is, a system of government in which the people as a whole have real power to control how they are governed. Putting the two considerations – order and democracy – together, I have argued, as a matter of normative political theory, that any large and complex society ought to possess a formally good legal system, as I shall define it.[21]

With respect to the formally good legal system, we are talking here not about the moral or other content of ordinary laws or even of procedural rules, but about the way in which simply having an orderly and public *system* of rules produces social benefits, such as social co-ordination, facilitation of co-operation and systematic control of harmful conduct. A formally good legal system should consist of a framework of intelligible and applicable rules by means of which we can co-ordinate our behaviour, enter into workable agreements and know what we cannot do or must do in order to avoid official disapproval and sanctions. These objectives can be achieved, it is argued, only if we have an agreed set of specific rules capable of being understood, followed and applied by people, whether or not they agree with their content.

We will, of course, also want the content of the rules not only to be compatible with the aims of co-ordination, facilitation and regulation, but actually to produce results that we think optimal with respect to our social and political values. However, whatever these substantive values may be, we require formally good law: rules that are general, clear, specific, applicable and stable. This is the familiar

---

21 See TD Campbell, *The Legal Theory of Ethical Positivism*, Aldershot: Dartmouth, 1996.

theme that clear, predictable law promotes order and stability in society. Rules enable us to know where we stand and to plan accordingly.

The conception of a formally good legal system is also fundamental to a particular sort of justice: what is called formal justice is that which treats like cases alike in terms of pre-existent criteria. This justice cannot be achieved unless there is an operative system of general rules impartially applied. Without that, we cannot claim to be even attempting as a society to treat like cases alike in a systematic way.

Of course, a *really* good legal system, a system that is good overall, will have laws that are not only general, specific and clear, but actually have content we like because it includes the right generalisations, the right classifications and the right remedies. If we could only agree what such substantively good laws would be then our political problems would be at an end, but in what Jeremy Waldron calls 'the circumstances of politics' we disagree fundamentally about the proper content of law.[22] Democracy is a system set up to handle and resolve these disagreements in so far as this is possible while still being able to have an operative set of rules which serve until such time as they are changed by appropriately democratic means.

This takes us to the second argument for ethical positivism: that a system of good positive law is essential for the realisation of democratic government in a large and complex society. There are many reasons for adopting this view. For instance, collectives or their representatives cannot routinely make decisions about particulars, but only about types of persons and situations. Further, choice of rules is not only a manageable focus for political discussion and choice, but is one which functions so as to mitigate the role of naked self-interest in politics by making explicit the choices that have to be made between how different categories of person and behaviour are to be subject to, or beneficiaries of state power. Finally, only if democracy is centred on the choice of rules can it begin to approach the ideal of providing real political power to the people as a whole. If the rules thus created are not followed or are subverted by processes that enlarge judicial discretion at the expense of rule-governed decision-making then democracy is thereby diminished.

In many ways, both reasons for adopting the rule of positive law are hardly controversial. Clearly, all tolerably fair and effective societies need a publicly knowable system of followable rules that can be identified in a publicly verifiable way.[23] Few would demure from the general thesis that the people, through their elected representatives, should make the rules, that it is the court's duty to apply them, and that democratic decision-making is more democratic if it is focused on making general rules than on *ad hoc* exercises of majority power.

---

22 J Waldron, *Law and Disagreement*, Oxford: Clarendon Press, 1999.

23 As is most lucidly argued in L Fuller, *The Morality of Law*, New Haven, CT: Yale University Press, 1969. But see also F Schauer, *Playing By the Rules: A Philosophical Examination of Rule-Based Decision-Making*, Oxford: Clarendon Press, 1991.

Even the most activist of judges usually endorse some such background set of political assumptions. This is, however, often followed by a string of caveats and qualifications that threaten to undermine the initial commitment to the democratic rule of law. Majorities get it wrong. Minorities suffer in consequence. Rules need to be kept up to date. Parliaments are slow to legislate. Technology moves too fast for government. Politicians are short-sighted. All these truisms, and many more, are used to justify departures from the accepted norm.

It is pointed out, for instance, that often there simply are no rules of a reasonably specific sort available to apply in many cases. In this situation, there is no logical space for negative activism (not applying the rules) or indeed positive activism (changing the rules) for there are none to be changed, and opportunistic activism becomes inevitable and pervasive. In this situation, legalism cannot be strict because it is bound to be incomplete.[24] This is why appellate judges, at any rate, always have decisions to make that are not significantly constrained by rules. Does this point by itself not undermine any hard form of ethical positivism? If there are no clear and relevant rules for judges to apply what are they meant to do?

## CONTEXTUALISM

There are indeed problems for ethical positivism with respect to formally defective legal systems, and since the rule of positive law is an ideal that can never be fully attained, the issue of what to do when the system falls short of the ideal is something that impacts on all legal systems to some extent all of the time. The issue is to identify the most acceptable strategy for judicial decision-making when the existing legal system is defective.

The first thing to note is that where there is an absence of clear, specific and practicable legal rules, then the system is defective and should be improved. A policy of leaving it to the judges to sort out is ineffective and unacceptable. The primary duties here fall on governments and legislatures. Democratic positivism is not a theory of law directed primarily at lawyers and courts, but at the democratic system as a whole, especially the legislature and the legislative drafters that serve them. It is the responsibility of the democratic system to produce clear, comprehensive and applicable rules.

---

24 Sir Owen Dixon, at his swearing in: 'Close adherence to legal reasoning is the only way to maintain the confidence of all parties in federal conflicts. It may be that the court is thought to be excessively legalistic. I should be sorry to think that it is anything else. There is no other safe guide to judicial decisions in great conflicts than a strict and complete legalism', *CLR*, Vol 85, 1952, xi, at xiv. Later he accepted 'the application of accepted principles to new cases or to reason from the more fundamental of settled legal principles to new conclusions or to decide that a category is not closed against unforeseen circumstances which might be subsumed thereunder. It is an entirely different thing for a judge, who is discontented with the result held to flow from a long accepted legal principle, deliberately to abandon the principle in the name of justice or social necessity or of social convenience', 'Concerning judicial method', *ALJ*, Vol 29, 1956, 468 at 472.

However, systems fail, often chronically, and governments evade their responsibilities. In the meantime, democratically-minded judges are in a difficult situation. The situation is not so problematic in the criminal law where charges not based on clear rules may be dismissed, but is less easy in private litigation when it may seem wrong always to leave a detriment where it lies, and may be inadequate with respect to the function of pressing dispute resolution. Nevertheless, no punishment and no remedy when there is no clear law is a good starting point, and we need to be cautious of filling the evident gaps in any system of law by the liberal exercise of judicial discretion or, at the higher level, in the making of new law.

Marginal creativity for the purpose of providing clarity and certainty is something that is required, even by legal positivism. The argument for having a formally good system of law itself legitimates a measure of rule creation, for instance, where this is necessary to resolve pressing disputes, although the argument from democracy suggests that any significant legal developments should be left with democratically elected bodies. Even the minimal creativity of judges should be provisional, in that it is subject to legislative review or, in the case of constitutional law, to constitutional amendment. Therefore, we need the constraint of minimalism and the assumption of provisionality.

There are more radical objections to the feasibility of ethical positivism than the occasional, or even frequent, absence of rules. Of particular philosophical interest is the argument that we can never have rules whose meanings limit decision-makers. Rules, we are told, are but strings of symbols, symbols are artificial cultural constructs whose meanings depend on how they are understood by their audience. All language must therefore be interpreted, and all interpretation is subjective in that it is vitally dependent on the mental operations of the particular individual seeking to understand the rule. It follows that there is no such thing as plain or ordinary meaning.[25]

Such rule-scepticism depends on sociological and philosophical arguments to the effect that all meanings depend on understandings of symbols that are embedded in cultural presuppositions and personal histories. It is evident that there is no 'objective' meaning that is independent of shared linguistic conventions and the shared social experience in which these conventions apply.

However, the fact that language is a social phenomenon with certain social underpinnings does not, in itself, show that culture, conventions and social experiences cannot result in a shared understanding of texts. 'Plain meaning' is certainly a culturally dependent phenomenon, indeed a communicative achievement, but it manifestly can succeed in social circumstances where there is shared understanding and the genuine desire to communicate.

That we often fail to achieve plain meaning, indeed that we often do not want to, or indeed that we often want to undermine or subvert it (which is exactly what

---

25 The literature here is vast, incorporating, as it does, legal realism, critical legal studies, and postmodernist critiques of legal determinacy. See J Boyle (ed), *Critical Legal Studies*, Aldershot: Dartmouth, 1992; and D Patterson (ed), *Post Modernism and Law*, Aldershot: Dartmouth, 1994.

lawyers are often paid to do), are evident facts of messy, lazy and adversarial social situations. However, this is not to say that effective communication – through the use of shared understandings closely associated with the language in which these understandings are expressed – cannot take place, or cannot be an ideal towards which effective progress is made to the point where it makes sense to talk of plain language. Indeed, to deny the possibility that a culture can be developed in which it makes sense to talk of plain meaning is in the end self-defeating, for it is a view that, *ex hypothesi,* cannot be communicated.

Nevertheless, the problems of achieving successful communication are real ones and do present a challenge to any form of legal positivism. How can we go about achieving legal clarity? Much depends on exactly what is being commended by way of interpretive method. To give the concept of judicial activism more substance, it is necessary to identify a positivist approach to judicial reasoning.

The approach to legal reasoning that fits best with ethical positivism is textualism, but a form of textualism that places texts in their contexts. I call it, enjoying the play on words, contextual textualism, or contextualism for short. Text in context, or contextualism, does not see the text as simply a way of getting at the subjective intention of the legislature. Democracy cannot be defended in terms of an appeal to some usually nonexistent subjective general will. Rather, we have a system where the people through their elected representatives have the duty of creating an official text, approved by a democratic vote, that is then constitutive of what they intend, and is therefore something for which they can be held responsible, at least when understood in accordance with its plain meaning (or lack of it). Contextualism is not intentionalism.

Neither is contextualism to be equated with 'literalism' if this means reading the words and sentences out of context, merely with the aid of a good dictionary, in ignorance of the social and political contexts. Indeed, most people we call literalists accept that the words of a piece of legislation can only be understood in the type of situation from which the legislation arose and to which it is intended to apply, the ends it is designed to serve, the controversies that led up to it, the alternative positions that might have been adopted, and the conventions of language shared by those involved, together with the conventions for the interpretation of such authorised texts in that jurisdiction.

However, contextualism is not purposive interpretation in any strong sense of 'purposive'. Contextualising does not mean use the text to find the ultimate or background overarching purpose of the legislation, then do whatever is necessary to achieve that purpose in this case or in similar cases. Rather, it means that if you have an appreciation of the social realities from which the legislation emerged, then you have the context that may enable you to understand the meaning of the text.

Contextualism is a form of originalism, but only in the sense that it generates reasons for emphasising the original texts, particularly of statutes and constitutions. It legitimates going back to the meaning of a text prior to the accretions of later and sometimes textually erroneous precedential decisions. To that extent, it endorses the so called literalism of the *Engineers* case that abandoned some tenuously based constitutional implications about intergovernmental immunities and reserved state powers, and returned to 'the meaning of the Constitution' read 'naturally in the light of the circumstances in which it was made'.[26]

In that sense, contextualism is not essentially conservative. It provides a basis for overturning a line of precedent that has gotten out of touch with the original text. Another example might be the way in which *Cole v Whitfield*[27] went back to the evident contextual meaning of s 92 that 'trade, commerce and intercourse amongst states shall be absolutely free', namely to promote free trade and avoid protectionisms between states rather than constitutionalise *laissez-faire* political economy. Cole may also be read as a contextualist return to the text that corrected the previous judicial activism evident in decisions such as the bank nationalisation case in 1948.[28]

There is of course a tension between a textualism of precedents and a textualism of original text, but the democratic standing of the Australian Constitution does give a basis for the *Engineers* case and *Cole v Whitfield* if we see these as returning to 'ordinary and natural meaning' of the democratically endorsed text. Indeed, the same may be said about the recent case of *Re Wakim ex p McNally* (1999) 73 ALJP 839; 63 ALR 270 in relation to cross-vesting. If the Constitution clearly does not allow for the Commonwealth DPP to prosecute under states' corporations legislation, there is a contextualist reason for deciding the issue on that basis, although it may be contested how far state constitutions exclude states conferring state jurisdiction on federal courts.[29] Certainly, the contextualism of ethical positivism does not mean following the interpretive method of the time. It is not conservative in that sense. As we have seen, it allows for putting to one side precedents based on non-positivistic or activist interpretations of authoritative texts.

It follows that while contextualism may be the contrary of 'judicial activism' it should not therefore be confused with judicial inactivity. Indeed, failure to apply existing law – negative judicial activism – is a culpable form of *inactivity*. Judicial law-abidingness often requires clear and decisive action in applying the text of the law. One aspect of the sad history of native title in Australia is the failure of courts to apply *correctly* existing law, by holding that the land was unoccupied or 'unsettled' when this was not in fact the case, although courts can hardly take the primary blame for that, given the assumptions of the time as to the nature of Aboriginal society.

As we have seen, judicial activism need not be opposed to judicial restraint. Judicial law-abidingness certainly does not involve holding back from the application of positive law simply because to apply the law would thereby

---

26 *Amalgamated Society of Engineers v Adelaide Steamship Co Ltd* (1920) 28 CLR 129.

27 *Cole v Whitfield* (1988) 165 CLR 360.

28 *Bank of New South Wales v Commonwealth* (1948) 76 CLR 1.

29 See D Rose, 'The bizarre destruction of cross-vesting', in A Stone and G Williams (eds), *The High Court at the Crossroads: Essays in Constitutional Law*, Sydney: Federation Press, 2000, 180–215.

constrain government or have major social and economic consequences. Judicial 'restraint' in this context is an abdication of judicial responsibility.

On the other hand, judicial law-abidingness does not require a court to give priority to its own interpretations of rules in situations where other reasonable interpretations are placed on these same rules by governments and administrators. The term 'judicial activism' was developed primarily in the area of constitutional law to formulate the thesis that courts should show respect for the interpretations of the constitutions developed by elected governments where these are not clearly contrary to the text of the constitution. That does not mean that governments or legislatures, any more than judges, may simply make the constitution mean what they choose and simply assert, for instance, that its legislation is within legislative power. That was tried in the *Communist Party* case,[30] and properly rejected by the High Court.

Interestingly, the legislation in question in that case[31] was declared invalid in part at least because it gave judicial power to the executive to decide who was a 'communist', that is, someone who belonged to a body of persons whose existence is prejudicial to the security and defence of the Commonwealth, a violation of the separation of powers that is clearly incompatible with democratic positivism. To that extent, the *Communist Party* decision is in line with democratic positivism. If judicial law-abidingness rules out courts putting their own favoured interpretation on such provisions and claiming their necessary superiority, then the use of vague and abstract constitutional provisions to support a preferred political goal is a form of judicial activism. It goes beyond what the text requires. In this context, deference to the elected branch is appropriate.

So there is a type of judicial activism, an opportunistic variety perhaps, that takes the form of utilising the necessarily broad provisions of a constitution to achieve purposes that have no firm basis in a contextual understanding of the constitution. Much of the implied rights jurisprudence of the Mason Court falls under this head of opportunistic judicial activism. It goes beyond what the text requires in the pursuit of a political objective. Certainly, free speech of some sort is clearly a presupposition of the representative government established in the Constitution, but what constitutes the *sort* of free speech that makes representative government a reality is a controversial matter that the founding fathers of Australia clearly left to the Parliament to decide under the constraints provided by the text of the Constitution and the representative system itself.

*Australian Capital Television*[32] invalidated, in the name of freedom of political communication, a no doubt imperfect law whose purpose was to restrict the impact of unequally distributed wealth on the outcome of elections by preventing political advertising during election periods. In so doing, the High Court of Australia opted for an American over a British model of dealing with election

---

30 *Australian Communist Party v Commonwealth* (1951) 83 CLR 1.

31 The Communist Party Dissolution Act 1950.

32 *Australian Capital Television v The Commonwealth* (1992) 177 CLR 106. Cf *Nationwide News v Wills* (1992) 177 CLR 1.

advertising, a preference that is not justified by a contextual understanding of its Constitution. Given the lack of rigour in the method of reasoning adopted, and the opportunistic way in which a new right was discovered in the Constitution, it does look as if at least this piece of implied rights jurisprudence was the result of a conscious attempt to alter the Constitution by unconstitutional means. This may be seen as a form of positive judicial activism and a palpable act of judicial treason comparable to what the New Zealand Court of Appeal did in *Baigent's Case*.[33]

The logical extension of this approach to implied rights was clearly articulated in the minority judgment of Dean and Toohey JJ in *Leeth*.[34] There the concept of judicial power was used to frame an implied right to equality before the law which, as they present it, would permit judges to render any legislation invalid on the basis that the distinctions it embodies are either not in the judge's view reasonable or because, in the judge's view, they are disproportionate to any legitimate end. This is precisely what a loose form of implied rights reasoning would endorse, thus subjecting the substance of all democratic decisions to the moral and political opinions of the higher judiciary. This was a dissenting opinion that has not been taken up favourably in later cases. In general, the Australian High Court, meantime, has since drawn back from that particular anti-democratic abyss.

The Australian implied rights jurisprudence can be seen as a move towards acquiring an entrenched bill of rights and it is important to articulate a response of ethical positivism with respect to court-centred entrenched bills of rights for the purpose of judicial review. Evidently, the values underlying ethical positivism are congruent with core human rights. Ethical positivism identifies a legal contribution to achieving a polity within which human beings are respected as being of equal worth and importance and must involve, in part, having legal rights that embody the values that underlie the discourse of human rights. Nevertheless, there are many human rights concerns about pursuing those moral rights that are human rights through the mechanism of entrenched bills of rights.

Here I only mention one of these concerns, which is that a court-centred bill of rights involving judicial review effectively requires judges to be judicial activists. It requires them to take broadly drawn statements of rights and turn them into concrete provisions that are not required by the text but represent the judges' moral readings, no doubt supported by a selective appeal to the moral readings of other judiciaries, and does so in a way that leaves citizens no legitimate way to resist them beyond constitutional amendment, a process that is itself powerless in the face of loose methods of constitutional interpretation, for the amended constitution can itself be creatively 'interpreted'.[35] Removing democratic rights in this way is a direct challenge to basic human rights and manifests a disrespect of

---

33 *Simpson v Attorney-General* [Baigent's Case] [1994] 3 NZLR 667. The court created a public law remedy for an alleged breach of the NZ statutory bill of rights for which, with clear parliamentary intention, the Act did not provide.

34 *Leeth v The Commonwealth* (1992) 174 CLR 455, 485–90.

35 This is amply illustrated in TD Campbell, KD Ewing and A Tomkins (eds), *Sceptical Essays on Human Rights*, Oxford: OUP, 2001.

the citizens whose autonomy, rationality and morality are called into question by having such constitutional arrangements. Within democratic positivism, human rights ought to be pursued through the ordinary procedures of politics in which the courts feature only after the enactment of appropriately specific legislation.[36]

## THE COMMON LAW DEFENCE

Of the many arguments that can be pitted against democratic positivism, one of the most powerful is based on the fact that the history of the common law may be seen as standing outside the theory. At best what I propose, it may be objected, is applicable only to statutory interpretation and maybe to constitutional law, but not to the common law. This is scarcely surprising, since the history of the common law largely predates the rise of democracy, a fact that is often forgotten when considering the relevance of common law traditions to contemporary judicial practice. Further, democratic positivism does not seek to be an explanatory theory that gives an account of either the history or the current performance of legal systems. Democratic positivism is a normative theory that sets up an ideal against which these phenomena can be evaluated. It does not, and is not intended to, describe accurately all that goes on. Democratic positivism sets forth an ideal to which we should strive. My complaint is that it is an ideal that is being put aside for no good reason and to the peril of our system of government.

Democratic positivism is entitled to be highly suspicious of the common law, especially in its resurgent form as a counterweight to the authority of Parliaments. This is not a suspicion with respect to its role as a method of statutory interpretation, if this is seen as a matter of seeking to render statutes clearer and more consistent in the course of interpretation within the confines of the text, contextually understood as applied to particular cases. Indeed, ethical positivism requires that courts insist that statutes be clear and unambiguous if they are seeking to change existing law, including existing common law, particularly where long established rights are involved.

Following in the tradition of Jeremy Bentham, democratic positivists are highly critical of the common law in a democracy if it is taken to be a significant source of new law with an open-ended method in relation to sources of law – culling from all over the world precedents that are to the liking of adventurous judges, and methods of precedential reasoning that provide no clear basis for *ad hoc* developments of law. And there is certainly reason to be suspicious if the common law is reoriented to become a bedrock of moral principles that trump actual rules and whose implications must be forever unclear due to their abstract and largely textless formulations.

Nevertheless, perhaps there is no great harm in the common law as long as its development is gradual and it is in clear subordination to legislation. Indeed, it may be a means to achieve greater clarity and consistency, and there may be

---

36 The most cogent expression of this view is to be found in J Waldron, 'A rights-based critique of constitutional rights', *Oxford Journal of Legal Studies*, Vol 13, 1993, 18–51.

benefit in the gradual development of rules in the light of the cases that come before the courts: unforeseen circumstances and changing social realities. There are strong arguments against this on the grounds that it gets us into lots of problems due to lack of policy expertise, as when incremental developments in the law of negligence have undermined the system of insurance that had made these developments possible. Judicial law-making can get us into a mess because justices generally do not have the competences or the resources to carry it out well, even if the values they bring to bear on policy-making are not in contention. Further, the issues that divide the parties in legal cases are only part of a wider and more complex picture about which the court is uninformed and with which it may be cognitively incompetent to deal.

On the purely practical ground that legislation and administration cannot effectively deal with all the matters that come before the courts, common law development may be no great problem if it is incremental and consensual. Even so, caution is required since incremental changes reach crucial thresholds that are tantamount to major changes in law and the required consent is difficult to ascertain. Ideally, therefore, in a flourishing democracy, common law should fade away into constrained statutory interpretation. Certainly democratic positivism fiercely resists attempts to entrench common law to the point where it is put beyond the reach of statutory revision.[37] It is one of the points that can be made against the development of implied constitutional rights jurisprudence that this can be used as a basis for developing the common law in a way that boosts its authority and makes it less amenable to legislative review.[38] A similar effect may be seen in the application of s 6 of the UK Human Rights Act 1998, which requires public authorities, including courts, to act consistently with Convention Rights when carrying out their duties.[39]

This link of the common law to human rights brings us to one of the most immediately persuasive arguments for judicial activism. Democracy, it is commonly argued, does not adequately protect vulnerable minorities. There is thus a case for retaining a measure of judicial activism whereby judiciaries can intervene to protect those whose votes are too small in number to prevent injustice being done to them. Sometimes this argument is based on a very simple view of democracy that assumes all voters are solely motivated by narrow self-interest with no interest in the public good or justice. However, even on a more optimistic view, we all agree that majorities can get it wrong, and that in this as in every area of life people do have limited altruism. As it happens, this is a main reason for insisting on the rule of positive law, and why it is that a principal duty of the courts is to ensure that general laws are fairly applied, especially in the case of

---

37 See *Bonham's Case* (1610), flirted with in *Union Steamship Co of Australia v King* (1988) 166 CLR 1, at 10. The court held that state legislative power could be 'subject to some restraints by reference to rights deeply rooted in our democratic system of government and the common law'.

38 Thus, Australian defamation law is becoming progressively constitutionalised through such decisions as *Theophanous v Herald & Weekly Times Ltd* (1994) 182 CLR 461.

39 'Section 6. Acts of Public Authorities (1) It is unlawful for a public authority to act in a way which is incompatible with a Convention right.'

vulnerable groups, just as it is similarly a reason for statutory provisions to outlaw discrimination on ground of race, gender, age and so on.

However, to go beyond strict statutory constructivism in order to shield vulnerable minorities and give courts a roving brief to change the law when they think a social group is being badly treated by the majority comes up against the key political difficulty that we do not have agreement about when and where such injustice exists, or what should be done about it if it does. Nor do we have any way of ensuring such discretionary powers are not then used for other less noble purposes.

It would not be a big concession for democratic positivism to allow that judicial belief in a grave injustice may justify at least ignoring mistaken precedents and correcting a past mistake in common law. It is possible to read *Mabo* partly in that way.[40] In contrast to the largely unfettered power given to judges who have to administer court-centred bills of rights, common law legal revisions in the cause of minority rights are subject to the override of Parliament, and *Mabo* has since been accepted by Parliament in a modified and developed form.[41] If it is problematic, it is not the most problematic form of judicial activism, particularly if it is confined either to minor changes or to changes that are based on mistakes of law or fact in cases decided many years earlier.

In the case of *Mabo*, there was not a long and impressive line of precedents, and the precedents could readily be interpreted as mistaken applications of contemporary law since they either made the false assumption that the territory of what is now Australia was effectively unsettled and without an existing system of rights in relation to the use of land, or erroneously held that it was a matter of law, not of fact, that Australia came into existence through settlement not conquest.[42] The precedential decisions were clearly erroneous in the factual assumptions made at the time in relation to the application of the *terra nullius* doctrine. What actually occurred was conquest, not the occupation of unsettled territory.

The decision in *Mabo* was certainly not incremental since it threatened the basis of Australian property law, but it can be considered positivist as it involved looking afresh at the application of the relevant law of occupation in the light of an improved knowledge of historical facts. Further, just because a decision has political consequences does not make it activist. Indeed, it would have been a form of negative activism not to make an obviously correct decision in law because it has major consequences. No doubt it would be better from the democratic positivist point of view that the legal changes deriving from *Mabo* had been initiated by the political process along the lines of more radical native title

---

40 *Mabo v Queensland (No 2)* (1992) 175 CLR 1, at 26: Brennan J: 'The facts as we know them today do not fit the "absence of law" or "barbarian" theory underpinning the colonial reception of the common law of England. That being so, there is no warrant for applying in these times rules of the English common law that were the product of that theory.'

41 Native Title Act 1993 (Cth), amended in 1998 following *Wik Peoples v Queensland* (1996) 187 CLR 1.

42 *Milirrpum v Nabalco* [1971] 17 FLR 141.

acts, but the methodology of the decision in question is not significantly suspect in ethical positivist terms.

Given what is at stake in protecting the rule of law, it may be regretted that such a concession is being made into the general principle that perceived injustice legitimates a major shift even in democratically correctable common law. Once we go beyond formal justice, then justice – substantive justice – takes us into the further consequences of changing the rules and straight into policy questions beyond the capacities of courts. Correcting a social injustice is a complex, non-incremental matter that cannot be distinguished from policy-making considerations, therefore we cannot sustain the position that judicial law-making is acceptable to correct substantive injustice but not with respect to determining public policy.

Further, as a general principle, it suffers from the defect of requiring to be interpreted in the light of the moral values of the person interpreting the principle. In other words, it is too subjective. There is great disagreement about substantive justice. There are no available criteria to pick and choose between the perceived injustices we allow the judiciary to correct and those we do not. The literature can readily draw verbal distinctions between the whims or personal or idiosyncratic opinions of judges and the reasonable, consensual and enduring values of civilised peoples, but these are often no more than emotive terms for those views we do not share and those we do. Indeed, the concept of enduring values is particularly suspect as it ignores the important factor of moral development. Many of our enduring values are far from admirable. As a test for which values we think should license activism, the fact they are old will not do. The fact that values are still with us looks more hopeful, but why exclude recent developments from the values to which we give weight – as issues of discrimination, which is relatively new in relation to race and gender, and very recent with respect to disability and sexual preference, illustrate? Moreover, enduring values cannot readily be detached from those values that are held in common by the vast majority of a population, thus rendering them impotent with respect to protecting those minorities who believe that their values are being overridden by majority views, the very factor that is said to justify common law intervention on behalf of vulnerable minorities.

There is a problem with the respect to the unjust treatment of minorities. Requiring democracy to be operationalised via rule-governance is one way of seeking to render political power more equal and so to protect minorities. However, it is not a problem that can be overcome by increasing the discretionary rule-making power of judges. Overall, judicial activism is not a satisfactory response to perceived substantive injustice. Other, more democratic, mechanisms need to be explored.

## CONCLUSION

I have sought to make the case for an analysis of judicial activism in terms of departures from law-abidingness. Where the law in question is good positivist law, the sort of justice that courts should provide is formal and procedural justice, and we should make it possible for them to do so by providing them with good positive law.

This gives us a basis for being highly critical of the move to broad discretionary type law as well as straight-out judicial law-breaking in law-making. It provides a particularly strong argument against bills of rights, where these are used to strike down or radically change otherwise valid law.

Sometimes it seems that there are really two sins: undermining certainty and clarity on the one hand, and ignoring democratic decisions on the other. After all, the absence of clarity and certainty in law is a defect of law in non-democratic societies as well as democratic ones, and making new law may add to clarity and certainty, at least in the future. However, in a democracy there is an additional reason for good formal law in that effective democratic decisions simply cannot take place unless they can make rules that are actually applied, and this requires that the posited law be clear, comprehensible and applicable.

One advantage of this analysis is that it applies not only at the giddy heights of appellate courts but in every courtroom where laws are enforced (or not, as the case may be). Maybe judicial activism is particularly dangerous in appellate courts because they make law not just in the instant case but by establishing new rules and principles that others then follow. Perhaps judicial activism is especially bad in constitutional matters; these are difficult to change after the event even through constitutional amendment.

Hence the need for tough public scrutiny and critique, not of the motives of judges, or of their off-duty activities, but of their judicial conduct on the job. Where necessary, we need to criticise and shame unethical judicial conduct, for that is the way that ethics are promoted.

One way we can do this is by suggesting that judges who cannot bring themselves to enforce existing law ought to resign. At least in the straightforward cases of negative activism – failure to apply clear and relevant authoritative rules – judges always do have a choice. If applying a clear law goes against their moral convictions, then they can and should resign rather than put the law to one side or replace it with another.

In the words of the current Chief Justice of Australia: 'in the administration of any law there comes a point beyond which discretion cannot travel. At this point, if a judge is unable in good conscience to implement the law, he or she may resign. There may be no other course properly available. Judges whose authority comes from the will of the people, and who exercise authority upon trust that they will administer justice according to law, have no right to subvert the law because they disagree with a particular rule. No judge has a choice between implementing the law and disobeying it.[43] Clearly, Chief Justice Gleeson is an antipodean positivist.

---

43 M Gleeson, *The Rule of Law and the Constitution*, Sydney: ABC Books, 2000, 127.

# PART 2:
# RIGHTS

# 7

# THE LEGALISM OF RIGHTS

Rights in the literal sense (that is, positive as opposed to 'moral' rights) involve an essential reference to the presence or absence of societal rules, that is, rules concerning human interactions which are accepted as authoritative within a social group. Not every societal rule has to do with rights. Some social obligations (such as the duty to vote) can be analysed without reference to anyone's correlative rights, and there are many liberties and immunities which, because of their lack of relevance to the interests of those who possess them, we would not normally think of as rights. The question dealt with in this chapter is whether any sort of rule-following would be part of a socialist way of life. This requires a survey of the variety of purposes served by societal rules. Once we are satisfied that these purposes feature amongst socialist objectives and that rules are necessary for their successful pursuit, then we can turn to the relationship between socialist societal rules and the concept of rights.

## FORMAL JUSTICE

Before examining utilitarian or instrumental reasons for having societal rules, we must first take up the legalistic criticism of pure legalism, or the idea of rights in their strongest form – a doctrine which can be designated pejoratively as 'rule-worship' or 'legal-fetishism'. Pure legalism is the belief that conformity to societal rules is intrinsically desirable, an end in itself, which has sufficient import to justify the creation of rules, and gives rule-conformity a significance which conflicts with and perhaps overrides other desirable social objectives.[1]

Pure legalism in its most sweeping form is the view that all aspects of social life ought to be governed by rules and that actions are to be judged good or bad, desirable or undesirable, according as they do or do not conform to pre-existing rules. Thus, morality is a matter of following rules embodying community standards and the purpose of law is to ensure general adherence to whatever rules are recognised as binding within a society.[2] The prime values of legalism are adherence to, and the impartial application of, existing authoritative societal rules. Legalism is opposed to the exercise of discretion in the following and

---

1 For a discussion of legalism and ideology see JN Shklar, *Legalism*, Cambridge, MA: Harvard University Press, 1964. Shklar defines legalism as 'the ethical outlook that holds moral conduct to be a matter of rule-following, and moral relationships to consist of duties and rights determined by rules' (at 1). She argues that the legalistic policy of justice is 'to resolve as many conflicts by judicial means as possible' (at 117). For the idea of 'legal fetishism' see EB Pashukanis and C Arthur (eds), *Law and Marxism*, London: Ink Links, 1978, 117.

2 For a persuasive argument that morality is not, in general, a matter of adhering to rules, see GJ Warnock, *The Object of Morality*, London: Methuen, 1971, Chapters 4 and 5.

applying of rules, actions based on the calculation of consequences, *ad hoc* adaptations of rules to suit the peculiarities of individuals in situations not covered by the rules, and the creation of new rules to judge the propriety of past behaviour.[3] Its nature is exemplified in those aspects of bureaucratic organisation which require strict adherence to a book of rules rather than assigning an area of discretion to a hierarchy of officials, deontological moralities which emphasise conformity to a set of shared social norms, and in the formal or deductive theory of judicial reasoning according to which the purpose of the courts is the rigid application of general rules to particular circumstances. Legalism appears, therefore, to be the antithesis of the freedom, spontaneity and purposive outlook which many theorists see as hallmarks of socialism. The legalists' devotion to rules rather than to the solution of problems and the furtherance of human welfare seems inhuman and misplaced, hence the designation 'legal-fetishism'.[4]

It is not easy to see why pure legalism should be accepted as a serious doctrine. To anyone – liberal or socialist – with a regard for human freedom, it must seem that the subordination of human choice to societal rules always requires further justification. Such plausibility as pure legalism has may derive from the mistaken belief that it is entailed by one or other of two more fundamental and more attractive propositions: first, that rational beings ought to act consistently, and secondly, that morality requires the moral agent to universalise his or her moral judgments. The idea that rational beings must be consistent, however, does not mean that a rational being must always act in an identical manner in identical situations, as if to throw one stone in the sea commits the rational agent to throwing all similar stones into the sea.[5] Rather, the consistency required of rational beings, in so far as it goes beyond refraining from self-contradiction, is that where there is a reason for acting in a particular manner then that reason must be accepted as applying to all similar situations. Such requirements, however, apply solely to the thoughts and behaviour of the individual and imply no commitment to setting up and following shared or societal rules for all rational beings. It may be that, if there are rules which all rational beings must follow, then they will in practice conform to the same rules, but they will not do so because these rules are shared but because they, as rational beings, hold them to be justified.

Similarly, it is a truism of moral philosophy that if a person makes the moral judgment that 'X is right' then he is committed to believing that all Xs are right, and to doing X whenever the opportunity arises unless there are other moral

---

3 A sympathetic analysis of the principles of legalism is to be found in L Fuller, *The Morality of Law*, revised edition, New Haven, CT: Yale University Press, 1969. Fuller argues that the requirements that rules be general, promulgated, prospective, clear, non-contradictory, constant, congruent with each other and demand only conduct within the powers of the affected party, follow from the undertaking of 'subjecting human conduct to the governance of rules' (96ff).

4 See Shklar, *op cit* fn 1, 13ff: 'The more the bar concentrates on formal perfection of established rules and procedures, the more removed it may become from the social ends that law serves.'

5 See C Perelman, *The Idea of Justice and the Problem of Argument*, London: Routledge and Kegan Paul, 1963, essays 1 and 3; and the criticism of Perelman's position in DD Raphael, *Problems of Political Philosophy*, London: Pall Mall, 1970, 175ff.

reasons that take precedence. This requirement of universalisability is one which all moral beliefs must satisfy.[6] Universalisability can be expressed by saying that the moral agent must guide his action by moral rules or maxims, but it is not the following of rules that makes his actions right. If it is right for the agent to keep a particular promise, then it must be right for him to keep such promises in all similar circumstances; this is not because in so doing he will be rule-abiding, but rather because if it is correct in the first situation to keep his promise then it is a logical consequence that it is correct to do so in all similar circumstances. The rule merely expresses the requirement of universalisability. There is no suggestion that the requirement of universalisability entails a commitment to follow any rules other than the agent lays down for himself. Indeed, to follow societal rules simply because they are societal rules is, in effect, for the moral agent to abdicate his duty to make up his own mind on moral issues.

There are two less radical forms of pure legalism to which the socialist must give more detailed attention. The first is the concept of the rule of law and the second the idea of formal justice. The doctrine of the rule of law, which derives from Aristotle, is that government ought to be through general rules and not through the arbitrary decision of individuals: the rule of law not the rule of men.[7] This doctrine takes it for granted that every society will have a government, but recognises that the powers of government are often abused. These abuses are to be limited by restricting governmental power to the promulgation of general rules which are applied by an authority independent of both the legislative and executive branches of government and ensuring that the actions of the executive officers of governments remain within the parameters laid down by the legislative authority. It is generally agreed amongst liberal theorists that the rule of law prevents some abuses and does have the advantage of treating the citizen as an intelligent person who is able to conduct her affairs in the light of known rules. It has even been argued that the rule of law guarantees a certain minimum moral content to the law.[8] However, given the stress on the control of the abuse of power by political authorities, presupposing as it does both the existence of political power and the tendency of those holding power to use it for their own ends, the socialist may feel that the safeguards of the rule of law will be unnecessary in a socialist society in which there would be either no government or, if there were a government, one which is in the hands of genuinely altruistic and trustworthy people to whom it would be reasonable to give discretionary powers which they could exercise for the common good in overriding or ignoring any societal rules that there happen to be.[9] We cannot, therefore, take a view on the importance that

---

6 See RM Hare, *Freedom and Reason*, Oxford: OUP, 1963, 7–50.

7 Aristotle, 'Politics', III and XVI, 1257a: 'it is more proper that law should govern than any one of the citizens.'

8 See PP Nicholson, 'The internal morality of law: Fuller and his critics', *Ethics*, Vol 84, 1973–74, 307–26.

9 For a socialist's defence of the importance of the role of law in pre-socialist societies, see EP Thompson, *Whigs and Hunters*, London: Allen Lane, 1975, especially 258–69: 'The inhibitions upon power imposed by law seem to me a legacy as substantial as any handed down from the struggles of the seventeenth century' (at 265).

the socialist would attach to the rule of law until we have determined whether a socialist society would require binding rules and political authority.

It is possible to give more immediate attention to the view that pure legalism is a prerequisite of the attainment of formal justice. Analyses of justice often distinguish between material or substantive justice, which refers to the content of societal rules, and pure or formal justice, which refers to the impartial and hence fair application of rules whatever their content.[10] It is a characteristic argument of legal positivists that only the latter has any genuine and objective meaningfulness since there can be agreement on what constitutes the accurate application of a rule but not about the so called 'justice' or otherwise of its content.[11] It is a corollary of this position that the significance of legal systems is primarily a matter of formal, rather than material, justice and that the attainment of formal justice in the impartial administration of rules is in itself a laudable objective.

Such a legalistic idea gets some support from the common assumption that it is just – in Aristotle's terms – to treat equals equally and unequals unequally.[12] On this view, where there are rules applied in any degree to a social group, it is unfair to those who suffer the burdens or do not enjoy the benefits that application of these rules will produce, if the actual administration of the rules does not place similar burdens or benefits on all those who should suffer or enjoy these things according to that rule. Thus, irrespective of the material justice of a tax regulation, it is said to be unfair if one person to whom the regulation applies is required to pay, while another to whom the regulation also applies is not required to do so. Or, when one group of employees gain a large increase in wages or salaries it is often assumed that, irrespective of the rights or wrongs of this increase, other similar groups are unfairly treated if they do not receive an equivalent award. The argument is not that if it is right to treat A in a certain manner logically it must be right to treat all other As in a similar manner (universalisability) but that, because one group has been treated in a particular way, other similar groups must be treated in the same way. Comparability of this type is grounded in a sense of formal justice.

Pure legalism interpreted in terms of formal justice represents an end-point for the positivist's efforts to expunge value judgments from legal analysis whilst retaining the supposition that there is some basis for the belief that justice is the objective of law. It has the advantage of expressing the neutrality of law, and of societal rules in general, as between different policy objectives, the law being a form or mechanism that can be used for an endless variety of social ends. Courts can then be limited to the pursuit of formal rather than material justice, hence the lawyer's conception of 'natural justice' as the procedural rules which must be followed in the interests of producing a fair, in the sense of an accurate and

---

10 See Perelman, *op cit* fn 5, essay 1. For a similar distinction between the concept of justice and conceptions of justice see J Rawls, *A Theory of Justice*, Oxford: Clarendon Press, 1979, 5ff.

11 See A Ross, *On Law and Justice*, London: Stevens & Son, 272: 'applied to characterise a general rule or order the words "just" or "unjust" are entirely devoid of meaning ... A person who maintains that a certain rule or order ... is unjust does not indicate any discernible quality in the order ... but merely gives to it an emotional expression.'

12 See *Politics*, III, 12, 1282b.

consistent, application of legal rules. Thus, no one should be a judge in her own case or show partiality to either party in a dispute by taking into account anything other than the relevant rules and the appropriate factual evidence. Accused persons should have notice of any charges and the opportunity to answer them and cross-examine witnesses.[13] These rules of natural justice are sometimes said to be important because they generate support for the decisions made on the part of those involved, particularly of accused persons,[14] but they can also be seen as ways of attempting to make sure that like cases are treated alike and that people receive only what they are entitled to according to the relevant rules. Similar arguments can be used against granting extensive discretionary powers to officials in the distribution of benefits and burdens or at the stages of investigation, prosecution and disposal in criminal law. Although there are many arguments given in favour of the exercise of discretion in these fields – such as the cost involved in subordinating all official actions to the requirement of rules and the lack of flexibility this gives to government administration and the treatment of offenders – it is a recurring theme of liberal commentators that such discretion is contrary to the ideal of justice, by which they mean formal justice, and should be kept to a minimum.[15]

It is perhaps a fine point of moral intuition whether or not formal justice is significant in itself, but there are several reasons why a socialist is likely to be less sympathetic to this ideal than a liberal theorist, and the emphasis given to formal justice in positivist legal theory has done much to explain the hostility of socialists to law and rule-governance in general. Formal justice is an inherently conservative notion and the fact that it is compatible with extensive real inequalities and material injustices means that it seems of little value to those with radical social objectives. A socialist is therefore inclined to regard formal justice as the quintessence of misplaced social priorities and dehumanised social relationships.

Certainly, formal justice is in itself a conservative ideal.[16] This is because rule-change is bound to give rise to formal injustice as between those who are treated under the first rule and those who are treated under the reformed rule. For instance, the murderer executed for her crime before the abolition of capital punishment could – if she were around to do so – regard it as unfair that she should suffer this fate while those guilty of the same offence at a later date received a lesser penalty. The same sort of injustice occurs when rules are made more burdensome, since those treated under the new rules suffer more than those

---

13 For an account of the interpretation and scope of these principles, see P Jackson, *Natural Justice*, 2nd edn, London: Sweet & Maxwell, 1979.

14 See JR Lucas, *On Justice*, Oxford: Clarendon Press, 1980, 97: 'These rules of procedure do not guarantee that decisions will be just. Rather they constitute necessary, or near necessary, conditions of the decision making process with which a man could be expected to identify.'

15 See K Davis, *Discretionary Justice*, Baton Rouge, LA: Louisiana State University Press, 1969; TD Campbell, 'Discretionary "rights"', in N Timms and D Watson (eds), *Philosophy in Social Work*, London: Routledge and Kegan Paul, 1978, 50–77; and TD Campbell, 'Discretion and rights within the children's hearing system', *Philosophical Journal*, Vol 14, 1977, 1–21.

16 See TD Campbell, 'Formal justice and rule-change', *Analysis*, Vol 33, 1973, 113–18.

who chanced to be in the same situation at an earlier time. Nor is there any doubt that formal justice is compatible with great material injustice, such as extreme inequalities of wealth and life opportunities. Thus, the ideal of liberal capitalism that all men are equal before the law, since it was combined with laws which were designed to make all equally able to enter into contracts and to use their resources as they wished, meant that those with superior wealth and superior talents were able to achieve positions far above those whose resources were more limited and whose capacities were less. If formal justice has any importance to the socialist it is likely, therefore, to be relatively superficial in contrast to his evaluation of the outcome of the fair application of the rules in question. If the distributive rules of an authority are substantively unjust, then it seems to him a matter of trivial importance that these rules are not consistently applied.

Nevertheless, there is some evidence that Marx approximates to the legal positivist's view of justice in refusing to regard the relationships of capitalist society as unjust.[17] It has been argued that Marx considers that the concept of justice is relative to the system of production operative in a society at a particular time. This would mean that there is feudal justice and capitalist justice and, perhaps, socialist justice. Along with the positivist, therefore, he considers it absurd to regard capitalist distribution as in itself unjust. Thus, in *Capital*, when Marx is discussing the idea that the payment of interest on borrowed money is a 'self-evident principle of natural justice' he argues that an exchange is 'just whenever it corresponds to the mode of production ... unjust whenever it contradicts that mode'.[18] This passage is certainly in line with his scepticism about the ideals of justice and in particular the assumption that there are natural principles of justice that transcend historical epochs. However, it is possible to regard these remarks on the so called justice of capitalism as in fact ironic,[19] and it can certainly be argued that they do not exclude the possibility that where the rules of distribution are materially just, perhaps in a socialist society, then formal justice has an important role to play. We cannot say, therefore, that Marx is definitively opposed to formal justice as a means for attaining material justice, but this is, of course, different from the view that formal justice has an importance independent of the content of the rules in question.

---

17 See RC Tucker, *Philosophy and Myth in Karl Marx*, Cambridge: CUP, 1961, 18–20.

18 See AW Wood, 'The Marxian critique of justice', *Philosophy and Public Affairs*, Vol 1, 1971–72, 244–82; at 257: 'For Marx, the justice or injustice of an action or institution does not consist in its exemplification of a juridical form or its conformity to a universal principle. Justice is not determined by the universal compatibility of human acts and interests, but by the concrete requirements of a historically conditioned mode of production.' In support of this thesis, Wood quotes the following passage from *Capital*: 'The justice of transactions which go on between agents of production rests on the fact that these transactions arise as natural consequences from the relations of production. The juristic forms in which these economic transactions appear as voluntary actions of the participants, as expressions of their common will and as contracts that may be enforced by the state against a single party, cannot, being mere forms, determine this content. They purely express it. This content is just whenever it corresponds to the mode of production, is adequate to it. It is unjust whenever it contradicts that node' (*Werke*, 25: 351ff).

19 See ZI Husami, 'Marx on distributive justice', *Philosophy and Public Affairs*, Vol 8, 1978, 27–64, especially 30 and 36.

If legalism is equated with the view that formal justice is of fundamental social and political value then socialists are not alone in their condemnation of legalism. Even those most committed to the moral significance of pure or formal justice never hold it to be an overriding consideration which renders unacceptable, for instance, all rule-change, or makes irrelevant any criticism of the content of rules. A revolutionary socialist critic of the legalism of rights cannot, therefore, direct his attacks simply at the ideal of pure formal justice. If he thinks that this is the core of the liberal notion of justice then in this, and in other matters, he is being misled by the limited horizons of certain legal positivists. Moreover, the rejection of formal justice as an independent value does not mean that the rigorous adherence to rules has no instrumental or utilitarian significance. It may be that there are advantages in general conformity to societal rules which override the importance of giving to the individual the ultimate authority to decide how he is to act in every circumstance. If legalism is taken to encompass adherence to rules for such ulterior purposes then, even if the socialist denies any intrinsic benefits to rule-following, she must be able to counter the instrumental arguments before she can dismiss rights because of their association with legalism. We must therefore turn to the alleged benefits which are said to flow from the creation and application of societal rules.

## SOCIAL CONTROL

The benefits and drawbacks of formal justice, and hence of a legalistic approach to rights, are part of the general assessment of the function of rules in society. In the remainder of this chapter I outline just some of these functions and relate them to images of a socialist society.[20]

If we take the law to be a body of rules prescribing, prohibiting and licensing certain types of behaviour which is, by and large, conformed to in the society to which it applies, then it is clear that a major element in the evaluation of particular legal systems, and the very idea of having a legal system at all, must be based on our evaluation of the types of conduct prescribed, prohibited or licensed. For instance, if it is the case that acts of a certain type (say homicide) are in themselves and prior to the existence of law considered harmful or immoral, then it is, *prima facie*, a desirable objective that all such acts be prohibited – the importance of having a law against homicide being that this is one way of reducing the number of such inherently undesirable acts. Looking at the law in this way is to regard it as a means of social control designed to maximise the incidence of beneficial acts and minimise the incidence of harmful ones or, if this sounds too question-begging in its utilitarian flavour, for encouraging desirable acts and discouraging undesirable ones. Rights are particularly germane to this way of regarding the law because they can be used to define what it is that is prescribed, prohibited or licensed by reference to the good or bad effects which actions and inactions may

---

20 For general treatments of the instrumental functions of rules, see R Summers and C Howard, *Law, Its Nature, Function and Limits*, 2nd edn, Englewood Cliffs, NJ: Prentice-Hall, 1972; and J Raz, 'On the functions of law', in AWB Simpson (ed), *Oxford Essays in Jurisprudence*, 2nd Series, Oxford: Clarendon Press, 1973, 278–304.

have on the welfare of others, for the language of rights serves to select out those interests that the law is designed to protect and further by its control of behaviour. Thus, all the multiple obligations which correlate with A's right to the ownership of her material possessions can be seen as various ways of ensuring that others act or refrain from acting so as to promote A's retention and enjoyment of these things. A's right to her possessions may thus be regarded as generating the correlative obligations in that these obligations are designed to protect A in the use of her possessions. Indeed, it is reasonable to argue that, if it is accepted that the purpose of law is to prevent harm and promote welfare, there should be no laws which do not protect or further human interests, thus giving the notion of rights a position logically prior to that of obligation.[21]

In so far as rules actually do protect interests, this accounts for the fact that rights, legalistically interpreted, may be valuable possessions of the individual in that they provide one means whereby his interests may be furthered. How valuable they are will depend, of course, on which of his interests are so furthered and this in turn depends on the content of the rules or laws. However, leaving aside for the moment the content of the law, the general point is that rules can be seen as an instrument for reducing the incidence of intrinsically harmful acts and encouraging the performance of beneficial ones, a function they fulfil in proportion to the degree of conformity that there is to the requirement of the rule. On this view there need be no virtue in legalism or rule-abidingness *per se*, although it is a necessary instrument for maximising behavioural patterns which are in themselves acceptable without reference to further objectives. The utility of legalism, on this view, is its instrumentality in encouraging and discouraging acts which have beneficial or harmful consequences prior to the existence of behaviour-directing rules.

This justification of rule-governance is vulnerable to the socialist argument that such forms of control are unnecessary for achieving these objectives since, in the right social and economic conditions, no rules or laws will be required to encourage and prevent the types of behaviour in question. Thus, it is often argued by Marxian socialists that, once the causes of human conflict and hostility have been removed by the socialist revolution and the development of communist society, there will be no need for laws to direct human behaviour since men's total endeavours will be directed towards the betterment of others through co-operative means, at which time men will be able to dispense with the dehumanising and impersonal legal ways of regarding and organising human conduct.[22] This will avoid the unfortunate side-effects of rigid adherence to rules in cases where the standard consequences do not pertain.

The Marxist view is that the phenomenon of man harming man is not a product of fixed human nature, but the consequence of economic and hence social

---

21 See DN MacCormick, 'Rights in legislation', in PMS Hacker and J Raz (eds), *Law, Morality and Society*, Oxford: Clarendon Press, 1977, 189–209.

22 For a discussion of this 'left idealism' see J Young, 'Left idealism, reformism and beyond: from the new criminology to Marxism', in R Fine *et al* (eds), *Capitalism and the Rule of Law*, London: Hutchinson, 1979.

circumstances which will be done away with in the advance to communist society, in which there will be no need for rules to restrict or encourage harmful and beneficial activities; the former will not occur and the latter will be done spontaneously, and for that reason more effectively.

In assessing this argument, we come right up against the problem of projecting ourselves imaginatively into a radically different form of society, a society in which economic scarcity is unknown and intentionally harmful behaviour unheard of, a society in which there is no property, no fear of the other, no desire to impose one's will. We can readily agree that where there is no 'mine' and 'thine' there can be no such thing as theft and where there is no motive to do acts which are manifestly harmful to others there might seem to be no need to have rules forbidding such acts. However, we have to consider whether there would be a residue of potentially harmful actions that would require to be kept in check by some regulatory means, and we also have to ask ourselves about the social mechanisms that would feature in the creation and maintenance of this fraternal type of society.

Even assuming that we may discount intentionally harmful acts within the main areas covered by criminal law, it is not within the bounds of reasonable probability to postulate that human beings could have unlearned or instinctive knowledge of the manifold ways in which such complex and developing creatures as men may be harmed and benefited. Moreover, the notion of 'harm' is evaluative as well as descriptive in that what counts as harm depends in part on the view taken of human wholeness or perfection. Even if we simply equate harm with pain then at the very least a socialist society would have to arrange for the study and communication of knowledge about the ways in which pain can be caused in order to teach its members how to avoid harming others. If 'harm' is broadened to take in all the ways in which men can fall short of an ideal human nature, such as the socialist norm of a fully developed creative and productive self-directed being, then we can readily see how the principle that harm should be minimised must generate a complex set of directives of a technical nature indicating how we should act in order to avoid harming others. These would become even more extensive if we take in ways of benefiting others, as seems appropriate in a community where the mere abstention from harming others seems an overly-limited objective. It is therefore possible to imagine rules against overfeeding children, or doing so much for others that they lose or never gain the capacity to direct their own lives; rules requiring men to meet the special needs of those with psychological and mental deficiencies not evident to the untutored eye; rules indicating methods whereby we can show an interest in the affairs of others without intruding on their need for solitude. Such rules would not be there to restrain malicious selfishness, but to ensure that human good is protected in ways which are not self-evident to the ordinary benevolent individual.

Moreover, it cannot be assumed that in a socialist society there would be no 'mine' or 'thine', no property whatsoever. Once it is allowed that there are some circumstances in which an individual or group has the use of particular objects, even if this is limited to specified occasions or purposes, then there must be some rules which indicate to others that this use is proper and hence that they should not seek to prevent it and, where appropriate, should facilitate such uses. Thus, if houses or even beds are allocated to persons for their temporary use, this requires that these objects 'belong' to certain individuals for certain periods of time. This may not involve the extensive property rights which include the right to buy and sell or to alter the objects possessed at will, but it does establish a line between 'mine' and 'thine' which must be drawn by rules indicating usage rights, otherwise there would be no way in which others, unintentionally or otherwise, could infringe such entitlements to the use of specific objects, and no amount of good will could prevent interference with entitlements of which men had no knowledge, even if we could make sense of such a notion.[23]

Such rules might not, of course, be regarded as instituting rights and would be educative and informative rather than coercive, but it is not the coerciveness of rules that is at present under discussion but simply whether there would be any role for rules within socialism. We have looked at some specific examples of rules for which there would be a need even in a benevolent community but, more generally, it is hard to see how the successful accomplishment of a harmonious socialist order, in which none harmed the other and all acted in a maximally beneficial way, could become a reality without an educational system to develop the potential goodness in children and bring them up to play a useful part in community life, and it is difficult to think of such a system dispensing altogether with behavioural rules. It is true that children would not be taught to follow rules for their own sake, but we have seen that the idea of rule-following as an end in itself is at most a small part of the justification for having rules and abiding by them, and the particular function of rule-following which we are at present discussing (the minimisation of harmful acts and the maximisation of beneficial ones) would seem to be of continuing relevance in any society in which men are not as naturally and instinctively knowledgable as they may be assumed to be spontaneously unselfish; although, again, it is hard to imagine that satisfactory motivation will not always require more than a nudge from an at least partly rule-based process of socialisation.

Inevitable limitations in human knowledge, the requirements for educating the young into the way of life of socialist societies and the need to establish normative standards of what counts as harm and benefit, plus the high standards set by socialists for mutual assistance, would generate in a socialist society rules whose content might differ from – but whose function would be the same as – those rules which are at present used to control human behaviour in order to minimise harm and maximise benefit. It may be that such rules would not require rigid adherence in that individuals could be trusted to interpret them in the light of particular circumstances, since they would not be liable to use this discretion for their own benefit, but it would still be the case that reasons would be required for not following societal rules and that persons would be subject to criticism where such deviations resulted in actions detrimental to the goals of socialism. Only such very general rules as 'do not gratuitously harm others' would require

---

23 For the variety of types of property right see AM Honour, 'Ownership', in AG Guest (ed), *Oxford Essays in Jurisprudence*, 1st Series, Oxford: Clarendon Press, 1961, 107–47.

universal conformity. More specific directives would tend to be regarded as rules of thumb rather than absolute requirements, but as long as the scope of discretion in the application of rules is limited by the requirement that departures from them be justified by the ends which the rules in general are clearly intended to serve, we can say that in a socialist society something like the social control function of rules would exist. As long as there is the possibility of acting otherwise than in the best interests of those affected, then there will be a need for rules by which to guide these actions. Rules against homicide and the deliberate infliction of injury might not be required, except perhaps for educational purposes, but prohibitions against spreading disease by insanitary habits, unpunctuality, types of carelessness which can result in injury and prescriptions requiring positive action in seeking out those who are in trouble and need help in specified circumstances – all these and many more are likely to feature in a conflict-free society of unselfish but otherwise human creatures liable to lapse through ignorance, tiredness, forgetfulness and inattention. On account of these same weaknesses, we can assume that conformity to these guiding rules could not be total, so that there would be a need for an appeal to the rules as a means to correct and compensate for the harm or absence of benefit caused by the deviations and to bring about greater conformity in the future. Uncoercive mutual monitoring and control of inter-personal behaviour would feature even in a community of 'brothers and sisters' and could not be achieved without a corpus of societal rules.

## ORGANISATIONAL RULES

Regarding the law as a means of minimising or maximising types of acts which are individually harmful or beneficial is only one way of approaching the possible benefits of legalism. Indeed, this is probably not the type of consideration that is most frequently associated with the justification of legalism. For instance, the benefits of law can be seen as organisational, in that they provide opportunities for co-operative social behaviour either of a private or a public nature. It is not just that ensuring a certain uniformity, and hence predictability, in behaviour allows the individual to make rational decisions about how to pursue his own interests, for sharing systems of rules makes possible new types of joint activities, either by ensuring that numbers of people act in unison to achieve objectives which they could not acquire alone (such as paying taxes to support medical services) or by developing rules which relate to separate roles within a complex social activity as in, for instance, the family, or economic division of labour. Here the point of rule-following is that it enables the individual to play a part in a corporate system which could not operate prior to the existence of rules and whose benefits cannot be described simply by the incidence of certain individually harmful or beneficial acts.

Such a view of the function of law tends to give rise to an emphasis on duties or obligations, particularly positive or affirmative obligations, for these indicate what the individual is to contribute to the co-operative enterprise. Because the benefits of the system may be remote from the fulfilment of the individual obligations on which it depends, they may not obviously correlate with anyone's rights. This function also explains the importance of the societal and legal powers by means of which people are able to enter into binding arrangements with others. The capacities to make gifts, to enter into contracts or to utilise the institution of promising can all have the effect of facilitating co-operative social relationships. All these processes involve rights in the sense of powers, and so the rules that determine how and when such capacities or powers are being exercised. It is only on the basis of such rules that actions of different role-occupants in complex social situations can be integrated in a purposeful manner and individuals occupying the same roles can make *ad hoc*, but not merely transitory, arrangements with each other.

In such situations, the benefits of rule-following are seldom the sum of each individual act of rule-conformity; rather, they depend on a variable but relatively high degree of adherence to rules since, in systems of any complexity, non-performance by a small number of those involved in the whole institutional organisation can vitiate the entire enterprise, and performance of the individual's obligations may in itself, in isolation from the contribution of others, be of no value at all. This truism of modern factory production applies to relatively simple systems in all spheres of social co-operation in which the contributions of a variety of operations carried out by different individuals are necessary for the functioning of the whole. Football teams as well as armies, social clubs as well as large-scale educational and political institutions, all require the input of very different forms of human activity which must form part of an integrated whole if the units are to function well, and sometimes if they are to function at all. These forms of human activity are definable in terms of the rules to which those performing them must adhere, rules which make it possible for us to assess their activities as done well or ill, and hence as conforming or not conforming to that which is expected of them, their obligations.

While not denying that rules are necessary to provide for co-operation between self-interested individuals, the socialist may argue that, in his society, co-operation will not be imposed and regulated but will be spontaneous or natural and hence more intense and intimate. A group united by strong ties of love and affection will, it is said, work together without recourse to regulations and rule-books which generate nothing but conflict, guarantee only minimal co-operation and are required only when a spontaneously affectionate relationship has broken down. In particular, there will be no need for those power-conferring rules which give some persons authority over others.

This argument has some force in small groups where the objectives and methods of co-operation are immediately obvious and everyone can, without prior principles of organisation, readily turn to the next job that requires to be done and call upon the assistance of others when necessary.[24] However, even here it may save much time spent in discussion and *ad hoc* arrangements if some

24 It is interesting that Putnam's example of non-regulated co-operation is that of helping to push a stalled car. (See p 5.) Anarchists in general have tended to oppose large bureaucratic organisations and advocate a society of small, face to face groupings. See A Carter, *The Political Theory of Anarchism*, London: Routledge and Kegan Paul, 1971, Chapter 3.

general co-operative principles and rules are adopted. For instance, it might prove helpful to have a rule that the person who is first to start a task draws up the plan of action for accomplishing it, or a rule that a technical disagreement about what needs to be done next be settled by a vote of those present or liable to be involved in the task. The contrary possibility of each deferring to the views of others gives no way of determining what is to be done. Moreover, such a willingly co-operative group is likely to find that it can best further its corporate ventures and ease the life of each of its members by adopting the standard conventions of civilised communal life; in particular, they would surely find it helpful to have some acknowledged way of coming to agreement, either by way of contract or promising, not because they could not trust each other to do what each thought best for the group but because a contract or promise would enable them to count on the performance of certain actions which might not otherwise have been done – since they would not necessarily appear to the person concerned to be beneficial – without some such formal agreement. Even a society of altruists would need to distinguish between a statement of intention and the making of a promise.[25] Making a promise would exclude the promisor from exercising his own judgment on whether to do the act in question, thus the promisee would be able to count on the performance of the act in a way which would not be possible if the matter was left to the discretion of the other, and this guarantee might enable him to pursue a line of action which is beneficial to the group but which would not be so if the act in question was not performed. The benefits of such institutions as promising are not always reducible to the self-interest of either party, and they have an application in the joint activities of small as well as large groups.

These considerations apply with greater force if we are thinking, as most socialists do, of large-scale industrialised societies with complex productive and social mechanisms in which the basis of co-operation must include established expectations that cannot arise simply from long experience of each other's ways and characteristics, particularly where the actions of one person are meant to harmonise or supplement those of another. Here it is even less plausible to think of untutored, unguided individuals being able to contribute to the community's inter-personal activities, the very sort of activities which are particularly valued by socialists. The vast range of possible forms of human organisation makes it impossible for there to be any large-scale co-operative behaviour, either on the roads, in factories, in group leisure or educational activities, which does not base itself on the common acceptance of shared rules whose content is to some extent arbitrary and could not, therefore, be arrived at by each individual separately, except by chance, and which does not require to be established *de novo* in each co-operative situation. Socialist ideals which look to some form of social organisation cannot avoid the incorporation of some such notion of rule-following.

At this point, the socialist might interject that such mutually acceptable organisational rules would not be imposed from without or forced on an

---

25 The general convenience of the institution of promising is lucidly demonstrated in D Hume and LA Selby-Bigge (eds), *A Treatise of Human Nature*, Oxford: Clarendon Press, 1888 (1739), III.ii.5, 516–25.

unwilling population. Using the example of conducting an orchestra, Marx accepts that all harmonious co-operation requires a directing authority.[26] However, it is possible for such necessary regulation to flow from the nature of the activity itself and as it is not imposed from without, it cannot be compared to the organisation of capitalist society in which the rules are not internal to the process – as is the case when socialists work together to produce the means of subsistence – but are an external imposition based on the private ownership of the means of production. The idea that some rules are imposed from outside a form of activity while others are part and parcel of particular activities, as the rules of good composition are to the writing of music or the drawing of a picture, is an interesting and helpful one, especially if it emerges that it is only the former type of rules that are under the cloud of socialist suspicion. If socialism allows for rules which are intrinsic to a process in that they are designed purely to facilitate the operation of that process in accordance with its own norms – for instance good music or efficient farming – and if such rules arise in co-operative ventures, as it would seem they must, and might even legitimate authority-conferring rules, then it becomes clear that the apparent objection to rules in general is not in fact to rules as such, but to irrelevant, oppressive or imposed rules. If it is established that those involved in harmonious communal enterprises are consciously following rules internal to the enterprise, then the fact that these rules are designed to assist the corporate project and are adhered to willingly by the participants in that venture does nothing to make their behaviour any less rule-governed or, if we prefer it, rule-guided.

In speaking of rules designed to maximise and minimise acceptable and unacceptable forms of behaviour I allowed that, in a socialist society, some discretion could be allowed to those following the rules, since particular circumstances may make following the rules less conducive to the welfare of those affected by it than not doing so – a process which is not fraught with the dangers of self-serving inconsistency as it would be in a society of selfish people. However, co-operative rules do not allow such extensive discretion since it is of their essence that others should be able to count on the rules being followed in order to make their own contribution to the total process. No doubt there may be occasions when promises may be broken because the situation has changed to such an extent that the intended benefit for which the promise was made could no longer be realised and no harm could come of ignoring it, but normally the whole point of obtaining a promise is to ensure that certain acts are done or not done and this is not achieved by leaving their performance to the judgment of the individual who has made the promise. The rules of promising would therefore, apart from exceptional circumstances, allow only the promisee to nullify the promisor's

26 See K Marx, *Capital*, Harmondsworth: Penguin, 1976, Vol I, Chapter 13, 445f: 'All directly social or communal labour on a large scale requires, to a greater or lesser degree, a directing authority, in order to secure the harmonious co-operation of activities of individuals, and to perform the general functions that have their origin in the motion of the total productive organism, as distinguished from the motion of its separate organs. A single violin player is his own conductor, an orchestra requires a separate one.' This idea is developed in EP Pashukanis's notion of technical as distinct from legal regulation. See his *Law and Marxism*, London: Ink Links, 1978, Chapter 2, esp 90–92.

obligation. More generally, exceptions to co-operative rule-following would only be by mutual agreement. Thus, the appeal to these rules would be rather stricter in its force, since the use of individual discretion is by and large excluded, hence any rights there may be under such rules (and I consider later whether it is appropriate to think of such rules granting rights) are more firmly established in the sense that they are less open to modification according to the judgment of those with the correlative obligations.

We should also note that in the case of co-operative rules it is often detrimental to the united purposes of those involved in a joint activity that a participant should, perhaps through a desire to do more than his share and thus go beyond merely doing his duty, use his own initiative to exceed that which the rules require of him, for this is to introduce an element of unpredictability, and perhaps of waste, into a situation that requires accurate foreknowledge of what the other will do. Thus, if I produce more nails for the communal workshop than can be used by others, or decline to take my right of way when driving a car, then, however laudable my motivation, the results are likely to be detrimental to those whom I seek to serve. This follows from the fact that such rules are not essentially designed to obtain a minimum contribution from antisocial beings, but rather to co-ordinate in the most productive way the willing contributions of a variety of different people. In the case of these rules, at any rate, we may be thinking of devices for enabling altruism to express itself rather than ways of minimising the harmful effects of selfish actions.

## DISTRIBUTIVE PATTERNS

A third and quite distinct justificatory basis for legalism, and hence for legalistic rights, is that rules are a necessary precondition for the attainment of material or substantive justice or for any patterned distribution of benefits or burdens. This is an argument used by those who equate law and justice, both in the formal sense in which it is said to be just to treat people in accordance with rules rather than as particular named individuals, and in the material sense in which what matters is that these rules be in accordance with some substantive standard of justice such as merit, contribution, or desert. The legal pursuit of formal justice – treating like persons alike irrespective of the nature of the likeness – is, arguably, as we have seen, an end in itself, and it can also be justified in a negative way if the alternative is considered to be unregulated decisions made on each specific occasion, which are liable to be random or to reflect the personal bias of prejudice of the distributor of benefits and burdens. However, leaving aside these aspects of formal justice, the impartial application of general rules is, failing unexplained coincidence or divine intervention, necessary for substantive justice according to which all receive that to which they are entitled under a correct distribution based on criteria such as merit or desert, or indeed for any patterned distribution. This function of rules incorporates many of the central areas of social policy concerning welfare, employment, housing and health services.

Logically, such patterned distribution could occur naturally, that is, without human contrivance. But even the most *laissez-faire* theories of society incorporate some rules whose enforcement is necessary for the outcome which is desired.[27] It is safe to conclude that a tolerably exact patterned distribution can only be obtained by the use of rules incorporating some reference to the relevant criteria for describing the pattern in question; thus, the allocation of punishment according to the degree of moral guilt needs the application of rules requiring the infliction of punishment in proportion to types and degrees of guilt. Here formal justice is not of significance for its own sake, but features because only strict adherence to such rules can produce the desired distribution of punishment. Similar considerations apply in the distribution of rewards according to status, need or any other quality or property of human beings according to which an allocation of benefits and burdens may be made. It therefore appears that, if a society seeks to achieve a certain distribution of desired goods, legalism may be justified as a means to achieve this distribution.

The argument from the desirability of achieving certain patterned distributions is not in itself unequivocal in its implications for the significance of strict adherence to the distributive rules. If what matters is the relative distribution, so that, for instance, the more deserving get a greater share than the less deserving, the less deserving a greater share than the undeserving, and so forth, then the rules would have to be applied in every case in order to achieve the desired rank-ordering in the distribution of available benefits; this would be the normal interpretation of the nature of distributive criteria. However, it is also possible to think of there being a correct proportion of a given benefit for a person with a certain quantity of a particular characteristic which can be achieved in individual cases without placing all those with varying degrees of the characteristic in a particular rank-ordering. In this less usual interpretation, each application of the distributive rule is of value as an independent contribution towards the total objective of everyone receiving that to which they are entitled, so that there is always a certain advantage in applying the rule to a particular case, as is the case when using rules for the purpose of social control. However, in the more normal, relativistic, idea of the appropriate quantity of any desired benefit to which particular types of individuals are entitled, it becomes much more important to apply the rules across the board since a particular application is unlikely in itself to make a positive difference to the desired distributive goal. In this case, the use of rules to achieve patterned distributions is nearer to the all-or-nothing effect we noted in the case of those organisational rules in which the effectiveness of any specific rule-application depends on the general, if not universal, application of the rules of the system.

---

27 Thus, FA Hayek, *Law, Legislation and Liberty*, Vol 2, London: Routledge and Kegan Paul, 1976, having dismissed the use of the notion of social or distributive justice as confused and dishonest, nevertheless regards his idea of 'catallaxy' – 'the special kind of spontaneous order provided by the market through people acting within the rules of property, tort and contract' (109) – as bringing about a distribution which reflects the knowledge and skill of individuals as well as their good fortune. For the idea that one purpose of equality of opportunity is to bring about a distribution which is in accordance with merit, see TD Campbell, 'Equality of opportunity', *Proceedings of the Aristotelian Society*, Vol 75, 1974, 51–68.

The third end served by adherence to rules or laws is, then, the achievement of patterned distributions of benefits and burdens. It might be thought that, in a socialist society, there would be no burdens (and hence no need to distribute them), and such abundance that no question would arise as to how desirable goods should be allocated.[28] However, this is an extreme view, and one which is particularly implausible since important material goods, such as land and energy, are limited in fact, and certain social goods, like high esteem and decision-making functions, are limited in principle. It can be acknowledged that as burdens and scarcities diminish, distributive rules become less important: where everyone has enough, no one need care about the distribution of the surplus; where the chores are slight, there is little need to concern oneself over their allocation. To this extent, the prophecy of abundance does undercut this basis of the need for rules. This is noted by those who claim that socialism is not so much about distribution as about liberty and the organisation of production. In this case, we would expect co-operative rules to feature more than distributive ones in a socialist society.

Many socialists, however, see themselves as involved in a movement to obtain a better or more just distribution of attainable goods and unavoidable evils. To this end, socialists sometimes oppose legalism on the grounds that it interferes with such distributions. Certainly, the socialist drive for social and economic equality can be hampered rather than aided by rule-following; thus the rule-guaranteed liberties of the individual and the rights of property owners can inhibit the redistribution of wealth.

The same sort of point is made from the opposite end of the political spectrum by those who see the engineering of social justice as in conflict with the rights of the individual.[29] The argument here is that, in the attempt to establish a certain distribution (to each according to his x or y, where x and y refer to characteristics of the individual), constant intervention is required in the normal processes of social and economic interactions. This means that the application of rules to human behaviour, and hence the guarantee of rights to the individual, is vitiated by the constant nullification of the outcome of everyday rule-governed activities by the intervention of officials who re-allocate legitimately acquired goods in order to establish some preconceived pattern of distribution. Thus, if people are given certain property rights, including the right to buy and sell, to set up in business, employ others and agree wages with them, this will inevitably produce a distribution of goods which fits no pattern because it is the outcome of the exercise of the rule-governed rights of the participants. To achieve a patterned distribution, it is necessary to take from some that which they have legitimately gained and to give it to others who are not entitled to it according to the rules of the processes in which all freely participated. Thus, the pursuit of patterned distributions is inimical to legalism for it involves constantly overturning the

---

28 To interpret Marx in this way requires us to view his endorsement of the distribution principle 'to each according to his needs' as applying only in a transitional state of socialism before genuine communism emerges and all distributive rules are transcended. See RC Tucker, *Philosophy and Myth in Karl Marx*, Cambridge: CUP, 1961, Introduction and Chapter X.

29 See FA Hayek, *op cit* fn 27, 85; and R Nozick, *Anarchy, State and Utopia*, New York: Basic Books, 1974, 160–64.

results and hence the legitimate expectations of those who have conducted themselves in accordance with the rules that apply to their normal activities.

It seems paradoxical when presenting a justification of societal rules on the grounds that they are necessary for achieving desired distributions of benefits and burdens to be faced with the criticism that the pursuit of such distributions runs up against rule-imposed limitations. The glib response to this paradox is to say that it is merely a conflict between rules with differing contents and not between having and not having rules. Therefore, property rules allowing individuals to use their possessions to produce commodities may lead to inequality, and if rules requiring redistribution simply return the situation to its original equality (assuming all start out with equal amounts of property) then the process seems pointless. However, it can be argued that any conflict there may be between property rules and distributive rules can readily be solved in a socialist way by rescinding the property rules and reorganising productive and distributive processes on lines which do not give rise to inequality.

However, the paradox goes deeper than this. It is a manifestation of a more pervasive tension between two ways of looking at rules, one which sees them as essentially telling the individual what she may or may not do in the pursuit of her own objectives, and the other as directing her as to how to contribute to a certain outcome or end-state. On the former model, the idea of rules (and hence also of rights) is to safeguard certain interests of the individual and then leave her free to direct her actions as she pleases. On the latter model, rules are designed to direct the individual to goals that are at once personal and social in that they enable her to make her distinctive contribution to the general welfare. If the socialist has to choose between these models she will opt for the latter, and is likely to incorporate an acceptable distributive pattern as part of her conception of the general welfare. This will involve giving end-state distributive rules priority where they conflict with the outcome of ordinary behavioural rules but, since most ordinary behavioural rules will be designed to facilitate the achievement of end-states embodying the application of distributive rules, such conflicts would not have the persistent and intractable nature of clashes between individual rights and social welfare in capitalist systems. Those socialists who share the *laissez-faire* liberal's distrust of distributive rules are unable to present us with a convincing picture of how a desirable ordering of benefits and burdens will occur. The metaphysically minded liberal can appeal to the concept of the natural harmony of interests or the workings of the 'invisible hand' of God or social evolution, but no such recourse is readily available to a socialist theorist.

## CONCLUSION

I have not, in this chapter, covered all of the many different functions of societal rules. For instance, I have largely omitted the use of power-conferring rules to grant authority to assigned individuals to play leading roles in social organisation, particularly in the creation of rules through legislation. I have also put to one side the utility of rules in the resolution of disagreements arising in the course of social interactions. A primary requirement of social life when confronted by such disagreements is for procedural rules laying down how disputes are to be brought to the point where they can be treated as settled, allowing normal interaction to continue. Even where the decision procedure adopted is dependent on the outcome of physical combat or on some form of lottery, there is a need for rules to set the format of the battle or indicate the winner in a determination by chance. Only in the most extreme state of nature could literal physical submission be the standard means for settling disputes. Where the authority for adjudicating in matters that seriously divide members of a social group is vested in individuals or officers, then some rule-governed mode of selection and signification of authoritative decisions will be required, even if no elaborate rules are necessary to guide the decisions of such persons or officers.

This function of societal rules might well be considered a candidate for extinction, assuming a socialist system in which there would be no serious disputes requiring to be settled by outside intervention. Compromise and mutual accommodation should be adequate to deal with any disagreements that might arise once class antagonisms no longer sour human relationships. This is, however, to assume that all disagreements are disputes about conflicts arising from the interactions of self-interested individuals but, given the other functions of rules outlined above, it is inevitable that even where there are no fiercely contended conflicts of opinion or clashes of incompatible interests between which arbitrary choices have to be made, there is still room for differences of view on the creation, interpretation and application of societal rules. If only for reasons of efficiency, there is a need for standard ways of resolving such divergencies of opinion. Moreover, the seriousness of a dispute need not be measured in terms of the private interest involved. Citizens of a socialist society might be expected to treat with gravity and care any differences they might have as to the ends and methods of their co-operative activities. The disputes might be different in content from those arising in non-socialist societies, but the significance attached to their resolution would still be sufficient to call into play agreed methods of coping with them. The resolution of disputes could therefore be added to the list of types of societal rule which would survive, albeit in a transformed fashion, within socialism.

Having considered, then, the independent claims of formal justice and some instrumental reasons for creating and sustaining societal rules, I take it as established that altruists in a conflict-free society require societal rules for social control, for organisational purposes, for long-term co-operative agreements, for bringing about the patterned distribution of benefits and burdens, probably also for the settlement of disagreements and, perhaps, as we shall see, for the allocation and operation of political authority. At least some of these objectives (particularly in the sphere of social co-operation) would require withholding from the individual the discretion to decide whether or not to follow established societal rules. This opens the way for the attributed rights of a socialist society where the rules in question benefit those individuals and groups whose interests are at stake, and who therefore may be said to have the rights correlative to the obligations identified in the rules.

# 8

# THE INDIVIDUALISM OF RIGHTS

Significant progress has been made towards securing a place for rights within the socialist ideal if we can establish that to endorse the institution of rights is not necessarily to commit oneself to the view that the rules which are logically inseparable from rights need be coercive or authoritarian. However, this is not yet sufficient to justify the claim that there would be rights in a socialist society for, although there cannot be rights without societal rules, there may be societal rules that are unconnected with rights. Not all behavioural directives or authoritative requirements for human action can be interpreted plausibly as involving the rights of others. While it can be argued that every right correlates with some obligation to respect that right,[1] it is much less convincing to say that every obligation correlates with a right. A socialist may, therefore, contend that the rules of a socialist society will offer authoritative guidance as to how citizens should act in furtherance of social objectives, and may even place obligations on the members of society, but insist that these obligations will not correlate with the rights of individuals. This would make duty, not rights, the essential concept of socialist community life.[2]

The rationale for stressing obligations and excluding rights is rooted in the third aspect of the socialist critique of rights: rights are to be rejected because they are an integral part of liberal individualism, the central ideology of capitalism. Rights, it is argued, are only of importance to those who are seeking to protect their self-interest against the predations of others; they express the ground-rules of a type of society that consists of isolated or atomic individuals in perpetual conflict with each other in a struggle for wealth and domination. Selfishness, competitiveness, acquisitiveness – these are the characteristics of capitalist man.

---

1 The possible exception being pure negative liberties. The different types of correlativity are discussed in D Lyons, 'The correlativity of rights and duties', *Nous*, Vol 4, 1970, 45–55.

2 Thus, socialist theorists always stress the need to incorporate duties as well as rights in constitutional provisions; see J Halals (ed), *The Socialist Concept of Rights*, Budapest: Akadémai Kiado, 1966, 49: 'Citizens' duties being devoid of any outstanding significance within bourgeois philosophy, the thinkers of the age of Enlightenment and bourgeois legal philosophers were at a loss as to how to deal with them.' See also Kruschev's address at the XX Congress of the Communist Party of the Soviet Union: 'We must develop among Soviet people Communist morality, at the foundation of which lie loyalty to Communism and uncompromising enmity to its foes, the consciousness of social duty, active participation in labour, the voluntary observance of the fundamental rules of human communal life, comradely help, honesty, truthfulness and intolerance of the disturbance of social order' (quoted in E Kamenka, *Ethical Foundations of Marxism*, 2nd edn, London: Routledge and Kegan Paul, 1972, 184).

The function of rights is to legitimise and regulate conflicts between such individuals.[3]

This attack on the individualism of rights is supported by an analysis of the language of rights: people 'stand on' their rights, 'insist' on their rights and enforce their rights against others, all of which appear to be self-regarding activities.[4] The close tie between a person's rights and his self-interest is also said to be reflected in the moral assumption that, whilst for someone to waive his rights is praiseworthy and to violate the rights of others is blameworthy, for him to insist on his rights is neither praiseworthy nor blameworthy. This is explained by pointing out that although unselfishness is generally admired and excessive selfishness blamed, a certain degree of self-interested behaviour is regarded as blameless. For the same reason, a person is said to be imprudent but not immoral if he fails to exercise his rights, but he is reprehended if he infringes the rights of others. This makes sense in a content of authorised competitiveness carried on within authorised bounds. The language of rights expresses these authorisations. In particular, liberty-rights provide the justification for right-bearers' pursuing of their own interests while the claim-rights of others mark the boundaries of legitimate self-interest. To remove this context is, it is argued, to remove the meaningfulness of rights.[5]

There is an immediate plausibility in this perspective on rights, but it is possible that the association of rights and competitive individualism is a contingent feature that serves to distinguish capitalist from socialist rights. Clearly, we would expect that in a society of self-centred persons attitudes to rights would be ungenerous and grasping, but this does not establish that possessive and selfish attitudes are presupposed by the institution of rights. Altruists might be expected to take a very different attitude to their rights. Nevertheless, it is clear that rights do have a close connection with individualism if only because they characteristically belong to individuals and all relate in some way to those aspects of rule-governed behaviour which centre on benefiting specific persons. What needs to be argued by the reformist is that this does not necessarily embroil rights in the sort of individualism that accepts or glorifies conflict between selfish and self-sufficient persons.

From the point of view of the logic of rights, a crucial issue here is the interpretation of what it is for an obligation to be 'owed to' another person, for it is the notion of an obligation being owed to the person with the correlative right that enables us to distinguish those obligation-imposing rules which do correlate

---

3 See CB Macpherson, *The Political Theory of Possessive Individualism*, Oxford: Clarendon Press, 1962, for this interpretation of Hobbes and Locke in terms of market relationships. Similar assumptions underlie later utilitarian theory of democracy; see J Mill, *Essay on Government*, Cambridge: CUP, 1937 (1819).

4 See R Flathman, *The Practice of Rights*, Cambridge: CUP, 1976, 70: 'A striking feature of such discourse has been the often unabashedly self-assertive and insistent character of the speech and other actions of those who hold rights. It is not only common but generally thought unexceptional for us to claim, maintain, assert, demand and insist upon our rights.'

5 Flathman argues that the language of rights pre-supposes that right-bearers have the capacity to be self-directing and assertive (*ibid*, 71ff).

with rights from those which do not. Therefore, it is through the analysis of what it is for B to owe to A the fulfilment of an obligation that we can explore the nature of the connection between rights and individual interests.

## CONTRACT AND POWER THEORIES OF RIGHTS

I discuss three competing theories of what it is that marks off those obligations which are owed to other people (the right-bearers) from other obligations. According to the contract theory, only those obligations that can be construed as arising from promises or contracts create rights. In contrast, the power or will theory is that right-correlating obligations are those which subordinate the will of the obliged person to the will or legal power of another. Lastly, the interest theory is that a right exists when an obligation is directed towards and grounded in the satisfaction or protection of the interests of another person, the right-holder. In this section I argue that the first two theories are inadequate even within the assumptions of liberal theory and in the next section it is contended that there is a form of the interest theory which is both in itself a more satisfactory theory and also the only theory congruent with the moral and sociological assumptions of the socialist ideal.

A paradigm example of a right is one arising from a promise, and by extending the notion of promising there have been erected contractual theories of rights which explicate what it is for an obligation to be owed to A by saying that a right arises from an agreement or contract in which B binds himself by giving his word to A, often in exchange for some reciprocal commitment; A, as the promisee or contractee, is the person to whom the obligation is owed, the person who has the right that B do or refrain from doing something in relation to the object of the right. The obligation is owed to A because B has made his promise to A, in consequence of which A has the right that B fulfil his commitment, but may, if he chooses, release B from his obligation.[6]

Although the notion of promising is itself problematic, it would be foolish to deny the attraction of the contractual approach to the understanding of rights, particularly when discussing justificatory theories about what rights people ought to have, or to underestimate the subtle developments of the crude theory outlined above to take in tacit and hypothetical promises. However, simply as an attempt to say what we mean by an obligation being owed to A, the right-holder, it is clearly inadequate, if only because we can readily understand and make clear what it is for A to have a right without invoking the concept of promising or contracting. The right of the hungry to be fed, the right of children to be educated, the right of a citizen to a fair trial in respect of any charge brought against him – all these make no essential reference to a prior promise-like commitment on the part of those with the relevant correlative obligations: they may be claimed,

6 If we discount Hobbes's natural rights as not being genuine rights since they do not correlate with any obligations, the Hobbesian version of the social contract exemplifies the contract theory of rights in its purest form. More commonly, it is a theory applied to conventional or positive rights as opposed to natural or moral rights.

asserted, upheld and in general understood without involving the notion of contract in any way, yet they are just as much rights as the rights of any promisee. The contract theory seems particularly inapplicable to liberty-rights, although it is common to avoid this difficulty by taking a natural law position on the right to liberty and a contractarian position on obligations which diminish liberty by establishing correlative positive rights.[7]

Of course, the enactment or adoption of a rule or law laying obligations on B towards A could be regarded as a promise or understanding given to A but, since the authority which initiates the rule is not necessarily the locus of the obligation established, it is not clear how this alleged or tacit promise explains the relation between B and A. Thus, when a government enacts a law which obliges B to do X for A, the promise, if there is one, is made by the state and not by B and so, on this theory, A's right is against the state and not against B, so that we have not explained what it is for B to owe the obligation to A.

To reject the contract theory as explaining the very nature of what it is to have a right is not necessarily to adopt the view that there are 'natural' rights which exist prior to the establishment of 'conventional' ones, for it may be that there are non-contractual positive laws which confer rights. In fact, the notion that all rights must originate in contracts can be cited as an example of the sort of individualism to which socialist theorists object.[8] The idea that we have no obligation to our fellow creatures except those that we have voluntarily agreed to take upon ourselves, presupposing as it does that the individual is an independent being who has an existence and self-sufficiency in abstraction from his social relationships, is totally opposed to the socialist concept of man as a social creature whose being is closely involved in the lives of others at a level of integration far deeper than that of the relatively superficial institutions of promising and contracting. While revolutionary socialists may, therefore, seize on the contract theory to demonstrate the unsocialist nature of rights, it is not a theory that has strong socialist credentials.

The second standard solution to the problem of explicating what it is for B's obligation to be owed to A, the right-holder, is the 'will' or 'power' theory, according to which A has a right only if there is a rule that makes A's choice or will pre-eminent over the actions or will of others in certain specified ways and circumstances. On this theory, to have a right is to be able to require others to act or refrain from acting in a certain way so that A is to be in a position to determine by his choice how B shall act and in this way limit B's freedom of choice.[9] The obligations correlative to rights are owed to those persons who have the legal or quasi-legal power to require that obligation to be fulfilled. Thus, only when there is an identifiable person A who can require B to act in certain ways and have at his

---

7 This is roughly the stance adopted in R Nozick, *Anarchy, State and Utopia*, New York: Basic Books, 1974, although, with Locke, Nozick allows that there are moral side-constraints on how individuals may use their natural liberty.

8 See S Lukes, *Individualism*, Oxford: Blackwell, 1973, especially Chapters 11 and 12.

9 For the idea of a right as a 'legally respected individual choice', see HLA Hart, 'Bentham on legal rights', in AWB Simpson (ed), *Oxford Essays in Jurisprudence*, 2nd series, Oxford: Clarendon Press, 1973, 171–201.

discretion whether or not so to require B's action or inaction can we speak of rights. Rights are discretionary powers, powers of a legal or quasi-legal type which the holders may or may not deploy as they wish. To have a right is to be able to require the correlative obligation or to waive it, hence we speak of B having an obligation to A.

The power theory has the advantage of having a straightforward positivist content which enables us to determine who has a right by consulting the relevant laws or rules rather than by inquiring into alleged past events, such as contracts (although such inquiries will be germane to establishing whether particular contractual rights exist). It also has the advantage that it enables us to distinguish clearly between analysing and justifying rights. Further, it has to its credit the capacity to explain a good deal of the standard language of rights, in particular the notion of waiving rights, but also the vast array of ways in which we speak of claiming rights, insisting upon, demanding, standing on, neglecting, exercising, defending and using rights, all of which accord with the idea of the right-holder having discretion over the use of legal-type powers over others. In this respect, it explains why rights are regarded as valuable possessions, for rights can be used to defend ourselves and carry out our wishes in a variety of circumstances, should we choose to do so; they are all gain and no loss.[10]

We can also use this idea of rights as discretionary powers over the actions of others to develop a positivist interpretation of rights by describing the practices characteristically used to enforce rights, the procedures for settling disputes about the existence and interpretation of the relevant rules and the use of enforcement agencies to require the fulfilment of such obligations as the right-holders legitimately demand. The right-holder is then seen as the person who has the legal standing which enables him to raise an action to compel the conformity of B to the rule in question or, in the case of social rights, to call on the forces of public opinion in his support. Thus, we can see how particular rights are part of a wider institution or practice of rights with recognised ways of claiming, assessing and, if appropriate, requiring the fulfilment of correlative obligations or obtaining compensation for non-fulfilment of obligations, all initiated by the acts of the right-holder and directed towards the satisfaction of his claims as established by the relevant authorities.

It is, however, even more obvious in the case of the power theory than in the case of the contract theory that such an interpretation of the nature of rights is too narrow to encompass all rights. There are rights for which there are no capacities on the part of the right-holder either to claim or to waive his rights. Even excluding the rights of animals as being too controversial, we must allow the rights of children, of the mentally retarded and of the aged. Indeed, in general we would not want to exclude the idea of rights of the powerless, including the legally powerless, who cannot activate the legal or public processes on their own

---

10 See Flathman, *op cit* fn 4, 79: 'There cannot be a right to an X unless having or doing X is in general, and in A's judgement, advantageous for A.'

behalf or make demands and waive obligations; they are beings who do not have the will to possess the sort of rights which accord with the power theory.[11]

Now it is, of course, possible for rights to be enforced or waived on the behalf of right-holders, so it might be argued that the idea of a right as a power is thus extendable to all rights. What is it to say that children have rights other than to say that specified persons have the legal power to compel the actions of others with respect to children? But this would mean that children's rights concern children but are not owed to them, for, on the theory under consideration, the essence of a right is the power of demand and waiver. If we separate the right-holder and the right-waiver (who we may call the administrator of the right) so that to have a right it is not necessary to have the power of claiming and waiving, then it becomes a contingent fact about rights that the right-holder is normally the person who may either insist or not insist on his rights. In this case, it is quite clear that when we speak of the correlative obligation being owed to A we are not simply indicating that A has this discretionary power over B, for we still say that the obligations of parents are owed to their children even when the discretionary power of enforcement is lodged elsewhere, perhaps in the state. Generalising this point, the thesis that A can choose whether or not to exercise a right presupposes that this right is something that can be described and analysed in isolation from A's legal capacity to exercise the right. Moreover, it makes perfect sense to say that A does not have the right to waive his right, indicating that the power of waiver is additional to, and may be separated from, the right itself. It would appear that the power theory is still in the shadow of the contract theory for it is in connection with promises and contracts that we normally assume a power of waiver on the part of the promisee or contractee.

For the reformist, the power theory is equally suspect from the point of view of ideological neutrality, since it has the implication that we should cease to think of the rights of those who have no capacity to make demands on others and limit the distribution of these valuable commodities to beings with rational wills capable of comprehending and involving themselves in quasi-legal procedures: the possessions of the intelligent, informed autonomous beings of the sort who make good entrepreneurs and lawyers. And it is the power theory which most frequently serves to explain the revolutionary's doubts about rights. Thus, Hirst minimises the significance of rights for socialism on the grounds that rights exemplify an area of claim and counterclaim.[12] In this he is only following

---

11 See AI Melden, *Rights and Persons*, Oxford: Blackwell, 1977, 72ff: 'The infant son surely has no obligation to his father, but he does have a right to the care and protection the father is able to give him; and this right exists as no mere augury of the future but as a right that he has then and there as an infant. Granted that certain conceptual linkages of this right are missing – for it makes no sense to speak of infants claiming or asserting their rights or forgiving those who violate them – the talk of the rights of infants is no mere *façon de parler* which could be put in a more straightforward and literal manner by speaking of what they need or ought to have in order that they may develop into beings who in a literal sense of the terms have rights.'

12 P Hirst, 'Law, socialism and rights', in P Carlen and M Collison (eds), *Radical Issues in Criminology*, Oxford: Martin Robertson, 1983, 100: '"Rights" in law establish a capacity for a person to advance in the courts a claim for relief or for an agent acting as a legal subject for that person to make the claim.'

Kelsen's thesis that a right (in the technical sense of a type of legal power conferred by a legal order to raise a suit for the execution of a sanction) is a 'specific technique' of the capitalist legal order 'insofar as this order guarantees the institution of private property and considers especially individual rights'.[13]

In fact, both the contract and the power theories of rights can be regarded as bourgeois theories in that they emphasise the legal role of the autonomous individual who has purely external and voluntary relations with other similar individuals entered into and maintained on the initiative of those involved. This model has particular relevance to the commercial exchanges which occur within capitalist societies where each individual, from the economic and legal points of view, is an independent owner of property (including the property he has in his own labour power), free to enter into any commercial transaction he chooses, transactions enforceable at the behest of those with whom he has contracted. Contract and power theories of rights are, on this view, a theoretical expression of bourgeois society in which the role of each individual as a property owner is that of a subject of rights. The idea of the rights of the individual, by which is meant primarily the equal right of all to buy and sell their labour and their products, is thus a feature of capitalism but not of the feudalism which preceded capitalism or the socialism which will supersede it. This is why the bourgeois revolutions of the 18th century championed the rights of man and why these same rights will cease to be relevant in post-capitalist society.[14]

The influential Soviet legal theorist EB Pashukanis (1891–1937) applies this theory of individual rights to the entire 'form of law', arguing that all legal (as distinct from administrative) rules have the form of commodity exchange.[15] Pashukanis's theory is a bold attempt to develop Marxian ideas concerning the essentially bourgeois nature of law and its incompatibility with socialist society. Pashukanis does not rest his case against law on its oppressive or coercive nature as an instrument of class rule but proposes the more subtle idea that law is a type

---

13 H Kelsen, *General Theory of Law and State*, A Wedberg (trans), Cambridge, MA: Harvard University Press, 1949, 136.

14 See K Marx, *Capital*, Book I, Part II, Chapter 6, Harmondsworth: Penguin, 1976, 280: 'The sphere of circulation or commodity exchange, within whose boundaries the sale and purchase of labour-power goes on, is in fact a very Eden of the innate rights of man. It is the exclusive realm of Freedom, Equality, Property and Bentham. Freedom, because both buyer and seller of a commodity, let us say of labour-power are determined only by their own free will. They contract as free persons, who are equal before the law. Their contract is the final result in which their joint will finds a common legal expression. Equality, because each enters into relation with the other, as with a simple owner of commodities, and they exchange equivalent for equivalent. Property, because each disposes only of what is his own. And Bentham, because each looks only to his own advantage. The only force bringing them together, and putting them into relation with each other, is the selfishness, the gain and the private interest of each. Each pays heed to himself only, and no one worries about the others. And precisely for that reason, either in accordance with the pre-established harmony of things, or under the auspices of an omniscient providence, they all work together to their mutual advantage, for the common weal, and in the common interest.'

15 See particularly *Law and Marxism, A General Theory*, B Einhorn (trans), London: Ink Links, 1978, translated from a German edition of 1929, which followed two previous editions in Russian. For discussions of Pashukanis's work, see CJ Arthur, 'Towards a materialist theory of law', *Critique*, Vol 7, 1976–77, 31–46; and R Kinsey, 'Marxism and the law', *British Journal of Law and Society*, Vol 5, 1978, 202–27.

of social relationship specific to capitalism.[16] From our point of view, the interesting aspect of his theory is that he regards law as a relationship between equal jural subjects who are the bearers of rights:[17]

> The legal system differs from every other form of social system precisely in that it deals with private, isolated subjects. The legal norm acquires its *differentia specifica,* marking it out from the general mass of ethical, aesthetic, utilitarian and other such regulations precisely because it presupposes a person endowed with rights on the basis of which he actively makes claims.

Arguing on Marxist lines, Pashukanis identifies legal relationships as a type of economic relationship. (He therefore rejects the idea of law as a system of rules or norms.) The basic economic relationships in capitalist society hold between those selling their labour (the proletarian class) and those purchasing it for the purpose of organising mechanised production (the capitalist class), and between the producers of commodities (that is, goods manufactured for sale in an open market) and participants in the marketplace. Law provides a framework for such exchanges, particularly in the resolution of disputes about commodity exchanges.[18] This is why law is adjudicative rather than administrative. In doing this, it treats each individual as a legal person entitled to the full (standard) compensation for his labour-power and the freedom to exchange his goods at whatever price he can obtain. Private law, especially the law of contract, which represents the essential form of law, assumes that each jural person is a distinct or isolated being, with interests opposed to other such beings, who is engaged in competition with all other owners.[19] Contract is thus integral to the ideal of law. The point of this system is to make possible the economic exchanges necessary for capitalist production, but the form of law is apparent in other social relationships, even in the family, all of which are viewed as involving the exchange of commodities at market prices.[20] Legal relationships are, at base, relationships between the possessors of commodities, therefore he treats law not as an appendage of human society in the abstract, but as a historical category corresponding to a particular social environment based on the conflict of private interests.[21]

Despite certain grave internal weaknesses in Pashukanis's theory (such as his difficulty in distinguishing between facts such as possession, and legal norms such as ownership),[22] his limitation of the concept of rights to rule-governed

---

16 See Pashukanis, *op cit* fn 15, Chapter 2.

17 Pashukanis, *op cit* fn 15, 100ff.

18 See Pashukanis, *op cit* fn 15, 81: 'A basic prerequisite for legal regulation is therefore the conflict of private interests ... the juridical factor in this regulation arises at the point when differentiation and opposition of interests begin.'

19 See Pashukanis, *op cit* fn 15, 117ff.

20 See Pashukanis, *op cit* fn 15, 103: 'If all economic life is to be built on the principle of agreement between autonomous wills, every social function, in reflecting this, assumes a legal character.'

21 See Pashukanis, *op cit* fn 15, 71ff: 'Law not as an appendage of human society in the abstract, but as an historical category corresponding to a particular social environment based on the conflict of private interests.'

22 See H Kelsen, *The Communist Theory of Law*, London: Stevens & Sons, 1955, 93: '"Ownership" in an "extra-judicial sense" is a contradiction in terms. Pashukanis must inevitably fall into this contradiction because he describes the legal relationship of ownership without recurring to the legal norms constituting this relationship.'

exchanges of a capitalist nature illuminates certain features of private law. However, it has little application to legal relationships between the state and the citizen and is strained to breaking point in its interpretation of criminal law as a process whereby a crime is 'exchanged' for a punishment of equivalent 'value'.[23]

The evident purpose of Pashukanis's theory is to vindicate a Marxian interpretation of law and to do so he, like so many revolutionary critics of rights, draws selectively on theories emanating from an alien ideological background. Such theories are evidence only of the sort of rights current in the types of society that Pashukanis wishes to contrast with socialism.

There is, in fact, little reason to accept Pashukanis's arbitrary refusal to regard as law the non-bourgeois systems of societal rules. His conclusions follow only if we accept contract and power theories of rights and give them a very special locus in certain economic relations of capitalism. He himself allows, following Engels, that where there are no clashes of commercial interests there will still have to be administration, that is, the organisation of joint activities on the basis of agreed objectives, as in an army, a religious order, or the running of a railway system.[24] We have already seen that such organisational activities generate rules and noted that some of these rules will include provisions for entering into agreements and having some legal powers over others. The fact that these institutions are not used for the purposes of bourgeois commerce is an insufficient reason to decline to call them legal, or refuse to regard them as establishing rights, for we still have to take into account the prospect of a theory of rights which is not confined to contractual and power rights.

Moreover, it is evident that Pashukanis assumes that bourgeois (and hence all) rights are pre-legal relationships to which law merely gives expression. This means that he is taking over for the purpose of his critique something like the theory of natural or moral rights according to which the idea of the individual as an equal bearer of rights is a metaphysical doctrine underlying law rather than a statement about the content of law. This is a point which has relevance to the revolutionary's view of human rights, which is discussed in the next chapter, but it does not have direct bearing on the concept of positive rights, which is the object of our present analysis.

## THE INTEREST THEORY OF RIGHTS

The inability of the contract and power theories to explain, at least in some cases, what it means to say that B has an obligation to A leaves as the main contender the 'interest' theory of rights according to which to have a right is to have an interest protected or furthered by the existence or nonexistence of a rule, law or under-

---

23 See Pashukanis, *op cit* fn 15, Chapter 7.

24 Thus, 'the prerequisite for technical regulation is unity of purpose. For this reason the legal norms governing the railways' liability are predicated on private claims, private differentiated interests, while the technical norms of rail traffic presuppose the common aims of, say, maximum efficiency of the enterprise' (Pashukanis, *op cit* fn 15, 81).

standing requiring action or inaction in ways that are designed to have a bearing on the interests of the right-holder; obligations, under these rules, are owed to the right-holder because they are obligations to further or protect A's interests, this being of the essence of the right in question rather than a secondary consequence of the fulfilment of the obligation.[25]

The strength of the interest theory is that it can cover all types of rights and explains the limited plausibility of contract and power theories. The protection that is given by rights may sometimes be afforded by giving A legal power over the wills of others (as the power theory contends is always the case) or it may involve practices such as the institution of promising or contracting whereby B undertakes to further A's interests in some specified way (which is how the contract theory construes all rights), but neither of these devices is essential to rights. As long as it is possible to interpret a positive obligation, like the obligation to feed the starving, or to leave adults alone to make their own decisions, as being for the interests of A, then such an obligation may be said to be owed to A, and A may be said to be the right-holder, his interests being the objective of the obligation. On this theory, not only are particular rights to be seen as ways of furthering the interests of right-holders, but the whole institution of rights is regarded as having the function of protecting interests of right-holders.

Further elucidation of what it is for a right to be for the protection of an interest requires us to distinguish the strictly legal or positivistic content that can be given to this conception from the background assumptions that go along with this understanding and application of rights, legal and non-legal. The specific consequences that flow from ascribing a right to A vary according to the type of right in question, but they can be spelled out in terms of the processes and assumptions which affect the application and interpretation of the correlative obligations. Where rights are explicitly mentioned in positive rules, this has the function of expressing either the legislator's intentions or the traditional understanding of the purpose of societal rules in a way which indicates that A's interests are to be considered as relevant in such judicial matters as: (a) who may raise issues in court about the non-fulfilment of the obligation (normally the right-holder or person authorised to act on his behalf, but perhaps any person in a position to show that A's interests have been detrimentally affected by B's behaviour); (b) how the content of the obligation is to be interpreted where this is in doubt (namely from the point of view of the interests of A that the rule is designed to protect); (c) how serious the violation is to be regarded when an obligation is not fulfilled (perhaps in proportion to the degree to which A's interests have suffered); (d) where questions of compensation or damages arise, who should benefit therefrom; and (e) the judicial creation of new obligations to protect interests previously protected by other obligations in different circumstances involving the same interests.

25 For an able defence of the interest theory of rights, see DN MacCormick, 'Rights in legislation', in PMS Hacker and J Raz (eds), *Law, Morality and Society*, Oxford: Clarendon Press, 1977, 189–209.

Quite apart from the specific implications in matters of procedure and application which the identification of whose rights are at stake in a particular situation may have – all of which may be seen as ways of ensuring that A's interests are safeguarded by legal or quasi-legal processes – the use of rights terminology in everyday discourse carries with it the connotation of the defence of right-holders' legitimate interests, which affects the whole approach to political and legal issues in those cases where the rights of those involved are explicitly stated to be at issue. Not only is the legal meaning of 'rights' cashable in terms of various mechanisms for taking A's interests into account in applying and interpreting rules, but the assumption that rights are for the protection of the interests of right-holders also points the whole process in the direction of guarding the advantages of those who are shown to have rights relevant to issues before courts, and permeates the background political and moral assumptions of the language of rights.

The general orientation which is introduced into the legal process by the concept of rights is continuous with the assumptions which go along with how we regard right-conferring rules in the course of non-legal social interactions independently of any issues which arise in the judicial process. Where rules employ the notion of rights, this is taken to mean that the purpose and hence the correct interpretation and significance of the rule is to assist or protect the right-holders in the pursuit of their interests. It indicates that it is A who has the warrant for action, or entitlement to receive or decline certain benefits or burdens, and that it is A's interests that are the *raison d'etre* of the required correlative obligations. This is not to say that there can be no ulterior purpose for ascribing rights to A, but to understand what it is to ascribe a right we must see this ulterior purpose as being served by a mechanism which gives precedence or standing in a stated manner to the relevant interests of the right-holder in specified circumstances. We can best understand the meaning of B's obligation to A (the right-holder) by saying that B's obligation is to act or refrain from acting so as to further or protect the interests of A in a way indicated by the content of the right in question, so that in the application and interpretation of the rules requiring B's activity or inactivity it is the interests of A that are to be taken into account.

The stress on individual interest in this analysis may seem to allow the revolutionary critic of rights all that he seeks or fears. It seems that rights are simply a way of institutionalising the overriding priority given to certain interests of competing individuals in situations of conflict: an institutionalisation of limited selfishness.[26]

---

26 This encapsulates Hume's idea of justice as an artificial virtue or social contrivance useful in view of man a limited altruism in situations of scarcity. See *A Treatise of Human Nature*, London, 1739, Book III, Part II. Bertell Ollman expresses the communist corrolary of this view: 'What happens … to the notion of private property in a society where no one ever claims a right to things he is using, wearing, eating or living in, where instead of refusing to share with others he is only too happy to give them what they want, where – if you like – all claims to use are equally legitimate? This is the situation of communism: the clash of competing interests has disappeared and with it the need to claim rights of any sort' (B Ollman, 'Marx's vision of communism', in *Social and Sexual Revolution*, Cambridge, MA: South End Press, 1979, 63).

However, this is so only if 'interest' is taken as being synonymous with self-interest, or selfishness, and it is assumed that obligations must be performed unwillingly. Neither of these contentions has to be accepted, although both are made naturally enough in a society in which individuals are primarily or even exclusively concerned about their own welfare in contrast to that of others and in which assistance is given to others only grudgingly, under coercion or in order to obtain reciprocal benefits. These assumptions are not, however, a necessary part of the conceptual tie between rights and interests. It is true that much of the history of the development of rights can readily be seen as reflecting successive attempts by one group after another to secure what they felt to be in their interests by imposing obligations on other groups with conflicting interests: historically, many rights can be seen as practices created for the regulation of conflicting self-interests and the imposition of the interests of the dominant group over those of others. Moreover, if we do take 'interest' to mean 'self-interest' and 'self-interest' to imply 'selfishness', then this accounts as well as any other theory for the typical associated terminology of rights: demands, claims, insistence, enforcement, imposition and so forth, and the idea that it is proper to waive one's rights but not to neglect obligations. It is, however, possible to detach 'interest' from 'selfishness' and 'obligation' from 'burden' and so open the way for a socialist concept of rights that retains the individualism inseparable from the idea of obligations being owed to others, but interprets the relevant interests in such a way that they do not amount to self-regarding behaviour and the correlative obligations in such a way that they are not typically viewed as burdensome.

While it is tautological to say that a person's interests are *his* interests, this is not to say that his interests are directed towards his own welfare, and while the 'selfish' interpretations of 'interests', in which it is assumed that a person's interests are self-regarding (that is, directed towards benefiting himself), are characteristic of a society in which 'individualism' implies the propriety of each seeking his own benefit except in so far as he is constrained by custom or law from harming others in the process, it would not be so in a society such as the socialist envisages. To allow for the possibility of unselfish 'interests', a more neutral and potentially more helpful way to regard 'interest' as it relates to the concept of rights is to concentrate on the idea of a person being 'interested in' something, rather than on the bare motion of something being in someone's interests in the sense of his welfare or wellbeing.[27] This enables us to produce an analysis of the concept and institution of rights that is adequate to existing systems and permits the development of a theory of rights that avoids the criticism that they are inherently and inevitably tied to the pursuit of self-interest or legitimate self-centredness, and at the same time maintains the essential connection between rights and the interests of their 'owners'.

For a being to have interests in the sense of being 'interested in' X or Y it is necessary for that being to be in some sort of conative relationship to an object, that is, to have some sort of desire, care or concern about that which he is

27 For a discussion of this distinction, see RG Frey, *Interests and Rights*, Oxford: Clarendon Press, 1980, Chapter 7.

'interested in'. This may be relatively passive, as when an object attracts or holds the attention of A, or relatively active, as when A has hopes, fears, aspirations, cares or concerns which prompt him to action or inaction in relation to the object of his interest. Having interests in this sense, therefore, depends on the arousal of his attention and usually also of some affective or emotional attitude towards features of his environment or of himself which are sufficient to motivate efforts towards or away from the objects of interest in appropriate circumstances. A person's interests are not simply those things which he considers in an abstract way significant or valuable, but items to which he devotes his own concrete attention and activity, the things he wants and cares about as part of his own way of life. They are the things in which he is disposed to be interested in that, given particular, usually recurring, circumstances of his life, he manifests attentiveness to, concern for and activity towards them, according to the nature of the objects and the opportunities available to him.

It is important to note that the idea of being interested in something does not necessarily carry the implication of self-regarding concerns which goes with the narrow idea of interests as that which is for the benefit of A. What a person is interested in may often be some condition of himself, but it need not be. He may be interested in the development of knowledge, the welfare of others, artistic conceptions, sports, animals, foreign countries, and so on, none of which can be seen as tied up with his self-interest in the sense of self-regarding interests.

The theory that what is common to all rights is that they relate positively to what the right-bearer is interested in is, in part, a descriptive generalisation about actual rights. As such, it is vulnerable to the readily available evidence that the social and legal rights of particular individuals do not always have direct bearing on what they are concerned about. A person may, for instance, have a legal right to a pension but, perhaps because he is wealthy, be entirely indifferent whether or not he receives that pension. The theory can, however, readily be developed to take account of such superficial objections.

In the first place, the ascription of A's right to X, although it presupposes that A is interested in or is concerned about X, often does so on the basis that the interests and concerns in question are dispositional. To be interested in X it is not necessary to be constantly thinking about X or always manifesting wants and desires about it, but simply to be disposed to have such thoughts, wants and desires on appropriate occasions. Thus, if I have a right to sell my labour, this does not imply that I always wish to do so but only that it is a wish that I have from time to time in appropriate circumstances.

We also speak of the right of A to X when A is a member of a class of beings all of whom are capable of being interested in X even though they do not all in fact have such an interest. This means that we sometimes ascribe a right to a being on the basis of the interests which he could have, in the sense that he is capable of having them, on the grounds that they are the sort of interests that ought to be protected and furthered by rights. This would, of course, normally be pointless if it is certain that the being in question never will have these interests, and the close relation between rights and interests can be seen from the fact that it would be misconceived to ascribe rights to X to a class of beings none of whose members are likely to be interested in X. Therefore I, as a human being, can have a right to freedom of speech even if I am not interested in free speech, for it is clearly the sort of thing that I could be interested in and which many human beings are interested in. The point of ascribing this right to me, as a person who is not interested in free speech, is to establish that if and when I do come to have such an interest, then my freedom to speak is something which ought to be protected by rights. Many rights are ascribed to persons in this way because of the interests they are capable of having.

We could regard these 'capacity rights' as being purely hypothetical rights that beings have if they have the appropriate interests but not otherwise, which preserves a close tie between rights and actual interests. This has the merit of bringing out the rationale for ascribing such rights to anyone although it is not a formulation that is likely to help with the drafting of readily applicable rules. It is also worth noting that there is another way in which what I have called 'capacity rights' are related to actual interests in that it is common for people to be concerned about the existence of rules imposing on others duties which will protect interests that they believe they are likely to have in the future; when this is the case it is not misleading to speak of A's right to X even although A has, at present, no disposition to be interested in X, provided that X is the sort of thing in which A could be interested.

Another way in which the connection between rights and interests is not always as direct as my formula suggests is that a person's right to X may not depend on his interest in X itself but in that to which X is causally related, or can be used to obtain. Thus, a person's right to a certain monetary income may be based not on his interest in having money as such, but on his interest in having those things which money can be used to buy. And a mentally subnormal person's right to medical treatment, about which he neither knows nor cares, may depend, for instance, on the fact that this treatment will help to make his life more comfortable, which is something in which he is interested. Therefore, the connection between rights and what right-bearers are interested in may not always be immediately apparent because it may be mediated by an assumed causal or instrumental relationship. Strictly speaking, therefore, we should say that to ascribe a right to X presupposes that the right-bearer is either interested in X, or in something to which X is causally or instrumentally related. Alternatively, it could be said that, where X is only indirectly related to what A (the right-bearer) is interested in, A has not got a right to X as such, but to that to which X is causally or instrumentally related. The point of putting it in this way would be to draw attention to the fact that the correct ascription of such 'instrumental rights' depends on the existence of the relationship which is said to hold between X and that in which A is interested. If money cannot be used to buy things that A is interested in having then there is no basis for saying that he has a right to it. Instrumental rights may therefore be regarded as secondary rights which presuppose the existence of prior and logically more fundamental rights to those things to whose protection or furtherance the instrumental rights are directed.

Despite these developments of the 'interested in' theory of rights, it would be difficult to claim that it is entirely successful as a description of all actual linguistic uses of rights language. In particular, legal systems have evolved the concept of a legal person to cover states, corporations, and other inanimate things which cannot be literally concerned about anything since they lack consciousness and desires. The rationale for such usages is generally that such rights indirectly, but in effect, have to do with the concerns of sentient beings. In the case of associations, for instance, the 'interests' of the collective entity can be given meaning in terms of the interests or concerns of its constituent members, assuming, that is, that these members are individual beings. However, it is more difficult to accommodate the extension of rights to purely inanimate things such as deserts and trees, as is sometimes proposed.[28] Many natural entities can be regarded as having interests in that they can be benefited and harmed, but they cannot be said to be interested in anything.

The reason for confining the literal use of rights language to those cases where the right-holders have concerns is in the end an evaluative one, which rests on the proposition that only the concerns of conscious, sentient beings have the moral significance to serve as the ends of a rule-governed order. That inanimate objects do not have this standing is ultimately as much a moral as a conceptual point, although the awkwardness of speaking of the interests of non-sentient entities indicates that it is an evaluation which is enshrined in the informal logic of our practical discourse.

The superiority of that version of the interest theory which interprets interests as concerns rests also on the extent to which it systematises at least some powerful intuitions to do with the proper criteria for membership of the class of possible right-bearers.[29] If we adopt the sense of 'interests' in which it means only the benefit of a thing, then we may plainly speak of the interests of flowers, buildings and rocks, for in each of these cases the entity in question may be preserved, and it even makes sense to think in terms of their protection and improvement. In this case, anything that can be benefited or harmed, improved or damaged, may be said to be a potential right-bearer. All that is required is that there be good or bad specimens of the type of thing in question and we are then able to speak of benefiting or harming it and thus of doing or not doing what is in or against its interests. This would mean that if any rule-protected interest constitutes a right, then any inanimate object might have rights. This cannot be said to be without sense, or without relevance in law, since legal systems have no difficulty in extending the application of legal personality to whatever type of entity it is expedient so to regard, but such extensions to entirely inanimate objects are so out of line with ordinary assumptions as to cast doubt on this interpretation of 'interest' as a criterion for demarcating the class of possible right-bearers. Indeed, it is one of the strengths of the 'interested in' theory of rights that it gives us a plausible criterion for defining the class of possible right-bearers. The requirement that right-bearers satisfy the condition of conative consciousness is broad enough

---

28 See, for instance, CD Stone, *Should Trees Have Standing? Toward Legal Rights for Natural Objects*, New York: Avon Books, 1975.

29 Some of the points which follow are argued at greater lengths in TD Campbell and AJM McKay, 'Antenatal injury and the rights of the foetus', *Philosophical Quarterly*, Vol 24, 1974, 17–30.

to encompass nearly all human beings who are biologically alive and gives us some sort of guideline to apply to such borderline cases as animals (the 'higher' animals clearly being included as potential right-bearers), human 'vegetables' (who may be defined as lacking consciousness and therefore as not having rights), and human foeti at various stages of development. Thus, we would have some basis for saying, on the suggested criterion, that foeti at the early stages of development can have no rights, and that whether or not they do so at later stages will depend on empirical assumptions about the emergence of consciousness. It has, further, the acceptable consequence of excluding from the class of right-bearers all inanimate objects including those 'living' things like plants and microbes, which it is possible to regard as being benefited but not as themselves having concerns, while at the same time allowing that there is an analogical basis for extending the range of right-bearers to include at least this limited category of rights-bearers, and allowing that the grounds for not doing so are as much moral as conceptual, in that the boundary between those entities which may have rights and those which do not is in the end to be decided by reference to the prior decision as to what sort of things are the proper objects of moral concern for their own sakes.

It is clear that taking the interests which are protected and furthered by rights as species of 'interests in' is sufficient to break the alleged analytical tie between rights and self-interest, since men may be interested in the welfare of others as much as in their own wellbeing, and concerned about the realisation of a multitude of objectives, such as the production of material goods or the growth of knowledge, which may have no direct connection with any condition of themselves. This is particularly true in the case of the concerns which people have as the occupants of social roles, such as those of mother, teacher or worker.

The 'interested in' theory of rights appears to have the consequence that a person's rights may not relate to his own welfare. This might be thought to introduce an unacceptable gap between a person's rights and that which benefits him. Surely it cannot be the case that A has a right that the welfare of B be furthered simply because A wishes B well. Rather, would we not say, more naturally, that it is the person who benefits who has the right? Indeed, is it not badly askew to say, for instance, that an environmentalist has a right that an endangered species about whose future he is concerned should be saved or that a football supporter has a right that the team of his choice win their match?

It is not being argued, however, that just any interest in a person or event will be an adequate ground for the acquisition of a right, but only that such interests are candidates for having the protection of right-conferring rules. In those cases where the interests in question do not relate to a condition which involves the right-holder, it still remains the case that the right is his because its justification relates to the fact that it is his interest in the person or event that is the grounds for establishing and maintaining the right. This is compatible with the existence of other rights relating to the same desired outcome which do belong to those directly involved in its realisation. It is not hard to give examples of existing rights that are based on the individual's concern for others, such as the rights that parents may have for support in the care of their children. The rights that arise under the institution of promising and contracting provide plenty of illustrations of one person's right that others be treated in certain ways. The fact that it may seem strange to regard the standard right as arising from a non-self-centred interest may derive more from the fact that, in the societies with which we are most familiar, self-directed interests are those which are most prized and protected, but there is no logical reason why this should be so. It makes perfect sense to say that there is a societal rule such that A owes it to B that C receive a certain benefit so that we may say that B has a right against A that C be benefited. This will be so where A's obligation to benefit C is grounded in B's interest in C's welfare rather than directly in B's welfare. The conceptual propriety of grounding B's rights in interests of this sort is a first step in countering the argument that a system of rights necessarily institutionalises competitive individualism. What it does presuppose is that the concerns of human beings are, at the very least, a factor of major moral importance. This form of individualism is inseparable from rights. It also accords well with the socialist ideal of man as an active, project-pursuing and creative being.

The proper target of the socialist onslaught on individualism is not on the institution of rights as such but the prior assumption that human nature is irredeemably egoistic. To reject the Hobbesian model of man as an unchanging bundle of desires for the pleasure of the desirer as no more than a historically conditioned image which is approximated to only at certain periods and in certain types of society, is not to reject that form of individualism which gives a central place to the satisfaction of desires and concerns. If we allow that man may develop a limited, even an extreme, altruism, this does nothing to downgrade the significance of so arranging organised social existence that the fulfilment of human interests is its central objective. The Marxist model of man as, at least potentially, a social being whose creative agency is most fully developed in co-operative, productive enterprises centres as much on the flourishing of the concerns and pursuits of individual human beings as any other social ideal. Indeed, the image of man as an agent or labourer whose fulfilment is attained through work fits neatly into the assumption that many societal rules are designed to encourage and defend the concerns of human beings. The individualism of rights requires no more than an acceptance of the organisational significance of some of the concerns and projects of sentient beings.

# DEMOCRACY, HUMAN RIGHTS AND POSITIVE LAW

## LEGAL POSITIVISM AND HUMAN RIGHTS

Those who care about human rights may instinctively welcome the Australian High Court's bold step in using the concept of implied rights within the Constitution to elicit a constitutional right to freedom of political communication. Reflection may dispel this good cheer, for it is not at all clear that this extension of High Court power places the elucidation of such human rights in safe or legitimate hands. Indeed, the substance of the decision, which disallows a change in the political broadcasting regulations, in part on the ground of its novelty, displays an indifference to existing inequalities of communicative capacity that manifests a limited, negative, property-oriented and unimaginative approach to the articulation of fundamental rights.[1]

Further, there are important reasons of democratic principle which cast doubt on the propriety of giving courts a veto over human rights interpretation. Courts have not the capacity, and should not have the authority, to overturn the duly enacted legislation of the parliament when this is within its constitutional powers. The fact that the legislation concerns human rights strengthens rather than weakens this stricture. Individual autonomy rights, on which so much of the human rights tradition rests, must include the right to an equal share in determining what is to count as, for instance, the fundamental right of freedom of communication.[2]

These familiar enough criticisms of court-defined fundamental rights are often countered with philosophical objections to their presupposed distinction between legislation and adjudication. The idea that the people's representatives can enact rights and courts merely apply them is dismissed as a jurisprudential anachronism which fails to perceive the current doctrine that every adjudication is an interpretation, in that rules and principles can be applied only with the meaning that is given to them by those who decide the particular case.[3] The

---

1 See *Australian Capital Television Pty Ltd v The Commonwealth* (1992) 66 ALJR 695 (hereinafter cited as *Australian Capital Television*) at 695: 'Pt IIID was invalid in its entirety because of the freedom *previously* enjoyed by citizens ...' (emphasis added). Perhaps more extreme is *Leeth v The Commonwealth* (1992) 174 CLR 455, at 498, particularly Gaudron J, who argued that an implied doctrine of equality entails that 'in constitutional context discrimination is constituted by different treatment of persons or things that are not relevantly different'. This may be a very acceptable moral principle but as a constitutional rule it enables courts to decide that any piece of legislation which they believe to be morally misconceived is invalid.

2 For an excellent recent articulation of this thesis, see J Waldron, 'A rights-based critique of constitutional rights', *Oxford Journal of Legal Studies*, Vol 13, 1993, 18.

3 For adjudication as interpretation see Donald Davidson on 'radical interpretation': D Davidson, *Inquiries into Truth and Interpretation*, Oxford: Clarendon Press, 1984, 141.

criticism that courts are not the proper forum for the development of fundamental constitutional rights is therefore put to one side as an expression of outmoded legal positivism.[4]

There is no doubt that legal positivism is on the decline as an intellectually respectable approach to law and adjudication. Moreover, this decline is evidently justified to the extent that the claims of positivism to be a descriptive theory of actual legal and political process are in many respects false and often covertly political, in that the theory helps to hide the political views of judges behind the misleading rhetoric of detached literalism.[5] Courts do not in practice restrict themselves to implementing the readily identifiable general commands of the sovereign, nor do they merely administer plain rules identified in a morally neutral way. Descriptive positivism is, to a significant degree, clearly false. However, this does not mean that we should discard legal positivism as an ideal worth pursuing. Indeed, legal positivism enables us to identify major inadequacies in existing legal systems where much legislation is badly drafted and many formally good laws are poorly and even unethically administered. Just because of these failures, positivism, in its democratic forms, remains an inspirational model to which political systems should, as far as is practically possible, approximate. Courts may not but should confine themselves to the accurate application of general rules, rules which should be clear, precise and empirically applicable expressions of the political 'will' of the people's representatives. Legislatures should take on full responsibility for the progressive development of the law and not leave such matters to the haphazard and unaccountable growth of the common law with its inchoate notions of justice and fairness as they are filtered through the judicial mind. This is neither the 'simple positivism' attributed by Shiner to John Austin, nor the more complex positivism to be found in the works of Hart, MacCormick and Raz.[6] Rather, it represents that aspect of the positivist tradition which sets out a political vision as to how states should be governed in accordance with laws created by citizens to serve human values. For the sake of a distinguishing label, I call this approach 'ethical positivism', a term that serves to indicate both the moral basis for the positivist ideal and the ethical commitments required for its instantiation.[7]

---

4 In Australia this often takes the form of a belated recognition of the truisms of American legal realism that judges can always decide cases as they like if they so choose, with a revival of the predemocratic style of common law reasoning repopularised by Lord Denning. See Mason CJ: 'The role of the judge at the turn of the century', the 5th Annual AJA Oration in Judicial Administration, Melbourne, 5 November 1993.

5 See A Hutchinson, *Dwelling on the Threshold: Critical Essays in Modern Legal Thought*, London: Sweet & Maxwell, 1988.

6 R Shiner, *Norm and Nature,* Oxford: Clarendon Press, 1992; J Austin, *The Province of Jurisprudence Determined*, London: Weidenfeld & Nicolson, 1955, introduction by HLA Hart; HLA Hart, *The Concept of Law,* Oxford: Clarendon Press, 1961; DN MacCormick, *Legal Reasoning and Legal Theory,* Oxford: OUP, 1978; and J Raz, *The Concept of a Legal System,* 2nd edn, Oxford: Clarendon Press, 1980.

7 The alternative term 'normative positivism' is ambiguous, as it is between the thesis that law is a system of norms and the view that positivism is an expression of normative commitment.

More specifically, in this essay I support the position that the decline of positivist orthodoxy has immense dangers for our democratic culture. This decline is reflected in an increasing acceptance that positivism has been dethroned from its assumed supremacy as the lawyers' theory of law, to the point where the problem for jurisprudence today is thought to be about finding a viable alternative to positivism. Many judges have ceased even to pretend that they are not making law, albeit within the flexible confines of traditional legal principle. Critical arguments to the effect that courts have made false claims to objectivity and neutrality are now captured by court apologists who take on board the critics' view that law and politics cannot be separated and turn the political tables by using this to legitimate the now overt legislative activity of courts.[8]

Some of these critical arguments against the positivist model relate purely to the complexities of interpretation,[9] others extend to a revival of the idea of the common law as an expression of community values, perhaps embodying principles which are constitutionally superior to the enactments of once sovereign legislatures.[10] Most commonly, the view is put forward that judiciaries are better placed than legislatures to formulate a list of fundamental rights which they can then use to invalidate otherwise authoritative legislation.[11] Together these views amount to an open invitation to the rule of lawyers, the increase of the corporate impact of the legal profession, particularly in its judicial mode, and involve the proposal that in one way or another we move beyond the political institutions which have emerged from a long struggle for democratisation.[12]

All this is partly the fault of positivists themselves, who have made dubious claims about their theory as an accurate empirical description of how modern

---

8 Paradoxically, this realist trend is reinforced by recent quasi-natural law theories that argue the essentially moral nature of the concept of law: See M Detmold, *The Unity of Law and Morality. A Refutation of Legal Positivism,* London: Routledge, 1984; and D Beyleveld and R Brownsword, *Law as a Moral Judgment,* London: Sweet & Maxwell, 1986. This form of natural law moves shakily from the analytic truth that moral judges, like all moral agents, must morally approve of their actions, including their judgments, to the conclusion that the moral judge must morally endorse the substance of her or his legal decisions. This ignores the possibility that it is the moral duty of judges to suppress their own moral views as to the propriety of the substance of the rules they are appointed to administer.

9 See D Kennedy, 'Freedom and constraint in adjudication: a critical phenomenology', *Journal of Legal Education,* Vol 36, 1986, 518.

10 TRS Allan, *Law, Liberty and Justice,* Oxford: Clarendon Press, 1993. Note the imputation of such noble ideals as equality to the ethically mixed and often politically partisan tradition of the common law by Deane and Toohey JJ in *Leeth v The Commonwealth* (1992) 66 ALJR 529, at 541–42. See also Toohey J, 'A government of laws, not of men?' Conference on Constitutional Change in the 1990s, 5 October 1992, in *Australian Legal News,* 27/10, 1992, 7–11.

11 This may be because they are believed to be more detached from political faction, perhaps because they are concerned with articulating individual rights rather than determining social policy; see R Dworkin, 'Political judges and the rule of law', *Proceedings of the British Academy,* Vol 64, 1978, 116.

12 See R Dworkin, *A Bill of Rights for Britain,* London: Chatto, 1990, 23. In the UK context Dworkin argues that incorporating the European Convention on Human Rights into the law of the UK will mean that 'Law and lawyers might then begin to play a different, more valuable role in society than they may now even aim to have ... might think in terms of principle and less in terms of narrow precedent' and so be 'the conscience, not just the servant, of government and industry'.

legal systems actually work. What we have lost in the process is a vision of the positivist model of law as an aspirational ideal which we *ought* to implement. The positivist insistence that law is one thing and morality quite another has been misunderstood as an amoral, even an immoral, thesis,[13] and this has detracted attention from the underlying moral rationale for legal positivism, namely that it is the task of the sovereign people and their representatives to articulate specific choices from within the options made conceivable through current community values and social practices; choices which, to be politically effective, must be expressed in the form of rules applied by independent judiciaries, a system which enables a formally just system of government, and effective organisation and democratic control of social and economic life in a way which has at least the prospect of being fair and guarantees at least an element of freedom with respect to the conduct which is not covered by the enacted rules.

To defend these strongly worded political and constitutional views is far beyond the scope of a single essay. It would require a defence of the intelligibility and plausibility of the view that rules *can* constrain decision-making.[14] It would require the demonstration that there is a line between interpretation and legislation.[15] It would require establishing working distinctions between politics and law.[16] Here I confine myself to developing and illustrating some points about fundamental rights in order to argue that commitment to human rights can be detached both from the narrow moral values with which they are normally associated and from the juridical device of court-administered entrenched rights that is generally considered necessary for their implementation. I argue that debate about the desirability of entrenched rights is skewed by certain common but false assumptions as to the political and theoretical affiliations of some of its key concepts. Because, in current political ideology, 'rights' are viewed as antithetical to the humane values of happiness and empathy,[17] and, in current legal theory, human rights are taken to be in conflict with strict legal positivism, the bill of rights debate is perceived as being a matter of rights versus utility, implicating a vision of an entrenched system of rights as a form of operationalised natural law, in contradistinction to parliamentary sovereignty which is associated with majoritarian utilitarianism and the positivist theory of law.[18]

I cut across these lines of combat and suggest that, on any defensible analysis, rights are entirely enmeshed within value conceptions, including those central to utilitarian axiology, and that there are strong rights-based reasons for opposing court-administered bills of rights,[19] some of which emanate from an essentially positivist model of law. These reasons apply *a fortiori* to implied constitutional rights and the use of background common law principles as ways of introducing

---

13 See L Fuller, 'Positivism and fidelity to law', *Harvard Law Review*, Vol 71, 1958, 630.

14 F Schauer, *Playing by the Rules: A Philosophical Examination of Rule-Based Decision-Making*, Oxford: Clarendon Press, 1991.

15 See A Marmor, *Interpretation and Legal Theory*, Oxford: Clarendon Press, 1992.

16 See K Greenawalt, *Law and Objectivity*, New York: OUP, 1992.

17 See C Sypnowitch, *The Concept of Socialist Law*, Oxford: Clarendon Press, 1990.

18 See TD Campbell, *The Left and Rights*, London: Routledge and Kegan Paul, 1983, 18–51.

19 See JAG Griffith, 'The political constitution', MLR, Vol 42, 1979, 1.

fundamental rights as legally superior even to unambiguous and democratically endorsed legislation.

This is particularly so if we wish to base rights less on the liberal moral values of individual autonomy and negative liberty, important as these may be, and more on a wider concern for the more humane values of happiness, caring and affirmative freedom. Human rights have been largely captured by an often unrealistic old-fashioned liberal model of the prerequisites of rational autonomous agents at the expense of a commitment to the elimination of suffering and the fulfilment of human desires of less exalted but more pressing types.[20] Court-based approaches to the definition of human rights exacerbate this imbalance.

## THE ARTICULATION OF HUMAN RIGHTS

In this part I draw on the example of the Australian High Court's recent decisions regarding implied constitutional rights, to argue that the articulation and defence of human rights ought to be a central task of any democratic process which regards the equal right of all to participate in political decision-making as fundamental. The fact that the method for expressing and securing rights is itself stated in terms of a fundamental right is no accident; indeed, it is one of the central arguments for my conclusion.[21]

The arguments which I put forward may be put under four adjectival headings: (a) epistemological; (b) democratic; (c) ideological; and (d) positivistic. These represent four types of argument against implied or explicit court-articulated fundamental rights. The example I take by way of illustration is *Australian Capital Television Pty Ltd v The Commonwealth* (1992)[22] in which the plaintiff challenged Pt IIID of the Broadcasting Act 1942 (Cth), introduced into the Act by the Political Broadcasts and Political Disclosures Act 1991. Part IIID prohibits political advertising on radio or television during an election period but allows for politically oriented radio programmes and the allocation of free television time for political parties. It was held by the High Court that:

> Pt IIID was invalid in its entirety because of its severe impairment of the freedoms previously enjoyed by citizens to discuss public and political affairs and to criticise federal institutions – freedoms embodied by constitutional implication in an implied guarantee of freedom of communication as to public and political discussion.[23]

We are dealing here with alleged implications within a federal constitution rather than the interpretation of an overt bill of rights, but the structural features of the

---

20 See A Gewirth, *Reason and Morality*, Chicago: Chicago University Press, 1978.

21 Waldron makes the point that the idea of civic participation is at the heart of the modern conception of rights and aptly comments that even if rights are trumps this does not decide which rights are trumps: Waldron, *op cit* fn 2, 33, 38, 51.

22 *Australian Capital Television Pty Ltd v The Commonwealth* (1992) 66 AJLR 695.

23 *Ibid*.

two cases are essentially similar with respect to the analysis of what is going on in the dynamics of such a decision. In both cases, authoritative constitutional words are being interpreted in the context of the alleged invalidity of an exercise of legislative power. Maybe it is more controversial to find a bill of rights within a constitution from which the drafters consciously excluded a bill of rights, but we may let that pass for the moment. Many of the arguments apply with even greater force to the more extreme argument, recently propounded by one member of the High Court, to the effect that implied human rights may be derived from the common law 'freedoms' which were assumed to have normative supremacy at the time the Constitution was approved.[24]

### A) The epistemological argument

The confidence with which human rights enthusiasts approve the adoption of court-centred fundamental rights is based on unsupportable assumptions about the distinctive epistemology of human rights. Only the assumed uncontroversial nature of content of human rights enables us to hold that courts are able to identify, in a non-partisan way, certain fundamental rights which may then be superimposed on normal political decision-making so as to keep the latter within its proper bounds. The justification for the courts being involved in this way is that they have the requisite skills for fact-finding and are used to applying given rules in a manner which is impartial enough to command our respect. All this rests on unsupportable ideas about the nature and justification of rights, namely that human rights may be captured in relatively pellucid and simple rules. The prime task in securing human rights is thus viewed not as knowing what these rights are, but in seeing that they are observed and remedies for their contravention implemented. Thus, it is assumed that we all know what torture is, and we all agree that torture is never justified; the remaining – and demanding – task is to find out when torture happens and provide mechanisms for its prevention.

This model of human rights as an intuited or agreed set of absolute prohibitions – which we may call the torture model – has important uses in the exposure of human rights abuses by such agencies as Amnesty International, and is of considerable importance in the realm of international relations, but it has little relevance to the pursuit of human rights in countries such as Australia. Once we move on from prohibitions on the grosser barbarities to the articulation of policies within a basically humane system we soon discover that the content and form of even the least controversial rights are matters of some difficulty and no agreed methodology. Does the right to life exclude capital punishment? Does it require the best available emergency medical care at no cost to the indigent? Does it give a right of action against a department of state that fails to prevent deadly child abuse? Indeed, as soon as we try to lift our standards from crude extremes, even the definition of 'torture' becomes problematic in relation to aggressive methods of interrogation and disgusting prison conditions.

---

24 Toohey J, *op cit* fn 10.

Further, there is no simple way in which such rights as are agreed have the form of absolute prohibitions on certain types of wrongful conduct. With highly indeterminate formulations exceptions are always allowed, especially in situations of conflicts with other rights. Absolutist formulations are fine in political rhetoric but they are always qualified in any formulations accepted by governments. In either case, in practice there will be many exceptions. So the vaunted absoluteness of human rights is no special protection until the specifics have been spelt out and difficult choices made, nor, unless we endorse an extreme libertarian ideology, are the correlative duties confined to negative ones of non-interference and inaction, so there is no agreement on the form of rights either.[25]

In fact, our consensus on human rights goes little further than a common cherishing of certain very important human interests which we value highly, and a commitment to some form of human equality and a highly unspecific notion of what is fair. These broad ideals are almost meaningless until they are worked out in detail in relation to different areas of activity and the endless competing priorities are brought into some form of working relationship. These values are inevitably socially acquired and articulated and we can only choose within the options our cultural context enables us to express. It follows that participation in the process of articulation and choice should be one of the most prized ideals of the human rights tradition, not simply the spectator sport that it becomes when these crucial choices are left to litigants, lawyers and courts.

Ostensibly, *Australian Capital Television* does not appear to be in the business of making political judgments based on the moral intuitions of the judges. Rather, what appears to be going on is the working out of the presuppositions of the idea of 'representative government', the explicit datum of the Constitution from which the relevant implied fundamental right is to be deduced. The determination of these presuppositions may be regarded as a factual matter within the normal provenance of judicial activity. Is the questionable legislation destructive of something that is causally necessary for representative government?

The court approaches these issues in two stages, first arguing that there is an implied right of freedom of political communication, and then going on to the view that Pt IIID violates that right in an unacceptable manner. In the first leg of the argument Mason CJ contends:

> The point is that the representatives who are Members of Parliament and Ministers of State are not only chosen by the people but exercise their legislative and executive powers as representatives of the people. And in the exercise of those powers the representatives of necessity are accountable to the people for what they do and have a responsibility to take account of the views of the people on whose behalf they act. Indispensable to that accountability and that responsibility is freedom of communication, at least in relation to public affairs and political discussion.[26]

In other words, freedom of communication is indispensable to representative government.

---

25 Consider M Menlowe and A McCall Smith, *The Duty to Rescue*, Aldershot: Dartmouth, 1993.

26 *Australian Capital Television Pty Ltd v The Commonwealth* (1992) 66 AJLR 695, 703.

This argument is unexceptionable if it is simply an assertion that some communication is a prerequisite of political representation but it does not establish some specific set of rights (dubbed 'freedom of communication') that is 'indispensable' in this regard. Indeed, it may be plausible to say that the more communication there is, the more representative the system will be, so that in a fully representative system there will be maximal communication. Mason CJ says:

> Absent such freedom of communication, representative government would fail to achieve its purpose of government of the people through their elected representatives; government would cease to be responsive to the needs and wishes of the people and, in that sense, to be *truly* representative.[27]

However, what he refers to is not actual or maximal communication but 'freedom' of communication, that is, some notion of normative order bearing on the governance of communication.

It is at this point that the assumption is made that the court simply 'knows' what this normative freedom of communication amounts to. The fundamental right is in this sense 'intuited' or, more accurately, taken as uncontroversially clear and beyond question. The 'intuited' moral judgment comes when the court simply discounts the corrupting influence of money in the election process, a corruption that does affect the equal competition of ideas which could be regarded as what freedom of communication is meant to be all about. The majority of the court 'knows' that what is involved in Pt IIID is a limitation of freedom of communication rather than an enhancement of it. The issue is dogmatically assumed to be freedom of communication versus competing public interests, such as political corruption.[28] The same confidence in the ability of the court to know what freedom of speech involves is demonstrated by its quick dismissal of the possibility that giving representatives special and cost-free access to the media enhances rather than reduces 'freedom of communication'.

Given that the court has this intuitive confidence in its judgment of what is involved in the fundamental right of freedom of communication, namely something like the existing rules relating to communication, the second stage of the argument for the invalidity of Pt IIID is relatively easy. If a law in any way further restricting communication is a violation of the right to freedom of political communication then it follows that outlawing political advertising even for a restricted period is a violation of freedom of communication. The only question then is whether there are any sufficiently good reasons for permitting such a violation. The majority opinions then centre on whether corruption of the political process or undue influence are sufficient grounds for going along with what is taken to be a clear incursion on the right to political communication.

The argument looks very different if we construe it as a debate about what constitutes freedom of communication. The majority on the court avoid the debate about whether freedom of communication might be enhanced by the legislation,

---

27 *Ibid*, 696, 703 (emphasis added).

28 *Ibid*, 705. The contrary view was put to the Senate Select Committee on Political Broadcasts and Political Disclosures November 1991 (1993) at 4.6.5 by Dr Ian Ward and Dr Ian Cook, both political scientists from the University of Queensland.

yet corruption may be a matter which is internal to the processes of communication. If it is communication that is corrupted, by being available only to those with large sums of money, then it is not a matter of freedom of communication versus corruption, but of articulating an acceptable set of free communication rights. However, even after allowing that the legislation may have bearing on access to the media and so to the problems of democratic politics in an age of expensive and restricted media outlets, Mason CJ blandly states that the common practice of regulating political advertising in nearly all other comparable democracies 'does not refute the proposition that Part IIID impairs the freedom of discussion of political and public affairs and freedom to criticise federal institutions in the respects previously mentioned'.[29] This displays a blithe confidence that the court 'knows' what freedom of communication involves and that, in particular, it is not a matter of providing access to the media. If the argument is made that Pt IIID would reduce the dependence of political parties on large contributors, this may be seen as tantamount to saying that it will *increase* freedom of communication in that what is available to electors will be less controlled by wealth. The fact that wealth and property dominate modern communications may be seen as a corruption of the political process precisely because it diminishes the sort of freedom of communication that 'truly' representative government requires.

Nor do the other majority opinions show any awareness that the argument that television advertising trivialises political debate[30] is an argument about the proper content of freedom of communication rights, something which needs to be determined after an examination of the rationales for freedom of communication in the political context – rationales to which they are happy to appeal when arguing for the existence of an implied right of communication but then ignore when passing over what constitutes that right.[31]

So the pivotal role of the court's assumption that it knows what freedom of communication is may be appreciated by noting the way in which this enables it to avoid addressing the question of whether or not the provisions of Pt IIID enhance or diminish the democratic system. My point here is not that the answer is obvious, but that it is not. If the question had been directly addressed then the speculative and political nature of the issues would have been so evident as to disqualify the court from having an authoritative opinion on the matter. As it is, the Chief Justice is able to accept the political and evaluative arguments of the Senate Standing Committee that considered the matter, but dismiss them as irrelevant. Had the court undertaken such a study itself, it would have been clearly involved in a political process more suited to the legislative branch of state. It would certainly have been evident that no answer could be read off from any uncontroversial formulation of a right to freedom of communication. The issue comes down to a matter of whether the legislation will make the Australian system more or less representative. This must be a highly speculative matter of

---

29 *Australian Capital Television Pty Ltd v The Commonwealth* (1992) 66 AJLR 695, 700.
30 *Ibid*, 703.
31 *Ibid*, 696.

political science and political philosophy, which is very dependent on questions about the particular conception of representative government and the economic realities of effective communication. While the dissenting judgments do not themselves directly address the conception of freedom of communication, they do show much more awareness of the political nature of the issues raised by the challenge to the legislation.[32]

In the event, the High Court made itself look rather foolish in being quite so bold in its claim that a system which is basically similar to that used in the UK, from whose Parliament the Australian Constitution may arguably derive its legitimacy and whose courts they cite in favour of the existence of a right to freedom of expression,[33] is so evidently contrary to freedom of communication as to warrant invalidating a piece of legislation that emanated from a lengthy and detailed democratic process.[34] It is certainly widely implausible to claim that the High Court's particular statement of what freedom of communication involves is *necessarily* implied by the Constitution. The case therefore nicely illustrates the way in which, when articulating the content and form of fundamental rights, courts permit their own unargued assumptions to fill the epistemological vacuum surrounding the discourse of human rights.

### B) The democratic argument

Perhaps the most powerful argument for having court-based fundamental rights is that democracy itself is neither self-justifying nor self-correcting. Democracy as a system of government cannot itself be justified by democratic means, without circularity. It follows that democracies are not entitled to choose to abandon democratic institutions. Further, even if democratic process is accepted as the sole basis for political legitimacy, this legitimacy depends on the system actually being democratic. The majorities that count are the majorities within properly constituted democratic regimes. It is evident, therefore, that there is reason to look for some institutional procedure to provide external oversight for electoral rules and procedures and to limit the capacity for even properly constituted democracies to resile from democratic norms.[35]

Moreover, actual democracies, in seeking to give institutional form to the justificatory idea of equal political power, have to operate according to some less than unanimous decision procedures that inevitably place the interests of minorities at risk. It can therefore be argued that it is actually democratic (in that it furthers the objective of equal power) to limit what majorities may do in relation to the interests of those individuals who are not of their number, hence the idea of

---

32 Brennan J, *ibid*, 724, and Dawson J, *ibid*, 703.

33 The case cited is *Attorney General v Times Newspapers Ltd* [1974] AC 273, 315.

34 Thus, the Joint Standing Committee on Electoral Matters, June 1989, Political Broadcasts and Political Disclosures Bill 1991, Senate Select Committee on Political Broadcasts and Political Disclosures, November 1991.

35 These definitional limits of 'democracy' are explored in I Chapman and R Wertheimer (eds), *Majorities and Minorities*, New York: New York University Press, 1990. See R Dworkin, *op cit* fn 12, 13: 'Democracy is not the same thing as majority rule.'

fundamental rights as a device to protect those interests, interests which not even majorities may thwart. Again, as part of democratic aspiration, it seems natural to look to courts to prevent majorities violating such rights. However, while these powerful considerations do point up important roles for the *idea* of fundamental rights as moral limits on unprincipled majorities, it is by no means clear that they legitimate a role for courts in actually developing the content rather than merely applying such right-centred rules as are deemed appropriate to protect the vulnerable interests in question.

Indeed, it is apparent that the solution of giving such power to a small number of unelected and unrepresentative persons drawn from the membership of a not always admired profession may turn out to be much more inimical to these rights than the undoubted problem with which we started. Given selfish or foolish majorities, neither courts nor Parliaments seem attractive mechanisms. If we are sure that we all know that rights are to be enforced, it is evidently proper to give courts the task of determining when such rights have been violated, but there are strong arguments for giving neither courts nor Parliaments the power to determine the content of these rights. The former are not democratically accountable at all and the latter only imperfectly. Giving either branch of state the power to determine the content of rights which trump majority decisions raises the eternal political dilemma: who is to control the controllers?

In these circumstances, the determination of fundamental rights by referendum has some advantages, although this in itself does not solve the problem of who establishes the electoral ground rules for referenda, nor does it overcome the problem of minority rights. Moreover, such referenda generally involve a decision for or against brief and unspecific rights which effectively place a great deal of unaccountable power in the hands of the interpreters who have the task of applying these indeterminate rights to specific circumstances.[36] It is more appropriate, therefore, to give the task of rendering fundamental rights more specific to the elected representatives of the people, who retain thereby at least some control over the all-important task of positivising priority rights. This removes from the courts the power to reject any legislation that can be viewed as an attempt to instantiate fundamental rights and retains the power to determine the content of fundamental rights as part of those political rights which are inseparable from democratic citizenship. Any viable justificatory theory of democracy centres on the idea of equality in the exercise of political power. Scarcely any aspect of political power is more important than the determination of what is to count as those priority interests which are to overrule and out-prioritise all other considerations. To hand this role over to a non-representative body is to hand over such a major aspect of political authority as to undermine the initial basis which is used to justify that move. To despair of the capacity of majorities to recognise rights for minorities is to despair of democracy itself. Indeed, if the populace does not retain an idea of and commitment to fundamental rights, courts are in no position to sustain the vitality and force of this essential element

---

36 On referenda, see G de Walker, *Initiative and Referendum: The People's Law*, Sydney: Centre for Independent Studies, 1987.

of democracy. Democracy was not achieved by judicial activism and is unlikely to be sustained by it. If the people and their representatives do not have a lively sense of human rights, and a strong sense of responsibility towards the values they represent, then fundamental constitutional rights, implied or otherwise, will be ineffective. And so, while it is true that democratic decision-making presupposes democratic process and majority sensitivity to the rights of minorities, it is mistaken to look to the maintenance of democratic culture and process outside of majoritarian electoral process.

In *Australian Capital Television*, the unelected judges decided what is an appropriate ordering of communication during election periods. They did so through an application of their conception of freedom of communication and its particular significance for representative government. In so doing, they took on the role of protecting democracy against a violation enacted by elected representatives. In the judgment, judicial suspicion of politicians is clear. *Per* Mason CJ:

> The Court should be astute not to accept at face value claims by the legislature and the Executive that freedom of communication, unless curtailed will bring about corruption and distortion of the political process.[37]

More particularly, the system of distributing free television time on the basis of previous elections was seen to favour the political status quo and hence the politicians who had enacted the legislation. All this fits the 'representation re-inforcing' thesis of John Hart Ely, which interprets the Bill of Rights as giving the US Supreme Court the task of sustaining the preconditions of fair elections.[38] Certainly, the High Court takes this as the paradigmatic area for the inquisition of legislative acts: 'The Court must scrutinise with scrupulous care restrictions affecting free communication in the conduct of elections for political office for it is in this area that the guarantee fulfils its primary purpose.'[39]

Now, of course, the High Court's suspicions may be justified in that the proposed reform would have benefited incumbent representatives (but not therefore always a particular political party). However, given that television time is a very scarce commodity and given the relevance of representative authority to the allocation of such a scarce resource, to say nothing of the highly restricted *de facto* access which holds at present, it is not clear what alternative system of allocation is appropriate. As Dawson J (dissenting) points out, the 'free access to the airwaves by all who wish to put a point of view during an election period is an impracticality, and, if there is to be free time, then there must be some method by which it is granted'.[40] Indeed, only by discounting the disproportionate influence of wealth is it possible to consider that the enacted reforms did not provide an appropriate move towards a 'more even playing field'. If so, this demonstrates that the court is taking a very particular and controversial line on a matter of how

---

37 *Australian Capital Television Pty Ltd v The Commonwealth* (1992) 66 AJLR 695, 696.

38 See J Ely, *Democracy and Distrust*, Cambridge, MA: Harvard University Press, 1980.

39 *Australian Capital Television Pty Ltd v The Commonwealth* (1992) 66 AJLR 695, 705.

40 *Ibid*, 725–26.

freedom of communication is to be spelt out. Further, there is no reason to believe that in so doing they were following the electors' view of fair political process as against that of their representatives.

In any case, it is part of my argument that it is corrupting to the political process that such matters are taken out of the political arena and settled by judges. Dawson J (dissenting) points out that the Constitution-makers explicitly rejected the American model (a point also emphasised by Mason CJ) and that this 'choice was deliberate and based on a faith in the democratic process to protect Australian citizens against unwarranted incursions upon the freedoms they enjoy'.[41] Dawson J does not deny that freedom of expression is as fundamental to a free society in Australia as it is in the United States, but rests his position on the Constitution's commitment to an alternative way of protecting rights: 'The fact, however, remains that in this country the guarantee of fundamental freedoms does not lie in any constitutional mandate but in the capacity of a democratic society to preserve for itself its own shared values.'[42] This seems not only an accurate account of what the Constitution implies but represents a political direction which is more thoroughly democratic than the alternatives. Dawson J again:

> To say as much is not for one moment to express disagreement with the view expressed by Murphy J that freedom of movement and freedom of communication are indispensable to any free society. It is merely to differ as to the institutions in which the founding fathers placed their faith for the protection of those freedoms.[43]

As it was Parliament rather than the High Court that enacted universal adult suffrage so it is to Parliament that we should look for dealing with the immense dangers facing democracy from the commercially dominated media, which now have an extraordinary power over public opinion. It is a matter for considerable regret that an initial (and no doubt imperfect) attempt to deal with this matter has met with such negative response under the guise of the protection of democratic rights.

## C) The ideological argument

*Australian Capital Television* demonstrates one way in which courts can claim to be impartial in relation to fundamental rights. Judges do not benefit or lose from changes in electoral process in a way that politicians may do so. More generally, courts may also be seen as detached from political conflict in a way which renders them able to take at least a relatively unbiased view of conflicts between majorities and minorities.[44] However, while such impartiality is a reason for entrusting courts with the application of specific rules to particular factual circumstances, it is not a sufficient basis for entrusting them with what is in effect legislative power, particularly when such judicial legislation is immune from review by legislatures.

---

41 *Ibid*, 722.
42 *Ibid*.
43 *Ibid*, 723–24.
44 See R Dworkin, *op cit* fn 12, 13.

The familiar arguments on this matter derive from the fact that any individual or group of individuals have their own value viewpoints, which means that they cannot be politically neutral when handed a specifically political task, such as legislation. It is no accusation of improper bias to say that courts, along with any other institutional collection of individuals, cannot be impartial in relation to the choice rather than the application of rules. It is not necessary to invoke any extreme realist argument as to the impossibility of any neutrality even in the interpretation and application of the clearest and most specific rules, in order to question unelected legislative power. Legal positivism does not require endorsing the myth that law is neutral as between social values.[45]

While this argument against implied constitutional rights does not depend on establishing that there are any specific value preferences involved in the exercise of judicial legislative power, it is arguable that the class, gender and age characteristics of court members are helpful in predicting and understanding their judgments on such matters. Certainly there are reasons for believing that court-based articulations of fundamental rights will tend to be both conservative and biased towards a negative idea of human rights, while a political process is more open to a more progressive and positive approach.[46]

In *Australian Capital Television*, the conservative tendency is illustrated in that the assumption is made that *existing* laws and practices represent a bundle of free speech rights which are the measure of what is justified in this sphere. It is the fact that the Act *alters* the existing rights of Australian citizens that makes it suspect and a *prima facie* violation of the right to freedom of communication. This is simply a status quo argument: 'Pt IIID was invalid in its entirety because of its severe impairment of the freedoms *previously* enjoyed by citizens to discuss public and political affairs and to criticise federal institutions.'[47] Further, this has the ring of truth only if freedom of communication is equated with the absence of legal prohibitions on any form of communication, the right of communication correlating with a duty on government not to prohibit any form of speech. However, fundamental rights are capable of being viewed as positive rights in the sense of correlating with the duty of government (or other governing body) to take positive steps to further communication by, for instance, the provision of free time on television. Such positive rights are not those with which courts deal routinely and reflect a creative community-oriented ideology which is not dominant within the legal profession. Indeed, although the plaintiff's submission that the provision of free time is a violation of their property rights is not explicitly addressed by the court, it is possible that the court's composition made it receptive to such views, as it is in general to US free speech jurisprudence which is similarly affected by the rights of media owners to control their own property.

Certainly, the court exhibits no awareness of ideological bias in detaching the definition of freedom of communication from the consequences of existing rules on the quantity, quality and distribution of the capacity to communicate within

---

45 See W Sadurski, *Moral Pluralism and Legal Neutrality*, Dordrecht: Kluwer, 1990.

46 See JAG Griffith, *The Politics of the Judiciary*, 4th edn, Glasgow: Collins, 1991.

47 *Australian Capital Television Pty Ltd v The Commonwealth* (1992) 66 AJLR 695, 695 (emphasis added).

the community. The centrality of the absence of prohibitions is evident in the court's disinterest in consequential arguments:

> The prohibition is no less antagonistic to and inconsistent with the freedom of political communication which is implicit in the Constitution's doctrine of representative government simply because the parliament or those in government genuinely apprehend that some persons or groups may make more, or the more effective use, of the freedom than others involved in the political process.[48]

In other words, it is formal, negative freedom that counts when fundamental rights are at stake.

## D) The argument from positivist values

If we view legal positivism as more of a prescriptive than a descriptive theory it may be characterised as the view that we are better governed through a system of explicit, precise and comprehensive rules which can be applied without recourse to the moral and political views of the adjudicators. The familiar benefits which are said to flow from this version of the rule of law are a serendipitous bundle: freedom for individuals and groups who can plan their conduct in the light of known legal consequences; formal equity in that differential treatment is according to some rule rather than official whim, with the prospect that if the rule is a good one then there will be substantive equity as well; and governmental effectiveness in that, with clear and specific binding rules, there is an increased prospect of altering conduct in an intended direction.

Less frequently noted are the democratic benefits of approximation to the positivist ideal. In its democratic form, positivism holds that the people or their elected representatives are the sole or at least the superior source of law. The positivist ideal of specific, impartially applicable rules enhances democracy by giving a focus to decisions which are sufficiently detailed to have some practical effect. In other words, choosing rules gives real and effective choices to the people or their representatives. Electing officials who are given wide discretionary power over individual matters involves a measure of accountability in so far as re-election is a matter of consequence to those officials, but far greater democratic control is obtained by requiring such officials to govern in accordance with rules which are subject to the outcome of democratic process. This control is, of course, even more important in the case of unelected officials, such as government bureaucrats and judges, who are not constrained by electoral discipline.

This last point is crucial in *Australian Capital Television*, if only in relation to the conduct of non-judicial officials, in that the absence of clear criteria for the allocation of 10% of free television time is given as a reason for rejecting the legislation. The court notes disapprovingly that the allocation of 10% of the free time depended on 'the exercise of discretion by the Tribunal'.[49] This means that it is not possible to anticipate how this discretion will be exercised.

---

48 *Ibid*, 719.
49 *Ibid*, 707.

However, essentially similar criticism may be made over allowing an interpretive discretion to courts that enables them by a process of very loose and inevitably political reasoning to make decisions which strike down legislation that is clear and precise. On the positivist model, the High Court is on strong grounds when it objects to what the Americans call 'unconstitutional vagueness', but the very same considerations count against court-centred bills of rights of court-engendered implied constitutional rights.[50]

The values that lie behind the desire for human rights can be captured within specific and neutrally applicable rules selected from existing social practices. Human rights can be positivised. Indeed, given that the crucial decisions are decisions about just what these values import, they must be positivised if they are to be effective, and if they are not to violate these values themselves, particularly those of freedom, equality and effective response to fundamental human needs. If we are given to such rhetorical talk, we might say that it is a human right to be governed by democratically chosen rules which approximate to the positivist ideals of clarity, specificity and consistency. There are fundamental human values and some of these need protection in laws of specific content.

However, this does not mean enacting bills of rights whose specific formulations become the object of legal interpretation as if this could take the place of political debate. It does mean identifying certain key valued interests which should be protected and furthered by duty-imposing rules which are adapted to particular social and economic circumstances. Thus, the Political Broadcasting and Political Disclosures Act 1991 (Cth) can be seen as an effort to instantiate a human right by democratising the election process so as to render more attainable political equality in a specific type of social circumstance. The assumption by the High Court of an arguable discretionary power to disallow such legislation is an affront to positivist ideals and a move away from the rule of law.

Of course, courts are able, albeit unsystematically, to positivise abstract rights through the standard processes of case law development, as happens routinely in those jurisdictions with entrenched rights. However, the more this happens the more the courts take on the role of legislators and, as the scope of these rights becomes interpreted in an expansive manner, there is scarcely a political decision that may not have to be re-argued in an ostensibly legal framework. Further, by drawing the courts into a more overtly political role we will in the long run reduce their capacity to fulfil their prime role of administering rules chosen for them in an impartial and non-political manner.

## CONCLUDING WORRIES AND POSSIBLE SOLUTIONS

This essay concentrates on important aspects of disquiet concerning the trend towards bills of rights and implied constitutional rights as a focus for political choice. However, it needs to be stressed that this is not to denigrate the

---

50 For the morality involved in interpreting vague rights, see M Perry, *The Constitution, the Courts and Human Rights*, New Haven, CT: Yale University Press, 1982.

importance of the idea of human rights and the significant value commitments they represent. Indeed, one of the more convincing reasons for being in favour of court-centred fundamental rights is that this may be a way of affirming the importance of these values. There is no doubt that the veneration for fundamental rights is to an extent tied in with the fact that they are seen as removed from the banalities and trade-offs of routine politics. It can be argued, therefore, that encouraging the Australian High Court to develop an implied bill of rights may have immense symbolic significance and help to regenerate a sense of the nature and significance of human rights in our society.[51]

On the other hand, the message that such an institutional arrangement gives is an essentially undemocratic one, not because majority decision-making is beyond reproach, but because it despairs of majorities being capable of thinking and voting in human rights terms, recognising the equal worth of all citizens, appreciating the need for attending to the basic needs of everyone and appreciating the importance of protecting the happiness as well as the autonomy of individuals. The symbolic impact of removing the articulation of human rights from the elected representatives of the people may be even more damaging than the symbolic advantages of setting up a countervailing political institution to oversee human rights.

Further, if we despair of politics then courts will not save us. A danger of entrenched bills of rights is that ordinary politics is given over to hard-nosed majoritarianism and unadulterated utilitarianism. It must remain part of any acceptable political culture that the democratic process in all its aspects is receptive of arguments that certain interests require the sort of protection which leads us to enshrine them in positive rights, that is, interests which are protected by specific mandatory duties on others to protect and further the interests in question without rendering these interests vulnerable to the calculation of utility (or any other calculation for that matter) in particular circumstances. The idea that only judges can be trusted to formulate and uphold rights is a facile and dangerous contention.[52]

The upshot of this discussion is the importance of finding an institutional way of emphasising and facilitating the democratic expression of human rights which does not involve major judicial input, an institutionalisation which preserves the idea of fundamental rights but reclaims it for democracy. There are a number of options and these cannot be explored here. Unentrenched bills of rights can help in focusing attention on human rights in that legislatures may be called upon to

---

51 The symbolic point is made in Dworkin, *op cit* fn 12, 56f.

52 S Chambers, 'Talking about rights: discourse ethics and the protection of rights', *Journal of Political Philosophy*, Vol 229, 1993, 247: 'People who doubt that inclusive rationalised debate is the means of strengthening our rights tradition must either doubt the capacities of human rationality or doubt that there are good reasons for justifying rights.'

reconsider their enactments if they seem to the courts to be in conflict with the current bill or charter.[53] This approach, however, still gives the judiciary the unfortunate task of reading what they can into highly unspecific rights. If, to avoid this, bills of rights are made very detailed, then they become generally indistinguishable from ordinary legislation.

A less dramatic alternative is to use the approved statement of rights in the context of a parliamentary committee which reviews all legislation in the light of the human rights perspective, something which goes neatly together with a review of draft legislation in relation to international treaty obligations emanating from the many human rights conventions to which countries are signatories.[54] To this can be added further functions for such a statement of rights, in particular their use as a guide to statutory interpretation and common law development, provided that this is subject to legislative review.

Without canvassing the pros and cons of these possibilities, I simply note that it is possible to find ways of institutionalising human rights considerations without making the courts the prime locus of their substantive articulation. A regard for humane values, and even a commitment to the ideal of autonomy which underlies much of the human rights conception, point definitively to the need for keeping the power of defining the content of fundamental rights within the mainstream of democratic politics. It is important that this be done, if only because it may serve to inhibit moves into what may be seen as a human rights vacuum within states that lack bills of rights on the American model, a vacuum which is more a matter of international comparison than actual neglect of human rights. Indeed, a main worry relating to the current Australian development is that genuinely democratically led human rights developments may be struck down by the High Court on the basis of its own unlegitimated ideology. This can only bring the ideal of human rights into disrepute, to the ultimate detriment of the humane values and human interests that they ought to serve.

---

53 As in the New Zealand Bill of Rights Act, 1990.

54 For one suggestion, see D Kinley, *The European Convention on Human Rights: Compliance without Incorporation*, Aldershot: Dartmouth, 1993; also A Lester, *Democracy and Individual Rights*, London: Fabian Society, 1968.

# 10

# HUMAN RIGHTS: A CULTURE OF CONTROVERSY

Many arguments in favour of constitutionally entrenched bills of rights are undermined by the inherently controversial nature of human rights with respect to their content, their form and their valence. Even in the case of civil and political rights, the concretisation of rights at the level of specificity required to decide particular cases must always be politically and morally controversial. There is no accepted moral or legal method that can be utilised to give the requisite objectivity to the value choices inherent in human rights jurisprudence. Positivisation of human rights increases their utility but compromises their moral status. It follows that legitimate articulation of human rights requires ongoing democratic dialogue and decision-making. Although perceived as a stop-gap measure, the UK Human Rights Act 1998 could facilitate an enduring partnership between courts and parliaments, placing human rights more firmly on the political agenda and establishing a proper balance between the inputs of courts and parliaments, which recognises that the development of positivised human rights must be primarily located in electorally-based politics.

The Human Rights Act 1998 may turn out to be a minor or a major change in the Constitution of the UK but, either way, it has to be viewed as part of a global trend towards the legal institutionalisation of the idea of human rights. This can only be welcomed if it places the identification and protection of fundamental human interests nearer the centre of the public agenda, but the entrenchment of court-based determinations of the content and form to be given to the concept of basic rights is a potentially dangerous development to the extent that it leads to the juridification of politics and the distancing of the prioritisation and concretisation of human rights from the domain of representative politics. Human rights will be the weaker if they are seen as the impositions of controversial interpretations of basic rights without the scope of democratic accountability.

The alternatives facing the UK with respect to the European Convention on Human Rights (ECHR) are quite restricted in the context of its membership of the European Union. Some constitutional changes are clearly required to remove the anomalies arising from British courts being unable to take significant cognisance of the ECHR even though its citizens may challenge their decisions at the European Court of Human Rights. The Human Rights Act 1998 appears to be at the modest end of the range of alternatives, but it may be no more than a staging post to a fully-fledged domestic bill of rights, in which case there will be a difficult debate on which specific rights and what mode of entrenchment are to be adopted. In fact, the emergence of a so called home-grown bill of rights seems an increasingly unlikely outcome as the problems of drawing up such a bill become more apparent. If a stop-gap Human Rights Act turns out to be a more permanent feature of the British Constitution, the ECHR may continue to have relatively slight impact on British courts, but its import will depend largely on the way that British judiciaries respond to the opportunities which it creates for more activist judicial roles. There is a possibility that the Act could encourage judicial creativity not only in statutory interpretation but also in the development of the common law in line with European human rights jurisprudence.

Whatever the outcome of the current constitutional fluidity, it is timely to reflect on the choice of mechanisms available to a country with a strong tradition of parliamentary democracy in adapting to an existing regional human rights system. This involves examining the shifting lines of debate about the nature and function of human rights and revisiting some of the familiar philosophical problems which dog the human rights movement by casting doubt on the epistemology of human rights. The principal point deriving from this reflection is that no institutional mechanisms that neglect the existence of radical and reasonable controversy as to the content, form, and valence of basic rights can be justified. A cognate suggestion is that there are aspects of the Human Rights Act 1998 which may serve to promote fruitful political dialogue between courts as primary monitors and parliaments as primary legislators of human rights, a partnership which permits the development of human rights law to reflect a fuller range of interests than the ECHR currently encompasses. If the use made of the new judicial powers is temperate and sensitive to the wider democratic context, it may turn out that there are good reasons for accepting something like the current Act as a working compromise between legal and political inputs to the articulation of human rights law.

## HUMAN RIGHTS CONTROVERSIES

Although the nature and significance of human rights has been debated for so long and in so many spheres, the lines of disagreement on the best way to conceive and institutionalise human rights are still far from clear. We may view the shifting areas of engagement in the dimensions of constitutional law, philosophical scrutiny and ideological compromise.[1]

In the constitutional debate, we have passed the stage where it is simply assumed that to be supportive of the human rights movement it is necessary to advocate a United States-style constitution with an entrenched bill of rights and a judicial override of legislative enactments. There is at least the beginnings of a debate within the human rights field as to the best method for the identification, articulation, and enforcement of human rights, particularly amongst those who give particular weight to the right of political self-determination.[2] Although it is widely assumed that, in recent times, courts have tended to make more

---

1 Much of the background theory for this essay draws on TD Campbell, *The Left and Rights: A Conceptual Analysis of the Idea of Socialist Rights*, London: Routledge and Kegan Paul, 1983. See Chapter 6.

2 Thus, C Nino, *The Constitution of Deliberative Democracy*, New Haven, CT: Yale University Press, 1993; and J Waldron, 'A rights-based critique of constitutional rights', *Oxford Journal of Legal Studies*, Vol 13, 1993, 18.

progressive decisions than legislatures on human rights, this has not always been the case and is far from guaranteed in the future.[3] It is also frequently acknowledged that changing the role of courts can have far-reaching and predictable effects on the nature of judicial appointments and on the conduct of those appointed to 'interpret' superficially attractive but worryingly vague statements of principle. History amply demonstrates that courts can thwart as well as facilitate progressive social, political, and economic changes. Indeed, it may be that those who turn in disillusionment from politicians to judges may find that the latter can offer little protection against the resurgences of regressive political movements which are more likely to emerge when we reduce our expectations of representative politics with respect to the furtherance and defence of fundamental civil, political, social, cultural and economic rights.

Nevertheless, while it is no longer axiomatic amongst supporters of human rights reform that such rights are best sustained through court-administered bills of rights, there is still an unjustifiably high burden of proof placed on those who are worried by the long-term constitutional consequences of making the progressive delineation of individual rights primarily the responsibility of courts by enacting constitutional changes which, it is generally agreed, transfer very significant political powers to courts, either within or without the boundaries of the state. Such far-reaching constitutional development may seem attractive, especially at a time when politics and politicians are held in such low regard, but their eventual impact on how citizens go about settling their political differences may well be seriously detrimental to electoral politics and thus to the legitimacy of governments. Further, it needs to be acknowledged that changes which entrench judicial power are harder to reverse than they are to implement. There is, therefore, reason to examine very carefully alternative ways of enunciating, protecting and furthering basic human interests.

In the philosophical debate, we have passed the stage where human rights are automatically associated with natural law and held to be incompatible with adherence to legal positivism.[4] Supporters of human rights do not now generally endorse a naturalistic moral epistemology whereby the content of human rights is read off from the essence of human nature or some religious view thereof. Many legal positivists welcome the use of human rights rhetoric to identify core societal goals and have no problems either with the institutionalisation of specified rights and duties as lexically prior to any conflicting legislation or with such rights and duties being given a special status within a democratic system of governance. Indeed, it is possible to see the progressive institutionalisation of human rights through the development by human rights courts of juristic doctrines and case law as a positivisation of purely moral rights whereby intangible generalised values are given specific content. The human rights rules thus concretised by the courts gain authority from a newly identified social source of law. In identifying a

---

3 For instance, see D Tucker, 'Natural law or common law: human rights in Australia,' in B Galligan and C Sampford (eds), *Rethinking Human Rights*, Sydney: Federation Press, 1997, 120–43.

4 For further analysis, see TD Campbell, *The Legal Theory of Ethical Positivism*, Aldershot: Dartmouth, 1996, 161–87.

social origin for human rights law, these developments may be seen as compatible with the 'sources thesis' that is commonly taken to define the theory of legal positivism.[5] On the other hand, the often nebulous content of human rights prescriptions comes up against the problems that such highly indeterminate legal norms present to a positivist ideal of the rule of law as an impartially administered system of clear, precise and determinate rules. In general, a positivist approach to human rights has the advantage of encouraging the creation of specific rules capable of guiding state conduct and providing bases for predictable remedies for violations of human rights without claiming that these can be deduced from self-evident or uncontroversial premises.

However, although legal positivists may welcome the moves to concretise or positivise human rights by rendering them more specific and justiciable,[6] this same process may also be seen as a way of weakening the capacity of courts to develop human rights law in accordance with enduring or emerging moral ideals.[7] The development of case law snares human rights in the tangled web of precedent and legal authority, thus threatening to devitalise its moral force in a way which is historically exemplified by the progressive positivisation of equity. There is therefore a powerful body of opinion in favour of having human rights law expressed only in the form of vague prescriptions which invite moral deliberation and textually unfettered discretionary decision-making by human rights courts without a major prior commitment to existing case law. From this point of view, to resist the creation of the massive judicial power inherent in such a discretionary model is taken to be a rejection of human rights *per se* rather than an attempt to uphold the rule of law through distinguishing the power to formulate rules from the duty to apply them.

Such a system of moral supervision is defensible, however, only to the extent that there is accessible knowledge of objective universal values available to courts. It may be seen as an achievement of the human rights movement that there is a widespread belief that such knowledge is indeed available. However, as we will see, this neo-natural law philosophy with its high confidence in the accessibility of human rights to human reason and the capacity of judges to reach an objective assessment of the content and priority of such rights far outstrips any available epistemological foundations which would justify taking such issues outside the domain of political disagreement.

In the ideological debate, we have passed the stage when human rights are associated primarily with a form of extreme libertarianism, wherein the essential purpose of human rights is to corral the activities of government into a highly constricted domain in order that individuals, either alone or in free association, may pursue their own good in their own way. While some demands for

---

5 J Raz, *The Authority of Law: Essays on Law and Morality*, Oxford: OUP, 1979, 47ff.

6 For examples, see TD Campbell *et al* (eds), *Human Rights: From Rhetoric to Reality*, London: Blackwell, 1986.

7 As in R Wasserstrom, 'Rights, human rights and racial discrimination', *Journal of Philosophy*, Vol 61, 1964, 630. See also J Feinberg, 'The nature and value of rights', *Journal of Value Enquiry*, Vol 4, 1970, 243.

court-articulated human rights do stem from the ideal of minimal government, whereby the egalitarian welfare policies sometimes favoured by popular majorities are seen as endangering fundamental rights and freedoms, it is now widely recognised that state activity is often required to realise many of the priority interests of all human beings and that these interests have as much right to be upheld as fundamental rights as the negative liberties of the traditional liberal state.[8]

It is true that the division between civil and political rights, on the one hand, and economic, social and cultural rights, on the other, remains politically salient. This division is marked at the international level in the different status of the International Covenant on Civil and Political Rights and the International Covenant on Economic, Social and Cultural Rights and at the European level in the distinction between the ECHR and the European Social Charter, which represent the continuing tendencies to regard civil liberties as intrinsically more basic than material needs and to assume that the prime role of the human rights movement is to limit the evil that governments do rather than encourage governments to become more proactive in the cause of fundamental human interests. Nevertheless, we may note the formal commitment of the United Nations to the equal importance of both types of rights[9] and the repeated attempts to demonstrate that there is no hard and fast distinction between costless civil and political rights and expensive economic and social rights which could justify the mandatory status of the former and the purely aspirational status of the latter.[10]

Moreover, current human rights regimes are beginning to have a dated look in that their emphasis remains on the sins of government rather than the evils of capitalism, if we may still use that term to identify the contemporary forms of private economic power. There is nothing in the concept, as distinct from the history, of human rights which requires us to identify states as the prime violators of such rights, and there is a serious incompleteness in an ideology which purports to identify and protect basic human interests while failing to address the suffering which is perpetrated by increasingly globalised private economic power. This is not to say that human rights are incompatible with capitalism any more than they are incompatible with government. Rather, it is to assert that economic power has the same systematic ambivalence for human good and ill as does political power.

There is a tendency to assume that the demise of Soviet-style communism represents a triumph of the way in which human rights have evolved within the jurisdictions of the Cold War victors. The globalisation of liberalism is often portrayed as the globalisation of libertarianism. However, freeing up the

---

8 Thus, C Fabre, 'Constitutionalising social rights', *Journal of Political Philosophy*, Vol 6, 1998, 263, 283: 'If one advocates constitutional civil and political rights as well as social rights, then one must advocate *constitutional* social rights.'

9 Vienna Declaration and Program of Action, *Human Rights Law Journal*, Vol 14, 1993, 352.

10 H Steiner and P Alston (eds), *International Human Rights in Context*, Oxford: OUP, 1996, 256–328.

association of human rights with libertarianism or negative liberalism has been assisted rather than retarded by the dissolution of the Cold War which has increased the prospect of new ideological configurations. The specifics of human rights no longer need to be drawn with an eye to their role in an ideological battle between capitalism and communism.

In this debate, the ideological implications of rights discourse are distorted by those who consider rights to be incompatible with life in a caring community of persons whose conduct is characterised by a degree of altruism and goodwill to others. This critique develops from Marx's scathing denunciation of inalienable rights as bourgeois ideology and is now common in communitarian and feminist writing.[11] These sceptical views of rights have much historical justification but miss the point, which is crucial for assessing the potential of rights, that the interests that are identified and protected by rights need not be construed in terms of narrow self-interest, but can include interests that caring persons have in assisting and supporting other people, interests which have a strong claim to be fundamental in a society of social beings.[12]

Moreover, the fact that citizens have rights does not require that they exercise these rights purely in their own interest. Indeed, it does not require that they exercise their rights as a matter of course since, in the great majority of cases, having a right includes the right to waive that right.[13] Critical discussions of the culture of rights too readily assume that the culture of rights is the culture of individual egotism, which encourages and promotes people to assert their own interests in conflict with those of others. It is possible to conceive of a system of rights as a framework of rules that can be drawn upon to promote fundamental human interests without a culture in which the citizens seek only their own self-advancement. Rights may be instrumental for a variety of purposes, including the capacity to confer benefits on others within a culture which includes a role for autonomous judgment by morally good people as to how and when they exercise their rights. A culture of rights need not be a culture of complaint.

There is another fascinating coincidence of seemingly incompatible trends in current political ideology in the acceptance of political globalisation in the form of democratic systems on the American model in conjunction with the affirmation of the neglected significance of cultural diversity. The circle is squared formally by affirming the universal significance of cultural diversity and materially by requiring that a democratic system ought not to permit rules or practices which discriminate on certain unacceptable grounds, such as race, ethnicity, national origins or gender. This leaves unresolved what to do with those cultural differences which embody incompatible positions on such matters as basic criminal law, the role of religious authority or the political legitimacy of different

---

11 For a balanced view of the latter debate see E Kingdom, *What's Wrong with Rights*, Edinburgh: Edinburgh University Press, 1991.

12 TD Campbell, *op cit* fn 1, 83.

13 MJ Meyer, 'When not to claim your rights: the abuse and the virtuous use of rights', *Journal of Political Philosophy*, Vol 5, 1997, 14.

forms of government. Nor does it enable us to deal with conflicting views of what are and what are not acceptable grounds for differential treatment. It also leaves unresolved the tension between the idea of protecting individual members of a cultural group from unacceptable discrimination in the wider society and the idea of promoting the distinctiveness of cultures which encourage precisely such discriminations within their own groups.

In summary, it remains true to say that it is often assumed that to be opposed to allocating power over the definition of human rights to courts is tantamount to being hostile to human rights as such, despite the significance and implications of the basic right to self-determination underlying all democratic theory. It is also assumed that human rights are and must remain primarily moral or natural rights in that courts must use their moral judgments or knowledge of natural law to determine which legislative enactments are permitted. This goes with the further assumption that human rights can be based on some objectivist morality whereby, through religious authority, moral intuition or natural science, a society, or identified segments of it, can, by adopting the proper epistemology of morals, be trusted to come up with the 'correct' reading and import of such matters as 'the right to life' or 'the right to food'. In this context, there are still those who equate relativism, the thesis that what is good and right for one group may not be good and right for another group, with subjectivism, the thesis that the epistemology of moral judgment privileges individual preferences, thus undermining the moral universalism on which human rights are based. Finally, it is also often assumed that a devotion to human rights is a commitment to some version of libertarianism whereby the interests of the non-responsible individual are paramount within the political system.

All these assumptions can be challenged, and need to be debated if we are to think clearly about how the future of human rights is best secured and which constitutional and cultural directions to take if we wish to promote our preferred versions of the content, form and force of such rights as we believe we ought to have. In making such challenges and furthering such debate, we must take note of the contestability of almost every aspect of human rights and look for ways of institutionalising human rights which retain primary political control over determining the content, form and valence of human rights within representative politics, and do so in a manner which recognises the inherently controversial nature of the specification of such rights, leaving scope for the further assimilation of social and economic rights and permitting a measure of cultural diversity within the domain of human rights.

## THE EPISTEMOLOGY OF HUMAN RIGHTS

The philosophical problems for human rights centre on the lack of a clear method for identifying the content of such rights and the associated phenomenon of ideological capture, whereby the all-important details of human rights are filled out in an evaluatively partisan way. Problematic also are the confusions arising from the existence of different conceptions of the form of rights and their correlative obligations, if any, with respect to their nature (for example, negative or positive) or their status (for example, moral or legal), matters which have significant political consequences.

It is difficult to grapple with these epistemological issues without adopting a position with respect to the ontology of human rights, the issue as to whether rights have some sort of independent and objective existence, as part, perhaps, of some socially pre-existent natural law, or whether they are entirely creatures of human creativity to be moulded and developed to human designs without the restrictions of a metaphysical reality which precedes and underpins them. Overlapping with both these areas of uncertainty are the specific conundrums involved with the alleged universality of human rights at a time when individual and group diversity is also a prized value.

These philosophical problems should not be ignored because they are expressed in an abstract and theoretical manner. Putting such issues to one side because there is general agreement that there is a role for human rights discourse in contemporary political systems ignores the practical problems which arise from genuine controversy over the content and form of human rights. Many questionable constitutional arguments are put forward by people who simply assume that we can know in advance what human rights are and have only to determine how best they may be enforced and promoted. Pronouncements are routinely made about the relative merits of courts and assemblies as guardians of human rights on the basis that we can inspect the outcomes of both approaches and observe which better secures the assumed objectives.[14] However, without a prior consensus as to precisely what these objectives are, which would require agreement at a level of specificity which is precise enough to guide conduct, such arguments carry little weight. In the absence of such a consensus, every constitutional recommendation must be made on the premise of the inherently controversial nature of the content and form of human rights at the level of implementation. Consensus on generalised standards and abstract affirmations is an inadequate basis for recommending any particular mechanism for the articulation and realisation of human rights.

The epistemological and ontological deficits of human rights not only undermine superficial arguments in favour of this or that method of institutionalising rights, but are manifest in the increasing controversiality of judicial decisions in the human rights field. It is the philosophical problems of human rights which explain the practical difficulties encountered in the attempts of courts and governments to reach evidently correct and widely accepted interpretations of fundamental rights in such realms as human reproduction, criminal law and procedure, positive discrimination, euthanasia, racial vilification and pornography.

There are practical solutions to these philosophical problems. These involve giving identifiable persons the authority to determine the meaning to be ascribed to human rights as they are to be applied. Human rights then become what

---

14 An example is S Freeman, 'Constitutional democracy and the legitimacy of judicial review', *Law and Philosophy*, Vol 9, 1990, 327. The appropriate critique is well made in J Waldron, 'Freeman's defense of judicial review', *Law and Philosophy*, Vol 13, 1994, 27.

specified courts, referenda or parliaments say they are. Disagreement is overcome by constitutionally authorised decision-making. Human rights, in the specific meaning in which they have application to actual social circumstances, are what the validating authority determines. Such positivisation of abstract human rights greatly assists their implementation, but the very act of concreting rights undermines their moral authority and reduces their capacity to provide a basis for external assessments of the workings of legal and political systems.

The continuing and exponential growth of human rights institutionalisation illustrates these pragmatic solutions to some of the theoretical problems. There may be no acceptable epistemology of human rights, but once we have positive rules and principles carrying the authorised human rights label then we can deploy familiar methods of legal reasoning to come to a determination of the content of human rights. We can then ascribe to human rights such ontological status as we ascribe to positive law in general. In this way, the development of human rights as a political and legal process appears to bypass philosophical anxieties. However, as we institutionalise human rights, they become just another set of rules and principles and just another set of human organisations which embody just another set of negotiated and enforced compromises between the dominant values of the time. Positivising human rights undermines the power of the concept to provide a source of morally imperious critiques of ordinary laws and legal systems.

The robustness of conflicting analyses of human rights makes it clear that neither the content nor the form of such rights as we wish to identify as 'human' or 'fundamental' are uncontroversial. Nor is there any methodology that can provide a more objective or more convincing way of settling these controversies than is available in the case of attempts to settle disagreements about any other set of rights and duties. Human rights, as positivised in conventions, codes or bills, have the potential to be used for or against the particular very different ideals treasured by all those who are prepared to sign up to some highly generalised commitments to human liberty, equality and wellbeing. Everything depends on precisely how the abstractions are given precision in relation to specific situations and how this is to be done cannot be deduced from the concept of human rights itself.

The basis of philosophical criticism of the idea of human rights has not been hostility to promoting the ideals of equality, liberty and the rule of law, nor has it involved rejecting the analytical and political goals of giving these rhetorical conceptions increased clarity and specificity. Rather, the basic criticism is that the identification and articulation of human rights in a form in which they have some application to real life circumstances is an inherently difficult and controversial matter on which rational individuals, even from within the same culture, can radically disagree. There are major choices to be made about what sort of rights we want, in form, content and application. Philosophical criticism is targeted at a naïve universalism which confuses agreement on vague statements of principle and evocations of positive emotional responses to abstract verbal formula with consensus as to how we ought to treat each other in practice and what sort of political and economic conduct is unacceptable. This basic criticism can take many different forms.

Thus, individual rights may be analysed in ways which demonstrate that agreement on the same formula masks disagreement about the meaning of that formula. The right to life is taken by some to mean the right not to be killed in any circumstance, thus excluding capital punishment and compulsory military service, and by others it is hedged around with numerous provisos and exceptions which legitimate the use of lethal force. For some people, the right to life applies to all stages and forms of human life, from conception through to brainstem death in a living body. Others prefer a qualitative definition of the sort of human life to which we have a right, involving a certain level of consciousness and/or capacity for thought and choice. There are those who interpret the right to life as the right not to be killed and those who see it as mandating the provision of the necessities of life, including adequate sustenance and medical care. Such differences of view amongst those who concur in affirming 'the' right to life can be traced to differing philosophical and political views, none of which exclude endorsing human rights as the basis of humane treatment and political legitimacy and none of which contravenes the standard catch phrases of 'human dignity' or 'equal concern and respect'.

Epistemological approaches to the critique of naïve universalism concentrate on demonstrating the theoretical and practical difficulties of establishing a way of selecting the content and form of rights. To survey this field would be to take in the whole moral philosophy, which may be seen as a cyclical history of failed attempts to establish an objective basis for moral judgment that has a foundation beyond the appeal to norms of an established culture. The strongest argument in favour of moral objectivity has always been the felt certainty of selected moral 'intuitions'. The insurmountable objection to the appeal to subjective certainty has always been the diverse content to which such certainty adheres.[15]

In recent times, the search for a universal foundation for moral norms has manifested itself in the attempt to establish an agreed basis in certain aspects of moral experience, such as basic rights, and concede irreversible diversity on other moral topics, such as the content of the good life. The objective is to identify a limited scope for justice or human rights, a core of self-evident foundational rights which can be set apart from politics and exempted from the subjectivist critique. If successful, this approach has profound political implications since it suggests that determinations of basic rights can be attained by a suitably impartial elite, while leaving the details of the good life to be worked out in the wider democratic process.

Unsurprisingly, the most powerful versions of the distinctive epistemology of rights are the products of a jurisdiction with a long history of an entrenched bill of rights. The most audacious effort in this regard is Rawls's rather short-lived claim to have revived the classical enlightenment methodologies to the point of providing a way of reaching justified agreement with respect to justice, including

15 The best brief account of this debate is to be found in JL Mackie, *Ethics: Inventing Right and Wrong*, Harmondsworth: Penguin, 1977.

the content of fundamental rights.[16] Interestingly, it was in the period when the Rawls-led return to substantive political philosophy was rehabilitated after the sceptical critiques of linguistic philosophers that academic defences of universal human rights re-emerged to give legitimacy to those who sought to commend a non-ideological consensus on human rights which could and should be extracted from the mess of actual politics.

Not much remains in current moral and political philosophy of the claims to provide a reliable epistemology of rights. Rawls has retreated to redescribe his theory as a pragmatic political technique within a certain type of liberal state.[17] In the legal community, however, there is still considerable attachment to Ronald Dworkin's version of the distinction between the right and the good, according to which there are matters of fundamental principle that are at base matters of individual rights which manifest the principle of equal concern and respect and are logically distinct from the valuations which focus on desirable outcomes of public policy.[18] In Dworkin's analysis, principles and rights have epistemological and therefore constitutional priority over competing views of the good life about which politicians and citizens may reasonably be left to contend. Dworkin's approach is saved from the unimaginable abstractions of Rawls's hypothetical original position, from which we are intended to construct the content of basic rights, by being historically tied to the progressive articulation of law within actual jurisdictions. His basic rights are constructed from an interpretation of particular legal traditions. From the point of view of human rights, however, this compromises the moral independence of the rights, for they are tied to the contingencies of a particular culture. Congruence with even selected strains from a specific legal history does not cut much philosophical ice as a basis for choice of rights within that jurisdiction, let alone in relation to transcultural objectivity.

The most promising theories of objectivist moral epistemology have been those that focus on information, choice and impartiality. The compelling attraction of Rawls's initial theory of justice as fairness derived from the way in which it associates preferred moral norms with being better informed, freely chosen and impartially arrived at. However, while moral judgments based on factual error can be rejected, information is in itself the object rather than the origin of moral judgment, for such judgment is an assertion of the acceptability or otherwise of certain states of affairs. Similarly, choice cannot in itself be a test of moral rightness since particular choices are themselves objects of moral assessment. Only the formal qualities of certain choices, such as its impartiality, can endow choice with moral status with respect to the content of that choice. By default, therefore, impartiality becomes the key category in the attempt to provide

16 J Rawls, *A Theory of Justice*, Oxford: Clarendon Press, 1971, marked the restoration of confidence in Kantian style methods as a means to obtaining objective consensus on basic rights and has had an important justificatory role in many defences of judicial review of legislative action.

17 J Rawls, *Political Liberalism*, New York: Columbia University Press, 1993.

18 The basic constitutional implications of Dworkinian jurisprudence are made clear in his influential essay: R Dworkin, *A Bill of Rights for Britain*, London: Chatto and Windus, 1990. See also his *Freedom's Law: The Moral Reading of the American Constitution*, Cambridge, MA: Harvard University Press, 1996.

objective bases for moral judgment, and impartiality is certainly a powerful idea with respect to the acceptability of moral judgments. Indeed, there is a good case for taking impartiality as a defining feature of morality, in that it is possible to classify an individual's preference for herself as amoral as well as immoral unless equivalent self-preference is allowed to all similar persons, hence the continuing force of Kant's universalisability principle.

However, the long history of critique of Kant's position and the shorter but more intense examination of Rawls's theory amply demonstrate that there is more to morality than impartiality. Partiality for one person or group of persons over another may exclude some putative moral positions as simply selfish, but such impartiality is compatible with an infinity of different evaluative commitments. Impartiality may take us as far as equality of rights but it does not get to the core of which rights are to be allocated on a basis of equality. Information, choice and impartiality may be essential ingredients in progressing moral belief systems; they do not in themselves settle any significant value disagreements.

The fact that human rights have flourished without sustained philosophical approval may be taken to prove the perennial appeal of the former and the general irrelevance of the latter. However, the philosophical scepticism concerning naïve enthusiasm for allegedly apolitical human rights is in no way undermined by their political popularity. The theoretical problems identified by critical philosophers manifest themselves in real-life controversies which threaten the usefulness and stability of human rights regimes.

## IDEOLOGY AND HUMAN RIGHTS

The international growth of the human rights movement since the end of the Second World War has been phenomenal with respect to its ideological acceptance, if not in relation to international compliance with its standards. This growth has come about alongside and despite consistent criticism of the philosophical base of key concept: the idea of universal, inalienable individual rights which have the epistemological characteristic of self-evidence, in that their content and form are inherently uncontroversial amongst reasonable people.

The moral power of the human rights ideology derives from the consensus that there are certain things that people have done to each other in the course of human history which are atrocious and ought not to be repeated. What may be called the torture paradigm connects human rights with a shared perception of totally unacceptable evils which are never justified and undermine the claims to political legitimacy of any system of government.[19] The constitutional insight of the human rights movement is that the determination of when these atrocities have been committed cannot be left to governments themselves, since they have

---

19 This is not to say that the question of what constitutes torture from the perspective of human rights is uncontested. See C MacKinnon, 'On torture: a feminist perspective on human rights', in K Mahoney and P Mahoney (eds), *Human Rights in the Twenty-First Century: A Global Challenge*, Dordrecht: Martinus Nijhoff, 1992, 21.

been the prime perpetrators. On the torture paradigm of human rights, setting up a superior court to adjudicate on the evils perpetrated by government seems warranted as a mechanism of accountability through procedurally acceptable findings of fact.

However, the scope of human rights has, with good reason, been extended beyond a few apparently uncontroversial evils characteristically brought about by the power of governments, and now covers a broad range of social, civil, political and economic interests which impact on every aspect of life in a modern society. Moreover, such rights are analysed as involving correlative duties that call for positive actions to secure the identified interests.[20] Thus, the human right to health not only prioritises health interests but places burdens on government to ensure that basic health care is available to all on the basis of medical need, irrespective of capacity to pay, and affirms that claims based on such rights have equal valence to other human rights-based interests. What may be called the health paradigm of human rights develops not only the content of human rights in the direction of wellbeing but also, in the shift from negative to positive rights, alters their form, and, with respect to relative importance in the deployment of scarce resources, their valence.[21]

The torture paradigm differs from the health paradigm not only with respect to the content and form of the rights to be protected but in relation to the dynamic of the human rights enterprise. In the torture paradigm, the emphasis is on achieving conformity to agreed minimal standards of conduct, such as the elimination of torture. The health paradigm is more of a developmental model which sees the role of human rights institutions domestically to be one of progressive development of law and social attitudes with respect to human equalities and the realisation of fundamental human interests, but nevertheless insisting on the imperative force of a basic minimum of achievement in relation to the available resources of the society. The health care paradigm is misrepresented when it is considered merely aspirational, for it relates not simply to ideals of a desirable form of social life, but represents genuine attempts to identify minimal acceptabilities of equal import to the original civil and political rights.

The shift to the health paradigm gives normality to the idea that all rights are costly to protect and brings a different emphasis to the interpretation and enforcement of civil and political rights, emphasising, for instance, that legal aid may be as much a prerequisite of a fair trial as the assumption of innocence. This fusion of the torture and health models of human rights serves to identify not simply the priority but the required goals for democratic governments. In total, the combination of torture and health care models require a society which is, for instance, free of discrimination, committed to the equal development of all, makes decisions only after open discussion, holds fair and open elections, and provides for quality education, culture and health care. Human rights thus become highly

---

20 See M Menlowe and A McCall Smith (eds), *The Duty to Rescue*, Aldershot: Dartmouth, 1993.

21 These themes are explored in VA Leay, 'Implications of a right to health', in K Mahoney and P Mahoney, *op cit* fn 19.

inclusive, omitting little that may be identified as a fundamental human interest. Moreover, there is nothing in the concept of human rights other than the perceived importance of the rights in question to bring to a close extensions of the scope of the domain of human rights from the torture to the health paradigm. Thus, in the international sphere we have already moved beyond social, economic and cultural rights to what is referred to as a third tier of human rights, involving collective entitlements to such things as development and environmental enhancement.[22]

While the progressive move towards equalising the importance of torture and health paradigms lends credibility to the ideological neutrality of rights discourse, it does exacerbate the epistemological problem of identifying the proper mode for determining the content, form and valence of such rights. Moreover, it produces intractable decision-problems in settling the inevitable clashes between rights and how far they are defeasible in the light of economic and political circumstances. Controversies of this sort reach a degree of sustained disagreement to the point where it seems reasonable to despair of the rights approach as an appropriate way to institutionalise the settlement of value disputes in society. Certainly, the task of monitoring and applying rights is overtaken by the need to determine their content, form and valence. In these circumstances, there must be heightened concerns about locating the articulation and development of such abstract rights in judicial organs, whose impartiality may enhance their capacity to make independent findings of fact and apply existing law, but in no way qualifies them to make value judgments on behalf of the community.

## CONSTITUTING HUMAN RIGHTS

The superior mystique of human rights is that they have been regarded as being in a class of their own, as in some way an exception to the contestability of other normative choices. If this is not the case then there is every reason to be cautious about exempting human rights from the normal processes of democratic scrutiny. While it may be an excellent strategy for the furtherance of equality, liberty and wellbeing to identify certain laws as more fundamental than others in that the community wishes to give them priority over any other norms with which they may come into conflict, we have noted that we cannot assume that there is some special epistemological access to human rights which makes it safe to abrogate their articulation to an entrenched legal process. There may be other more sceptical but ultimately more efficacious methods of giving institutional expression to the insight that it is important to identify and protect fundamental

22 These 'third generation' rights are not, so far, serious contenders for inclusion in justiciable human rights law, but there is no reason why, for instance, the right of non-nationals to humanitarian assistance, or certain environmental rights, should not be a candidate for juristic human rights and given equal weight to certain civil and political rights ('first generation'), and most economic and social rights ('second generation'). For the terminology, see K Vasak, 'Les differentes categories des Droits de l'Homme', in A Lapeyre *et al* (eds), *Les Dimensiones Universelles des Droits de l'Homme*, Vol 2, 1990, 297.

human interests and ensure that these are not lost sight of in the give and take of everyday politics.

Constitutional questions focus specifically on who should exercise which political powers in a jurisdiction, with legal interest centring on the separation of powers, particularly between legislative and judicial. We have seen that there is reason to doubt whether there is a readily delineable domain of human rights that can safely be assumed to be insufficiently controversial to excise from the electorally-oriented political systems of democratic accountability. Institutions set up to enforce the self-evident rights of citizens are not fitted to the role of deciding what the content and valence of these rights is to be. However, instead of being tribunals primarily to determine questions of fact as to human rights violations, human rights courts have become *de facto* legislatures, able to determine what is and what is not to count as a violation of human rights. While it seems intuitively right that we cannot entrust safeguarding democracy to those who currently hold elective office, since they have an evident interest in subverting the democratic process in order to retain and enhance their existing power, it seems equally clear that there is no reason why elite legal opinion as to the practical import of abstract rights should be allowed to determine what is and what is not democratic. Moreover, given the ever enlarging scope of human rights, court-based entrenchment of human rights in general is even more incongruous when this involves judicial settlement of political priorities in so many areas of political disagreement.

It is not suggested that there are easy solutions to these problems. The problem of guarding the guardians is as old as political philosophy itself. As Hobbes so graphically identified, human societies suffer the tragic fate of being vulnerable to the political and economic organisations on which they depend. We must expect, therefore, that there are intractable antinomies at the core of choices about institutionalising human rights. It is always possible to find good arguments against locating bottom-line power to any one locus or combination of loci. Protecting minorities seems to require endangering the legitimate interests of majorities and other minorities. Forms of entrenchment which require large majorities are ineffective with respect to the protection of highly unpopular minorities, intolerance often being enhanced by a dominant consensus. We may distrust politicians because they have short-term objectives and vested interests in the denial of democratic rights, but we may have more problems with the rule of lawyers, a somewhat despised occupational group with a proven record of professional self-interest. Judiciaries are normally excepted from this low esteem, but where they are given major political powers, their decisions come under public scrutiny and their special expertise (in the law) is questioned as the exclusive criterion of appointment. Given reasonable laws, judges are accepted as socially beneficial while they act positivistically, but not otherwise.[23] If we then go to the people by way of referenda, we arrive at the antithesis of the protection of minorities. Populist views on the specifics of social issues are rarely in accordance

---

23 See Chapters 3 and 4.

with the goals of most human rights activists, yet consent in some form must be the ultimate foundation of all political legitimacy.

These difficult choices are all manifest in the institutionalisation of human rights. If we retain only relatively costless negative rights then we under-emphasise social and economic interests. If we stress basic social and economic interests as equally significant human rights then we take judges into areas with which they are not equipped to deal and give them power over resources for which they are not responsible. If we seek to positivise human rights in a manner which accords with a version of the rule of law that favours predictability, uniformity and impartiality in applying and securing human rights, then the higher law becomes ordinary law, subject to all the weaknesses of over- and under-inclusiveness, legalism and inflexibility. If we leave human rights as open-ended invitations to the exercise of moral judgment by the current legal authorities, this undermines the usefulness of the legal system in providing a stable framework of expectations and remedies. If we emphasise the symbolism of rights, the importance they have for education, and the political impact they can have on political emotions, we need broadly based inclusive statements of rights which are of little use in generating justiciable tests of political legitimacy.

Ultimately, the formalities of a constitutional regime may be of secondary importance to the development of a culture of democracy in which there is a degree of commitment to open dialogue and compromise, as well as a realisation that, while acceptance of majority opinion may be the best closure mechanism for political disagreements, this lacks legitimacy if the majority seriously neglects the sort of claims which underlie the development of human rights law. Indeed, the principal significance of the choice of constitutional mechanisms may be their impact on such a democratic culture as the only enduring defence against authoritarianism and abuse. From this point of view, institutionalising human rights may be important mainly because of the ways in which it symbolises the inadequacies of pure majoritarianism, gives focus for the formation of public opinion on the basic interests of all citizens, and provides mechanisms for addressing individual grievances, objectives which may be met without formalising a counter-majoritarian veto on the electoral political procedures. The question is whether this can be achieved without giving too much influence to a globalised network of judicial authorities to the detriment of healthy representative politics.

## THE UK HUMAN RIGHTS ACT 1998

These reflections range far beyond the relatively modest step of incorporating the ECHR in the mild way envisaged in the UK Human Rights Act 1998, an Act which is concerned principally with interpretation of domestic law, not with its replacement.

However, it may not be easy to restrict the impact of the Act to minor questions of interpretation. Interpretation is itself a slippery term which is now used much more widely than simply in relation to making a selection between different readings of ambiguous statements, and is often equated with highly flexible forms of legal reasoning.[24] Interpretation may involve creative concretisations of vague statements in order to give justiciable meaning to those statements, a process which goes far beyond resolving ambiguities.[25] With respect to more specific statements of rights, 'interpretation' is taken to include how we read legal texts to determine whether or not there is an ambiguity which needs to be addressed as well as the process of resolving that ambiguity. The attempt to distance the ECHR from making or unmaking UK law and confining its use to the clarification of obscurities comes up against the thesis that obscurity is not something which comes on the face of a statement but emerges from the pre-existing state of mind of those who seek to give meaning to a form of words.

Although these points may be overstated in that they ignore the existence of relatively stable understandings of verbal patterns within particular cultures, there is no doubt that the existence of the ECHR does impact on how we read our domestic laws in the first place. The Convention affects what seems clear and what does not, as well as which clarifications are to be preferred. And so, while it is possible to sustain a fair working distinction between understanding and interpretation in a legal culture where there is sufficient precision and continuity of discourse, this process is undermined by the introduction of unspecific principles as a guide to the so called interpretation of pre-identified ambiguities and obscurities.

Further, it is not clear what will be made of the requirement of s 6 that public authorities must conform to the ECHR. This may be read (or 'interpreted') as permitting or even requiring courts, which are explicitly identified in the Act as public authorities, to develop the common law so that it is increasingly in harmony with the Convention. This may not be the intention of the Act's sponsors, but, in a fluid constitutional situation involving the changing role of courts, it is possible that judiciaries will modify their working assumptions as to how statutes, including the Human Rights Act 1998, are to be interpreted. Certainly, there are available theories of interpretation, particularly in the human rights sphere, which place few limitations on judges' power to understand the enactments of legislature in accordance with generalised norms which permit cognisance of purposes other than those in the mind of the legislators.

---

24 See A Marmor (ed), *Interpretation and Legal Theory*, Oxford: Clarendon Press, 1992; and B Bix (ed), *Law, Language and Legal Determinacy*, Oxford: Clarendon Press, 1993.

25 This and related problems are examined in an important article that casts doubt on the utility and clarity of the model on which much of the Human Rights Act 1998 is based: AS Butler, 'The bill of rights debate: why the New Zealand Bill of Rights Act 1990 is a bad model for Britain', *Oxford Journal of Legal Studies*, Vol 17, 1997, 323. See also G Huscroft and P Rishworth (eds), *Rights and Freedoms: The New Zealand Bill of Rights Act 1990 and the Human Rights Act 1993*, Wellington: Brooker's, 1995; and J Elkind, 'New Zealand's experience with a non-entrenched bill of rights,' in P Alston (ed), *Towards an Australian Bill of Rights*, Canberra and Sydney: Centre for International and Public Law, 1994, 235. Section 6 of the New Zealand Bill of Rights Act reads: '6. Interpretation consistent with Bill of Rights to be preferred – Wherever an enactment can be given a meaning consistent with the rights and freedoms contained in this Bill of Rights, the meaning shall be preferred to any other meaning.'

Putting these two points together, if British judiciaries choose to develop the common law in accordance with the precedents established in the European Court of Human Rights and the decisions of the Commission, and if they systematically 'interpret' any parliamentary modifications of the common law in such a way as to make them compatible with the ECHR, there is little that can be demonstrated to be legally wrong in their conduct. We could therefore have a situation where there is increased impetus to develop the common law without the sense of illegitimacy that at present accompanies significant changes unapproved by Parliament, and decreased capacity, legally and politically, for Parliament to exercise its theoretical sovereignty by passing legislation which can decisively override common law developments.

It is argued that this will not happen. In support, it is pointed out that current decisions of the European Court are not threatening in this way and that there is no will on the part of the British judiciaries to take on such wider powers. This may well be so in the short term, but relatively small constitutional changes have to be seen against the wider process of change, and we cannot easily extrapolate from current decisions and attitudes to what will be the case in 10, 20 or 50 years time. This might not matter if the constitutional changes are readily reversible, as is the case under the doctrine of the sovereignty of Parliament. However, what may emerge is a process of entrenchment whereby reversibility is disallowed or made more difficult. Already, the sovereignty of Parliament is no longer a fixed point of British constitutional law. It therefore becomes imperative to look at possible long-term consequences under different legal cultures, different judiciaries and different political situations, noting that some of these differences will themselves be the result of promoting a juridification of political issues by giving an ever-increasing law-making role to judges. It would appear that the Act gives encouragement to liberal methods of interpretation which have the potential to undermine the traditional ethics of adjudication which requires a basic commitment to respecting the intention of the legislature as expressed in the legislated text.

Working through these potential implications of the Act may require a new model of the separation of powers which can provide bounds within which judiciaries and legislatures can work co-operatively in a way which ensures that human rights are more at the centre of a political debate in which citizens can participate. This model requires elements of tension and partnership between the legislative, executive and judicial branches of government. An enhanced role for parliamentary committees is one emerging feature of such a model. The declaration of incompatibility outlined in s 4 of the Act could prove to be an ingredient which helps to shape the political agenda and attract parliamentary and media attention in a way which improves the quality of political discourse and encourages a human rights-centred focus for constitutional partnership. In such ways, the Human Rights Act 1998 may be an enduringly beneficial constitutional development which contributes to a relatively stable and sensible model of the relative roles of judges, parliamentarians and populace in the identification and development of what the community elects to identify as human rights.

## CONCLUSION: A CULTURE OF CONTROVERSY

This essay has taken an overview of the Human Rights Act 1998 in the context of the potential of human rights institutionalisation. It suggests that the Act may help to produce a framework which is compatible with the continuing centrality of parliament as the core democratic institution. It is accepted that any satisfactory contemporary constitutional arrangement is dependent on a widespread acceptance of the idea of human rights as central to political legitimacy, but this must involve the awareness that the content, form and valence of human rights are inherently controversial, so that any satisfactory regime of human rights must be the product of continuing debate, with respect to the precise formulation of human rights law, to which citizens and their representatives are the major contributors.

Effectively highlighting the importance of identifying and protecting fundamental human interests does require a generally understood culture of rights. However, we have seen that this need not mean accepting an ethos of narrow self interest which excludes a commitment to the public goods on which most fundamental human interests depend. Legitimate self-interest incorporates a degree of reciprocation and can even accommodate a degree of altruism. We have also seen that a culture of rights need not involve looking principally to courts rather than to representative politics for solutions to value disagreements and competing interests. In fact, it may require that courts be seen as essentially protectors rather than definers of rights, providing remedies on the basis of proven violations of existing positive rights as enunciated elsewhere. A human rights culture need not be a culture of litigation any more than it has to be a culture of dependence, a matter of looking to others rather than ourselves for solutions to our problems on the grounds that protecting our interests is primarily a duty of others rather than an achievement for ourselves. A culture of rights may be political rather than legal in its nature, preferring debate to litigation and voting in representative assemblies to voting in the court room, particularly when fundamental interests are at stake.

Seeing human rights as a vital part of a culture of controversy in which neither Parliaments, courts nor the people are to be trusted, and in which the core of politics must be oriented to reaching a series of legally enforceable but temporary agreements as to the rights which best protect and enhance the equal interests of all citizens, may enable us to view the Human Rights Act 1998 as a useful development which gives further institutional recognition to a democratic style of human rights regime in which Parliaments and electorates are encouraged to address human rights questions in an involved and responsible manner.

# 11

# INCORPORATION THROUGH INTERPRETATION

In the absence of express language or necessary implication to the contrary, the courts therefore presume that even the most general words were intended to be subject to the basic rights of the individual. In this way the courts of the United Kingdom, though acknowledging the sovereignty of Parliament, apply principles of constitutionality little different from those which exist in countries where the power of the legislature is expressly limited by a constitutional document. [Lord Hoffmann][1]

## INTRODUCTION

The Human Rights Act 1998 (HRA) is widely regarded as a characteristically British compromise, in this case between giving human rights more weight in the UK polity and preserving the constitutional primacy of the House of Commons.[2] Thus, the HRA gives the higher courts the power to declare an Act of Parliament to be incompatible with the European Convention on Human Rights (ECHR), but not to render it invalid.[3] Only Parliament can change its own legislation, an unrestricted constitutional right that, theoretically at least, remains intact. Similarly, while courts, along with other 'public authorities' have a duty to conform to the ECHR, a provision which is likely to prompt more adventurous development of the common law, they cannot override statutory law to achieve such an objective,[4] nor are they bound to follow, although they must take into account the jurisprudence of the European Court of Human Rights in so doing.[5]

---

1 *R v Secretary of State for the Home Department ex p Simms* [2000] 2 AC 115, at 131.

2 Lord Lester of Herne Hill, 'The art of the possible: interpretation of statutes under the Human Rights Act', *European Human Rights Law Review*, Vol 3, 1998, 665–75, at 668: 'The political compromise represented by an interpretive Bill of Rights of this kind was envisaged by Hersch Lauterpacht in his brilliantly original and prophetic study of the need for an "International Bill of Rights" published in 1945.' See also Lord Irvine of Lairg, 'The development of human rights in Britain under an incorporated convention of human rights', *Public Law*, 1998, 221; Sir W Wade, 'Human rights and the judiciary', *European Human Rights Law Review*, Vol 3, 1998, 520; and D Feldman, 'The Human Rights Act 1998 and constitutional principles', *Legal Studies*, Vol 19, 1999, 165–206, at 168–69.

3 UK Human Rights Act 1998, s 4(2): if the court is satisfied that the provision is incompatible with a Convention right, it may make a declaration of that incompatibility. Section 4(6): a declaration under this section ('a declaration of incompatibility'): (a) does not affect the validity, continuing operation or enforcement of the provision in respect of which it is given; and (b) is not binding on the parties of the proceedings in which it is made.

4 *Ibid*, s 6(1): It is unlawful for a public authority to act in a way which is incompatible with a Convention right.

5 *Ibid*, s 2.

Compromise is also apparent in that courts are required to have the ECHR in mind when interpreting Acts of Parliament. This must be done so as to read such Acts, 'so far as it is possible to do so', in a way which renders the Act compatible with the ECHR.[6] This 'interpretation requirement', as I shall call it, encourages courts to read legislation on the presumption that Parliament intends to legislate in accordance with the ECHR, but courts cannot actually ignore or invalidate statutes that are perceived to be clearly incompatible with the Convention. The most that can be done, in such cases, is to issue a 'declaration of incompatibility', which enables the government to use a fast-track parliamentary procedure to amend the offending statute, should it wish to do so.

Despite this complex balancing of powers and the general appearance of moderation and compromise that permeates the text and politics of the HRA, I argue in this chapter that the impact of the HRA will severely diminish the effective authority of elected representatives of the British people. This is concealed by the fact that courts are required to interpret but not to override Acts of Parliament. However, the interpretation requirement, when seen in the context of the theories of interpretation that accompany the judicialisation of human rights, has the capacity to bring about *de facto* full incorporation of the ECHR to the point where courts are in practice able to overturn legislation that they deem to be in violation of their reading of the ECHR.

The frequently made assertion that the HRA incorporates the ECHR is, strictly speaking, misleading, since the incorporation involved is largely confined to matters of interpretation. However, the interpretive possibilities now available to the judiciary have the potential to bring about full incorporation of the ECHR. The scope and power of the interpretive techniques that are licensed by the HRA will make judges the determinate body with respect to a wide range of policy issues which have hitherto been fully within the sphere of parliamentary responsibility. The HRA effectively incorporates the ECHR into British law through the interpretive norms that it brings with it. The Lord Chancellor is therefore mistaken in holding that, because the HRA takes an interpretive approach to fundamental rights, it is compatible with the tradition of parliamentary sovereignty.[7]

Some HRA sceptics argue that the HRA will in practice make very little difference to the law of the UK beyond a small range of matters, such as the tightening of procedural protections for accused persons in criminal process. The conservatism and traditional deference of the British judiciary to elected governments will be enough, it is argued, to ensure that the HRA does nothing more than to reduce the incidence of embarrassing findings against British government by the European Court of Human Rights. While there will be a great

---

6 *Ibid*, s 3: so far as it is possible to do so, primary legislation and subordinate legislation must be read and given effect in a way which is compatible with Convention rights.

7 Lord Irvine of Lairg, 'Activism and restraint: human rights and the interpretive process', *King's College Law Journal*, Vol 10, 1999, 177–97, at 178, n 3: 'It is this interpretive approach to fundamental rights which facilitates the coexistence of strong rights protection and respect for parliamentary sovereignty.'

deal of new legal activity and more complexity and expense in the British legal system through the addition of further grounds for legal argument, nothing much will change in relation to the protection and furtherance of human rights. My HRA scepticism is rather different. I argue that it allows an open-ended amount of judicial activism that has the potential to remove control over a broad range of issues from the domain of ordinary, non-legal politics. What actually transpires will depend crucially on the use that the judiciary makes of the central provisions of the HRA, but the constitutional scene is now set for the now legally legitimate but still democratically problematic exercise of greatly enhanced political power by judges in the British political system. Whereas it used to be commonplace to say that the absolute legal sovereignty of Parliament is in effect limited only by political considerations, the new interpretive powers granted to the courts by the HRA are powers that are now subject only to political factors, such as hostile public reaction to court decisions.

## THE SCOPE OF THE INTERPRETATION REQUIREMENT

Each of the central provisions of the HRA appears quite weak, and even together they may seem to be relatively insubstantial, even innocuous – no more than a quasi- or very partial incorporation of the ECHR. Parliament retains its sovereignty, the courts remain subordinate to the elected government and the ECHR is not directly a part of UK law. However, it may be difficult for governments to ignore declarations of incompatibility or to override through legislation alterations to the common law which have been made by courts with the explicit justification of rendering the common law compatible with the ECHR. At a time when judicially enforced 'human rights' have, in the eyes of the public and the media, greater political legitimacy than the outcome of partisan electoral political processes, governments may not wish to subject themselves to the politically damaging opprobrium which would arise from their ignoring a declaration of incompatibility or legislating to negate a development in the common law that has been presented as necessary to bring existing law into line with the ECHR. Being mindful of the prospect of an appeal to the European Court of Human Rights, and relieved to hand over responsibility for imposing morally controversial laws to the courts, governments are not, it is argued, likely to challenge changes to the common law or interpretations of Acts of Parliament which are said to derive from the provisions of the ECHR.

Nevertheless, these predictions may not unduly trouble the democratically minded citizen, since such effects are postulated on the assumption that governments will seek to avoid the electoral consequences of unpopular decisions, and that accords well enough with basic democratic norms of popular accountability. To be sure, it will mean that the HRA will give more political influence to courts with respect to setting agendas, but the ultimate determinations are made by Parliament, and this in the spotlight of media attention that itself can be regarded as a democratic enhancement. If courts come out with declarations of incompatibility and initiate common law developments that are unpopular, governments will suffer no electoral setbacks by ignoring or overriding them. This may make the anti-majoritarian goals of the ECHR more difficult to achieve, but this is not necessarily a serious concern to majoritarian democrats.

There are, however, more profound worries about the apparently balanced compromise provisions contained in the HRA. Some of these concerns arise from the fear that the interpretation requirement is much more potent than it looks. The instruction to read legislation 'in a way which is compatible with Convention rights' may appear to do little more than legitimate the standard practice of drawing on a number of external sources as aids to the interpretation of formally defective law, that is, law which is unclear, ambiguous, or in need of supplementation if it is to be effective.[8] On this view, it will make the ECHR, when relevant, the preferred 'third umpire' in cases of interpretive doubt, but it does not threaten to upset the standard practices of traditional statutory interpretation as they now operate, allowing the use of external materials and considerations when there is no available evident plain meaning.

The terms of the interpretation requirement suggest something much stronger than this.[9] Certainly, the parliamentary debates indicate a proactive role for judges which displaces the assumption that interpretation is a marginal aspect of adjudication that arises only in penumbral cases.[10] It seems clear that under the HRA legislation must, at the very least, be read from the perspective of the ECHR in something like the way that British courts view statutes as primarily additions to and only sometimes modifications of the common law, in that the presumption is that a statute does not alter the common law unless it explicitly and clearly does so on its face. In practice, this means that an effort is made to see if there is a feasible meaning of the text of the statute which does not overturn existing common law and, if there is such a meaning, to adopt it as the 'correct' interpretation. More widely, this is an approach that can be taken to all new law on the grounds that this protects the cohesion and integrity of a legal system. Moreover, the same sort of presumption applies in a stronger form to the displacement of established common law principles in the light of new legislation. Here the rationale goes beyond protecting the integrity of the legal system and is seen as offering some protection for fundamental rights.

---

8 See Sir A Hooper, 'The impact of the human rights act on judicial decision-making', *European Human Rights Law Review*, Vol 3, 1998, 676–86, at 686. While Hooper points out that, in some ways, statutory interpretation will be radically altered by the HRA, he argues that 'the higher courts are already very familiar with the Convention and have been reaching decisions which they would have reached post-incorporation'.

9 The wording of s 3 of the HRA is certainly stronger than the South African equivalent, which requires 'a reasonable interpretation of the legislation that is consistent with international law over any alternative interpretation that is inconsistent with international law' (Art 233 of the Constitution of the Republic of South Africa 1996), and probably stronger than the New Zealand equivalent: 'Wherever an enactment can be given a meaning that is consistent with the rights and freedoms contained in this Bill of Rights, that meaning shall be preferred to any other meaning' (Bill of Rights Act 1990, s 6). Note also Lord Steyn in *R v DP ex p Kebeline* [1999] 3 WLR 972: 'Section 3(1) enacts a strong interpretive obligation.'

10 Thus, the Secretary of State for the Home Department (Mr Jack Straw): 'we want the courts to strive to find an interpretation of legislation that is consistent with Convention rights, so far as the plain words of the legislation allow, and only in the last resort to conclude that the legislation is simply incompatible with them ...' (HC Deb, 3 June 1998, cols 421–22).

In the case of the ECHR, the parallel assumption would be that, unless the text indicates clearly to the contrary, there is strong presumption that statutes are read as if they were intended to be in accordance with the ECHR, which is a statement of fundamental rights that is sometimes said to be derived from traditional common law principles. The interpretation requirement will then work in much the same way as current principles of statutory interpretation, whereby statutes are construed so that they do not alter fundamental common law principles or rights unless there is a clear and unequivocal intention apparent in the text of the statute that has such effect.[11] Thus, implied overturning of basic common law is not permitted, although Parliament may alter any part of the common law provided it does so explicitly and clearly. If this approach is adopted with the ECHR, courts will make strenuous efforts to read statutes in ways that are compatible with the ECHR, but where there is an explicit and clear statutory text which is not compatible the ECHR then that text will be applied as law, notwithstanding that incompatibility, although, of course, a declaration of incompatibility may follow. There seems no doubt that a strong presumption of this sort is in accordance with a minimalist reading of the interpretation requirement.[12] Certainly, the view that Parliament will be taken to intend not to legislate contrary to the ECHR is underlined by the provision of the HRA that the government is required to make a 'statement of compatibility' on precisely this matter when introducing legislation.[13]

The rationales for maintaining traditional principles of common law, unless there is a clear parliamentary intention to the contrary that is manifest in the text of a statute, are similar to those for giving the ECHR a similar status, in that both may claim to be loci of fundamental principles. However, in the case of the common law, there is an assumption that there is in existence a relatively cohesive body of rules and principles whose coherence and integrity is to be maintained so that new law is fitted into this framework in a way which does not fragment the existing corpus of law. The same assumption cannot reasonably be made about existing ECHR jurisprudence, although it is to be expected that, in the leeway allowed in the HRA for departures from the body of case law derived from the ECHR, there will be a gradual merging of common law and British ECHR jurisprudence to produce a body of existing judge-made law that is more powerfully resistant to legislative alteration than is existing common law. This scenario fits with the common judicial contention that British common law is by and large completely compatible with the ECHR.[14] For this reason the ECHR may

---

11 See *Derbyshire County Council v Times Newspapers Ltd* [1992] QB 770.

12 Indeed, it has been put forward as the proper approach for UK courts to take to the ECHR well before the enactment of the HRA. See Lord Browne-Wilkinson, 'The infiltration of a bill of rights', *Public Law*, 1992, 397–410.

13 HRA, s 19(1).

14 See Lord Browne-Wilkinson, *op cit* fn 12, 465: 'It is now inconceivable that any court in this country would hold that, apart from a statutory provision, the individual freedoms of a private person are any less extensive than the basic human rights protected by the ECHR.' See also *Attorney General v Guardian Newspapers Ltd (No 2)* [1995] AC 109, at 283. A worrying implication of this assumption is the implication that legislation amending current common law is immediately suspect as being in violation of the ECHR.

come to be seen more and more as closely associated with the common law for purposes of interpretation.

Again, democrats may not be unduly worried by such developments if these interpretive methods are undertaken in good faith, for they should act as a spur to increased clarity, directness and openness in legislative drafting and enactment. This would make it easier for governments to be held to account for the legislative outcomes, and may generally improve the formal quality of legislation in which crucial issues are frequently fudged as the result of political compromises and poor legislative drafting. Parliaments have a duty to enact clear and unambiguous laws in terms of which they can be judged and held responsible by the electorate. The desirability of explicit and clear law reform is uncontroversial with respect to the idea of the rule of law, even if this ideal is often frustrated by the need to gain political consensus in favour of legislation with carefully constructed ambiguities.

Such a sanguine prognosis of the import of the interpretation requirement of the HRA follows from a belief that fundamental interpretive methods of British courts will be largely unchanged by the introduction of the HRA. However, it cannot be assumed that traditional principles of interpretation will be followed, and courts will continue to apply statutes in accordance with their evident textual meaning. Currently, the orthodox method is still substantially in place, so that it is only where there is an ambiguity, or obscurity, that courts may look for guidance from external sources, such as *Hansard*, or the ECHR, yet it cannot be taken for granted that the ECHR may be admitted to British courts for the purposes of interpretation without bringing with it the interpretive methods which go hand in hand with current rationales for having and deploying bills of rights. These methods give far less weight to textually evident meaning, and much more deference to the assumed purposive intentions of legislators with respect to the stated or assumed objectives of the legislation in question. If such purposes are now taken to include conformity with the ECHR, then it follows that the legislation whose compatibility with the ECHR is in question will from the start be read so as to make it compatible with the ECHR. In other words, there will be no firm textual basis to serve as the clear and settled meaning of a piece of legislation against which to go on and raise the question of its compatibility with the ECHR. Legislation will already have been 'read down', implications drawn from the intention to comply with the ECHR will already have been 'read into' the text, even before issues of compatibility are addressed.[15]

It follows that the HRA gives the ECHR a higher status than existing common law. Indeed, the expectation behind the Act as a whole would appear to be that the ECHR should begin to permeate the whole process of law-making and law application, to the point that it is not simply a set of side-constraints on law enacted with other objectives in mind but the favoured telos of all legislation and adjudication. Thus, it will be expected of any enactment that it is an attempt to instantiate the ECHR and that it is a court's duty to carry this objective forward by reading legislation either narrowly or expansively in the light of the broad

15 See RA Edwards, 'Reading down legislation under the Human Rights Act', *Legal Studies*, Vol 20, 2000, 353–71.

purposes of the ECHR itself. This will mean 'interpreting' legislation in a way which sits rather lightly on actual words, particular intentions or the traditional constraints thought to be set in place through deference to the plain and ordinary meanings of the legislation in question. The dynamic picture is not that of the ECHR as existing law to be modified from time to time by explicit legislation, a legitimate process comparable to clear legislative changes being made to the common law. Rather, the ECHR is to be seen as directing, limiting and augmenting legislation in a much more positive way than existing common law, with no assumption that legislation contrary to and overriding and replacing ECHR provisions is to be routine and intentional.[16]

This may seem rather fanciful to those steeped in the ideas of the distinction between legislation and adjudication and the division of powers between courts and legislatures based on that distinction. However, this would be to ignore the steady trend towards more open-ended interpretive methods increasingly deployed in British courts.[17] It is also unmindful of the impetus which will be added to this trend by placing the ECHR more firmly within the purview of ordinary courts. The new interpretive role of the ECHR is not a matter of introducing further legal materials on which existing interpretive methods are brought to bear, but involves the adoption of distinct interpretive methods that have been developed to deal with the particular problems which arise in applying abstract statements of rights to concrete cases. It is not simply that the quantity and range of the materials available for interpretation have been enlarged. Rather, the radical developments in store for British jurisprudence have much more to do with the further development of interpretive norms. Texts of statutes will come to be seen as no more than fallible and defeasible guides to ascertaining an implied legislative 'intent' in the light of the courts' reading of the ECHR.

Those who have seen the adoption of more purposive methods of interpretation without apparent damage to the administration of justice may find such talk unnecessarily alarmist. Already it is generally accepted that interpretation must have regard to underlying purpose as well as evident meaning. Indeed, it is generally accepted that often enough the meaning of a legislative text is not evident if we are not aware of the background purpose of an enactment, the reasons why it was introduced, the objectives that its proponents have in mind, and the debates that went on about its terms. Literal meanings are always to some extent relative to the purposeful context which creates and sustains legislation.

Such purposive interpretation, which is aimed at understanding the meaning of a text in the light of the context from which it emanates, is not inherently

---

16 This is already evident in the substantive tests for administrative review where Convention rights are in point: *R v Minister of Defence ex p Smith* [1998] QB 517, at 554 (concerning what is '*Wednesbury* unreasonable'); see also *R v Chief Constable of North Wales Police and Others* [1997] 4 All ER 691.

17 A trend that accelerated once it became acceptable for law officers to acknowledge openly the judicial role in law-making. See Lord Reid, 'The judge as law maker', *Journal of the Society of Public Teachers of Law,* Vol 12, 1972, 22; and A Lester, 'English judges as lawmakers', *Public Law*, 1993, 269.

disturbing to democrats if the text that is being interpreted is the enactment of an elected assembly. Indeed, attention to purposive context may well help to limit the range of feasible meanings that may be given to a legislative provision in ways which respect the democratic process. There are, of course, legitimate concerns in cases where appeal is made to legislative 'purpose' in a way which draws on the (perhaps suspect) ulterior purposes or motives of legislators. Further, insuperable problems may arise in determining what exactly is 'the' purpose of any piece of legislation. However, in general the purposive approach has not made an enormous difference to interpretive practice, and where it has been in evidence this has often been to the enhancement rather than the overruling of 'plain meaning' by bringing into focus the context in which the legislation was brought forward. To know the problems being addressed, and to grasp the objectives of a piece of legislation, often clarifies the text of an enactment and renders it more transparent at the point of application.

The situation is very different when the purposes in question are not those of the Act that is being interpreted but those which derive from the broad purposes thought to be enshrined in the HRA itself. And, as we have seen, even in common law jurisdictions it is accepted that the interpretation of abstract rights must be done in an open and generous way so as effectively to protect the rights of those who are vulnerable to the activities of the state. This is in part because of the very abstraction of these statements of rights, but is also affected by the court's view of its role in providing effective remedies for human rights violations.[18] Interpretation in the human rights context is an expansive and creative process governed by the assumed functions of bills of rights, such as protecting the perceived interests of vulnerable minorities and groups against the majoritarian pretensions, or upholding some overriding and overarching principles of equality and justice, in a way which turns legal reasoning, in this context, into a form of legally legitimated moral discourse. Moreover, the view that constitutional rights have to be seen as enshrining developing moral and political standards negates the power of precedent in such settings,[19] hence the injunction of the HRA that courts should 'take into account' rather than actually follow the decisions of such bodies as the European Court of Human Rights.[20] For such reasons, while the HRA may seem to confine the use of the ECHR to the interpretive function, it cannot control an expansive view of what counts as interpretation when it comes to reading and bringing to bear a list of fundamental rights and their associated jurisprudence.

Once this sort of textually relaxed and morally purposive approach is adopted with respect to human rights, it will not be easily confined to the interpretation of

---

18 This is evidenced by developments in Hong Kong that incorporated the International Covenant on Civil and Political Rights: the Hong Kong Bill of Rights Ordinance 1991. See *Ng Ka Ling v Director of Immigration* [1999] 1 HKLR 315, 339–40, which rejects a 'literal, technical, rigid and narrow approach' in favour of a 'generous interpretation of … constitutional guarantees'.

19 The classic reference here is B Carduzo, *The Nature of the Judicial Process*, New Haven, CT: Yale University Press, 1921, 98–141. For an adaptation of this approach to the interpretation of the ECHR, see *Tyrer v United Kingdom* (1978) 2 EHRR 1.

20 HRA, s 2.

those rights themselves, so that there will be a major impact on legal interpretation in general. Thus, in practice, there will be no clear line between identifying an ambiguity, gap or other formal deficiency on the one hand, and using extraneous material to deal with such problems on the other. The HRA will bring the ECHR to bear on the process of discovering and establishing that there is something resembling an ambiguity in the statutory text. The presence of the ECHR will therefore affect not only the resolution of formal deficiencies of domestic legislation but the creation of these perceived deficiencies. Now that interpretation via the ECHR is in place, we will find that such open-ended interpretation comes to pervade the legal process in a quite imperialistic manner. Indeed, it is realistic to assume that the prime long-term impact of the ECHR will derive less from its content than from its displacement of the centrality of plain, literal or ordinary meaning in favour of a textually unrestrained process of enforcing particular judicial views of the proper goals of a democratic society.

The opening up of the interpretive method which is part and parcel of the HRA is thus a more serious long-term threat to the protection and development of electorally-based democracy than the projected deference of Parliament to declarations of incompatibility. The right of Parliament to determine the law of the UK appears better founded than the maintenance of current interpretive methodology, yet the former is vulnerable to the latter. At the extreme, Parliament may pass any legislation it likes in the plainest of terms and have this rendered null by courts that read the legislation in a 'possible' way that reflects a judicial reading of the ECHR. This is all the more likely to happen if, as is predicted, courts will be reluctant to make declarations of incompatibility.[21]

Further, the right of judges to interpret the law is as politically entrenched as the right of Parliament to make law. Interpretation is almost universally seen as the prerogative of the courts because it is part of adjudication, and that is taken to be their exclusive function. It is therefore not only politically difficult but also constitutionally questionable for Parliaments to reject a court's particular interpretations or even question a court's interpretive methods. Judicial power that is built on the right to interpret is therefore not vulnerable to democratic pressures, although this could change as the public becomes aware of the nature of human rights interpretation.

If the increased judicial powers that are licensed by the HRA become in these ways invasive of legislative authority, this makes the HRA a more impressive instrument for containing elected governments, but it makes for greatly heightened fears as to its democratic credentials. From this perspective, the HRA may turn out to be less of a compromise with than a capitulation to the courts. Thus, scepticism as to the feasibility of cabining the ECHR in the role of an interpretive aid follows from the expansive theories of interpretation which come with the global trend to legalise and constitutionalise moral rights. These theories of interpretation enable courts to take to themselves matters previously reserved for democratic decision-making as to how such moral rights ought to be

---

21 As is foreshadowed in recent decisions such as *R v Secretary of State far the Home Department ex p Simms* [2000] 2 AC 115.

concretised and implemented. This chapter expounds and illustrates this thesis, and suggests ways of heading off such developments before they take on the legitimacy of accepted judicial and constitutional practice.

## DEMOCRATIC SCEPTICISM

To appreciate the constitutional issues at stake in the way we approach the HRA, it is necessary to be aware of the principal democratic and rule-of-law qualms concerning judicially articulated bills of rights in general.

Central to the main arguments against bills of rights is the uncertain ontological and epistemological status of human or fundamental rights themselves. These difficulties do not concern the idea that some types of positive rights and duties be given a status which enables courts to use them to override other rights and duties, or even the idea that there are rights we might wish to ascribe to and secure for all human beings. Nor do they involve questioning the values embodied in the idea of human rights, such as equal human worth and the relief of suffering and domination. Rather, the difficulties arise when we try to reach agreement as to precisely what these higher-status rights should be and how the values we associate with human rights are to be understood and brought to bear on institutional arrangements and particular decisions. Whatever agreement can be reached at the level of abstract statements, the content, valence and scope of particular human rights are incurably contestable when it comes down to giving them specific applicable meanings.[22]

This may appear a tendentious way to formulate the issue because it rules out the perspective that the prime task is to find out what these rights actually are, rather than to decide what they should be. From a traditional natural law perspective, for instance, the central task is to find out what our natural rights are and always have been, whether or not they have been recognised or observed in any particular society at any particular time.[23] On this view, we might accept a positivistic analysis of 'fundamental rights' as those rights that are, as a matter of fact, given superior or protected status within existing constitutional arrangements, but keep the terminology 'human rights' for pre-existing and historically non-contingent entities called natural or human rights which serve as the grounds or justification for the fundamental rights that we have or ought to have. These human rights are moral entities that have an existence which is independent of human action or belief, and are as much a part of the structure of the universe as the entities whose existence is presupposed and investigated by the physical sciences. However, it is claimed that we do not need scientific or other specialist training to have acquaintance with and knowledge of human rights, for

22 See TD Campbell, 'Human rights: a culture of controversy', *Journal of Law and Society*, Vol 26, 1999, 6.

23 Rooted in the classic natural law theories of Thomas Aquinas but developed in more secular terms throughout the Enlightenment period, the range of philosophers I have in mind includes Hobbes, Locke and Rousseau.

they are the objects (or perhaps the presuppositions) of the universal human capacity for moral knowledge which is manifest in our foundational insights into or intuitions of moral truth. This means that we can hope to justify the ascription of fundamental rights on the basis that there are human rights that not only in some literal sense already exist but do so in a way which renders them accessible to our cognitive capacities.

Whatever the philosophical attractions of this ontology may be, no agreed method for obtaining knowledge of the specific content of human rights has established itself. Unless we accept that there are authorities with special knowledge of these rights to whom we should all defer, a belief in the existence of human rights is epistemologically and politically insufficient. While it is not possible to disprove the existence of such moral entities and it is possible to make some sense of the claim that there are such things if we adopt certain theological metaphysics which allow us to conceive of a timeless god or gods who have authorised or created such facts/norms, there is no generally accepted method or approach to 'discovering' what these entities are, apart from standard but inconclusive methods of everyday moral reflection and debate. We may simply believe on the basis of religious or some other form of external authority that there are such human rights of which those with the requisite authority have 'knowledge', but this is to reject the possibility of acquiring a philosophical or rational basis for such beliefs.

Of course, other, less metaphysical, theories may be deployed to provide grounds for the intelligibility of the idea of ahistorical human rights and their superior moral legitimacy,[24] but these have the same epistemological deficiencies which leave disagreements about the content, form and valence of human rights unresolved and lack the fallback position of religious or moral authority to make such determinations for us. Again, it is possible to withdraw from the modern imperative to provide objective justifications for moral and political positions and adopt a purely pragmatic posture towards the idea and legitimacy of human rights.[25] This form of postmodernism, which abandons the modernist pursuit of rational and universal justification but seeks to retain the form and rhetoric of such core enlightenment concepts as human rights, is in a particularly weak position to deal with the contested pluralisms of contemporary human rights discourse.

In practice, epistemological disagreement means that we must put aside arguments about the existence or legitimacy of human rights as morally privileged entities or insights and address ourselves to the more tangible issue as to what rights we should adopt as the fundamental positive rights of all human beings and how we should go about making such decisions. This leads to deep and pervasive disagreements, but it does focus us on the sort of issue about which it makes sense to debate and settle between ourselves as best we can. And so we

24 Recent attempts of this sort are epitomised by J Rawls, *A Theory of Justice*, Oxford: OUP, 1971; and R Nozick, *Anarchy, State and Utopia*, Oxford: Blackwell, 1974.

25 See, eg, R Rorty, 'Postmodern bourgeois liberalism', in R Hollinger (ed), *Hermeneutics and Praxis*, Notre Dame, IN: University of Notre Dame Press, 1985.

arrive back to the question of how we are going to go about deciding precisely what our positivised fundamental rights should be.

This may still be viewed as a contentious way of putting the matter, since it assumes that we should seek to be precise about fundamental human rights, but is this wise? Is the purpose of human rights discourse not to express broad social and political values on which we can all agree as the basis for legitimate government? Do human rights not represent a broad moral consensus about equality, liberty, fairness, toleration, ownership, justice and life itself? It is the unhelpful demand to render these abstract concepts into something more precise, it may be argued, that leads to disagreement, division and even scepticism as to the status of human rights generally. Should we not be content with statements of general rights that clearly capture our deepest moral commitments to life, liberty and equality as the consensual basis for a civilised polity?

Certainly, highly abstract statements of rights can serve important social and political functions analogous to grand credal statements that can be affirmed as the condition of membership of a broad church, although even these usually contain historically important specifics and have given rise to sustained disagreements and bloody wars. Indeed, a prime role for human rights discourse, and one which may be lost in the move to positivise human rights, is to express broad value commitments which form a basis and inspiration for establishing more precise political objectives through debate, compromise and working agreements. Once human rights are identified with a particular set of case law, for instance, there is the danger of diminishing its moral force and utility. Abstract affirmations of equality, liberty, community, the rule of law and so on can be powerful rhetorical vehicles for engendering moral commitments in ways which help to moralise otherwise coercive and oppressive political systems and generate trust and co-operation that foster a sense of legitimacy.

However, this is not the role for human rights discourse that is envisaged by proponents of the HRA, who see judicial review of legislation as a crucial part of realising human rights. This judicialisation strategy requires courts to pronounce upon the sense and then the validity of legislation as applied to concrete situations, which involves giving sufficiently precise meaning to statements of abstract rights to determine highly specific controversies between particular legal persons. The demand for precision is the result of the move to justiciability that turns human rights from moral principles into rules that bind rather than ideals which inspire. The ambition for precision is laudable in that human rights ideals may make little difference to people's lives unless their particular sufferings can be authoritatively identified as unacceptable and remedies provided. Aspirational human rights lose much of their significance if they do not encourage action to remedy specific evils.

The ECHR does not, however, meet the standards of precision required for transparent judicial application. Statements of human rights such as the ECHR in themselves are far from precise, and the process of specifying their content in sufficient detail to begin to know how they apply to specific circumstances is both necessary and extremely difficult. We simply do not possess conceptions of individual human rights that are sufficiently clear, precise and intelligible to guide and constrain legal judgments by any process of reasoning that can be classified as legal 'interpretation' of a type that can be distinguished from general political and moral debate. Abstract statements of human rights do not make 'good' law because they suffer from the major formal defect of vagueness and imprecision.

Again, this may appear contentious. There are respected theorists who canvass the benefits of having few, simple and abstract laws which can be used by judiciaries to reach humane, just and efficient decisions in a flexible way in the light of the particular circumstances of those involved.[26] There is considerable hostility to the provision of specific rules to cover every circumstance on account of the technical 'legalism' involved, which gets in the way of commonsense justice. On such a view, what matters is impartiality, fairness, wisdom and experience, qualities which are hindered and constrained by adherence to multiple, complex, and specific systems of law that fail to see the wood (justice) for the trees (rules).

The contrary arguments for a more positivistic version of the rule of specific laws, according to which the important functions of law, such as the limitation of official power and the establishment of a clear system of interpersonal rules that can be administered and known without recourse to judicial determinations as to countless individual circumstances, are extensive and well known.[27] All that needs to be noted here is that the project of incorporating the ECHR is highly problematic in relation to these considerations. Moreover, this is not simply a matter of human rights coming into conflict with other values. The importance of the rule of law, as construed in concrete positive terms, has been central to certain ideas of liberty (the republican ideal of citizen assurance that they can act in the knowledge of what conduct is likely to attract sanctions) and democracy (that governments must act within the confines of existing laws). All these rights are themselves part of the human rights corpus.

Of course, it will be said that these problems will be addressed and solved through the development of a British human rights jurisprudence in which the ECHR will be given justiciable form through incremental case law. This process will have a flying start through having to 'take into account' the human rights jurisprudence of the European Court, the European Commission of Human Rights, and the persuasive force of the prolific case law of jurisdictions throughout the world with similar entrenched rights. What we can expect is a British slant on a well established and reasonably precise system of legal rules derived from previous legal decisions. Indeed, if this is not forthcoming then history will undermine one of the principal arguments for the HRA: that domesticating the ECHR will reduce adverse findings against the British government in the European Court of Human Rights.

Merely to state this position is to make clear how far the case law model of human rights is removed from the idea of abstract human rights as moral entities.

---

26 Eg, J Shklar, *Legalism*, Cambridge, MA: Harvard University Press, 1986; and, from a more pragmatic perspective, RA Epstein, *Simple Rules for a Complex Society*, Cambridge, MA: Harvard University Press, 1995.

27 See, eg, F Schauer, *Playing by the Rules. A Philosophical Examination of Rule-Based Decision-Making*, Oxford: Clarendon Press, 1991.

To identify human rights with a historically contingent set of judicial decisions that may or may not accord with the variety of considered views as to what these rights may be is to gain the benefits of positivisation to the detriment of using human rights as a basis for external moral critique of existing law. Can the moral force of human rights survive the process of juridification? Such questions turn our attention back on the issue of the 'interpretive' process whereby statements of abstract rights are shaped into a justiciable form that gives birth to a usable set of judicial determinations.

## 'INTERPRETATION', HUMAN RIGHTS STYLE

Just how far proponents of judicial review of legislation on the basis of bills of rights have developed the idea of what counts as legal interpretation can be gleaned from the work of the influential advocate of a bill of rights for Britain, Ronald Dworkin.[28] Any democrat who is comforted by the notion that the ECHR is 'only' an interpretive Act may be considerably discomfited on learning what such enthusiasts for judicially articulated and enforced bills of rights regard as within the legitimate scope of legal interpretation.

A principal attraction of Dworkin's position[29] is that he appears both to incorporate a measure of accommodation to existing law, in that every decision made by a court should 'fit' with the existing corpus of authoritative legal constitutions, enactments and decisions, and at the same time to advocate a method of interpreting these materials so that they are 'the best that they can be' in terms of the underlying principles of the legal and political system in question. The 'fit' requirement serves to distinguish legal reasoning from other forms of practical reason, which are not constrained in this way, while the 'best' requirement provides the grounds on which a court can decide which of the many determinations that can reasonably be held to fit existing legal and political sources should be adopted in this particular case, there being no assumption that there is any one correct outcome from applying the criterion of fit alone, even when we apply the test of coherence or consistency to the mass of raw legal data.

The thesis, it should be noted, is not that a court should decide what decision is best overall. That would be too open-ended to count as legal reasoning and could have no precedential value. Rather, the decision has to follow from the best interpretation of the existing legal materials that are relevant to the case in point. The grounding in existing legal materials is what makes the method 'interpretive', for interpretation, it is asserted, must be of a text.

On the other hand, the interpretation of these texts takes the form of a strenuous intellectual and moral analysis that is required if we are to give any legally useful

---

28 R Dworkin, *A Bill of Rights for Britain*, London: Chatto & Windus, 1990.

29 There is no one Dworkinian position to be found within his extensive corpus. The brief overview given here is intended to reflect the common and influential understanding of Dworkin's position by those who see his theory of law as providing the basis for model human rights adjudication. It draws largely on R Dworkin, *Law's Empire*, London: Fontana, 1986.

and politically legitimate meaning to a text. Intellectually, the task is to bring together all relevant rules, principles, statutes, case law, legislative debates and so on. Morally, the task is to mould these into the coherent pattern that can be justified by reference to the underlying moral principles that provide the best justification for these historical materials. That justification of those materials is then applied to give an interpretation of the text in question that maximally furthers the objectives assumed by that justification. This is not a cut and dried process but a complex of moral reflection in which different and competing moral/legal principles are pitted and weighed against each other in an effort to provide a morally coherent outcome that Dworkin calls 'integrity'.[30] Even at the stage of determining the fit between an interpretation of a particular text and the accumulated legal materials, the judge is seeking a moral coherence which requires finding an interpretation that fits the principles that best justify that material. This moral telos becomes even more dominant as the judge comes to a final decision as to which reading of a text is best, once all these relevant facts and the foundational principle of the legal and political system have been taken into account. Relevant factors here include the integrity of the political system, its procedural fairness, and the beliefs of the community it serves. Ultimately, judges' 'interpretations' of legal texts are efforts to achieve a morally coherent decision that fits best into their interpretation of the values of the culture within which they operate.

The outcome may be to override the immediately relevant rules of law,[31] or to give an unexpected reading to a legal text in order to make it exemplify the justificatory principles at work in the law more generally. In Dworkin's examples, most of the work in legal reasoning goes into deciding which interpretation is the best one, remembering that interpretation is not a matter of closer textual examination or of discovering and following the intentions of legislators. It involves bringing to bear on the text principles, such as equality and respect for persons, which are believed to offer the best justification of the existing body of law. Here the term 'justification' relates primarily to moral criteria of political relevance and not to any distinctively legal standards, although the whole idea of developing a morally coherent body of authoritative norms is Dworkin's own interpretation of what law is.

Importantly, there is no assumption involved that the body of legal material which counts as part of the raw material for interpretation is sufficiently consistent to meet any rigorous test of coherence, so that any justification will involve not only giving more weight to some legal data than to other parts of the historical aggregate of constitutional provisions, statutes and case law but actually disregarding recalcitrant aspects of the tradition in question. 'Fit' does not apply to all the inherited material, but only to that part of it that is in

---

30 *Ibid*, 96: 'It [integrity] argues that rights and responsibilities flow from past decisions and so count as legal, not just when they are explicit in these decisions but also when they follow from the principles of personal and public morality that the explicit decisions presuppose by way of justification.'

31 Dworkin's most cited example of this is *Riggs v Palmer* 115 NY 506, 22 NE 188 (1889). See R Dworkin, *Taking Rights Seriously*, London: Duckworth, 1977, 23. This example is used by Dworkin to exemplify the role of principles in adjudication. It now requires to be seen in the wider context of the theory of law as integrity.

accordance with the basic principles derivable from that system of law in the round. Clearly, there are elements of pick and choose here in that some precedents can be discarded, and countless decisions have to be made about what weight to ascribe to past enactments and decisions. This inevitably involves drawing on the personal preferences of the judges involved to determine which of the principles available within their legal and political culture seem to them to offer the most acceptable justification of the relevant law, although a judge is meant to discount any of his or her moral beliefs which are atypical. So, while the principles used to interpret a particular law are said to be derived from the body of law in question, they also serve to determine what constitutes the acceptable part of that law, a somewhat circular process which gives scope for enormous disagreement and generates considerable doubt about the Dworkinian belief that there is always one 'right answer' to such interpretive exercises.

For our purposes, it is important to note that, when it comes to applying the law, construed as being in accordance with the best justification of the legal data that survive this process of interpretation, it is incumbent on a court to modify the most immediately relevant law to the case in hand if it does not cohere with the interpretation favoured by the judge in question. This means that statute law can be overridden by the principles that have been found to underlie the common law, so interpreted, and even more so by provisions of the constitution as they are perceived in the interpretation in question. In consequence, all legal cases are potentially 'hard' cases, for any legal decision may be called into question by the invocation of a moral principle developed in the process of deciding how existing law can be presented as the best that it can be.

While it is not exclusively directed towards constitutional law, Dworkin's account of legal interpretation has to be seen primarily as a model for interpreting and applying constitutional provisions. Here at least Dworkin makes it clear that, whatever judges may say to the contrary, legal reasoning is a form of moral reasoning.[32] Thus, he regards the American Bill of Rights as an invitation of moral judgment. This has the advantage of making sense of the idea of a 'best' interpretation of vague and inconsistent legal materials. It is also supported by his general criticism of the idea of law consisting entirely of legal rules that can be understood and applied without an element of moral assessment being involved. This is because the terminology involved in expressing legal principles, and indeed the very concept of law itself, are all 'interpretive' in his technical sense that there can be no agreed empirical criteria determining their correct application. It follows that, in this most fundamental area of law at least, moral judgment is the decisive ingredient, and hence, just because such law is fundamental or overriding, all legal judgment has a decisive moral aspect.

This brief account of Dworkin's theory of legal interpretation is presented as an important and influential example of what counts as legal interpretation within the human rights methodology of those who favour court-administered bills of rights. Such theories are vulnerable to the criticism that they extend the

32 See R Dworkin, *Freedom's Law: The Moral Reading of the American Constitution*, Cambridge, MA: Harvard University Press, 1996.

conception of 'interpretation' so far that they destroy the distinction between understanding and interpretation on which the tradition of positive law is founded. It can also be argued that there are alternative and better-grounded approaches that confine the role of judicial interpretation through giving much greater weight to the potential of enacting relatively clear and unambiguous rules which have democratic endorsement. Dworkin, it should be noted, contends that such systems are not available to us.[33]

It is not possible to follow through this debate here, but we can note the existence of powerful arguments to the effect that the sort of moral disagreements which Dworkin thinks are best settled in courts are more properly matters for political debate and decision. Accepting the importance of having a system of laws that is at least consistent in regard to what it prohibits and permits, and coherent in its moral goals, does not require us to accept that achieving this cohesion is a judicial duty which requires courts to substitute their moral vision for that of legislatures. The principal argument Dworkin uses to give judges this role is that the law, as a coercive system, must be rendered justifiable to its subjects, which can only be done by a 'community of principle' that does not give the last word to political majorities.[34] This, of course, dismisses alternative accounts of legitimacy in terms of the democratic source of legislation,[35] accounts that have to be put to one side in order to justify the interpretive mechanisms of the HRA. Conversely, Dworkin's theories have been relied upon in many arguments favouring the incorporation of the ECHR into British law. The HRA thus adds legitimacy to the adoption of Dworkinian styles of judicial reasoning in British courts, especially in relation to the ECHR.[36] For most advocates of judicial review of legislation, applying abstract human rights to concrete circumstances is ultimately a matter of applying general moral principles. Dworkin himself is perfectly open about this, as, increasingly, are his practitioner disciples.[37]

## INTERPRETIVE POSSIBILITIES

Where does this take our understanding of what it is to interpret an Act of Parliament as compatible with the ECHR 'where possible'?[38] In brief, my

---

33 R Dworkin, *op cit* fn 29, Chapters 4 and 9.

34 R Dworkin, *op cit* fn 20, 190–216.

35 See, eg, J Waldron, *Law and Disagreement*, Oxford: Clarendon Press, 1999.

36 For an example, see F Bennion, 'What interpretation is "possible" under section 3(1) of the Human Rights Act 1998?', *Public Law*, 2000, 77.

37 Dworkin's account of 'integrity' may illuminate the rather obscure 'principle of legality' that has recently been introduced to justify activist interpretive methods. See *R v Secretary of State for the Home Department ex p Simms* [2000] AC 115, *per* Lord Steyn: 'in these circumstances even in the absence of ambiguity there comes into play a presumption of general application operating as a constitutional principle ... This is called the principle of "legality".' See also *R v Secretary of State for the Home Department ex p Pierson* [1998] AC 539, at 573G–575D and 587C–590A.

38 For an incisive and scathing analysis of this section of the HRA, see G Marshall, 'Interpreting interpretation in the Human Rights Bill', *Public Law*, 1998, 167; and 'Two kinds of compatibility: more about section 3 of the Human Rights Act 1998', *Public Law*, 1999, 377–83.

argument is that this provision can operate effectively only on the assumption of an approach to statutory interpretation that is in fact rejected by those who seek to juridify rather than democratise human rights. Only if we have an independent way of determining what a legal text means can we address the question of whether or not it is compatible with another text, and if that other text (in this case, the ECHR) is implicated in determining what the original statutory text actually means, this undermines the basis for comparing the two texts. The idea of what is possible or impossible in the interpretation of a statute is itself affected by the Convention with which courts are asked to compare the statute. In other words, at the extreme, in this context anything is 'possible' provided it can be believed to be in accordance with the ECHR.

'Possibility/impossibility' is a multifaceted concept whose meaning can vary from tight logical sense deriving from the notion of self-contradiction, through scientific meanings related to compatibility or incompatibility with established theory or overwhelming empirical evidence, to more everyday meanings of 'unlikely but feasible/not-feasible' or simply 'one of a number of likely or unlikely outcomes'. Thus, in everyday discourse, the injunction to do something 'if possible' can vary from 'do it if you have the capacity and opportunity to do so' to 'do it if it does not interfere with what you would have otherwise have been doing'. In interpretation, as it operates in relation to human rights, most things are 'possible' in the sense of compatible with an available and respected theory of adjudication. At the other extreme, in more interpretive contexts, 'possible' might be taken to require that the statements of law in question, when read according to their plain or natural meaning, should not logically contradict each other.

What limits, then, does 'where possible' place on a court which has to carry through the injunction to interpret a piece of legislation as being in accordance with the ECHR? The most restrictive meaning of 'possible' in this context, in the sense of the meaning with least impact on how statutes are interpreted in the UK, would be that reading a statute according to its plain, natural or ordinary meaning comes out with a result that does not directly contradict the provisions of the ECHR as understood in the light of the relevant ECHR case law. On one side of the equation, 'interpretation' is given a positivist rendering, giving *prima facie* priority to natural meaning of the statute. On the other side of the equation, no attempt is made to give justiciable meaning to a statement of abstract right, and full weight is given to particular decisions of the European Court of Human Rights as binding precedents. The injunction to make a reading which is compatible amounts in the simplest case to seeing whether the plain meaning of the statute is compatible with existing ECHR case law. On this view, it is not possible to read a statute as in accordance with the ECHR if its natural meaning is in conflict with that of a precedential case. It would be 'possible' in the sense of feasible for the courts to abandon respect for natural meaning, or for existing linguistic practices, but this is not held to be 'possible' because it is illegitimate so to do. Unless there is lack of clarity, ambiguity, or evident absurdity, the natural meaning stands as the benchmark on both sides of the equation for establishing compatibility.

However, this strict and clear meaning of 'possible' is clearly not what the government intended in legislating the HRA.[39] Courts are expected to use their new interpretive powers to achieve readings of legislation which effectively protect Convention rights. There are, however, a variety of ways in which the idea of possibility in this context could be made more elastic and the bounds of possibility enlarged to serve the objectives of the Act. The question is whether the degree and form of elasticity that is adopted renders the apparent limits on judicial power ineffectual and takes us down the path of *de facto* full incorporation.

Thus, on the ECHR side of the equation, more emphasis could be given to the licence which is given to British courts to take account of, but nevertheless go beyond, the jurisprudence of the ECHR and develop a home-grown body of case law on the basis of independent ideas as to how the ECHR should be read and applied in the British context. There is enormous scope for revisiting and developing the abstract statements of right in the ECHR in accordance with the moral understandings of the judges involved and their view of the limits which can reasonably be placed on Convention rights in a democratic society. There is thus a large speculative aspect as to what it is that legislation is required to be compatible with. Nevertheless, a plain-meaning approach to legislation could provide many clear limitations on the actual application of these case law developments. If human rights-style interpretation is combined, on the other side of the equation, with a plain-meaning approach to statutory interpretation, then there is the potential for unforeseen and frequent declarations of incompatibility between legislation, traditionally interpreted, and an open-ended content of the ECHR as viewed through the moral lenses of British justices.

However, another and more likely outcome is a dearth of such declarations on account of the requirement that judges interpret statutes so as to make them compatible with whatever they take the ECHR to require.[40] Armed with Dworkinian methods of statutory interpretation in the shadow of fundamental rights, it will not be difficult to imply content into the text on the assumption that

---

39 See *Rights Brought Home: The Human Rights Bill* (Cm 3782, 1997), para 2.7: 'The Bill provides for legislation – both Acts of Parliament and secondary legislation – to be interpreted so far as possible so as to be compatible with the Convention. This goes far beyond the present rule which enables the courts to take the Convention into account in resolving an ambiguity in legislative provision. The courts will be required to interpret legislation so as to uphold the Convention rights unless the legislation itself is so clearly incompatible with the Convention that it is impossible to do so.'

40 Thus, Lord Cooke of Thorndon: 'Traditionally, the search has been for the true meaning; now it will be for a possible meaning that would prevent the making of a declaration of incompatibility' (HL Deb 3 Nov 1997, col 1272). He has since put this into practice in *R v DPP ex p Kebeline* [2000] 2 AC 326, where in his judgment the writings of a distinguished commentator are taken as sufficient evidence that what must be regarded as a 'strained' interpretation is 'distinctly possible': see Hooper, *op cit* fn 8 at 9. For an early example in the context of the application of the ECHR through the Scotland Act 1998, see also *Brown v Stott* [2000] JC 328, at 354: 'The Solicitor General accepted that, since the section does not say expressly that the Crown can use the information in a prosecution, it would be possible to read the section restrictively, as simply permitting the police officer to require the keeper to give the information and not as permitting the Crown to use the information to incriminate the keeper at any subsequent trial.'

Parliament intended to legislate in accordance with the ECHR. The Lord Chancellor allows that apparently 'strained' meanings will be acceptable because they are not simply possible but desirable in terms of the objectives of the HRA. While he does not consider that the HRA will license readings which are 'fanciful' or 'perverse', it is clear that he would not apply these terms to readings which derive from an approved method of interpretation that seeks to make a statute 'the best that it can be'. Indeed, such creativity may be represented as the reverse of perversity and the height of judicial virtue, to be classified as 'imaginative, inventive and sympathetic' rather than fanciful.[41] If, with the Lord Chancellor's blessing, declarations of incompatibility are treated as a 'last resort', it will not be beyond the wit of the British judiciary to adopt highly constructive 'interpretations' of what others may see as texts with a good claim to have the sort of plain meaning which hitherto legislatures were taken to intend. All this could be regarded as in accordance with the 'spirit' of the HRA, which carries with it not simply a text but an invocation to change the fundamentals of statutory interpretation.

Moreover, it is important to note the direction in which there is pressure to adapt meanings to obtain 'compatibility'. There is no suggestion that what is needed is a compromise between possible interpretations of statutes on the one side and the ECHR on the other. It is not that readings of the ECHR will be preferred if they are more in accordance with the statute in the same way as readings of the statute will be preferred if they are closer to the interpretation being given to the HRA. Rather, the idea is that it is the legislation rather than the ECHR that should bend to accommodate the goal of compatibility.

Taking this to its logical conclusion, we can see that there is no stable basis on either side of the equation in which statutes are to be compared with the ECHR to see if it is possible to make the two compatible by giving an appropriate 'possible' meaning to the legislation in question. Without a more or less positivist method of approaching legislation there can be no basis for claiming that the text of legislation will provide any sort of restriction on the judicial capacity to make it mean what they deem it good that it should mean. Indeed, the interpretation requirement does not really make sense in a judicial culture that gives no great weight to some conception of plain or contextually evident meaning. Some form of interpretive legal positivism, a theory which is largely incompatible with the philosophy of those in favour of human rights juridification, must be presupposed to give workable content to the injunction to read legislation 'wherever possible' as compatible with the ECHR.

In practice, it is likely that the legislative text will be manipulated to make it compatible with judicial interpretations of the ECHR, with an even more interventionist approach to subordinate legislation. The most common tactic will be to read in exceptions to clear rules of law along the lines of 'except in so far as an application of the rule conflicts with the ECHR, as interpreted by the court'.

---

41 HL Deb Vol 583, cols 535, 840, 306, 280. See A Lester, *op cit* fn 17, 271.

Parliament could only effectively counter this device by an explicit statement that the provision applies 'notwithstanding the ECHR'.[42]

## A MORE DEMOCRATIC INTERPRETATION OF THE HRA

In order to preserve the democratic right of the citizens of the UK to determine the basic principles on which their society is to be governed and to have an equal say in how these principles are to be embodied in binding rules, it will be necessary to hold onto a plain-meaning approach to the interpretation of statutes, and to openly acknowledge that interpreting the ECHR is a matter of moral reasoning in which courts have no special expertise and in connection with which their decisions have no political legitimacy.

From this perspective, it would be best if declarations of incompatibility were to be seen as routine and unproblematic. If moral disagreement over what the provisions of the ECHR should be taken to mean is accepted as commonplace, because of the inherently controversial nature of the issues which call to be determined in making such interpretations, then courts should be regarded as having the right to make only provisional determinations of what it is that human rights asserted in the ECHR require us to do. These determinations may, with perfect propriety, be challenged and overturned by elected governments after public debate.

This approach, which preserves the ultimate human right of citizens to determine what their fundamental rights and duties are to be, can be conceptualised as giving them either the right to interpret the ECHR or to override that convention in the light of their understanding of what human rights and whose human rights are to be respected in their polity. The first approach will be preferred by those who equate the ECHR with its subsequent jurisprudence. The second approach will be preferred by those who see the ECHR as an evolving convention attempting to give progressive expression to a certain shared sense that there are moral human rights which we must constantly seek to approximate. The result will be much the same either way, for both approaches place the democratic political process at the centre of the articulation of the controversial specific content of fundamental rights.

It is of considerable democratic importance that British judges should not see the interpretive opportunities licensed by the HRA as an occasion for regarding themselves as moral authorities, and that the interacting functions of the interpretation requirement and the declaration of incompatibility be accepted as giving legitimate scope for involving everyone in the determination of fundamental rights. This requires that Parliament and people be able to hold

---

42 This would be comparable to the Canadian Charter of Rights and Freedoms, s 33(1): 'Parliament or the legislature of a province may expressly declare in an Act of Parliament or of the legislature, as the case may be; that the Act or a provision thereof shall operate notwithstanding a provision included in section 2 or sections 7 to 15 of this Charter.'

judges to the public meaning of what is enacted as law by the legislature, and that it be accepted as politically as well as legally legitimate for Parliament to exercise its ultimate authority over the question of what nebulously expressed but crucially important fundamental values are to mean in the hard world in which coercion is used to enforce the views and interests of some people over those of others.

It may be objected that this approach will undermine the whole point of the HRA, which is to restrict the capacity of governments to abuse the human rights of vulnerable groups. Surely we do not want to allow even elected representatives to ignore and violate human rights? For all its rhetorical force, this argument simply bypasses the problem of what are to count as human rights and what are to count as violations of them. The unavoidable question is whose interpretation of 'human rights' should prevail when it comes to the decisions that are enforced as law? There are, of course, good reasons for not giving the authority to determine such questions to anyone, since we may disagree with their opinions on the matter, an argument which applies to granting anyone political power. Indeed, human rights are introduced into political systems precisely because of the fallibility and corruption of elected governments, but the problem of giving final powers of review to another branch of government is that it too may get it wrong, ignore abuses of human rights, and perpetrate injustice in its turn. Judges may appear relatively benign and enlightened, perhaps because they are not subject to the pressure of elections, but when their decisions are widely believed to be unacceptable, perhaps because of the limited moral vision and practical experience of what is in effect an elite corpus of lawyers, they are not accountable or subject to replacement and correction beyond the sphere of their own peers.

These debates take us beyond the analysis of the HRA to the whole question of the benefits and drawbacks of having entrenched bills of rights. That this is where my argument has led amply illustrates the point of this chapter: to demonstrate that all these basic constitutional issues are indeed relevant to the HRA, which, despite its mild and compromising appearance, substantially incorporates the ECHR into British law. In evaluating the HRA we must, therefore, engage in the larger constitutional debate as to the locus of ultimate political power. If we wish to confine the HRA to an interpretive role that does not override legislative authority and to ensure that the development of human rights in the UK expresses the developing moral convictions of the British people, then we need to focus directly on the right of Parliament and people to have a binding view as to what is to count as a 'possible' legal 'interpretation' in the performance of the judicial role, particularly with respect to the ECHR.

# PART 3:
# DEMOCRACY

# DEMOCRACY IN A WORLD OF GLOBAL MARKETS

Dissatisfaction with electoral democracy is often based on the optimistic belief that there is something better on offer, such as 'mixed' systems of governance (incorporating substantial elements of judicial oversight, managerialism or delegation to international and transnational organisations). Contemporary concerns for democracy are more and more associated with the pessimistic belief that, due to global market forces, there is little of significance that sovereign states, especially liberal democracies, can decide for themselves.[1] This combination of beliefs is dangerous for a system of government that depends on a degree of citizen participation, and even enthusiasm.

Equally insidious is the deleterious effect of global market ideology on the operative models of democracy. By implication, these increasingly incorporate market analogies, such as depicting the voter as consumer and the politician as salesperson, thus condone the acceptance of actual market forces in the political sphere, so that there are fewer and fewer barriers to the control of politics by financial power.

By way of resistance to false optimism as to alternative systems, unnecessary pessimism as to the powerlessness of states, and the ideological imperialism of global markets, this chapter reaffirms electoral democracy as a desirable and potentially effective way of institutionalising collective power for the purpose of self-protection. The particular focus is on a legally (but not judicially) oriented theory of democracy in which citizens are legislators and jurors rather than merely political consumers and thereby often economic pawns.

## TRADITIONAL BATTLE-LINES

Classic theories of democracy can be divided into self-determination or autonomy models on the one hand, and self-protection or utilitarian models on the other. The former stress the independent significance of people deciding their own destiny, whether or not they govern effectively; the latter stress the importance of having mechanisms whereby people, as individuals or groups, do in fact protect and further their interests. For self-determinationists, democracy is a matter of peoples making choices for themselves, shaping their own lives and making their own mistakes, while for the self-protectionists it is about citizens having effective means to defend and benefit themselves politically and economically.

---

1 S Sassen, *Losing Control? Sovereignty in an Age of Globalisation*, New York: Columbia University Press, 1996.

In meta-moral terms, self-determinationism smacks of deontology, particularly rights associated with autonomy and freedom, while self-protection has the flavour of consequentialism, particularly the minimisation of harm. Self-determinism is associated with the language of inalienable rights, while self-protectionism is more at home with notions such as the common good and the general interest. Such contrasts can be expatiated copiously. Thus, the supporters of self-determination regard voting as an expressive act manifesting autonomy, and government as an embodiment of their will, while self-protectionists look upon voting as a power or instrument, and government as an external force, perhaps a necessary evil, which requires surveillance and containment.

## THE PRESENT CONFLICT

To many contemporary commentators, the conflict between self-determination and self-protection models is yesterday's war fought with outmoded and ineffectual weaponry over terrain that no longer has strategic import. Few people nowadays, it is said, have reason to voluntarily engage in voting either as a means of self-affirmation or as a significant self-protection. Democratic politics as a vocation is discredited to the point of ridicule. People look in fear or hope to wider, generally economic, factors in order to understand the insecurity of their presents and discern the shape of their futures.

Moreover, the more academic amongst the democratic theorists point to the phoney aspects of a conflict in which competing ideologies falsely highlight their alleged differences whereas in fact they represent rather similar forces engaged in a messy, confused and maybe unnecessary domestic conflict. After all, real self-determination, if it is to have any significance, must involve the successful exercise of power to achieve chosen objectives. Politics is not token self-expression but achievement of social and economic goals against or with other people.

Further, if there are any genuinely deontic rights, then the right to self-defence must be amongst the more foundational of these, and the successful exercise of the power of voting may be seen as the archetype of minimal self-determination.[2] This reduces the contrast between the two models largely to one between bungling self-determinationists and effective self-protectionists. This cannot be a satisfactory analysis, although there is point to the contrast between the idealism of self-determinationism and the more realistic goals of self-protectionism, which makes self-protectionism simply a particular form of self-determination.

In any case, the emerging consensus is that the choices presented to contemporary electorates are minimal, whatever their normative political rationale may be. The policies of parties with any chance of electoral success differ only at the margins, and the power of governments to implement their policies is greatly exaggerated. This is where the discourse of globalisation enters into the analysis. The freedom of sovereign states is said to be so diminished, in the face of

---

2 A point constantly and lucidly made by Jeremy Waldron: see J Waldron, *Democracy and Disagreement*, Oxford: OUP, 1999, Part III.

powerful global economic forces that compel conformity to transnational market realities as the price of sustaining acceptable levels of economic productivity and consumption, that the states' primary role of economic management is usurped. Countries have to compete for the favours of global economic organisations on terms that are set by the economically dominant states whose governments are, in turn, dependent on private corporate conglomerates.[3]

Contemporary analysts do not, however, agree as to either the novel armouries or the revised objectives for what pass as postmodern democracies. Indeed, it is exciting to note that at a time when globalisation is said to be a homogenising force, there is still some divergence in the competing political philosophies on offer. First in line is the human rights approach. Although human rights philosophies have their modern origins contemporaneously with the institution of representative democracies, they are now viewable as offering an alternative path to what is seen as a 'majoritarian' and hence oppressive system of government. Based on a powerful critique of winner-take-all political systems and backed up by extensive evidence of the plight of identifiable minority groups, the human rights movement seeks to pinpoint those individual interests which have fundamental moral status and to institutionalise their protection and furtherance in ways that counter elective dictatorship and systemic discrimination, hence the enthusiasm for entrenched individual rights being placed in the institutional hands of judicial guardians who are believed to be above the political brawl.[4] This strategy accords with the global trend to link the idea of universal human rights to judicial rather than legislative or political authority.

It is impossible to be opposed to human rights in the context of efforts to counter state terrorism and inhumanity, yet there is much that is troubling about adequacy of human rights philosophy. In particular, there is the embarrassing persistence, indeed exponential increase, of disagreement as to their content at the level of precision at which they have to be applied to concrete situations. The particularisation of human rights reveals that abstract slogans do not offer operationalisable rights and duties, and the process of concretising abstract rights reveals that this is all too evidently a matter of politically contentious moral judgment.[5] All can agree, for instance, that there is, or should be, a right to life, but disagreement abounds over capital punishment, voluntary euthanasia and the duty of states to provide the prerequisites of a healthy existence.

At this point, we encounter twin and complementary strategies. One is an apparent retreat into purely procedural human rights, which are then seen as means for both restraining and democratising government procedures. By confining human rights to the function of maintaining democratic process, either

---

3 For balanced discussions of these trends, see D Held, *Political Theory and the Modern State*, Cambridge: Polity Press, 1989, Chapter 8; and D Goldblatt, D Held, AG McGrew and J Perraton, *Global Flows and Global Transformations: Concepts, Arguments and Evidence*, Cambridge: Polity Press, 1998.

4 RM Dworkin, *Freedom's Law. The Moral Reading of the American Constitution*, Cambridge, MA: Harvard University Press, 1996

5 TD Campbell, 'Human rights: a culture of controversy', *Journal of Law and Society*, Vol 26, 1999, 6–26.

through identifying and entrenching political equality of speech, association and participation, or through the rule of law and the constitutional separation and even division of powers, issues of substance are avoided and left to the procedures of the properly constituted electoral system.[6] This move comes at the cost of dissociating human rights from the criterion of those rights which are not only universal but protect the most important human interests, and hence the exclusion of some of the traditionally most prized human rights. This may not be a price worth paying if procedural rights turn out to be as contentious in their detail as substantive rights.

The other strategy is the intellectualisation of democratic process by taking the focus of democratic government away from the instrumental power of the vote and towards public debate aimed at articulating an agreed content to basic rights and establishing legitimate discursive mechanisms for reaching consensus as to the common good. The deliberative focus goes with a general revival of the classical republican participatory ideal of a citizenry that is actively engaged in political life. This second strategy is particularly germane to that postmodern irony of a globalised world, the phenomenon of normative pluralism, that is, the recognition of the divergences of incompatible group-centred world views which are, in the tradition of liberal toleration, to be accorded equal respect.[7]

## THE PROMISE OF DISCOURSE

Discourse democracy offers a number of encouragements that transcend the dichotomies of rights and consequences on the one side, and of self-determination and self-protection on the other. First of all, deliberative democracy opens up the prospect of mutual accommodation based on working agreement rather than ideological unity, an enterprise that is associated with the notions of incompletely theorised agreement[8] and overlapping consensus.[9] Dialogue may lead to a *modus vivendi* amongst political opponents, which generates temporary acquiescence to a working agreement between the divergences that abound in pluralist societies.

No doubt this working agreement is soiled by a measure of bargaining in which advantages are traded not only on an equal basis, but also in recognition of the inescapable realities of existing economic and other social inequalities. Nevertheless, realistic political accommodation produces a *modus vivendi,* which can be a marginal improvement if not a just outcome for all parties. Partly in response to moral disquiet at the legitimisation of agreements reached between unequal parties, some discourse democrats bring in a second and more epistemological rationale for fundamental procedural rights, namely the function

---

6 In recent times, this mode of reading the Constitution of the United States has stemmed from JH Ely, *Democracy and Distrust. A Theory of Judicial Review,* Cambridge, MA: Harvard University Press, 1981.

7 Thus, J Habermas, *Between Facts and Norms,* Cambridge: Polity Press, 1996.

8 C Sunstein, *Legal Reasoning and Political Conflict,* New York: New York University Press, 1996.

9 J Rawls, *Political Liberalism,* New York: Columbia University Press, 1993.

of dialogue in furthering the causes of truth and justice.[10] The arguments are familiar and to some extent enticing. Freedom of speech, especially where each person affected by a decision actually makes an equal input, leads to the pooling of information and the rational, empirically-based critique of claims to knowledge, so that the outcome of an open and equal debate amongst all those affected by a decision is likely to at least increase the chances of a decision being taken on the basis of reliable information.[11]

Further, in a dialogue approaching to the Habermasian ideal speech situation, each person has to justify to every other his or her views as to what collective decision, if any, should be reached. This procedure is derived from what is involved in according a person equal respect, a basic equality which requires that we seek to reason with each other. This is said to have the effect of excluding evidently partial viewpoints and purely self-serving demands.[12] Just as no scientific view is correct merely because a particular person holds or believes it, so no political view is acceptable simply because it is the view of a particular person. In dialogue, scientific or political, reasons must be given, reasons which could be accepted by any person and which therefore exhibit impartiality, even objectivity, the hallmarks of justice as well as of truth.[13]

There are practical and epistemological difficulties here. The practical difficulties relate to the unrealisable nature of the ideal speech situation in contemporary market societies in which there is great inequality of capacity to engage in such debate and generally insufficient time and opportunity to do so. Of course, this can be rectified by radical egalitarian changes and the attainment of a civic culture in which dialogue is a common practice for all citizens, a programme that has the happy requirement of adding economic to political equality. While there are technological developments which might be conducive to such communicative egalitarianism, it is clear that the current market trend is towards commodifying the means of communication, a development which is highly inegalitarian. Further, if the economic prerequisites of the ideal speech situation are to be written into fundamental rights, this involves the awkwardness of expanding the scope of human rights beyond procedural formalities and into the social and economic spheres, thus landing us with the political disagreements from which we were seeking to extricate ourselves by retreating into traditional civil and political rights.

The epistemological difficulties of deliberative democracy centre on the fact that there is much more to moral and political disagreement than disconfirmable information and self-referential partiality. What this something more amounts to,

---

10 C Nino, *The Constitution of Deliberative Democracy*, New Haven, CT: Yale University Press, 1994.

11 The classic statement of this thesis is JS Mill, 1859, 'On liberty', in JS Mill, *Utilitarianism, Liberty, Representative Government*, London: Dent, 1910.

12 An effect that Jon Elster praises as the 'civilising force of hypocrisy': 'Strategic uses of argument', in K Arrow, R Mnookin, L Ross, A Tversky and R Wilson (eds), *Barriers to the Negotiated Resolution of Conflict*, New York: Norton, 1995, 236–57.

13 A Gutmann and DE Thompson, *Democracy and Disagreement*, Cambridge, MA: Harvard University Press, 1996.

how significant it is, and what can be done about it, are the sleeping and unanswered issues that cast doubt on the moral sufficiency of democratic dialogue. Some disagreement can be overcome by adopting a point of view that is impartial in that it seeks to take the interests of everyone equally into account. Some moral views can be dismissed for their evident partiality. There are moral disagreements which can be overcome because they rest on factual disagreements that are corrigible, at least to the extent that evidence is available to settle the matter at issue (for example, urgency of combating ozone-layer depletion). Consequentialist moral beliefs are particularly subject to revision in the light of changes of empirical beliefs. Even deontic claims can be undermined by demonstrating that the nature of the actions praised or condemned are not in themselves what the holders of these beliefs take them to be. All moral judgments have an element of supervenience in that they are evaluations of some empirically describable phenomena. Change your comprehension of what is involved in autonomous action, free trade, capital punishment or homosexuality and you may well change your deontic assessment of such phenomena. Or, then again, moral judgment may not respond to the clarification of factual issues for empirical information, even when viewed from a non-personalised perspective; it may not, therefore, necessitate or even always contribute to moral agreement.

Many philosophers have argued that factual agreement does generate moral consensus, but such positions depend on outmoded beliefs in a uniform human nature made up of basic emotional responses which, in the absence of identifiable distorting circumstances, produce universal responses of acceptance or rejection to identified forms of conduct, motive and even belief.[14] Such views are not simply pre-postmodern; they are pre-latemodern, pre-Marx, and pre-social science. It matters not whether the diversity of human responses to similar fact situations is based on individual genetic differences, group culturation, the differential exercise of capacities for moral reason or rooted in profound differences in epistemological capabilities, the result is the same: there is, quite legitimately, more to moral judgment that impartiality plus information.

## DEMOCRACY AS COLLECTIVE SELF-PROTECTION

All this does not entirely demolish the pretensions of deliberative democracy. Even the elimination of some bases of moral mistake must be seen as advantageous. Moreover, there is the empirically testable claim that an increase in consensus derives from the right sort of deliberation in the right sort of setting, and consensus on political matters, however it comes about, is generally seen as a moral plus. Whether or not that consensus is a sign of objective truth and justice, it is at least a way of avoiding either coercive intervention or acquiescence in an unjust status quo.

---

14 Such efforts may be traced in, for instance, A Smith, *The Theory of Moral Sentiments*, Oxford: Clarendon Press, (6th edn 1790), 1979; and J Rawls, *A Theory of Justice*, Oxford: OUP, 1974.

The insufficiency of deliberation with respect to epistemological justification does, however, deflect attention back to the exercise of power in politics, that is, the imposition of a binding requirement on a non-consenting minority. It is natural to analyse such situations as involving the unwarranted imposition of majority over minority interests but, outside total consensus, we have no way of deciding if the minority is morally in the right, or represents a different but equally valid moral position, or is defending vested interests and unjustifiable self-preferences. In this context, 'minority' does not analytically refer to disadvantaged and deprived groups, of which there are multitudes, but simply those aggregates that happen to be outside the majority consensus. Indeed, such aggregates normally include the most privileged and wealthy persons in any society.

At this point there are grounds for a reassertion of the self-protection model of democracy, enlarged, perhaps, to take into account not only protection against the partiality or ignorance of the current holders of economic and political power, but against the moral values of others mediated through the apparatus of state, church, media, law and authorised education.[15] It is important to assert that this majority protection function of electoral democracy is of fundamental importance not simply because the dialogue model does not live up to its prerequisite of free, equal and informed dialogue but because, even if it did realise these utopian prerequisites of the ideal speech situation, it could not deliver a consensus based on objectively justified moral agreement. Even so, majority rule can still be justified as a way of maximising the protection of people's interests, including the protection of what they morally value, including their conceptions of justice.

The import of this analysis is wide ranging and fundamental. Political debate should be conducted in a way that recognises that not all disagreement is based on illicit self-preference or misinformation. Therefore, politics should not be conducted on the basis that debate can replace the exercise of decisive power through majority decision-making procedures. Further, there is no methodology of impartial informed dialogue, no form of routinised reflective equilibrium, no form of interpreting the history of law as the best that it can be, and no impartial decision-making procedure that can be taken to justify removing or diminishing the power of majorities to protect themselves against the evils and incompetences of governments, courts and employers. This renders problematic efforts to curb the power of majorities so that they do less harm to oppressed minorities: these same measures diminish the capacity of majorities to protect themselves against those minorities which are neither poor, oppressed, nor benign.

This is not to deny that there are important ways in which a social culture and a set of political institutions can be adjudged better or worse with respect to maximising the extent and effectiveness of self-protection, nor does it diminish the particular concern that has to be attached to protection of vulnerable minorities. The democratic ideal is, after all, self-protection for all, not just the self-protection of a majority. Majorities are, in this respect, always second-best devices,

---

15 For example, the landslide victory for reformists over fundamentalists in Iran's February 2000 parliamentary elections.

but the problem of moral epistemology does mean that we have to see democratic systems as primarily mechanisms for the generation and utilisation of power on the part of the bulk of the people. This means that our efforts should be directed to maximising the causal efficacy of a vote and providing the means whereby votes can be used for the effective protection of the interests of voters, hence the absolute centrality of information, not primarily to reach a rational consensus, but to give citizens a basis on which to assess the impact of government conduct on their lives.

That said, it is clearly imperative to develop a political culture in which it is recognised that the interests of all count equally and that the value of each individual person is not diminished simply by being in a minority. This involves the acceptance of such platitudinous truths as that not all self-protection is morally defensible and that everyone's morally justifiable self-protection is equally important. This is the stuff of a sense of justice. It is a virtue of majoritarian self-protection theory that if votes are cast not on the basis of a view of justice but with a view purely to maximising the amoral interests of the voter, then the result may still be better than one in which the amoral preferences of a minority triumph. However, majoritarian protectionism is more defensible if it operates in a culture in which votes are cast on the basis of self-interest moderated to the point of moral justifiability, that is, with a view to a fair assessment of the impact of the outcome of the interests of all others, impartially considered by giving their interests equal weight. Moreover, this model can be extended to incorporate a regard not simply for different interests but for different values or, amounting to the same thing in many respects, the interests of others as they are rather than how we conceive these interests.

At this point in the analysis we can accept the full force of the dialogue model as an element in a morally admirable form of electoral democracy. Such a dialogue encourages voters to put their self-interest in a context that enables them to judge its comparative worth and to exercise their voting power in the light of this judgment.[16] The outcome could be less discrimination against vulnerable minorities without diminishing the protection of majority interests and values.

In this context, we must emphasise the significance of the subject matter of democratic choice, or that which the voting is actually about. One of the traditional ways of seeking to ensure that majorities have regard to minority interests is to require that they choose general rules rather than make particular decisions directly bearing on what happens to identifiable individuals. This is part of the complex rule of law ideal, which serves many different functions. One of these functions is that political choices of *rules* are more satisfactory than individual political determinations because they are less likely to be discriminatory. Most effective in this regard are universal general rules that apply

---

16 This approach rejects both the public choice axiom of voter self-preference (JM Buchanan and G Tullock, *The Calculus of Consent*, Ann Arbor, MI: University of Michigan Press, 1962) and the Dworkinian downgrading of 'external' or other-directed preferences (RM Dworkin, *A Matter of Principle*, Cambridge, MA: Harvard University Press, 1985, 234–36).

equally to all citizens, especially in societies where citizens are, as in Rousseau's republic, in essentially similar circumstances.[17]

Currently, it may be argued, it is an obstacle to democratic power that voters get to choose only representatives who become members of a legislative assembly and occupy high executive office, thus leaving citizens at the mercy of whatever those elected persons come up with by way of executive action and legislation, with only a generalised and periodic opportunity to alter the rulers and thereby only indirectly the rules. One of the great democratic opportunities of new communication technologies is that voters might be given more direct access to debate on and choice of legislation, as Rousseau envisaged.[18]

## GLOBAL VICTORY

However, all this, it will be said, is beside the point or, at least, beside the points raised by globalisation as to the emptiness of the choices left to political procedures of any sort. The essentials of our lives are decided in the boardrooms of the multinationals, the power politics of World Trade Organisation 'agreements' and the exigencies of the laws of supply and demand in global markets.

This critique deserves a multiple response. First, it needs to be said that there have been few states that have ever had political sovereignty in the sense of an actual capacity to successfully pursue their prime objectives. The limitations on the achievements of politics may now be more global than local, but they are not necessarily greater. The argument for democracy does depend on there being open-ended possibilities as to what can be achieved politically. Further, there is a tendency to overlook the potential for interstate co-operation for the protection of their mutual interest in not being at the mercy of a system of international competition that favours existing economic powers.

Secondly, the inevitability of global capitalism on current conceptions of the free trade model may be perceived as a legitimating ideology on a par with 'iron tendencies' identified in Marx's *Communist Manifesto* as leading to the inevitable downfall of capitalism and the equally determined emergence of communism. The same arguments applied to Marx's historical determinism can be applied to liberal capitalist historical determinism. Both are effective propaganda; neither is established hypothesis.

Thirdly, and relatedly, the propaganda of 'no real choice' is posited on a circular affirmation that the people's preference is always and inevitably for increased productivity and increased consumer goods, rather than better lives and happier communities. This may be ridiculed by saying that, of course, countries are free to be poor, but this again assumes that we all agree as to what constitutes poverty and how much consumer goods contribute to human happiness.

17 TD Campbell, *The Legal Theory of Ethical Positivism*, Aldershot: Dartmouth, 1996, 58–61.
18 J Fishkin, *Democracy and Deliberation*, New Haven, CT: Yale University Press, 1991.

Nevertheless, we have to take cognisance of the fact that states are no longer sovereign in even the legal sense that they are free to extricate themselves from international law, particularly international trade law, a law which is almost entirely detached from any form of democratic control and rides along on the coat-tails of the globalisation of 'human rights'.

The eventual way forward in this situation may be no different in principle from the way forward within undemocratic polities in general, in that the weak must gather their strength collectively against the individually strong through the development of institutions which provide an equal say for all affected parties, independent of wealth, race, gender or age. Here we have to discover the essentially collectivist element in democracy, albeit with an eye to redrawing the boundaries of the relevant polities to take account of increasing economic interdependence. Cosmopolitan theory points down this path to globalising democracy.[19]

Evidently, there are a multitude of problems confronting the development of global democracy. One concern is the amplification of existing problems of public choice theory. Individualistically oriented theorists of democracy, especially, it must be said, utilitarian self-protectionist theorists, have always been foxed by the connection between voting and individual interest. Voting, it is said, is an irrational activity, because one person's vote almost never affects the outcome and therefore there is no causal connection between voting and protecting interests.[20]

We should note that a similar form of argument can be used against many other examples of apparently irrational individual conduct, like joining an army to fight a just war, or paying taxes when you could evade detection if you did not. The standard justification to the model is to admit an element of moral fairness into the domain of rationality, but we need not go that far. The logic of collective action can be based on the ineffectiveness, not the immorality, of an individual approach to politics. Majorities in democratic theory have to be seen as more than the sum of the largest number of aggregate preferences, but as a form of collective action whereby 'the people' jointly rid themselves of unwanted rulers or rules.

The rational choice model cannot be simply translated to the international sphere, because of the disparate sizes of independent polities and the differences between the ontology of persons and that of states. However, the international vision of democracy can be of a system whereby the interests of the most numerous collectivities, taking account of their divergent sizes, can be brought to bear on those powerful minorities whose interests are given disproportionate weight in a world which is globalised in the sense that economic power is less and less cabinable and economic inequality is irrationally dependent on the accident of birthplace. So, even if globalisation in the sense of interconnectedness of states is largely irreversible, something which is doubtless greatly exaggerated, there are

19 D Held, *Democracy and Global Order: From the Modern State to Cosmopolitan Governance*, Stanford, CA: Stanford University Press, 1995.

20 R Wollheim, 'A paradox in the theory of democracy', in P Laslett and G Runciman (eds), *Philosophy, Politics and Society*, Oxford: Blackwell, 1969.

no *a priori* reasons why democratisation of the globe should not feature as part of the solution to less palatable consequences of globalisation. Meanwhile, there is always the possibility of inter-state co-operation, a form of solidarity among poorer nations which echoes the unionisation of industrial workers in capitalist systems.

However, such far-sighted hopes have little prospect of success if democracy does not regain credibility within the nation-state. This takes us to one of my initial points: the, on balance, pernicious global impact of the market model on democratic politics. I say 'on balance' because there are undoubted benefits to viewing citizens as political consumers in so far as this both affirms that it is citizen preferences that count, and in presenting the vote as a power to be utilised by its possessor. Indeed, at first sight, and in its historical development, the self-protection model can be viewed as a market model. The Benthamite vision of artificially harmonising the interests of citizen and ruler by making the latter subject to re-election by the former, with free speech as a prerequisite of informed electoral choice, is at the core of the self-protection model. Modern developments which stress that, in a pluralist society, winning a constitutionally sufficient majority requires governments to appeal to as many different interests as possible enhance the market flavour of the reigning theories of democracy.

The flaw in any acceptably precise application of the market theory of democracy has always been the fact that, in an electoral outcome, there is only one purchase, one elected government and, in relation to the goods provided by the elected government between elections, not everyone does or can receive that for which their vote might reasonably be considered sufficient payment. Elections are collective purchases. Indeed, they cannot be properly regarded as purchases at all, since the resulting political establishment is a public good, enjoyed or suffered by those who did not pay for it as well as those who did. Governments are not owned, at least not by voters.

Moreover, the market model can be viewed as corrupting in so far as it legitimates voting as a form of self-preference, indeed requires it as a necessary prerequisite of the outcome, hence the normative attractiveness of the deliberative counter-theories which foster impartiality and other moral attitudes in the democratic citizenry. By moving away from the idea that a vote is a means of obtaining personal benefit towards seeing the vote as an expression of opinion as to the general interest – as an interim decision-making process which temporarily interrupts a free and equal debate between all those affected by the decision in question – deliberative democracy gains the moral high ground.

Further, the market model encourages the acquiescence in the assumption that the goods to be fought for and won in the political arena are economic goods, either by way of redistribution or in relation to facilitating the attainment of wealth through economic activity. Democratic politics is the pursuit of economic advantage by other means. It encourages the view that the worth of a vote to citizens is what they can purchase with it by way of economic advantage. This means that it is in effect acceptable to 'buy' and 'sell' votes both analogically and literally.

This viewpoint extends to the basic accoutrements of democratic politics. Political office is not only a source of gainful employment to the elected representative, but a means for the disbursement of economic favours. Information is needed by voters to make the instrumentally best choices and is therefore a valuable commodity to be created for gain, bought and sold, borrowed and lent. Speech as the instrument of persuasion in an essentially economic process must be available to all citizens, but its availability can be at a price, for speech is as much a commodity as the vote itself. So we enter the world of highly rewarded opinion leaders with hidden paymasters, lobbyists on contract, public relations experts paid by results, political party fundraising, advertising expenditure, media owners and payments for asking parliamentary questions as a natural mode of democratic politics. Some of these activities are legal and others illegal, depending on where you are and when. Some of them are little more than a necessary economic base for non-economic political activity. However, in total, they amount to a commodification of available and effective political discourse, which carries the idea of a vote as a purchase to its logical conclusion.

If this is the democracy that is being globalised, then representative democracy is in real trouble since the market theory itself requires that economic and political currencies not be interchangeable. Democracy is a system of political equality, and political equality is unobtainable where the exercise of the equal rights involved can be bought and sold, hence the understandable concern about campaign finances, political advertising, economic gerrymandering and media ownership.

In theory, we can look to procedural human rights for assistance here, but the values of freedom have overcome the values of equality with respect to the human rights which are being globally prioritised. In particular, freedom of the market makes any real measures to control political advertising and media ownership unrealisable. Consequently, deliberative democracy is in no position to sustain its preconditions of equal access and participation in the relevant debates. Despite its many attractions, therefore, the market model is inevitably implicated in the commodification of politics in ways that must depress democratic expectations.

There are, however, some positive lines of thought yet to be explored, some of which take us to some crucial connections of law and democracy. Thus, there is scope for a *rapprochement* between self-determination, self-protection and deliberative theory. To achieve this we must first curb the pretensions of deliberative democracy to be the only theory which does not simply take preferences as given and seek a mechanism to turn private into collective decisions, but involves a developing interaction of views which progress towards a novel outcome. For instance, in utilitarian theory, freedom of expression has long been ascribed the role of rendering individual preferences and beliefs more rational and more co-ordinated. There is no problem, in principle, in developing this openness to include debate as to what constitutes a just agreement between participating parties. The self that is expressed or protected can be a self that cares about others as well as itself and is capable of giving equal consideration to the interests of others. Such self-interest can involve tolerance of the different values of others, but cannot be expected to endorse those values. Nor, as we have seen, is it to be expected that good faith and well-informed debate can resolve such value disagreements as remain, hence the need to retain the vote as an exercise of equal power which minimises the inevitable harm arising from the fact that not everyone can get their own way in a polity. Nevertheless, informed and impartial dialogue can serve to improve self-protectionism in terms of its own objectives, without being able to resolve basic value disagreements. Having lured elements of deliberative democracy into the self-protection camp, we are then faced with the utopianism of seeking to approximate to an ideal speech situation in a world of globalised markets. Two suggestions may be made in this respect, one relating to the form and the other to the content of law.

The rule of law is essential to democracy for a variety of reasons. One reason is that, where law is the prime object of democratic deliberation and choice, there is a greater chance of self-preferences rising to a measure of impartiality simply by dint of the fact that the matters at issue are presented in terms of categories and classes rather than individuals and particulars. At its most artificial, as regards a universal law which applies equally to all citizens with respect to a matter in which they are all similarly situated, even selfish self-interests will, as Rousseau notes, opt for that law which is in the general interest. At its most aspirational, having decisions generalised, and the categories of choice explicit, makes the citizen face up – preferably in public – to the moral choices involved in selecting relevant criteria.

If this has merit, the radical implication is that citizens should participate in debate and choice of rules directly rather than via their elected representatives, a procedure that also has the advantage of reducing the current slippage between what parties promise and what they actually deliver, thus diminishing the power of political parties, the influence of well-financed pressure groups and the opportunities for corruption.

The second positive suggestion, which responds to the charge of utopianism against deliberative democracy, has to do with the content of democratic law. It concerns, *contra* the tendencies of globalised market parameters, the strict separation of politics from financial inputs designed to influence the outcome in favour of one party or policy. All political choices must be made in the light of their economic consequences, *inter alia*. This does not mean that economic power should be permitted to influence those choices. Such a policy requires draconian restrictions on party political finance, political donations, availability of paid advertising and ownership control of media outlets, including editorial content. Without such measures, even the limited potentials of deliberative democracy are unrealisable and the self-protective function of the vote is vitiated by absence of reliable information and adequate debate.[21]

Taken together, choice of law, not choice of law-makers, and financially uncorrupted information and opinion flow, may seem an unfeasible order. However, there is one aspect of globalised markets that potentially works in their favour, namely the ever-increasing availability of economical and efficient means of communication. The Trojan horse of economic market power may turn out to

---

21 C Sunstein, *Democracy and the Problem of Free Speech*, New York: Free Press, 1993.

be the information technologies it has spawned. With a multimedia communication system in every home, the prospect of widely-viewed debate between and with random selected representatives, and electronic voting, there could exist the means if not the will for a shift to a more direct form of municipal democracy. This in turn may enhance the chances of democratising the international order so as to redirect global markets to serve the wellbeing of those vast populations who do not share in the creation and consumption of the goods that are and could be available to them, rather than the profitability of transnational companies and the governments who, increasingly, serve them.

# 13

# LEGAL POSITIVISM AND DELIBERATIVE DEMOCRACY

When celebrating the great intellectual tradition stemming from the work of Jeremy Bentham, it is appropriate to remind ourselves that legal philosophies often gain their significance and import from their place within wider political theories. It was Bentham's utilitarian philosophy that fuelled his theory of law as well as his eventual commitment to democracy. In contemporary legal philosophy the increasing importance of what we may call political philosophies of law follows on a decline in respect for purely analytical approaches to legal concepts, uncritical empiricist studies of law, and closed-circuit doctrinal exposition. The topical question in legal theory at the end of the millennium is not so much 'what is law?' as 'what sort of law do we want and why?'

In this context, it may seem curious to focus on legal positivism, an approach to law which has come to be identified with empty formalism, theorising by definition, morally detached linguistic analysis, and the unreflective science of calculable observations. However, legal positivism can be viewed, at base, as a morally grounded approach to law that sets out an ideal type of legal system. On this interpretation, legal positivism is a living political philosophy available to be re-articulated in relation to current political conditions. In particular, there is exciting work to be done relating the insights of legal positivism to the re-emerging participatory models of politics as they feature in deliberative or discourse theories of democracy.[1]

Legal positivism is generally regarded as an inadequate analytical and empirical theory whose distinctive feature is the avoidance of moral commitment. However, Benthamite positivism is not alone amongst positivisms in presenting a revisionary model of law in the context of a normative political theory of government, in his case as a system of regulated power which, amongst other things, serves to enhance democratic control of government. This mode of legal positivism may be called 'ethical positivism', principally to make it clear that the theory involves an evaluative commitment to a certain type of law – positive law – that is framed in such a way that it can be identified and followed or applied without recourse to contentious moral and political judgments.[2]

The term 'ethical positivism' also helps to signify that law, so conceived, is an institution within which the roles of judge, legislator and citizen bring with them certain ultimately unenforceable but indispensable moral duties of a type which are often referred to as 'ethical' because they relate to the performance of a role

---

1 For an excellent collection of essays, see J Bohman and W Rehg (eds), *Deliberative Democracy*, Cambridge, MA: MIT Press, 1997; also, C Nino, *The Constitution of Deliberative Democracy*, New Haven, CT: Yale University Press, 1996.

2 TD Campbell, *The Legal Theory of Ethical Positivism*, Aldershot: Dartmouth, 1996.

within the complex of roles that constitutes a social institution. Included in the role moralities of ethical positivism are the judicial duty to recognise and enforce only positive law, the legislative duty to enact laws which can be applied more or less without recourse to controversial moral and political judgments, and the citizens' duty to participate in an ongoing process of fair bargaining and open debate to determine the rules which are to be mandatory within their communities and to be loyal to the outcome of such a democratic process.

To establish that ethical positivism is a significant element within the positivist tradition, reference may be made to Gerald Postema's lucid exposition of Bentham's legal theory along just these lines.[3] More recently, Jeremy Waldron has advanced an analysis of the later work of Immanuel Kant, which convincingly presents Kant as what he calls a 'normative positivist', by which he means a positivist who uses 'value judgements that support the positivist position that evaluations of the former type [which identify some proposition as a valid legal norm] should not be necessary'. Waldron insists that:

> To present Kant as a legal positivist is thus not to neglect Kant the moraliser or Kant the theorist of value and right. Instead it is a matter of showing why – that is, on what evaluative grounds – Kant defended the idea of positive laws – that is, laws that people could identify as such whatever their particular moral views.[4]

Placing Kant and Bentham under the same ancestral umbrella may be thought to sacrifice precision for the sake of intellectual pedigree, but ethical positivism is in itself a partial and limited legal theory which has the potential to play the role of a unifying theory within which seriously different political philosophies and moral epistemologies may coexist or contend.[5] Currently, without their permission, we may identify the work of Neil MacCormick, Joseph Raz, Frederick Schauer and Jeremy Waldron as exemplifying significant elements of ethical positivism.[6]

On this basis, it is appropriate to explore the theory of ethical positivism in relation to two broad and schematic types of democratic theory – market theory and deliberative theory – and, in particular, consider the implications of deliberative theory for the role of courts in the development of the law and the constitutional propriety of substantive judicial review of legislation through

---

3 GJ Postema, *Bentham and the Common Law Tradition*, Oxford: Clarendon Press, 1986, 328–36.

4 J Waldron, 'Kant's legal positivism', *Harvard Law Review*, Vol 109, 1996, 1535–66, at 1541.

5 TD Campbell, 'Legal change and legal theory: the context for a revised legal positivism', in W Krawietz, DN MacCormick and GH von Wright (eds), *Prescriptive Formality and Normative Rationality in Modern Legal Systems*, Berlin: Dunker and Humbolt, 1994.

6 Thus, see for instance DN MacCormick, 'The ethics of legalism', *Ratio Juris*, Vol 2, 1989, 184–93; F Schauer, *Playing By the Rules: A Philosophical Examination of Rule-Based Decision-Making*, Oxford: Clarendon Press, 1991, 197; J Raz, 'Authority, law and morality', *Monist*, Vol 68, 1985, 39–40, and *The Authority of Law: Essays on Law and Morality*, Oxford: OUP, 1979; and J Waldron, 'The rule of law in contemporary liberal theory', *Ratio Juris*, Vol 2, 1989, 79–96.

court-administered bills of rights. It is suggested that the perceived descriptive accuracy of market theories, coupled with their evident moral inadequacies, underpins many of the arguments in favour of the development of judicial power in the service of democratic objectives. In this context, deliberative theories of democracy are often called in to vindicate the role of the courts as impartial arbiters of the common good and protectors of fundamental rights against majority indifference and market failure.

However, the more defensible forms of deliberative theory, such as that articulated by Jurgen Habermas,[7] indicate that the prime locus of democratic deliberation is the total community of persons affected by the exercise of political power. This suggests that, in so far as deliberative theories are thought to have significant application to the actual practice of politics, we should see them as diminishing the case for increased judicial power arising from the assumed descriptive accuracy and moral inadequacy of market theories, and supporting attempts to confine the constitutional role of courts to the protection of the conditions of democratic deliberation and electoral choice in the wider community.

This thesis may be supplemented and enhanced by an appreciation of the role of positive law in the promotion of democratic goals as it is articulated in the theory of ethical positivism.

## ETHICAL POSITIVISM AND DEMOCRACY

*The Legal Theory of Ethical Positivism* attempts a rehabilitation of a maligned theory of law which, in its crude and caricatured form, is regarded as descriptively and philosophically flawed. Legal positivism, according to its critics, is the thesis that law is an autonomous system of rules operating separately from the moral and political values which may be used to justify them. It is argued that this thesis does not capture the way in which legal systems actually operate. In particular, judges are not simply the mechanical appliers of rules mechanically identified as valid within the jurisdiction. Nor, it is said, does the positivist analysis of legal rules as having meanings which are there to be discovered accord with contemporary theories of meaning which locate the meaningfulness of symbols in the interactions of members of linguistic communities, sharing a way of life, in which meaning is negotiated along with much else besides. More generally, positivism is identified with an overdependence on analytic definitions and abstract conceptualism, which turns theorising about law into a matter of defining its key terms and the development of law into unpacking the implications of abstract ideas. Alternatively, legal positivism is identified with blinkered empiricism which purports to trace external patterns of causation from the origins to the outcome of legal process. The sins of autonomism, deductivism, formalism, conceptualism and empiricism are heaped on the head of the scapegoat theory of

---

7 See J Habermas, *Between Facts and Norms*, Cambridge, MA: MIT Press, 1997.

legal positivism recently referred to by one of its lonely American defenders as a 'pariah' theory.[8]

Ethical positivism seeks to rescue legal positivism from these caricatures by representing positivism as a normative political philosophy about the manner in which political power should be exercised:

> In brief and highly simplified terms [the legal theory of ethical positivism] presents an aspirational model of law according to which it is a presumptive condition of the legitimacy of governments that they function through the medium of specific rules capable of being identified and applied by citizens and officials without recourse to contentious personal or group political presuppositions, beliefs and commitments.[9]

In other words, ethical positivism is about striving towards the rule of law, specifically the rule of positive law, as a set of constitutional norms, a model which requires that political power be rule-governed, and in which we seek to establish rather than presuppose a body of ordinary and constitutional mandatory rules that can be recognised and applied in a value-neutral manner.

The political relevance of this ideal does presuppose that we are able to make significant progress towards operationally distinguishing the making of law from its application, separating the identification of the sources of law from the interpretation of particular laws and applying the same to particular fact situations. It also requires that we are able to formulate rules that have sufficient *de facto* meaning for the target audience that they can be understood and followed by members of that community whatever their own distinctive beliefs and perspectives. To that extent, the theory is empirically grounded, but it is not vulnerable to evidence that any particular system does not achieve these thresholds.

An adequate exposition of ethical positivism involves outlining both the moral reasons for having rules – the *justifications* of rule-governance – and the moral standards required of those who live under and operate such a system – the *ethics* of rule-governance.

In tackling the first question – 'why rules?' – we come across a surprisingly large number of rationales for having rule-centred polities. The familiar reasons highlight the role of rules in promoting co-ordination, social control, conflict avoidance and conflict resolution, and the way in which rules can offer partial defences against the injustices and fears perpetrated by arbitrary (that is, non-rule-governed) exercises of power; if rules are operating in a context where everything that is not forbidden is permitted, rule-governance allows for a sphere of autonomy in which individuals and collectivities can act as they please and be assured that they can so do.[10]

---

8 F Schauer, 'Positivism as a pariah', in RP George (ed), *The Autonomy of Law: Essays on Legal Positivism*, Oxford: OUP, 1996, Chapter 2.

9 TD Campbell, *op cit* fn 2, 2.

10 From the vast literature on these topics we may select as the best recent account of the role of rules F Schauer, *op cit* fn 8.

In addition to these familiar rule-rationales, there are some justifications of rule-governance which relate more specifically to the idea of democracy as distinct from the rule of law *per se.* In particular, there are impressive arguments which point to the ways in which a politics of rules, that is, a political system directed to the choice of rules rather than merely a choice of rulers, is more likely to come up with morally justified outcomes in terms of the democratic values of self-government, general wellbeing, and just equality.

These democratic virtues of rule-governance come about in a number of ways. First, there is what may be called the 'democratic control advantage', which relates to the fact that majorities can exercise more power through the choice of rules than they can through the choice of representative alone. Not only is control over representatives enhanced by requiring them to act in accordance with rules, as Dicey insists,[11] and to govern via legislation rather than official discretion but, in so far as there is an expectation that policies be presented in terms of the rules that will be enacted to implement them, control over elected representatives is potentially increased and a clearer basis provided for assessing their performance in ongoing public debate and prior to further electoral choice.[12]

A second democratic advantage of rule-governance relates to what may be called the 'moral form advantage' of having rules, a phenomenon which has application beyond, but is particularly germane to, democratic systems of government. The moral form advantage derives from the fact that all conduct affecting others, including the justifiable exercise of power, must, if it is to be a candidate for moral acceptance, embody some principle or maxim whereby its moral status may be assessed. As a matter of morality, acts are right or wrong only in so far as they exemplify acceptable or unacceptable *types* of conduct, where the type is identified through the morally relevant features of the act and actors. The moral form advantage takes up the idea of universalisability from moral philosophy and, in the tradition of Kant, applies it not only to the practice of legislation but to the content of what is legislated.

It follows from the criterion of universalisability that the conduct required of citizens by governments must be universalisable, in that their supporters must be prepared to see it applied to all persons in similar circumstances. Government policy, to pass moral scrutiny, cannot require citizens to behave in ways which are not at least candidates for such moral legitimacy. General rules, in so far as they specify required and permitted conduct in terms of classes of persons and types of conduct, can readily exemplify or be related to maxims which are at least candidates for universalisability.[13] In deciding which rules are to be mandatory in their jurisdiction, citizens are offered political choices which are presented in the appropriate moral form.

The moral form advantage is particularly potent where the political system affords real opportunities to debate the rules which are to be implemented in that

---

11 See AV Dicey, *Introduction to the Study of Law and the Constitution*, 10th edn, London: Macmillan, 1959.

12 See TD Campbell, *op cit* fn 2, 61.

13 See TD Campbell, *op cit* fn 2, 60.

polity. Discussion and decision in legislative assemblies, direct or indirect, is moralised through the requirement that decisions are about rules not about particulars, especially where the generalities are such that legislators and citizens are covered equally by the rules in question. Where citizens and legislators together are actually equally affected by the rules of their community, because the rules are literally universal in content and/or because all citizens are in basically the same situation with respect to the distinctions embodied in the rule, then rule-choice is a way of ensuring equality of outcome. Since it was Rousseau who sought to ensure that democratic assemblies focused on the common good, as distinct from the good of all individually, and sought to achieve such an egalitarian outcome by requiring that all citizens in his republic were in roughly equal economic and social circumstances, this virtue of rule-governance, a version of the moral form advantage, may be dubbed the 'Rousseau technique'.[14] In actual democracies, rule-making requires distinctions to be drawn which do not affect all citizens equally, but the ideal remains in the presumptions that all such distinctions must be justified and, other things being equal, the same set of rules should apply to legislators and citizens alike.

A further way in which rule-governance may be connected with democracy is in its centrality to constitutional forms of government. It may be claimed that democracy is a system of government which is particularly dependent on constitutionality, not only because the basic rules of an electoral system must be kept within bounds which can be considered to manifest political equality, but also because democracy presupposes a bundle of civil and political rights as prerequisites of the legitimacy of electoral outcomes.[15]

And so we have at least three reasons – democratic control, moral form and democratic constitutionality – that demonstrate a need for positivist rules in democratic systems. How precisely these points are developed and supplemented, and in particular how we are to tackle the question of who should have the power to make these rules, depends on a number of factors, including the conceptions of democracy that are adopted.

## THEORIES OF DEMOCRACY

Theories of democracy come in a bewildering variety of terms, with very different definitions, justifications, and institutional arrangements. Initially we may usefully think in terms of two simple models of democracy which apply principally to the understanding of electoral systems, but also have bearing on the

---

14 See J Waldron, 'Rights and minorities: Rousseau revisited', in J Chapman and R Wertheimer (eds), *Majorities and Minorities*, New York: New York University Press, 1991.

15 TD Campbell, *op cit* fn 2, 61: '[a]s in all constitutional politics, rules are required to state with some precision the prerequisites of that process. In the case of democracy this involves giving specific substance to such ideals as freedom of speech, responsible government and equal electoral capacity. This constitutional framework is an indispensable prerequisite for democracy, both with respect to its mechanisms and with respect to the rights of participation which must be firmly guaranteed for equal participation to be more than a formal possibility.'

everyday interactions of people and governments in democratic systems. Market theories provide an economics-style analysis of democratic choice and process, principally in representative systems. They are theories of choice and preference. Deliberative theories are those contemporary forms of participatory theory that stress the role of inclusive debate as to the content of the common good, traditionally in more direct democratic polities. They are theories of discussion, consensus, and sometimes of knowledge.

Discourse, or deliberative, theories,[16] which hold that democracy is essentially about open deliberation concerning the common good, purport to provide either a pragmatic or else an epistemological basis for consensual government. They have communitarian and civic elements which are initially more attractive than the rampant individualism and factionalism of market alternatives, according to which democracy is about buying and selling candidates or parties or elites so that as many people as possible get what they want. They also fit nicely with the trend to give more authority to legal process as a form of institutionalised debate. However, discourse theory is ambivalent with respect to judicial activism, by which I mean the practice of judges either making manifestly new law or using the leeway provided by the necessity of interpretation to bring their own or other extraneous moral, social, political and economic views into the substance of adjudication.

Nor does the theory of deliberative democracy provide a clear rationale for substantive judicial review, by which I mean giving courts the power to override legislation on the ground that it violates, for instance, fundamental rights, whether by way of common law principles or bills of rights, unless these latter are precisely formulated and electorally approved and can therefore be applied according to positivist methods of statutory interpretation.[17]

Moreover, deliberative democracy, in its pure form at any rate, is flawed in at least two ways. It is flawed in its utopianism, in that the standards required for genuine communicative action are often unrealisable in a political community. This means that it may be necessary to fall back on a degree of market realism in order to explain and justify democracies as they actually operate. Secondly, deliberative democracy is flawed in so far as it makes epistemological claims. Along with countless other political epistemologies that seek to institutionalise impartiality and information maximisation as the keys to justice and justification, deliberative theories fail to see that there are reasons for moral and political disagreement other than bias and ignorance.[18]

---

16 See J Bohman and W Rehg, *op cit* fn 1; and C Nino, *op cit* fn 1. Also, J Habermas, *op cit* fn 7; J Cohen, 'Deliberation and democratic legitimacy', in A Hamlin and P Pettit (eds), *The Good Polity*, Oxford: Blackwell, 1989; C Sunstein, *The Partial Constitution*, Cambridge, MA: Harvard University Press, 1993; and A Gutmann and D Thompson, *Democracy and Disagreement*, Cambridge, MA: Harvard University Press, 1996.

17 Formal judicial review, which relates to the scrutiny of legislation to see if it is within a head of power sanctioned by a constitution, is another matter.

18 This sweeping critique applies to all moral epistemologies that seek to extract comprehensive moral conclusions from the concepts of impartiality and consent alone.

While moral and political progress in relation to shared knowledge of the common good can be made through discursive debate in the right institutional setting, supplementation is needed, perhaps by maximising consent in the form of majority affirmation, if we are to establish a decisive and acceptable theory of democratic decision-making. This is not, however, simply another of those disappointing compromises that have to be made in political life, for there are attractive elements in the market theory of democracy – a theory which, in the proper framework, gives real content to the concept of self-determination. Market theory offers recognition to the desirability, other things being equal, of people having choices and getting what they want. This makes it a plausible device for resolving persistent value disagreement in a pluralistic society, in which case some combination of discourse and market theory may serve both to analyse and to justify the way that law can and should be made in a democracy.

Whatever theory of democracy is morally preferred, it is the perceived plausibility of market theory as a description of what actually goes on in liberal democracies, combined with the perceived moral deficiencies of pure market realism, with its undoubted insensitivity to the needs of vulnerable minorities and its blindness to the possibilities of genuinely just outcomes from the political process, which serves to promote interest in judicial activism and substantive judicial review as a means whereby courts can be sources of protection for those who miss out in the majoritarian market process.

We may be able to counter this trend if we combine elements of the two approaches and adopt a theory of democracy which is market at the core, but tempered by discourse elements which are sufficiently powerful to counter the factors of market theory which appear to call for the remedies of judicial activism and judicial review; then we may arrive at a more realistic and more appealing theory which, in conjunction with the commitment to rule-governance, may be called democratic positivism. By 'positivism' here is meant the normative theory that law ought to be a system of rules which can be followed and applied without recourse to the moral or political views of those involved. 'Democratic positivism' is a positivist system of law in which the overriding source of law is the people, defined in terms of competitive and free elections for the appointment of representatives who make law and for the establishment, directly or indirectly, of executive authority, all in a context which has at least some of the elements of open dialogue and freedom of association as part of the essential cultural background to the somewhat brutal closure mechanisms of elections and majority voting.

In summary, the theory of democratic positivism modifies the model of market democracy with discourse elements which are sufficient to sustain a balance clearly against judicial activism, beyond certain limited exceptions which give the courts delegated power to deal with ambiguities and gaps in existing law where it is unnecessary or unjust to await legislative clarification and development, and also against judicial review when it strays beyond the formalities of *ultra vires* and procedural justice. The market theory is, perhaps correctly, believed to be descriptively superior, but it has certain moral defects. Discourse theory is generally more admirable as an ideal but is often irrelevant because unreal, and has major epistemological insufficiencies. Nevertheless, there may be sufficient force in the deliberative approach to democracy for us to look at an improved political system in which judges continue to have a politically subordinate place but the discourse elements of democracy are more fully institutionalised and deployed amongst all those who are principally affected by the decisions in question.

## MARKET THEORIES OF DEMOCRACY

The still largely current form of market theories of democracy was established in the 1960s and is typified by the view of Joseph Schumpeter that democracy is a competitive struggle for the people's vote, a competition between elites which then debate, vote, and legislate, ostensibly on behalf of the people.[19] In general, political theorists at that time held the view that democracy is constituted by an electoral system whose justification, if it has one, depends on the benefits which result, principally to the majorities whose votes determine the outcome of the elections which decide who has the right to rule. The advantage of democracy, conceived of as a market-style interaction between candidates offering policies and citizens buying the most attractive package, is that this is the best way of realising the preferences of the largest number of people. How far and quite how it achieves this is a matter of disagreement internal to market theories but, in its classical form, it is a neat combination of institutionalising individual voter/consumer autonomy in a system which ultimately serves the general wellbeing through reflecting the preferences of reasonably prudent and knowledgeable voters.

Schumpeter's approach is a sceptical version of the market theory of democracy which goes back to the ideas propounded by early 19th century utilitarians, such as Jeremy Bentham and James Mill, who saw democracy as an institutional device to maximise the general happiness.[20] The classical utilitarian model of democracy is simple and to that extent attractive. Its postulates are credible and contemporary: all individuals are primarily interested in their own happiness or wellbeing and seek to secure it by more or less rational choice, selecting the means they believe to be best suited to obtain what they want. Included in what these self-interested persons want is security, regularity, the stability which makes commerce and family life possible, and the knowledge that agreements will be kept. In other words, they want governments, they want rules, they want protection, they want organised co-operation, but this involves giving authority to some of their number to make and enforce the requisite binding rules.

However, those who are given that authority are themselves self-interested rationalists, and are not to be trusted to do that which is for the welfare of others. Indeed, all rulers may be expected to use power to look after themselves at the

---

19 JA Schumpeter, *Capitalism, Socialism and Democracy,* 2nd edn, New York: Harper and Row, 1950.

20 See, for instance, J Mill, 'Essay on government', London: Encyclopedia Britannica, 1820; D Held, *Models of Democracy,* 2nd edn, London: Polity Press, 1996; and R Harrison, *Democracy,* London: Routledge, 1993, Chapter 6.

expense of others. Democracy is simply an institutional device for harmonising the self-interested actions of rulers with the self-interested desires of the ruled. The institution of periodic elections ensures that only those rulers who maximise the felt wellbeing of others will be re-elected and, of course, all rulers want to be re-elected. Democracy, according to this normative version of the market theory, is a set of procedures for achieving an artificial harmony of interests as between rulers and ruled.

With respect to the implications of the pure classical market theory of democracy for the role of courts, it seems clear that the internal implications of the theory are hostile to judicial activism and substantive judicial review. Within the market theory, the judicial role is essentially to facilitate the decisions of the sovereign people as expressed by them or their representatives. This is most evident in relation to the pure classical form of utilitarian market theory, but it remains applicable to Schumpeter's competition between elites if it is assumed that it is elections rather than judicial appointment that determine who rules. Of course, rejecting substantive judicial review is compatible with the uncontroversial role of courts in ensuring that government is conducted within the rule of law, in that legislatures act within the requirements of the constitution and the executive branch carries out its tasks only in accordance with the properly enacted laws of that state, a matter of formal review, but this stops far short of judicial activism and substantive judicial review.

However, while market theories in themselves exclude both judicial activism and substantive judicial review, it is clear that, in practice, many rationales for encouraging judicial activism in statutory and constitutional interpretation, and in the development of the common law, presuppose, in one way or another, the accuracy of some version of this market theory of democracy according to which the right to govern is the outcome of electoral competition. Paradoxically, although market theories do not themselves favour judicial activism and substantial judicial review, the market theory is taken for granted, as an accurate description of how democracies actually function, by most theorists who commend an activist and substantive law-making role for courts. They do so not because they take the theory to be descriptively false, at least not in Schumpeter's version, but because they take it to be morally inadequate.

For such theorists, courts may be required to correct the deficiencies which arise even in free and efficient political markets. In particular, courts may be given special briefs:

(a) to protect those minorities who lose out in the electoral process (hence the idea of courts as guardians of fundamental rights in common law or through bills of rights);

(b) to safeguard all individuals against a style of government which is serviced by self-interested bureaucracies and geared to give as little as it can in order to obtain the necessary quota of votes (hence formal and substantive judicial review of administrative conduct);

(c) to counter the short-sightedness and erratic performance of democratic governments as they pursue immediate political advantage (hence the practice of interpreting statutes so that they fit more readily into existing law conceived as a systematic whole).

In general, the perceived moral deficiencies of market democracy make it natural to look to the courts to protect minorities. What better role to give courts than the protection of human rights seen as those interests which are vital to the happiness and wellbeing of every individual?

This would certainly seem to be the line taken by Sir Gerard Brennan, the former Chief Justice of the High Court of Australia, although he does no more than hint at its more radical implications. In 'Courts, democracy and the law',[21] Brennan describes democracy, in Lord Hailsham's terms, as an elective dictatorship, and courts as the protectors of minorities from executive power. The courts' role in a democracy is to render protection available to those who believe themselves to be oppressed by the government that is not representing their interests.[22] Although he rejects substantive judicial review of legislative action, on the ground that the courts' role is the administration not the making of law, he regards the courts' control of executive power deriving from the use of interpretive techniques which draw on the fundamental principles of the common law.

The route whereby Brennan gets to this strong view of the courts' role with such a weak view of their capacities to control the executive is interesting. He identifies the Westminster model of responsible and representative government as inspired by Dicey's conception of an executive answerable to the Parliament and a supreme law-making Parliament representing the electorate in whom political power rests by reflecting their wishes in an effective manner. He then accepts the analysis that this situation applies no longer. Executives do not accurately reflect the wishes of the people and are not controlled by the people's representatives. Explicitly adopting Schumpeter's definition of democracy as 'that institutional arrangement for arriving at political decisions in which individuals acquire the power to decide by means of a competitive struggle for the people's vote' in opposition to Dicey's model of representation and sovereignty,[23] he calls for a 'more realistic view of democracy in our time' and a re-appraisal of the constitutional safeguards of freedom. Since the Parliament does not reflect the people's wishes, and does not in any case control the executive, who but the courts can protect the oppressed?

In fact, Brennan does not think that courts should fail to apply duly enacted laws within the constitutional powers of the Parliament on the grounds that they are unjust. There can be no 'interference with lawful policy: that is the proper domain of the political branches'.[24] The Constitution of Australia simply does not allow for substantive judicial review of that sort. What courts do is 'subject the political branches of government to the rule of law', but what does this involve? No more, it appears, than ensuring that the Parliament stays within its

---

21 Brennan CJ, 'Courts, democracy and the law', *Australian Law Journal*, Vol 65, 1991, 32–42.

22 *Ibid*, 32.

23 JA Schumpeter, *op cit* fn 19, 269.

24 Brennan CJ, *op cit* fn 21, 36.

constitutionally enunciated powers and the executive remains within the law enacted by the Parliament, assuming these are within its constitutionally allocated powers. Brennan does toy with the idea of fundamental common law rights which are superior to Parliament's enactments,[25] and he does hold to a very exalted overview of the values enshrined in the common law as including 'the dignity and integrity of every person, substantive equality before the law, the absence of unjustified discrimination, the peaceful possession of one's property, the benefit of natural justice, the immunity from retrospective and unreasonable operation of laws',[26] but he restricts the import of common law rights to the piecemeal development of the common law and the process of statutory interpretation.[27] What he has in mind here are the presumptions against retrospective operation, against the creation of a criminal offence, against a right to search and seize, and against the expropriation of property, none of which count against clear and explicit legislation with respect to these matters. This is really quite tame in the light of his diagnosis of the collapse of the system of responsible and representative government and his vision of the courts as 'applying the law in preservation of a free and democratic society'.[28]

Chief Justice Brennan's paper is simply one example of the thesis that the introduction of the idea of deep common law rights, along with proposals for enacting a bill of rights, or developing a more vigorous approach to implied constitutional rights, can often stem from an acceptance of market theories of democracy as fairly accurate pictures of what actually takes place in representative government. These proposed reforms and doctrinal developments are then presented either as ways of both securing a genuine political market and/or making up for the perceived deficiencies of fully realised political markets, particularly in relation to those who miss out in the competitive process.[29]

## DELIBERATIVE THEORIES OF DEMOCRACY

Of course, despite common assumptions to the contrary, market theories, particularly in their classical forms, may not be descriptively adequate. Market theories of democracy have been subjected to sustained criticism on descriptive as well as evaluative grounds. There is not too much evidence that voters act as rational maximisers of their own utilities, either with respect to their prudential rationality (are we really that bright?), or with respect to their motivations and outlook (are we really that selfish?), and there is some evidence that voters have

---

25 See TRS Allan, *Law, Liberty and Justice: Legal Foundations of British Constitutionalism*, Oxford: Clarendon Press, 1993.

26 Brennan CJ, *op cit* fn 21, 40.

27 'The values of the common law inform the rules of statutory interpretation': Brennan CJ, *op cit* fn 21, 37.

28 Brennan CJ, *op cit* fn 21, 41.

29 For a similar theme, see The Hon Sir John Laws, 'The Constitution: morals and rights', *Public Law*, 1996, 622.

some concern for social justice and the welfare of others.[30] Indeed, it has often been pointed out that if we are all rational maximisers to whom voting is bothersome, then, if voting were not compulsory, we would never vote unless we believed that our vote would make a difference to the outcome which, of course, it almost never does.[31]

In addition to these doubts as to the economic model of human behaviour, there are difficulties with the analogy between a market and an election in that, with a market, we can generally make our choice as individuals as to what we buy, so that one person can buy item A and another item B, whereas in an election only one item or packages of items are bought as a result of the aggregation of individual choices.

And so, even in the descriptive mode, market theories are less than satisfactory, and this is one reason why they are displaced by discourse theories according to which democratic government is a process of open and uncoerced deliberation aimed at reaching a rational consensus concerning the common good or public interest in which elections and majority voting are no more than second-best devices to reach some binding decisions in a process of deliberation which ideally ought to go on until unanimous agreement is obtained.

This deliberative model is radically different from the market model in the following respects:

(a) It is not about making individual demands, or making mutually beneficial agreements (as in contracting or bargaining), but about choosing between rival conceptions of the common good.

(b) It utilises voting only in a context of ongoing deliberation in which preferences are not taken as given, fixed inputs, but change and develop in the process of seeking agreement. To engage in deliberation is to accept propositions only on the basis of impersonal reasons, which involves a willingness to change your own views as well as an effort to change the views of others. Deliberative democracy is not a process for translating fixed individual preferences into an aggregate which gives a particular social outcome; rather, it is a process of dialogue whereby people change their preferences in the light of the arguments and information presented to them.

(c) It rejects the assumption that people are wholly egotistical and calculating, and assumes a capacity for impersonal reflection and a mutual recognition of the value of each individual as able to engage in such reasoned deliberations.

(d) It is communitarian in its commitment to truth as a socially deliberative outcome (although sometimes consensus takes the place of truth as the objective of deliberation).

---

30 D Held, *op cit* fn 20, Chapter 5.

31 For instance, R Wollheim, 'A paradox in the theory of democracy', in P Laslett and WG Runciman (eds), *Philosophy, Politics and Society*, 2nd series, Oxford: Blackwell, 1962, 71–87.

(e) It has more radical assumptions about what sort of equality is required for democratic process. Not only must there be mutual recognition of each other as sources of reasons for selecting this or that conception of the public good, but there must be a social reality in which individuals are free from those pressures which would prevent them responding to better reasons rather than to greater pressures, and in which there is genuine opportunity for all citizens to participate in the process of dialogue.[32]

Deliberative interpretations of democratic process undermine many of the reasons commonly given for strengthening the creative role of courts in the democratic process. This is because the institutionalising of discourse in the political system around the common good counters the perceived problems of market theories with respect to minorities and the protection of fundamental values. Dialogue theories enable us to claim that the broadly participatory political process is epistemically the best source of law from these points of view. The articulation and protection of human rights, for instance, is a more likely outcome of democratic political debate than elitist legal discourse.

In a deliberative democracy, courts may still be required to secure the conditions of free and open debate, but the nature of these conditions is best determined through political discourse. Courts may still be required to protect fundamental rights, but the content of these rights is a controversial matter on which rational consensus must be sought. Courts must keep bureaucracies within the rule of law, but that law is the creation of the deliberative process. Further, the defects which arise from the market model of democracy as a competition between self-interested political consumers and retailers do not arise to the same extent in a system in which decisions are made on the basis of reasons addressed to the content of the common good which all those affected can be expected to recognise and affirm.

In brief, if the discourse theory is accepted, then there may be less reason to fear for the welfare of minorities, although there may be continuing, perhaps increased, reason to question the legitimacy of 'democratic' decisions which do not match up to the premises of democratic dialogue. Indeed, while setting these standards is properly the outcome of democratic process, where a political system falls below a minimum threshold of open debate it may in some circumstances be democratically proper for judiciaries to take the lead in setting these standards as well as applying them.

## DELIBERATIVE DEMOCRACY AND THE JUDICIAL ROLE

It is possible to be quite sceptical about discourse theory and the deliberative turn in democratic theory, which can look like an irrelevant fantasy in the context of the banalities of number-crunching politics and the realities of Parliaments where the low level of debate is often an embarrassment. Given the very real inadequacies of

32 This skeletal model of discourse democracy draws heavily on C Nino, *op cit* fn 1.

actual democratic process, it remains tempting to look to courts to supplement or improve on the defective dialogue which characterises the normal political process, and, if we are looking for a discourse theory which is more elitist than the dialogue of representatives, judges may readily be adopted as an alternative elite. Judges, it may be thought, are professional practitioners of public dialogue, accustomed to giving reasons and making decisions on the merits of the case rather than bowing to external pressures. Indeed, the economic and institutional independence of the judiciary can be seen as a ground for giving political legitimacy to their dialogues over and against that of politicians and voters.

Courts, a discourse theorist may argue, should have an enhanced role in a deliberative democracy because:

(a) reason and debate are inherent in the judicial method, at least at the appellate level;

(b) the independence of judiciaries from economic and political pressure puts them in a situation of impartiality from which they have a better view of what constitutes the public interest than other people;

(c) the rules of natural justice ensure that judges hear all sides of a case and disqualify themselves if they have a personal interest in the outcome of the case.

Models for judicial dialogue can be derived from a number of philosophical sources. John Rawls's theory of how we should approach the choice of fundamental principles to determine the basic rights and duties in society seems particularly apposite.[33] If we consider, for instance, how to institutionalise the Rawlsian method of reflective equilibrium and the device of the veil of ignorance, who could do this better than specialists in the rules of evidence who are trained to put out of their minds what is deemed to be inadmissible or irrelevant?

Adding together the norms of judicial independence, according to which judges must not be beholden to external pressures, and the rules of natural justice (such as the rule excluding a judge who has a personal interest in the outcome of a case) comes near enough to the package of qualifications required of the impartial spectator, whose judgments often attract moral respect, to make it reasonable to claim that there is at least a substantial overlap between the legal and the moral points of view. One familiar version of this approach allocates to judges the role of articulating, as well as applying, fundamental rights, leaving as the sole reserved territory for representative legislatures the task of deciding those policy issues which do not affect fundamental rights. Conjoined with the thesis that, where they conflict, rights trump policies, this justifies giving enormous legislative power to courts.[34]

A market theorist will be suspicious of such judicial power on the grounds that judges are not exempt from the sway of self-interest and are not open to the

---

33 J Rawls, *A Theory of Justice*, New York: OUP, 1972.

34 See R Dworkin, *Taking Rights Seriously*, New York: New York University Press, 1978, and *Law's Empire*, London: Fontana, 1986.

discipline of electoral accountability. While a dialogue theorist may be more sanguine on the matter if the courts in question approximate to a process of open dialogue untrammelled by the constrictions of precise legal authorities, nevertheless, the closed circle of those who can join in such judicial debates is bound to remain a worry for the dialogue theorist. In order to be a satisfactory part of democratic dialogue, courts would have to be open to wider sources of opinion and evidence than is currently the case. However, if judges are to make their decisions in accordance with law rather than by a direct appeal to reason and the common good, which must surely remain their prime function, then judicial dialogue is not the sort of open-ended debate that the proponents of discursive democracy have in mind. It may be that in hard cases, where judges must reach beyond existing law, judges should mimic democratic dialogue with respect to their interpretative role, and even use the same methods to fill in gaps and maybe to dispense with obsolete laws, but such judicial creativity can easily get out of hand if it permits giving direct appeals to public notions of justice and the common good which bypass the process of democratic debate and substitute specialist legal talk for open political dialogue.

The main problem with this initially attractive scenario is that, while factors (such as tenure and secured salary) which are considered central to judicial independence are of enormous importance with respect to promoting the accurate implementation of existing law by protecting judges from external pressures, they do not constitute a sufficiently superior vantage point for the determination of the common good to provide grounds for giving the judiciary such a major share in the creation and development of entrenched law. Many theories of the epistemology of moral judgment, including those involved in discourse democracy, put great stress on the significance of impartiality as the grounding for the legitimacy of moral opinions. The Kantian imperative to act on that maxim which you can will as a universal law, which is used in relation to the justification for rule-governance, is only one example of the conceptual and epistemological link often alleged to hold between impartial assessment of human conduct and reliable moral judgment.[35]

From an epistemological point of view, it can be argued that, while partiality, in the sense of having a personal interest in the outcome, can be accepted as a disqualification as far as moral judgment goes, it is far from clear that impartiality, considered as personal non-involvement in the particular case and giving equal weight to the interests of all those involved, is sufficient in itself to generate moral truth or create moral authority. Kant's universalisability principle has never prevented disagreement between equally impartial individuals as to what they would be prepared to universalise. However independent they may be, judges are in no better position than anyone else to choose between competing values or conflicting moral rights. Judicial impartiality may negate selfishness, but it cannot distinguish values and decide on the precise content of basic rights. It follows that there are reasons for either seeking to exclude the matter in hand from the scope of legal obligation and leaving it to individual choice, or deferring

---

35 For a recent example, see B Barry, *Justice as Impartiality*, Oxford: OUP, 1994.

to the views of the majority, a procedure which at least maximises pre satisfaction.

The standard liberal move at this point in the argument is to draw on the distinction revived and popularised by Rawls between the right and the good, according to which the morality that may be required of citizens relates to rightness and wrongness, while the morality that is left to individual choice is between what is good and bad or, sometimes, in a less moral form, what one wants or does not want.[36] The right is infused with the rigours and force of deontological language – the discourse of imperatives – and closely associated with the cognate concepts of rights and duties, whereas the good is linked to consequentialist theories, according to which conduct is not right or wrong in itself but only in relation to the niceness or nastiness of its results.

With some such dichotomy in place it is then claimed that impartial courts are well fitted to determining right, while legislatures are more suited to dealing with the maximisation of the good, conceived as the sum of individual utilities. Courts are not well informed on the consequences of conduct, but they know right and wrong when they see them. In particular, they are experts on legal right and wrong, which is spelled out in terms of a system of rights and duties that requires a knowledge of rules and principles, which is their domain. The political function of the distinction between right and good becomes clear. Individuals by themselves and through their representatives are left to pursue their personal ideas of the good life; the state provides a framework of rights and duties to ensure that, in so doing, they do not harm their neighbours. All this paves the way for the claim that the methods of impartiality are adequate, and indeed superior, with respect to justice and rights, while allowing that differences of values should be left to the political process.

Great political weight is given to this frail distinction. We do not need to be Benthamites to see that judgments about good and bad, worthwhile and not worthwhile, valuable and not valuable, enter deeply into the determination of what conduct is right and wrong, and thus into the determination of what rights and duties we ought to institutionalise. It is true that there are matters which ought to be left to individuals, and technical matters concerning the best means to, say, economic ends which are appropriate matters for legislatures backed up by massive bureaucracies. It is also true that once we adopt a system of rights and duties, then, until we decide to change them, these rights and duties should be enforced without calculation of consequences other than those referred to in the content of the rights and duties themselves.[37] This does not mean, however, that decisions about which fundamental values ought to be protected and secured by rights and duties can be determined by impartiality methodologies alone, any more than it means that we can determine basic rights and duties by some Kantian or Rawlsian device which judges could become rather good at it if they only tried, perhaps with a bit of philosophical coaching.

---

36 This is a central theme in J Rawls, *op cit* fn 33.

37 See TD Campbell, *The Left and Rights*, London: Routledge, 1983, Chapter 3.

## CONCLUSION

This selective summary of some prime contentious territory of legal and political philosophy at the turn of the millennium may be rounded off with a brief consideration of the recent work of Jurgen Habermas, the leading exponent of discourse ethics and the deliberative theory of democracy.

In some ways, the work of Habermas can be viewed as simply one further attempt to derive substantial substantive conclusions from the concepts of consent and impartiality, in his case via the idea of ideal speech act theory, but his approach is distinctive and exciting, both because of its philosophical grounding and its location within continental European social theory. The philosophical method is a Kantian-style transcendental deduction of the presupposed communicative ideals of uncoerced dialogue in which the equal participants are committed to truth, sincerity and normative rightness. The social theory gives context to what would otherwise be a historically detached analysis of law and explains his refusal to detach this communicative ideal from the actualities of real-life dialogue.

Habermas's basic claim is that engaging in dialogue commits us to a co-operative search for truth and justice, for 'every speech act involves the raising of criticisable validity claims aimed at inter-subjective recognition'[38] but, unlike those who take what he calls the philosophical approach to such matters, he is concerned with justice in a world where facticity is central to legitimacy, in that we are dealing – particularly in the sphere of law – with the stabilising of expectations through established social practices. The 'facts' in *Between Facts and Norms* include the sort of instantiated positive law that is fundamental to legal positivism. However, the success of law as fact in promoting social cohesion depends on an acceptance of law as legitimate or just, and here we have the tie-in with deliberation for, in a pluralist world, acceptable norms of justice are the outcome only of communicative rationality, hence legitimacy requires general deliberation amongst those affected.

The argument is long, cumulative, and extremely scholarly, and I refer to Habermas only to ask what, in the light of this discourse theory, he makes of the judicial role in a democracy. If deliberative democracy requires open dialogue between all those affected by the outcome, we should find in Habermas a clear example of a broadly populist approach to the articulation of what is just and a rejection of the idea that concretisation of basic rights can be done by courts as representative deliberators. Indeed, this is how his argument ultimately does go. Thus, while he broadly admires Dworkin's judge Hercules, who takes legal facticity very seriously in his respect for precedent and statute and yet is prepared to transcend such positive sources of law in the light of a more universal conception of justice, he echoes Michelman's quip that Hercules is a 'loner', the implication being that the dialogue necessary to transcend the status quo must be undertaken by the general populace, not the expert elites.

---

38 J Habermas, *op cit* fn 7, 18.

Certainly, Habermas does not think that any individual or group, judicial or otherwise, can use his method to read off substantive principles of justice in the way that Rawls or Dworkin methodologies may be deployed. Substantive principles can be the product only of actual social deliberation, 'the *argumentative process* of the co-operative search for truth'.[39] He rejects as insufficient the liberal individualist paradigm of a pre-existing known set of individual rights; he rejects also as insufficient the social welfare paradigm of law as an instrument for maximising wellbeing. In their place he has a purely procedural model of law, with the procedure of law-making coming through the discursive will-formation of a free and equal dialogue: '[i]f we follow a procedural theory, the legitimacy of legal norms is gauged by the rationality of the democratic procedure of political legislation.'[40]

The significance of widespread social dialogue follows from the fact that the public political discourse is not a matter of abstract philosophical thought but is an attempt at agreement in a particular society with its particular customs along the lines of the communitarian pursuit of self-understanding.[41] In the perhaps unfortunate terminology used by Habermas, legitimating discourse involves 'ethical' discussion, by which he means that it concerns the customs or ethos of a concrete society as well as a 'moral' discussion, that is, in his view, norms with connotations of universality in abstraction from specific perceptions of what is good and bad or, in the case of law, with norms of universal justice which relate to fundamental rights and duties.[42]

Further, Habermas sees that there is no need to make an exception to socially inclusive dialogue simply because we are dealing with fundamental rights.[43] He also rejects the view of Ackerman and Michelman that constitutional courts can act as representatives of the people in protecting their interests in a paternalistic manner. For Habermas, this involves the false assumption that democratic will-formation is a matter of putting into place prior settled mores, whereas, in accordance with deliberative theory, actual debate leads to revised outcomes.[44]

However, Habermas does acknowledge the need for interpretation in the course of the 'discourse of application', as he terms the basic function of the judiciary, and he accepts the propriety of the pressure to achieve internal legal coherence in the process of applying norms. Nevertheless, he retains the separation of powers, presenting law as a 'system of rights that ... is interpreted and elaborated in procedures of democratic legislation and impartial norm application',[45] thus

---

39 J Habermas, *op cit* fn 7, 280.

40 J Habermas, *op cit* fn 7, 232.

41 J Habermas, *op cit* fn 7, 280.

42 J Habermas, *op cit* fn 7, 282: 'Unlike ethical questions, questions of justice are not inherently related to a specific collectivity and its form of life. The law of a concrete legal community must, if it is to be legitimate, at least be compatible with moral standards that claim universal validity beyond the legal community.'

43 J Habermas realises that the argument of *Marbury v Madison*, 1 US 137 1803 is not logically watertight: see *op cit* fn 7, 240–41. See also C Nino, *op cit* fn 1, Chapter 6.

44 J Habermas, *op cit* fn 7, 277–78.

45 J Habermas, *op cit* fn 7, 234.

sustaining a clear distinction between the democratic process of legislation and the application of established rights and duties to concrete situations. Moreover, the legitimacy of the procedures adopted in the judicial application of legislation is itself a matter which is determined by the democratic deliberative process.

However, Habermas does not make it entirely clear whether assessment of the legitimacy of judicial interpretation relates to the substance of the outcome or the method of legal reasoning deployed. No doubt this will depend on whether the judicial method of interpretation adopted involves appeal to substantive moral principles not determinately identified in law. This is not made clear so, while it is possible to read most of what Habermas says as concurring with the view that judicial method is limited to arriving at a procedurally proper method of determining how particular laws are to be understood and applied, it sometimes appears that the legitimacy required of each legal decision means that judges must transcend such legally internal interpretative norms as Herculean consistency and coherence, and utilise purely judicial dialogue to arrive at a substantively just outcome *contra* established law. In the constitutional context, his discussion of these matters presupposes rather than argues for a distinct constitutional law on American and German lines. In general, his position is hostile to the 'value' jurisprudence of German constitutional law in so far as this involves the application of generalised values rather than a debate centred on norms. In this sense, he severely circumscribes the role of the constitutional courts so that it is no more than an intensified form of the ordinary courts' interpretative role of rendering the law coherent:

> The court reopens the package of reasons that legitimate legislative decisions so that it might mobilise them for a coherent ruling on the individual case in agreement with existing principles of law; it may not, however, use these reasons in an implicitly legislative manner that directly elaborates and develops the system of rights.[46]

His considered position, therefore, would appear to be that legal discourse can lay claim to a comparatively high presumption of rationality, because application discourses are specialised questions of norm application and can thus be institutionalised within the surveyable framework of the classical distribution of rules between the involved parties and an impartial third party. For the same reason, however, they cannot substitute for political discourses that, 'geared for the justification of norms and policies, demand the inclusion of all those affected'.[47]

On the other hand, Habermas commends a protective role for constitutional courts in overseeing the democratic process. According to his procedural understanding of the constitution, 'the constitutional court should keep watch over just that system of rights that makes citizens' private and public autonomy equally possible'.[48] In a somewhat more specific formulation than John Hart Ely's

---

46 J Habermas, *op cit* fn 7, 262.
47 J Habermas, *op cit* fn 7, 266.
48 J Habermas, *op cit* fn 7, 283.

representation reinforcing theory of constitutional interpretation,[49] Habermas contends that 'the constitutional court must work within the limits of its authority to ensure that the process of law-making takes place under the legitimating conditions *of deliberative politics*'.[50] The pursuit of this goal does not seem to be limited by the existing, perhaps defective, political process, and appears to afford considerable leeway for interventionist courts, but this needs to be spelled out and defended in much greater detail, especially as his theory that private autonomy and public autonomy go hand in hand involves the view that autonomy requires significant material provision if all individuals are to share in these autonomies. If a measure of social and economic equality is required to reach the appropriate threshold of ideal speech conditions to provide democratic legitimacy, then the power to review legislation in the light of its procedural democratic credentials could impact on core economic and social policy.

Also, if Habermas takes the political arguments for sustaining the facticity of law seriously, it may be argued that judicial review must include judicial oversight of the positivistic form of democratic outputs. If legislatures do not come up with specific rules interpretable and applicable without recourse to contentious moral and political judgments, then they may be regarded as functioning outside the scope of constitutional democracy, a violation of what it is that deliberative politics is meant to be about.

Even such restricted powers of review still leave us with the perennial question of who is to control the controllers and keep the judges within their required roles of applying positive law and guarding the prerequisites of deliberative democracy and its market substratum. Ultimately, that role must be self-enforced, hence the most ethical role in the interlocking set of the ethical roles of courts, legislatures, and citizens is the duty of the judge to positive law, a duty with which judges should be more at home than they are with the role of moral arbiter over the contentious content of vague statements of entrenched rights.

Overall, the current work of Jurgen Habermas supports the conclusion that the theory of deliberative democracy implies that we ought to be striving to improve the quality of dialogue in representative politics, rather than locating the resolution of political issues in the debates of specialist lawyers, even if they do have a measure of political and economic independence enjoyed by few other groups in society. Indeed, it could be highly detrimental to the ideals of democracy if the case for judicial independence relating to such matters as tenure, appointment, salaries and pensions was thought to be part of an argument for increasing the power of courts in relation to such controversial political issues as the proper content of fundamental rights, rather than preserving their role as impartial adjudicators of fact and administrators of pre-existing positive law.

---

49 JH Ely, *Democracy and Distrust: A Theory of Judicial Review*, Cambridge, MA: Harvard University Press, 1980.

50 J Habermas, *op cit* fn 7, 274.

14

# DEMOCRATIC ASPECTS OF ETHICAL POSITIVISM[1]

There are important constitutional questions about the role of judiciaries and legislatures in contemporary democracies. Here these issues are discussed in the context of the suggestion that the tradition of legal positivism has an important bearing on the formulation of principles specifying how judges and legislatures ought to carry out their tasks.

This is a formidable undertaking. It requires the articulation and deployment of both a theory of law and a theory of democracy, and this in an age in which theories of any sort are suspect. It is a particularly formidable task because the theory of law in question is legal positivism, a paradigm which has been systematically questioned as a result of developments in philosophy and the social sciences. Today, legal positivism is widely regarded as intellectually, empirically and morally untenable, and legal positivists no longer have the confidence which arises from espousing what used to be the reigning orthodoxy of leading practitioners.

The intellectual problems of legal positivism arise principally from the role that legal positivists ascribe to rules as a means of controlling conduct, including the conduct of governments, which runs counter to contemporary views on the indeterminacy of language. The empirical problems of legal positivism centre on their perceived failure to identify the boundaries between law, morality and politics in actual legal systems. Morally, legal positivism is frequently portrayed as bankrupt, having in the past tolerated slavery,[2] Hitler's democratic socialism[3] and South Africa's apartheid system,[4] and currently resisting the progressive institutionalisation of the human rights movement. It is also held responsible for the failure of legal systems to adapt to changing circumstances, the insensitivity of judges to the personal and social realities affecting the litigants who pass through their courts, and the amorality or immorality of lawyers whose professional conduct is often regarded with contempt.[5]

---

1 This chapter benefited greatly from the enthusiastic participation of everyone who attended the Workshop on 'Judicial activism and judicial review in Australian democracy', particularly Fred Schauer, who has been highly supportive of the project at every stage.

2 R Cover, *Justice Accused*, New Haven, CT: Yale University Press, 1975.

3 See HLA Hart, 'Positivism and the separation of law and morals', *Harvard Law Review*, Vol 71, 1958, 593; and LL Fuller, 'Positivism and fidelity to law: a reply to Professor Hart', *Harvard Law Review*, Vol 71, 1958, 630.

4 See D Dyzenhaus, *Hard Cases in Wicked Legal Systems: South African Law in the Perspective of Legal Philosophy*, Oxford: Clarendon Press, 1991.

5 See W Simon, *The Practice of Justice: A Theory of Lawyers' Ethics*, Cambridge, MA: Harvard University Press, 1998.

Democracy gets a rather better press, although its almost universal popularity makes it harder, rather than easier, to find our way through to a satisfactory theory of democracy. Beyond the conceptual link between democratic government and political equality and a high level of agreement that it is desirable that governments be subject to periodic popular elections, accompanied by a minimum threshold of civil liberties and political rights, there is no single coherent theory of democracy which can both guide us as to what sort of democratic system we should have and, at the same time, elicit the general support of specialist participants and ordinary citizens which would be required to put it into practice. We seem doomed to operate with an uneasy mixture of incompatible democratic ideals with, on the one hand, a market model according to which political power is a commodity and voters are consumers out to satisfy their individual desires by purchasing the political package that seems to offer them most of what they want and, on the other hand, a participatory or deliberative theory which relies on the unlikely prospect of giving a controlling political influence to a public discourse which is directed to the achievement of a consensus as to what constitutes justice and the common good.

Notwithstanding these difficulties, this chapter suggests a framework for deriving some tentative answers to some rather familiar questions – answers which have some prospect of commanding general approval and generating practical guidance. These answers and guidance are designed to be relatively neutral in terms of the particular substantive matters which divide citizens as to the content of first-order political and legal decisions, but enable the setting up of democratically acceptable legal processes and procedures for the resolution of such disagreements and direct those who operate such institutions as to how they should conduct their business.

I call the politico-legal framework of principles proposed 'democratic positivism'. Democratic positivism is positivistic in the tradition of a legal positivism that is wedded to the political significance of channelling governmental power through specific unambiguous conduct-governing mandatory rules, with genuine exclusionary force, capable of being applied without recourse to contentious moral and political judgments – rules which have their source in empirically identifiable and constitutionally defined human acts.[6] Democratic positivism is democratic in that it affirms that the source of these authoritative rules is empirically identifiable institutional acts which are the outcome of democratic procedures. Democratic procedures are taken to be procedures that serve to maximise the involvement of all those affected by the rules that bind them in a way which approximates to the ideal of giving their choices equal weight with respect to rules and decisions which are binding on them. This confines the term democracy to those systems of government that seek to approach equality of individual self-determination, either through direct

---

6 More technically, democratic positivism is a form of prescriptive hard positivism which presupposes soft positivism (the thesis that a legal system may, with conceptual propriety, incorporate morality as a criterion of the rule of recognition) but contends that no legal system ought to incorporate such criteria. See TD Campbell, 'The point of legal positivism', *King's College Law Journal*, Vol 9, 1998, 61–87, at 68–70.

participation in the legislative and executive process, or through the election of representatives whose role is to legislate and govern on their behalf, subject to periodic election, ongoing opportunities for criticism and systems of answerability which require public responses to criticism, both prior and subsequent to electoral accountability.[7]

## DEMOCRATIC POSITIVISM

Democratic positivism is a theory in tension in so far as the positivist aspects involved can come into conflict with its democratic elements. For instance, a democratic political process may come up with a decision to depart from the rule of positive law in favour of more particular and less formal outcomes. Or the requirement of the rule of positive law may prevent elected governments from exercising judicial functions or passing laws embodying vague moral standards.

We can reduce this tension between democracy and positivism by excluding from the normal democratic process those rules which constitute the electoral procedures and the systemic prerequisites, such as freedom of speech, which give legitimacy to putatively democratic decision-making. These prerequisites, which could even include the governance of rules as a means of promoting political equality, may be exempt from democratic change on the grounds that they are constitutive of democracy and cannot therefore be dispensed with without undermining the democratic credentials of the system. This move does not solve that core problem of democratic theory which concerns the appropriate decision procedures for determining precisely what these untouchable democratic fundamentals should be, but it is an indispensable part of any genuinely democratic theory that self-destructive 'democratic' decisions are not democratic at all. Further, in so far as it can be shown that legal positivism is itself a democratic prerequisite, and therefore partially constitutive of any acceptably democratic system, the tension between legal positivism and democracy is eliminated. Moreover, it is arguable that a system of law and government which embodies the norms of prescriptive legality is part of the presuppositions which constitute democratic systems. On this view, the issue of whether government must be conducted in accordance with a system of positive law is not open to democratic disposal.

To follow through this analysis, we must move from clarification of terms enabling empirical descriptions of political and legal institutions to the substance of the rationales and justifications of democracy and legal positivism which are indispensable to the further specification of both concepts. In relation to legal

---

7 A more familiar term than democratic positivism would be constitutional democracy, but this does not sufficiently capture the fact that the constitutions in question are concerned to establish governance through rules or, more specifically, governance through positive rules. Another description for my politico-legal ideal might be democracy within the rule of law, but this is apposite only if we give a positivistic interpretation to the rule of law whereby the law in question fits the positivist model of the application of pre-existing specific rules capable of being understood and implemented without direct recourse to contentious value judgments.

positivism, the main justificatory task relates to the social utility and moral significance of societal rules, as opposed to unfettered individual autonomy or the discretionary power of officials, and the moral appropriateness of rule-governance in the distribution, exercise and control of political power. In *The Legal Theory of Ethical Positivism*,[8] I explore such instrumental virtues of rule-governance with respect to predictability, regularity co-ordination, conduct control, conduct facilitation, dispute resolution, individual autonomy, economic efficiency, power allocation, the formal preconditions of substantive justice and the focus of democratic dialogue. There I argue that these are the principal reasons why it is good for a society to have systems of specific mandatory rules which preclude individual members from exercising their own judgment over certain matters with respect to their own conduct.

I do not rehearse all these rationales here, although they are central to the understanding of democratic positivism, including its account of legal authority and legal obligation. However, it is worth highlighting those justifications of rule-governance which are particularly germane to democracy. These rationales focus on the thesis that empowering officials with wide-ranging discretion, although it holds out the prospect of utilising expert opinion and making fine-tuned decisions in the light of the particular circumstances of each situation, is inappropriate where the decisions call for value judgments whose content depends both on the personal or collective outlook of those exercising that discretion and their susceptibility to the influence of interested parties, so that what varies is not so much the circumstances of the case as the personal beliefs and interests of the officials who have the discretionary power and the pressures which are brought to bear on them.

In the arena of political conflict and evaluative disagreement, the advantages of expertise and particularised justice promised by the wise deployment of such discretionary power are negated for the democratic positivist by the scope provided thereby for the impact of opinions and influences which have no legitimacy within the system. Abstracting from the content of rules, which may or may not be themselves embodiments of class, gender and racist attitudes, the absence of rules increases the vulnerability of parties to controversial political or discriminatory attitudes and beliefs which are as endemic within legal institutions as they are in society at large. The contention is that rule-governance can be an effective way to promote the neutralisation of unauthorised ideology, prejudice and illegitimate self-interest in the exercise of power.

Pointing out the various benefits of rule-governance does not imply that social life as a whole should be strictly rule-based or that there should be a system of positivistic rules covering every aspect of social life. The thesis is, rather, that where there is government – that is, non-optionality enforced by punishment and detriment – then it must be rule-governed. Indeed, legal positivism fits neatly with a political theory which favours a limited domain for government along the

---

8 TD Campbell, *The Legal Theory of Ethical Positivism*, Aldershot: Dartmouth, 1996. See also F Schauer, *Playing by the Rules: A Philosophical Examination of Rule-Based Decision-Making*, Oxford: Clarendon Press, 1991.

few simple rules model developed by Epstein.[9] However, in the light of the pervasive role of unjustifiable domination in social relations, in most complex societies the domain of law should be far more extensive than anything envisaged by libertarians.

Further, it is important to note that, in practice, rules and democracy converge in so far as rules are a powerful instrument for bringing about predictable change and democracy is justified in part by self-determination, in the sense that it allows people to collectively achieve their goals in and through the public sphere. If rule-governance has a positive correlation with effective governance, defined in terms of meeting the objectives of those with legitimate power, then it makes for a more effective democracy (if that is the system in operation) just as it can make for a more effective tyranny.[10] Arguments based on the alleged effectiveness of rules in producing desired outcomes are vulnerable to evidence that they do not do so either in general instances or contexts. Why, then, is the democratic process not a source of legitimate decision-making as to whether positive rule-governance is or is not desirable in this or that circumstance? After all, there is much interesting, and apparently evenly balanced, discussion about whether certain policy objectives are better served by setting general standards rather than enacting specific rules.

The answers to this essentially empirical challenge to the supremacy of rules direct us towards less contingent rationales for rule-governance which have more to do with the issues of political authority that generate theories of democracy. It can be argued, for instance, that any exercise of political power must have its substance approved by the consent of the governed, and that this can only be achieved prospectively by the democratic authorisation not just of rulers, but of rules. Anything less subjects the citizen to a degree of illegitimate coercion. The system violates the principle of political legitimacy that no one should be subject to the democratically unconstrained will of another to the precise extent that state officials – that is, persons whose decisions are backed by coercive sanctions or non-voluntary detriments – have discretionary power. If rules are a necessary element in the control of government officials, it follows that exclusionary rules are necessary conditions of democratic coercive authority.

A version of this thesis is to be found in those aspects of Rousseau's social contract model[11] that relate to the problem of securing equality of self-

---

9 RA Epstein, *Simple Rules for a Complex World,* Cambridge, MA: Harvard University Press, 1995.

10 Moreover, it can be argued that democracy, as the rule of the many, is more dependent than other systems on rule-governance for it is easier to institutionalise the shared power of all citizens in the choice of rules than it is in the aggregate of decisions on a case-by-case basis. Of course, democracy could consist only in the election of fixed-term dictators, and some will argue that this is the system that many democratic systems resemble, but that is to make the scope of the democratic choice less than it need be. At the other extreme, all citizens could decide on each particular matter, but that is impractical. A choice of rules seems to be a compromise which maximises efficiency by reducing input costs and maximises the impact of the decisions.

11 J Waldron, 'Rights and minorities: Rousseau revisited', in J Chapman and R Wertheimer (eds), *Majorities and Minorities,* New York: New York University Press, 1991.

determination in the democratic process. Rousseau dissociates himself from what we now call the populist majoritarian vision of democracy, where the decision that is made is the one which attracts the majority of self-interested endorsements. Such a process might elicit the rule of all but it would not realise the general will – a will aimed at the common good. It is unnecessary to base democratic positivism on something so intangible and idealistic as an electorally-based process that realises the common good, whatever that might be.[12] However, we can go as far as a modified version of the model and claim that an assembly formulating a choice of rules is intrinsically more acceptable than one making singular decisions. This thesis can be supported on three grounds. One is that, potentially, all members of the assembly are affected by the rule and are therefore going to scrutinise it carefully. Rousseau made this contingently true by insisting on economic and social homogeneity in his republic so that all rules did impact on all citizens in the same way – something to which we might seek to approximate but can hardly require.

A second reason why we might restrict assemblies to the choice of rules – that is, norms relating to categories of person and types of situation – is that dealing with these types of rule guards against decisions being made purely on the basis of the identity of individuals or named groups who would thereby be vulnerable to the exploitation of self-interested majorities. Although such restraints as rules might place on victimisation and discrimination can be evaded formally by the selection of general rules which uniquely or disproportionately identify the targeted persons or groups, this requirement does institutionalise the unacceptability of victimisation and discrimination, and serves to reduce their incidence by requiring the legislative debate to be about types and categories rather than particulars.

This takes us to the third and more basic ground for restricting democratic assemblies to the choice of rules, which is that the moral legitimacy of coercive power depends on the exercise of that power conforming with a normative form which is capable of being morally justified. This form must be general, not particular. A minimum requirement of morality is treatment in accordance with an acceptable reason which the person concerned is committed to applying to similar circumstances on different occasions, or at least until such time as they change their moral beliefs. The political version of this universalisability requirement is that government's treatment of citizens be in accordance with reasons relating to the characteristics of persons and circumstances, and this can be done systematically only through treatment in accordance with rules. Rule-governance, therefore, is a precondition, although by no means a guarantee, of morally justified political authority. A system which does not frame its choices in this way is simply not a candidate for moral legitimacy.

This third ground for preferring rules, which I call the moral form advantage, can be further developed in the context of deliberative democracy which makes actual debate a prerequisite of legitimate democratic process. It can be argued that

---

12 For the classic critique of this approach, see J Schumpeter, *Capitalism, Socialism and Democracy*, 5th edn, London: Allen & Unwin, 1976.

such a debate is moralised by being confined to a choice of rules which requires principled reasons to be given to justify the categories that feature in the alternative rule formulations. If the rationale for the debate requirement is epistemological, in that it is grounded on the claim that public discourse involving all those affected by a decision promotes the development of morally just outcomes, then we are close to full-blown Rousseauism.

If we put these arguments together then we have a powerful combination of moral and political reasons for rule-governance as an essential part of democracy – some demonstrating that a choice of rules enhances the power of populations and some demonstrating that it helps moralise majoritarianism, either by increasing the size of the majority or by subjecting the substance of the choices to moral scrutiny. This is comforting to the extent that it shows an affinity between positivism and democracy and reduces the scope of the tension between democracy and positivism which is latent in democratic positivism.

The force of such arguments is limited in so far as they establish only the practically necessary conditions for political legitimacy and can offer no guarantees of acceptable outcomes with respect to the content of the rules and the overall efficacy of rule-governance in terms of the ideas it is intended to serve. On the other hand, given the inherent difficulty not only of dealing with the pervasive social and economic forces which generate inequality and injustice, but also the fundamental epistemological problems over establishing the content of the moral and political values through which we can evaluate political outcomes, they do constitute a powerful *prima facie* case for democratic positivism.

All this clears the way for addressing some of the apparently intractable problems – philosophical, empirical and evaluative – which are routinely used as a reason either to bury positivism or to demonstrate that there is no theory of democracy that both describes democracies as they are or might be and offers convincing justifications for systems that are compatible with rule-governance. In doing this, some orienting principles for good legislating and good adjudication emerge.

## PHILOSOPHICAL PROBLEMS OF LEGAL POSITIVISM

The philosophical problems of legal positivism relate mainly to the epistemology and ontology of rules. The epistemological problem is that rules have no meaning in themselves but acquire meaning through the conceptual and linguistic apparatus that people within particular cultures bring to the texts which constitute their verbal formulations. It is not just that rules have a core meaning that can be interpreted differently at the margins by different individuals and groups. The core meaning is itself relative to the cognitive contribution brought by the individuals and groups who give their meanings to the symbols in question, and this cognitive contribution varies both between groups and between individuals. Traditionally, it has been possible to work with a distinction between the undeniably correct reading of a text in so far as it is clear and precise, and the areas of uncertainty which require us to deploy various techniques of interpretation to arrive at a reasonable, but not conclusively correct, reading of a text which is not entirely clear and precise.

However, on the radical epistemological critique, there is no distinction between understanding and interpretation. Every linguistic act is a matter of ascribing meaning. Moreover, interpretation is irredeemably creative and subjective. There are no fixed meanings 'out there', only what individuals, in the light of their personal and cultural constitution, make of the signs and signifiers that, in abstraction from the linguistic practices of specific groups and individuals, are the only things that enable us to identify a rule as the same rule. This relativity of meanings seems to undermine the idea that rules can impose significant limits on conduct, even with good-faith commitment to understanding the rules. There is always an in-built flexibility to all readings of all texts which renders such concepts as plain, natural or ordinary meaning, which are central to traditional expositions of legal positivism, suspect to the point of ridicule.

This philosophical problem for positivism opens up an enormous and difficult terrain. Here I address not the substance of the philosophy of language but its relevance to the credibility of legal positivism. The strength of philosophical scepticism about human communication is such that we might feel forced to conclude that we only think that we understand each other, whereas in fact, for the most part, we do not. Perhaps we are protected from the emotionally devastating loneliness of this subjectivity by the illusions of shared understandings. However, in fact, it is argued on philosophical grounds that we have no justification for such no doubt life-enhancing beliefs beyond the explanations provided by evolutionary epistemology or psychoanalysis.

It is tempting, however, to take the line that the alleged inability of philosophers to justify our claims to shared understandings capable of being communicated verbally demonstrates the failure of philosophy rather than the failure of communication. If the philosophical theories cannot account for the palpable experience of mutual understanding based on verbal exchanges, often mediated by texts, then it is the theories rather than the experience which are found wanting. In general, we might say that the philosophy of language seems to leave us where we began – namely, with a sense that we have no real understanding of the mysteries of our existence and the nature of our capacities. All philosophical theories of language do no more than scratch the surface of the awesome experience of interpersonal communication. It would therefore be foolish to stop trying to communicate on the grounds that no one has given a satisfactory explanation of how we manage to do this.

While there might be even some philosophical strength to this reaffirmation of common sense, which is itself a cyclical occurrence in the history of philosophy, the trouble with such a no-nonsense approach to the perceived failure of the philosophy of language is that this failure is more a manifestation than a cause of communication scepticism. We do have many real doubts about our capacity to transcend quite limited cultural confines by way of discourse and shared texts, and sceptical theories of meaning may serve to explain why we could be right to have these doubts rather than undermine an otherwise confident and successful process.

Moreover, if we take a more positive approach to the philosophical argument we will see that its critiques do not all point to the futility of attempting to improve the level of shared understanding. Indeed, the core Wittgensteinian position, linking language to shared ways of life, can be read as a vindication, implicit in its endeavour to provide an explanation for genuine communication within its proper contexts. Further, if we regard communication not as a given which is there to be enjoyed but as a possibility to be more or less achieved, then we can view the critiques as providing signposts for improvement rather than reasons for retreat.

In the case of law, for instance, we may theorise the whole enterprise as involving a systematic exercise in mass communication. Law, involving as it does the audacious objective of regulating whole societies through clarifying what is required, permitted and institutionally enabled, is evidently a grandiose project which invites communicative failure. On the positivist model, law has particularly ambitious communicative goals in that it requires attempts to state general rules in a relatively context-free manner so that they can be understood by large numbers of people in approximately the same way. This is far removed from the situations in which we learn to speak and where we have the greatest sense of our communicative achievements – namely, where we are engaged in a practical activity with a small number of people with similar life experiences.

Our confidence that we can achieve some success with such communicative feats in which there are agreed rules with agreed meanings governing large populations may be bolstered by the claim that this population of persons already has other rules of language which they share and by reference to which they can all end up with something like the same reading of the same text. So we explain the communicability of some rules, legal rules, by the prior existence of other rules, language rules. It is, however, at the level of linguistic rules that the philosophical critique which undermines the communicability of legal rules has its greatest impact. We cannot account for linguistic rules by bringing in yet other rules, and so on into an infinite regress. At this level of explanation, language rules must be seen as simply attempts to give incomplete and inadequate expression to a set of skills which are learned in concrete social situations by people with shared experiences involved in face-to-face interactions. However, if language itself is not a matter of applying rules and thereby deducing a correct meaning, we can still maintain that law is a matter of applying other rules, rules of conduct, which have acquired meanings prior to, and independently of, the description of conduct in question.[13]

The suggestion is that, if we regard human communication as a fragile and even endangered achievement which requires constant renewal and reinforcement, and view the rules of language principally as attempts to

13 The debate requirement can also be interpreted in the context of a consumer model of democracy as having to do with the pooling of information, in which case we are not saddled with quite such an idealistic theory of democracy. This latter option puts more weight on the second reason for rule democracy – namely, that it reduces the likely impact of selfish majorities or, even worse, selfish minorities or individuals.

formulate these achievements rather than create them, then we will, as practical theorists, look to the philosophy of language as a source of ideas of how to achieve the seemingly impossible and transcend the convention of our immediate social networks by successfully communicating with a wider range of persons. The crucial questions in legal philosophy then become who should have the tasks of formulating these communications and how should they go about the processes of creating and/or applying them.

In this case, it makes sense to see law as a process of communication between law-maker and legal subjects mediated, in cases of dispute and enforcement, by adjudicators whose task is to discern the intentions of the law-maker in so far as they are expressed in the authorised text, these intentions not being the ulterior purposes, if any, that the legislation is designed to achieve, but the meaning that the text is intended to convey to its audience. Such a process has to proceed on the basis of an infinity of shared assumptions which, for all their contingency, enable us to think in terms of what we may call the intended plain meanings of legal enactments as legal enactments. This is not because there are such things as plain meanings automatically attached to particular words and sentences. The role of the notion of plain meaning in legislative communication is by way of a paradigm assumption that what legislators intend to communicate is what they have reason to believe the selected text will be taken to mean, which relates to what will seem the 'plain' or 'natural' meaning to the audience addressed – an assumption on which subjects, including judges, are entitled and required to rely. Legislators could try to communicate in code, and this might do if the code was clearly understood and universally known. However, it so happens that the mutual focus on 'plain meaning' is the best practicable basis for maximising communicative success over time.

The priority of plain meaning in statutory interpretation can thus be seen as a contingent device required for the successful communication of rules. Plain meaning represents a 'common ground' on the basis of which disputes can be resolved and conduct controlled and facilitated.[14] It is the presuppositions of successful communication to a large and diverse audience that dictate the function of the idea of plain or ordinary language as the primary and default criterion for a correct reading of a legal text. Where there is no basis for communication of this sort because of the absence or inadequacies of shared systems of meaning, then other criteria, such as stipulative definition, enter the picture.

Further, plain meaning can be contextualised in at least two senses without undermining the communicative objects of legislation. In the first place, fixing on a common meaning has to start with shared assumptions about, and experiences of, types of social situations in which that discourse is active. The fact that law seeks to transcend particular contexts does not mean that it can be decontextualised in relation to types of situation. Secondly, legislation has to be read in the context of the practice of legislation itself – that is, with an

---

14 See F Schauer, 'Statutory construction and the co-ordinating function of plain meaning', *Supreme Court Review*, 1990, 231; and DA Strauss, 'Why plain meaning?', *Notre Dame Law Review*, Vol 72, 1997, 1565.

understanding of the function of legislation and the particular form of legislative institutions that are in operation. This does not require that the meaning of a positive rule be subject to significant revision in the light of earlier legislation and case law, but it does enable rules to be read as modifications of existing bodies of law. Thus, democratic positivism allows that the ideal of plain meaning has to be related to particular conceptions of the roles of legislation and the historically contingent devices for improving communications between legislatures and subjects adopted in that jurisdiction.

However, considerable difficulties arise in adopting plain meaning where the legislation is intended to counteract assumptions and patterns of conduct accepted as normal in a society or parts thereof, for language embodies the existing outlooks and ideologies of the people whose language it is. This is why it is plausible to argue that no rules can be read in an ideologically neutral manner and that there is no way in which legal reasoning can be autonomous in the sense of being entirely cut off from the (always problematic) cultural assumptions of the society in question. However, what a political system can do is select from the variety of socially available discourses those which embody the beliefs and assumptions that the legislature chooses to favour. This is largely a matter of piecemeal changes to, or clarifications of, pre-existing socially accepted meaning.

On such a basis we may formulate the basic positivist principle of adjudication as applying a pre-existent rule in accordance with the plain or stipulated meaning of the authorised text in relation to the intended audience in the context of the legal enterprise, positivistically conceived. This does not mean that this goal is always achievable. Some rules may not have plain or stipulated meaning. Rules which do have such meanings may not be readily applied to unforeseen situations. The basic principle does make clearer, however, what legislators ought to be trying to do and is required as a basis for a working distinction between the application, non-application and creation of law in the process of adjudication, thus enabling us to give some cognitive content to the rather emotive term 'judicial activism', that content being judicial determinations which do, or do not, seek to have as their primary and overriding objective the application of laws in accordance with such plain and stipulated meaning as they may have.

Within this broad definition we may distinguish negative judicial activism, which is the failure to apply law in its plain and stipulated meaning, and positive judicial activism, which is making a judicial decision, either in a particular instant or through the creation of a ruling that becomes a precedent, which is not warranted by existing authoritative legal texts. Negative judicial activism is failure to apply the law; positive judicial activism is creation of new law. The two forms of judicial activism may operate together but may be identified and evaluated separately.[15] For instance, it may be argued that negative judicial activism is harder to justify than positive judicial activism when the latter is directed to supplementing, rather than overriding, existing rules. The concept of

15 For the purpose of clarification, it may be necessary to distinguish judicial activism, in any form, from the sort of decisions that have to be made in applying a general term to any particular thing, however clear and specific these general terms may be – what may be called the process of concretisation.

judicial activism pre-supposes that it makes sense to seek to identify the specific content of pre-existing law, and may have little application where there is no such law. I take it that legal positivism seeks to maximise the extent to which it does make sense to speak of judicial activism, giving it a prime focus on law-making.

No assumption is being made here that everyday discourse is replete with plain meanings, and such positivistic objectives must take into account the fact that everyday plain meanings usually depend on the occurrence of communication within a social context familiar to the participants. Rather, the language of positivistically good legislation is selected because of its suitability to communicating across contexts and communities, which involves, amongst other things, a reluctance to use broad evaluative language, a preference for empirically verifiable properties and a willingness to offer definitions where terminology is in doubt.

The difficulties that arise in achieving communication of this sort can sometimes be overcome by conventional devices for reading texts which are designed to reduce lack of clarity and ambiguity – devices which, if known to the legislature, enable it to make its intended meaning more transparent, hence the various techniques of statutory interpretation, sometimes presented as systemic gatekeepers whose function is to preserve the autonomy of law, can be seen as a natural extension of those many conventions of language that are designed to promote mutual communication.

This approach immediately undercuts the standard caricature of legal positivism as an approach to law which assumes that words have intrinsic meanings that are simply there for all to see and follow mechanically without regard to context and social differences. Rather, if large-scale communication in general terms is a socially achieved goal which has little that is mechanical about it, plain meaning is as much an object as a supposition of the law, although law is not alone in pursuing such goals; it rides on the back of the ongoing processes of socially constructed meanings on whose success the feasibility of the legal enterprise depends.

Indeed, the role of adjudication in such a process must be quite limited and has to be seen in the context of a general political process that is geared to articulating choices between different existing and potential patterns of shared activities to the point where certain alternatives can be clarified and identified as authoritative norms within the system. Political dialogue and the process of legislating may not readily be seen as an exercise in improving communication (although they are more readily seen as the articulation and making of choices) but the idea of law as a communicative process with the objective of clearly articulating the general requirements and permissions of social and economic activity depends on just such a context. Positivism needs, before a theory of adjudication, a theory of legislation which focuses on, and renders coherent, what we are doing when we arrive at a text which is to serve as an authoritative instrument for mandatory and coercive order.

In this way, the philosophical problems of positivism may be deconstructed or perhaps reconstructed, until they represent more of a practical challenge for the achievement of large-scale interpersonal communication in a world in which there are powerful vested interests (lawyers and their clients included) operating against such a goal.

This leaves open the question of precisely who is communicating with whom. The Benthamite model assumes the centrality of a legislative sovereign distinct from the administrators of law, which leaves the courts a law-making function only with respect to the clarification of statutes, essentially by rendering them more specific and unambiguous. However, positivism has also been used as the basis for common law legal developments through extrapolation of rules from individual decisions using the basis of precedent. Precedents too may be exclusionary, if decisions, once made, restrict the range of factors that a court may take into account when making subsequent decisions on similar cases.

It may be thought that the choice between statute and common law depends on democratic, rather than positivist, norms. Common law judgments can have all the specificity that derives from a clear decision on a particular case, although there is room for continuing scepticism about the precision of the way in which individual decisions come to have legal authority and how the rules alleged to be implicit in these precedents are articulated with respect to the form of their generality and specificity. However, it is not clear that common law and statute law have equal claims to embody positivist ideals for there is an internal contradiction in a system which depends on precedents that were not themselves the outcome of precedential reasoning to identify the pre-existing law. The idea of the development of the common law necessarily embodies elements of both negative and positive judicial activism. This can largely be overcome by confining judicial activism to the highest court and redescribing it as sharing in legislative sovereignty, although this could have problems for jurisdictions which have a constitutional commitment to the separation of legislative and judicial power.[16]

This, then, requires us to explicate the highest courts' law-making methodology as something other than fully precedential. The end result of these conceptual manoeuvres may satisfy the positivist norms in principle, and the issue of whether or not judge-made law is desirable then becomes a matter to be determined by reference to the democratic ingredients of the democratic positivism. Currently, it is probably correct to say that common law reasoning aspires more to a Dworkinian model than a positivist one, with an ever increasing use of generalised moral principles and a widening range of possible sources of new common law being brought into play, so that legal positivism is becoming increasingly inadequate as a description of common law reasoning in relation to these fluid, revitalised and diffuse common law approaches. This does not exclude, however, a reassertion of the Benthamite critique of the common law on both positivistic and democratic grounds. To the legal positivist, there is an unfortunate lack of precision, clarity and predictability in common law and statutory interpretation modelled on common law methods. To the democrat

16 See TD Campbell, 'Legal positivism and political power', in A Vincent, *Political Theory: Tradition and Diversity*, Cambridge: CUP, 1997, 172–92.

there is something alarming in a common law system with increasingly open-ended sources, drawing on whatever jurisdictional innovations seem attractive to the judiciary and including a variegated transnational human rights jurisprudence which threatens to entrench judicial law-making in a way that makes it less democratically accountable.[17]

## EMPIRICAL PROBLEMS OF LEGAL POSITIVISM

Having reconstructed some of the philosophical problems of positivism as stimuli to renewed efforts at communicative development, our critical focus must be turned to legal process, positivistically conceived, and the implications for legal positivism of the evidence that, in the area of the social construction of agreed meanings, positivist ideals are not realised in legal practice. Traditionally, legal positivism has claimed primarily to describe and explain the nature of all developed legal systems. The empirical critique is that it fails lamentably in these respects.

Thus, with respect to the goal of large-scale communication, is the function of the lawyer in an adversarial system not to undermine such agreed meanings as may appear to be established? If one reading does not help her client, is the lawyer not bound to commend a different reading? And do not judges – particularly appellate judges in postmodern jurisdictions – openly use the flexibility of communicative process to produce individualised justice and provide constructive solutions to social and economic disputes without seeking to follow, or even create, specific rules, which are widely seen as a distraction from the political choices that have to be made in the application of any pre-existing law? Moreover, is there not evidence that the required process of justifying decisions by reference to precedent and statute in fact misrepresents the reality of the forces which lead to particular decisions that are better explained in terms of ideological assumptions, class, ethnic and gender affiliations and the realities of what courts can achieve in given political and economic circumstances?

This is the domain of the empirical problems which beset legal positivism. Law, it is contended, simply has little resemblance to what legal positivists would have us believe. Legal rules are seldom clear, and judges do not always follow them even when they are clear: they change the law in the process of adjudication, and give reasons in their judgments which underdetermine the result and are often no more than rationalisations for decisions taken on other grounds, so that there is endless scope in the system, through the manipulation of process and the purchase of technical expertise, to achieve a result which is in no way evident on a rule-centred analysis.

The short answer to such points is to say that they do not apply to contemporary legal positivism as a vital prescriptive legal theory which sets

---

17 This may apply to both the current defamation law regime in Australia and the Human Rights Act 1998 in the UK. See TD Campbell, 'Human rights: a culture of controversy', *Journal of Law and Society*, Vol 26, 1999, 6–26.

standards against which to assess and – if the allegations above are correct – criticise existing practice. Therefore, the label 'ethical positivism', which serves to indicate that we are dealing with those elements of legal positivism which are aspirational with respect to a formally good system of law, that is, law which is not derived from any analysis of the concept of law or description of current practice but rather from a political philosophy that is conscious of the paradox of political life – namely, that we need states but have reason to fear them – whose partial solution depends on establishing the rule of positive law. In brief, showing that actual legal systems do not operate positivistically does not negate the claim that they ought to do so. It is therefore wrong to assume that legal positivism is either purely a descriptive or an inherently conservative approach.[18]

The legal theory of ethical positivism is ethical in a further sense in that it is accepted that no system of rules can in itself produce any beneficial results or protect from any of the evils of government without the ethical commitment of functionaries of the system and its subjects and citizens. If subjects routinely seek to evade their legal obligations wherever possible, if citizens take no interest or part in the creation of law through the democratic process, if lawyers successfully work to subvert the application of law and judges are practising legal realists, then no system of rules will operate effectively with respect to the values posited in the rationales of rule-governance. Indeed, the sins that are often placed at the door of legal positivism, such as gender, race and class bias, are perhaps better seen as unwarranted departures from rules which exclude such factors as irrelevant than as failures of rule-governance to combat such improper partialities.

That said, however, we have to note that there are two types of empirical test for a theory – one relates to actualities and the other to potentialities. The argument that existing systems are not positivistic may be deemed irrelevant to ethical positivism, but the argument that no system can conform to the ideal of ethical positivism is less readily dismissed. There is no point in extolling an ideal which is idealistic in the pejorative sense that it is unattainable to the extent that no useful progress can be made towards its implementation.

Legal positivism is so vulnerable to this line of attack that, historically, the theory may have evaded the issue by making the coincidence of the existence of law and conformity to law a matter of definition. Thus, the thesis that the existence of a sovereign, and hence the existence of legal obligation, depends on efficacy (or general obedience to authoritative commands) makes the existence of law depend on the existence of a certain level of conformity to identifiable human authority, hence the slogan that validity presupposes efficacy.[19]

This rather circular contention can be reinterpreted on the basis of the Hobbesian distinction between laws which oblige *in foro interno* and those which oblige *in foro externo* – a distinction which can be illustrated by saying that our commitment to keep our promises is conditional on others doing so as well, the

18 A point well made in AJ Sebok, 'Misunderstanding legal positivism', *Michigan Law Review*, Vol 92, 1995, 2054.

19 HLA Hart, *The Concept of Law*, Oxford: Clarendon Press, 1962, 100–01.

argument being not one of moral reciprocity or fairness, but the basic fact that the benefits of promising are not to be had unless people in general keep their promises. We can generalise this line and say that the rule rationales that play such a substantial part in the justification of legal positivism presuppose that there can be such conformity to rules as is necessary for the promised benefits of rules to be realised.

In some cases of conduct-controlling rules there are benefits to almost every single act of conformity and harms to almost every contravention. The law of homicide is an example in point. The moral form advantage, also, may not be undermined by patchy conformity. However, in many other types of rationale, such as rules of co-operation, co-ordination, dispute avoidance and resolution, the benefits do not come from individual conformity but from general, and sometimes near universal, conformity, as in the case of most road traffic rules.

In so far as the rule rationales on which ethical positivism depends involve consequentialist assumptions about the effects of rule-following, its general appeal is vulnerable to empirical study and its relevance may vary according to the areas of social and economic life in question and the type of society to which it is applied. This means that it is important for legal positivism to identify the various thresholds of conformity at which the benefits of rule-governance kick in with respect to the different consequentialist rule rationales. Several questions need answering: 'what are these thresholds?', 'are they attainable?' and 'what should we do if conformity falls short of these thresholds?' 'Who are "we" anyway'? These issues are explored further below.

## ETHICAL POSITIVISM IN AN IMPERFECT WORLD

The analysis of some of the empirical presuppositions of ethical positivism brings us to a fundamental issue in the articulation of democratic positivism – namely, its response to positivist shortfalls in actual systems, including the failure to meet co-ordination thresholds, the non-existence of appropriately positivistic laws, the failure of legal and judicial ethics, and the absence of realistic mechanisms for constitutional change. Considering each of these in turn, I suggest how the practical implications of ethical positivism vary with different types of defect. What emerges is something like a strong form of Schauer's presumptive positivism,[20] in which the adjudicative norms of ethical positivism emerge as defeasible in the light of positivist shortfalls. This approach threatens to undermine the whole logic of exclusionary rules by providing bases on which citizens and judiciaries can opt out of their obligations, but accepting practical limitations to the applicability of exclusionary rules need not lead to the introduction of generalised discretion within a legal system.

20 See F Schauer, 'Rules and the rule of law', *Harvard Journal of Law and Public Policy*, Vol 17, 1991, 645.

## Co-ordination thresholds

In a perfect positivist world, no law would be promulgated which could not attain an efficacy threshold of conformity. In the real world, compliance can be a major problem. In this real world, it may be argued, there is no obligation on the subject to conform to any rules that are promulgated without attaining that threshold. Such a response is within the positivist tradition of making efficacy a condition of validity and hence of obligation. On the other hand, condoning individuals choosing not to conform to mandatory rules on the basis of their own assessment of efficacy thresholds threatens the achievement of the necessary threshold conformity. The idea of law as mandatory relates to such matters as law's function in solving co-ordination problems as set out in the various versions of the prisoners' dilemma. Permitting the subject the right to make up her own mind is to give up the compulsory co-ordination strategy which seeks to overcome the prisoners' dilemma. Permitting individual judgment makes co-ordination vulnerable to the self-partiality of those who are prone, even in good faith, to delude themselves as to the consequences of their conduct, to say nothing of those who follow their immediate self-interest. For such reasons, there are good grounds for staying with a very sticky form of presumptive positivism in order to maximise conformity so that, for instance, administrators and judiciaries should not fail to enforce a law on the basis of perceived non-conformity in other instances. Enforcement agencies have duties to avoid selective enforcement, which threatens the non-discrimination goals of legal positivism. However, legislatures have a political duty not to enact and retain certain types of laws when these fail the test of practical conformity necessary for their efficacy.

Despite the critical significance of compliance thresholds for the justification of co-ordination rules, decisions about what these levels are and whether they have been met are not best taken at the point of assessing what is to be done in particular cases. Responses to the ineffectiveness of co-ordination rules as a result of failures of compliance is a law enforcement and political problem, not a matter for individual agents or courts of law.

## The absence of positivistically good law

What are subjects and judges to do when there is a dispute to be settled but no rule to apply, or where the apparently relevant rule is vague or in other ways unclear? A traditional answer, favoured by Kelsen, is that they, or judges at any rate, should do nothing. No criminal conviction should follow in such circumstances, and in civil disputes the loss will have to lie where it falls, for there can be no remedy on the basis of judicial invention.

This seems unsatisfactory in the light of at least some of the values which underpin the case for having rules. If we are to have rules to aid dispute resolution, what are we to do when such rules are not available and we are faced by a dispute that needs to be resolved? In this context it seems inadequate to depend on the principle of 'no rule, no resolution', although it may be defensible to draw back from coercively imposed solutions to disputes if we take on board all the negative arguments about discretion as a vehicle of bias and arbitrariness.

On balance, where disputes threaten serious injustice or social disorder, it is tempting to underwrite, in such second-best situations, positive judicial activism in the sense of making decisions without specific legal authority and even creating new law through the system of precedent. This may aid the existing dispute settlement, avoid future conflicts and be compatible with democracy, provided such precedent-setting decisions are subject to legislative review.

The questions that arise here relate principally to variations in the appropriateness of judicial activism in relation to imperfect positive law according to the areas and types of law concerned and the feasibility of effective legislative review of such developments. Problems of inaction focus on the substantive injustice of providing no remedies for what are apparently evident wrongs and having no acceptable alternative way of settling damaging disputes. Problems of action lie more in the opportunities it gives for those with ready access to the courts to use their economic power to thwart the legitimate expectations and interests of others.[21]

In the case of gaps in existing law, something may depend on the reason for these gaps. Advocates of positive judicial activism will point to the failure of legislatures to address important issues whose solution involves making choices that will, however they are decided, lose electoral support or bring out divisions within political parties, thus creating a legislative vacuum which it is proper for courts to fill. However, the counter-argument is that legislation lacks democratic legitimacy where it is opposed by intense minorities and that picking and choosing between proper and improper inaction on the part of legislatures involves illegitimate value judgments as to the importance of the neglected issue and the proper response to disagreement about how they should be addressed.

## *Failures in legal and judicial ethics*

The legal and judicial ethics I have in mind here relate to the proper perception and execution of the legal and judicial roles with respect to the application of positive law. This conception of legal ethics relates directly to the role of legal participants with respect to the rule of law and therefore depends on the value judgments required to select appropriate judicial method and litigation norms, as well as conformity to such methods and norms as are chosen. For the ethical positivist, the prime ethical duty of judges, for instance, is to apply positivist methods of judicial determination to such positive law as is available to them.

The initial plausibility of legal realism rests substantially on the evident truth that, at least in the short term, the law in any particular case is the finding of a

21 Many legal positivists have seen such second-best scenarios as potentially beneficial opportunities which enable helpful developments of law to be made by wise judges, benefits which provide welcome flexibility to meet individual circumstances in the interests of justice, or make the law as a whole more coherent. This leads to an interesting argument about whether law is better made in response to individual situations known in detail to hopefully impartial judges, or in the light of policy goals articulated by legislative bodies who are often far removed from knowledge of individual circumstances.

court with respect to that case. This departs from the positivist model in so far as that decision does not apply the relevant rules in the light of an accurate finding as to the relevant facts of the case as identified by the rules in question. The failure of the positivist model in a particular case may be due to the inappropriate theory of judging utilised by the court, or by a failure to follow an acceptably positivistic model for some other reason, including departures from the appropriate norms of litigation. Such matters concern the ethics of lawyering and, in particular, of judging, because they cannot be easily controlled from outside the confines of peer pressure and systems of judicial appeal to which the legal realist truism also applies.

While, in many onslaughts on the performance of legal systems, it is difficult to distinguish criticisms of the content of law from criticism of its administration, many of the failures identified by those who see legal systems as favouring the economically powerful and culturally dominant groups in a society relate not to the inadequacies of positivistic models of proper process but to the failure of those who operate the system.

Dealing with deficiencies in judicial ethics is one of the least tractable problems with respect to rule-governance. Internally, to the system, the hierarchy of courts and possibility of appeals are of paramount importance but, where the legal culture accepts legal realism as a liberating norm rather than as an unpleasant fact, there are real difficulties in rectifying the situation. Courts must be given the power ultimately to determine particular cases, otherwise the separation of powers collapse. On the other hand, if courts have the last word on the methods they use, then they can clearly usurp the powers that rightfully belong to a legislature under any theory of democracy by choosing to ignore or revise any rules with which they are presented, by using the techniques of free-ranging interpretative methods.

There is no clearly optimal response to unethical judging, for any attempt to rectify the matter – except, perhaps, by way of public discourse – tends to undermine the very independence of the judiciary which is required for positivist systems of law. Legal positivism may rely on ethics in this sphere simply because there is no acceptable alternative. In theory, ethical positivism holds to the view that legal method is a legitimate matter of concern for the entire polity, including the legislature. Further, there is no good reason to give the judiciary the power to determine its methods other than that there is good reason not to give such power to legislatures. Perhaps there is a constitutional need for a workable system of calling judges to account for their operative methodology. However, even if we do not have to trust judges to set the proper standards for judicial process and judgment, policing conformity to these standards has to be largely a matter of judicial self-regulation.

The problem of having to rely on judicial ethics is reduced by the possibility of legislative review of judicial action, but the practicalities of legislative review, with packed agendas and powerful pressure groups, are such that unethical judicial reasoning often rules by default. In this context, positivists may argue for the political propriety and efficiency of the routine legislative review of judicial activism as a normal and acceptable device, with judicial activism being explicitly signalled and then subjected to legislative scrutiny. Such transparencies can be viewed as part of the ideology of democratic positivism.

## Constitutional constipation

The final category of second-best scenarios relates to the problem of what constitutional courts are to do when there is no effective mechanism for legitimate constitutional change – a problem which arises in an acute form if we are looking for a legitimate source of positivist rules for the judicial review of legislation.

If we assume that constitutions should be interpreted in the same way as any other piece of positive law, then we encounter the problem that there is no legislative review of constitutional decisions by courts, other than constitutional amendment. This can be seen as a problem both with respect to the discipline of constitutional courts and the difficulty of keeping constitutions up-to-date.

For reasons such as this, it is argued that legal positivism is particularly inappropriate in the constitutional area. For functional reasons, constitutions, as the basis for historically long-term political association, tend to include some highly imprecise terminology. The very idea of constitutionality restricts the role of executives and legislatures in determining constitutional matters. The problems of inter-generational communication render the plain meaning ideal of legal positivism less applicable. No wonder, then, that courts feel bound to develop constitutions in line with their perception of current needs, particularly when the formal procedures of constitutional change stack the cards against change. Of course, it can be argued that this is precisely what constitutions are meant to do, otherwise there would be no point in entrenchment. On the other hand, it is easy to be persuaded that flexibility of interpretation is more appropriate in constitutional than in other areas of law.[22]

This is a problem which could be greatly reduced were it feasible to redraw the rules for constitutional changes so as to provide for frequent constitutional amendment through plebiscites, subject to whatever entrenchment procedures are considered appropriate. This would enable politics to move towards some precision and contemporary relevance with respect to the rules governing contentious constitutional institutions and concepts such as representation, equality and judicial power. If regular amendment can be institutionalised, there is no reason, in principle, why constitutions should not be reasonably specific, clear and up-to-date.

In the nature of the case, such change is not normally attainable, hence the phenomenon of constitutional constipation accompanied by incurable imprecision of terminology. In these circumstances, second-best solutions are called for, but what they should be is far from clear. To take just one example, from examination of the Australian constitutional cases which are so central to questions of judicial activism in that jurisdiction, it seems evident that any system of constitutional interpretation that depends on the judicial unpacking of such

---

22 But see F Schauer, 'Constitutional positivism', *Cornell Law Review*, Vol 25, 1993, 797.

broad concepts as representative government, and the social and political preconditions of their instantiation, are potentially so sweeping as to undermine the operation of ordinary law when conceived on the positivist model by making large areas of ordinary law vulnerable to unending constitutional challenge.[23]

The prospects for containing this form of second-best judicial activism through restricting it to some working conception of human rights or fundamental values are not good, partly because, in many jurisdictions, constitutional interpretation extends to federal matters and cannot therefore be confined to individual rights, but also because the scope and range of human rights, democratic and otherwise, are either inherently controversial or far too extensive to remove from legislative oversight. It is salutary to note that, despite the ever increasing role of the concept of human rights in world politics and the undeniable importance for any political system to identify the priority human interests that require defending and promotion, the powerful philosophical arguments against the existence of any privileged knowledge of what these rights might be, both in content and form, have not been adequately answered. If there was a list of specific universal rights which could be known to be true or correct by any rational person, then the rationale for placing the administration of these rights in the hands of a small group of specialist adjudicators would be strong, although, due to problems of selecting the specialists and insuring against their human frailties, not overwhelming.

However, as things are, all the points about diversity and difference which feature in the justification of having a system of democratically derived positive law to provide a framework for economic and social life apply *a fortiori* to the basic value judgments involved in concretising human rights. Shared reflection may produce agreement with respect to an affirmation of the principle of equality but this does not mean that agreement will be forthcoming as to what similarities and differences between individuals and groups are proper grounds for similar and different treatment. All the questions of relevance and degree which arise in decisions about rulings, and which have sufficient specificity to affect people's actual situations, are inherently controversial in that there is no basis for removing their resolution from whatever political processes we think best suited to arrive at politically authoritative determinations.

All this becomes progressively clearer as covenants, charters and declarations of rights become more concrete. It is not being hostile to the value commitments which underpin the development of human rights, conceived of as the priority interests to be protected and furthered in a political community, to hold that the articulation and specification of the applicable content of these rights is properly a matter for the political, rather than the judicial, process. However, this still leaves us with the question as to what that political process should be and the problem of what to do if we do not have a usable process for constitutional change.

---

23 For a discussion of these cases, such as *Australian Capital Television Pty Ltd v Commonwealth* (1992) 177 CLR 106 and *Theophanous v Herald & Weekly Times Ltd* (1994) 182 CLT 104, see Chapters 17 and 18 of TD Campbell and J Goldsworthy (eds), *Judicial Power, Democracy and Legal Positivism*, Aldershot: Dartmouth, 2000.

This survey of reasons for why we might seek to depart from the model of ethical positivism prompts a change of focus towards political reforms which will reduce the incidence of such pressures but does not suggest that the presumption of positivism need be systematically overridden. This leads us on to the democratic ingredients of democratic positivism; these ingredients have to be examined further before we can come to a final view on the various second-best solutions to the positivistic deficits of actual legal and political systems.

## THE DEMOCRATIC SETTING

While there may be, as I have argued, more than a mere affinity between legal positivism and democracy, one further factor which may require courts to depart from their duties to positive law is the absence of proper democratic process. Even those who accept that it undermines positivism to give courts wide powers to review legislation in the light of broad value standards, which they use to crystallise vaguely worded fundamental rights, nevertheless look to courts to conserve the democratic framework that is a precondition of the political legitimacy of law, if only by scrutinising the formal or procedural validity of putative laws.

As we have noted, democratic positivism is directed as much at the legislative and general political process as it is at the activities of courts. In this sphere, deficits can arise both from failures with respect to the enactment of positivistically good laws, and with respect to inadequate democratic process which may precede the enactment of what may be formally satisfactory laws. Just as it seems inadequate to make judiciaries the arbiters of their own conduct with respect to adjudication, so it seems inadequate to entrust democratic decision-making to the self-scrutiny of legislatures.

Legislation may be undemocratic either in its origins (perhaps because it was not adequately debated) or in its content (perhaps because it restricts freedom of assembly). Both defects give rise to the prospect of judicial review as a response to second-best situations, either where legislatures are undemocratic in their composition or procedures or, while being democratic in these respects, enact substantively undemocratic laws. These are the prime, but not the only, circumstances in which judicial review of legislation, with the power to declare undemocratic legislation invalid, is held to be a proper constitutional device and a legitimate part of the separation of powers. For instance, with democratic positivism, there is scope for making the constitutional validity of ordinary laws dependent on sufficient specificity and clarity.

At one level, there is no positivist difficulty with judicial review, provided this is governed by specific procedural and substantive rules. Thus, courts may have the power to apply certain tests to all legislation, provided these tests are clearly set out and can be applied without recourse to contentious moral and political opinions. Indeed, some such powers are inevitable in enabling courts to recognise the putative sources of law as authoritative, hence the role of rules of recognition in legal positivism.

Judicial review of legislative action, when it goes beyond questions of federal power, may seem particularly straightforward in the case of legislation which is undemocratic in the first sense – that is, it is the product of a procedurally undemocratic process – provided these procedural requirements are uncontentious in their meaning, although there are immense problems in requiring anything more than the fulfilment of formalities of due democratic and legislative process.

Judicial review is not much more problematic in the case of legislation which is undemocratic in content, provided that content relates to changes in the democratic process as identified in the constitution – for instance, by electoral boundary changes which do not take account of population distribution. Again, there could be concerns about the precision of such review rules which may be no more than broad standards of political equality, but this can be dealt with within the theory by rendering the review rules more precise. Indeed, it is difficult to see why judicial review of a democratic positivist sort – namely, judicial review governed by clear and specific rules – should, in principle, be confined to matters of democratic form and substance, for there is nothing anti-positivist or anti-democratic is establishing rules which are lexically prior to other laws. Objections arise only when these are entrenched in a non-democratic manner or include vague conceptions, such as equality or non-discrimination which can be used to override just about any legislation with which the judges involved disagree.[24] Objection to judicial review of legislative action must be based on the constitutional illegitimacy or the substantive vagueness of the rules for review rather than the institutional fact of there being such rules.

This is not to legitimate, however, systems of judicial review of legislation which are the creations of courts and which courts seek to make fireproof against legislative revision by claiming an inherent constitutional priority to judicial review on the basis of a political philosophy rather than a historical constitution or statute. Neither the nature of judging nor the concept of the separation of powers, for instance, gives a sufficient basis for requiring judiciaries, by constitutional default, to be the guardians of either formal or substantive democracy. *Marbury v Madison* is a clever piece of politics but not a watertight piece of reasoning.[25] It seems right to argue that Congress cannot be judge in its own case if its actions are under constitutional scrutiny, but the same logic applies to a Supreme Court making a judgment as to its own powers. No political system can deal with the problem of who guards the guardians except by the inculcation of appropriate ethics. There is simply no institutionalisable answer to the ultimate political conundrum as to who is to judge the constitutionality of the actions of any branch of government at the highest level, in the absence of express

24 Thus, in a minority opinion in *Leeth v Commonwealth* (1992) 174 CLR 455, at 502, Gaudron J takes the judicial power which is entrenched in the Australian Constitution to include 'the concept of equal justice' along the lines of substantive interpretations of the 14th Amendment of the Constitution of the United States, which guarantees every citizen the equal protection of the law.

25 See C Nino, *The Constitution of Deliberative Democracy*, New Haven, CT: Yale University Press, 1996.

constitutional provision. However, there is nothing within democratic positivism to reject the idea of judicial review of legislative action in principle. The problems lie in how to specify what these rules might be and how they are to be authorised and applied.

The realities of judicial reviews of legislation are that their standards are rarely democratically authenticated and, where they are so authenticated, they take such unspecific form as to remove from the normal democratic process matters whose determination are at the heart of self-determination. This is particularly evident where the democratic content is extended to include a range of fundamental rights which go beyond the sort of democratic process to which clear content can be given. If we have an expansive idea of what is involved in democracy, and the fundamental democratic rights are stated in broad and by no means purely procedural terms, then to remove judgments about the proper content of democratic laws from legislatures and give it to judges on the grounds that they are guardians of democracy is to remove most of the most important political issues from the democratic process and thus possibly to undermine a more basic right – the right to self-government.[26]

This conclusion may not be unwelcome to the majority of citizens in contemporary jurisdictions, for legislatures and democratic politicians do not currently have a good reputation as sources of law, particularly where their self-interest is at issue. The more checks the better, it may be thought, in the case of a class of persons whose role obliges them to act in unprincipled, unreliable and partisan ways. To many people, impartial judiciaries seem to be better sources of law than populist assemblies, particularly with respect to democratic process where there are reasons within democratic theory to distrust political practitioners. If the articulation of democratic positivism does provoke such a patently anti-democratic response, this may indicate that some such sentiments underlie both the enthusiasm for giving further discretionary power to judges and the willingness to acquiesce in the increasing power of judicial review over legislative enactments.

The thesis that judges are better placed to make good law than politicians takes us to the core of the democratic debate, which is addressed below. First, there are two arguments to be considered. One is the argument derived from the supposed impartiality of judges; the other is the argument derived from the veniality of politicians.

While philosophy may be ineffectual in accounting for communicative realities, it can be self-referentially very powerful in cutting down the pretensions and claims of its own practitioners. Thus, analytical and critical philosophy effectively counter the claims that information and impartiality are sufficient bases for claims to such superior moral knowledge as to justify the imposition of obligations on others. Before and since the founding father of legal positivism, Thomas Hobbes, tried to deduce the authority of the state and the validity of core

---

26 See J Waldron, 'A right-based critique of constitutional rights', *Oxford Journal of Legal Studies*, Vol 13, 1993, 18.

social and legal obligations from enlightened self-interest, philosophers have been trying to prove alternative and more exalted channels for the justification of morality and the provision of guidance as to how we should criticise and develop our moral convictions without resorting to untestable appeals to human reason. The core modern example is Kant's contention that an act is right if all rational persons are willing to see it universalised or, in other words, applied to all similar persons in similar circumstances. More recently, the liberal philosopher John Rawls has drawn this together with other enlightenment insights about the impartiality of the moral point of view, in that it does not give any preference to one individual or type of person over another.

These theorists have taught us much and, while they have all undoubtedly provided tests that can help us not only identify moral questions but also improve the quality of moral judgments, it has been decisively shown, again and again, that they do not enable us to settle genuine moral disagreements in a manner which gives satisfactory grounds for systems of mandatory rules backed with coercive sanctions. In particular, defining impartiality, as we normally do, in terms of absence of personal attachment to the individuals involved in the dispute in question and an ability not to make an exception of oneself or another person simply because we are ourselves or have particular attachments to that other person, is a sound basis for determining some issues of public morality. However, such tests are perfectly compatible with unending value disagreements – that is, disagreements about what is worthwhile, important and significant in human life. Given diversities of cultures, individuals and tastes, impartiality does not solve the problems involved in adopting shared values, although it may be helpful in deciding how what we value should be shared.

Impartiality, in a judicial context where positivistic rules are available, is able to generate objectively justifiable decision-making but only because the available rules make it possible for judges to approximate to a position of value neutrality. Such institutionalised value neutrality, however, renders proper judicial method ineffectual in dealing with substantive moral disagreements. Further, requiring judges to abandon value neutrality threatens their capacity to act in those matters where impartiality is of the essence – namely, in the ethically proper interpretation of rules and their accurate implementation to specific fact situations without recourse to contentious personal opinions.

Curbing the pretensions of judicial impartiality leaves us with the problem of the partialities and ignorance of Parliaments, the selfishness of majorities, and the often greater selfishness of powerful minorities. If we are not to encourage constitutional change which enables judges to make major value choices for us, then how are we to reorient and reinvigorate democratic processes so that they produce rules which are not only positivistically good but also tolerable in content? On some (market-style) democratic theories, it is to be expected and welcomed that politicians are unprincipled or adaptive, in that it is their job to respond to changes in popular opinion, and it is to be expected and welcomed that politicians are self-interested at least with respect to being motivated by the desire for re-election, for this is what makes government responsive to general opinion. However, can such creatures also fulfil the role of legislators and leaders without a framework that forces them to act against their politically-oriented roles in such a way as to manipulate the majorities that support them and neglect the minorities who do not? This leads us to the issue of what to do about democratic deficits.

We may restart the overview of the democratic setting of ethical positivism by working through the consequences of accepting the argument that informed impartiality is insufficient to vindicate a right to make value judgments on behalf of others. What does the rejection of such an epistemology of values imply for the theory of democracy? One possibility is that it amounts to a form of moral relativism which requires us to abandon anything beyond contingent agreement as to shared values and ideals of social justice, accepting the individual's assessment of what he or she considers worthwhile and providing a system which gives as many as possible of these individuals what they want. Democracy is, then, the aggregation of desires – the ideal of desire maximisation.

This is the model of democracy historically associated with legal positivism in its classical utilitarian manifestation. For any theory that retains an emphasis on individual autonomy, it remains a telling element in favour of individuals having an equal say in government that this maximises the realisation of desires. In this model, the crucial element is an effective political market with good information on the proffered packages, freedom of choice in the expenditure of votes, and equality of opportunity between potential political candidates.

However, our scepticism over reaching objectively justified agreement on values means that we may endorse, but cannot justify, the utilitarian principle on which the classical theory depends. The principle that we ought to maximise the greatest happiness of the greatest number is simply one amongst the many principles that have been commended by those who have striven to attain the required standpoint of informed, but sympathetic, impartiality. We can bypass this difficulty to some extent if we can obtain intersubjective agreement and if that agreement includes agreement as to the desirability of achieving such agreement, but does this give us the basis for coercing those who do not share in the hoped-for consensus? Probably not, but then, in a world where values cannot be objectively justified, there can be no establishable objection to the coercion of a minority by a majority, or vice versa. In this context, the idea of maximising preferences may seem a pragmatic approach to the problem of disagreement, and we may proceed with the utilitarian justification of democracy that, by making rulers subject to re-election, we make it more likely than with any other method of government that rulers will rule in the interests of the majority.

A significant flaw in this pragmatic market approach is that, in purchasing a package for themselves, the individual voters are at the same time selecting the same package for others, hence the problem of the absence of consensus leading to the rule of majorities and the incompatibility of that with the initial premise of political equality; hence also the temptation to modify the pure market approach and say that voting in a political election is giving an opinion as to what is in the common good rather than expressing a preference related to individual self-interest. Add the contestable premise that the view of the common good which is shared by the largest number of people is epistemologically superior, in that majority voting is actually a guide to correctness in the determination of what is the common good and what will best promote that objective, and we have a more promising basis for justifying majority decision-making because the losing minorities can be assured that the outcome is the one most likely to serve the common good.

For the purpose of this chapter, normative democratic positivism involves a commitment to maximising individual autonomy, subject to a democratic override. This implies that, other things being equal, government should maximise negative liberty and provide for equal political power in relation to the determination of whether other things *are* equal and, if not, what legislation is warranted, while at the same time seeking to mitigate the unfortunate side-effects of the majoritarianism which gives practical effect to equal political power by introducing as many as possible of the mechanisms and culture which render individual preferences more oriented towards conceptions of the common good.

This may be considered inconsistent, since one model requires individuals to vote and perhaps debate in accordance with their self-interest so that the results maximise the sum of self-interest, while the other model requires the voter to select and debate according to an ideal in which his or her interests play only a small part. However, there is no formal difficulty here, as people can take satisfaction in the well-being of others, thus rendering their self-interest inclusive of the interests of others. Problems do arise, however, when some vote on a purely self-oriented basis and others on a more altruistic assessment of the common good, thus skewing the aggregate decision towards those with a narrow conception of self-interest.

Assuming this problem can be contained, what sorts of device might suffice to channel democratic process towards the common good model and how do these impact on issues of judicial activism and judicial review? I have already suggested one tactic: the governance of positivistically good rules. We have seen that this approach does not favour judicial activism (except perhaps as a rectificatory or second-best technique). What rule-governance does suggest, however, is the propriety of formal judicial review of legislative action with respect to the clarity and specificity of law. In such a system, courts would be required to declare invalid putative laws which are directed at named individuals, perhaps even named groups, such as bills of attainder, and also, more controversially, putative laws which are seriously unclear or too general to provide genuine guidance for subjects and courts (the issue of constitutional vagueness). We may call this type of formal judicial review of legislation 'rule-testing'.[27]

Another common good device, which is more usually used when seeking to improve the acceptability of majority voting, is the requirement of effective deliberation and public criticism as an essential part of the democratic process. This is particularly interesting because it is the model which is thought to lead us

27 For a recent Australian example, see *Polyukhovich v Commonwealth (War Crimes Case)* (1991) 172 CLR 501, at 535, in which there was majority support for the view of Mason CJ that the Commonwealth could not enact a law 'adjudging a specific person or specific persons guilty of an offence constituted by past conduct and imposing punishment in respect of that offence'.

towards a broad-ranging system of judicial review which, with its emphasis on universal knowledge of fundamental rights, seems to derive from the natural law tradition. However, deliberation, as such, features also in classical utilitarian market models of democracy, principally as a source of information which enhances consumers' capacity to get what they really want, and hence what will satisfy their desires. Such information may also, of course, be relevant to discussions aimed at the discovery of a common good, but deliberation is given to other functions, such as the pursuit of consensus, which reduces the problem of minority oppression or, more ambitiously, to obtaining collectively an improved conception of the common good. The latter makes an epistemic claim for deliberation on the basis that the outcome of genuine deliberation between all parties affected by a decision as to the terms of collective existence is more likely to provide a correct apprehension or construction of the common good.

If this has sufficient plausibility, then there is good reason to require that democratic legitimacy includes a public discussion requirement not only in the electoral phases of democracy but also in the ongoing processes from which legislation emerges. However, the constructive criteria of any form of deliberative democracy – particularly one that makes claims to epistemic authority – are such that they would be very difficult to capture in a set of positivistically good rules that could be applied in a satisfactory scheme of judicial review.

The norms which courts apply to their own deliberations, such as giving their reasons in terms of preceding authorities, are inappropriate for deliberative democracy, as they have a more limited function and are designed in part to restrict the range of arguments that can be introduced. In some ways, courts may be expert reasoning forums, but the constraints of reasoning within the domain of law, and the restrictions on who may participate in the deliberations, mean that courts do not have the sort of open dialogue with respect to available arguments and available sources of argument that discourse theory requires. Further, as we have seen, there is no reason to think that any form of deliberative method enables us to delegate our moral reasoning to any restricted group of people, with or without legal qualifications and experience. Indeed, the most persuasive forms of deliberative democracy are those which see the requisite discussion as diffuse within a society, with deliberation leading up to, but itself part of, the decisions which embody the reflective preferences of those liable to be affected by the group decision in question.[28]

Nevertheless, it is possible to conceive of specific formal requirements for public debate and consultation, disclosure of relevant information and explicit reference to a checklist of factors which must be considered in the course of legislative drafting, parliamentary process and enactment. It is consonant with the deliberative democratic positivist critique of substantive judicial review to have a system whereby a pre-enacted convention or charter of specific rights is used by a constitutional court to review legislation in the light of its implications for these specified rights and either provisionally override, refer back, reinterpret or simply

28 Particularly J Habermas, *Between Facts and Norms*, London: Polity Press, 1996.

give a declaratory opinion on legislation which appears to conflict with such rights, thus establishing a dialogue between courts and legislatures in which legislatures, nevertheless, have the last word. Such processes can contribute to the articulation and implementation of basic rights without returning to the political authority of elected legislatures, thus providing a form of judicial review without positive judicial activism.[29]

In democratic positivism, these basic rights might include those democratic rights which relate to adequate public discussion, information and consultation regarding new legislation. If weight is given to the deliberative aspects of democratic theory, these democratic rights could be cashed out in part as requirements that must be met in the enactment of new legislation, going beyond formal rights of political participation to require actual processes of communal debate beyond the legislative assembly itself. Such requirements could be supplemented by the proposed interactive process for the development of legislation whereby some judicially dominated body has the power to return to the legislatures enacted laws which seem to violate defined fundamental positive rights. Democratic positivists might also explore ways in which the legislative assemblies are better focused on their legislative task and more open and orderly in their deliberative procedures. These are radical suggestions, and are made primarily to illustrate the point that there are responses to positivistic and democratic deficits other than looking to the remedial activism of courts, the nature of whose impartiality is inadequate to settle value disagreements and ought to be preserved for other important and more specialist tasks, particularly the application of existing law, with all its controversial embodiments of value commitments, to specific situations, which, it is argued, is a necessary ingredient of a genuinely democratic system.

29 Numerous actual alternatives are on offer in Sweden, New Zealand, Canada and, most recently, in the UK in relation to the Human Rights Act 1998.

# 15

# LEGISLATING HUMAN RIGHTS

Even the most ardent advocates of constitutional bills of rights see that there is a place for human rights legislation, that is, for legislation that is aimed primarily at the protection and implementation of human rights. A constitutional bill of rights would not, for instance, do away with the need for a Racial Discrimination Act or Equal Opportunity or Land Rights legislation. For those who have serious doubts about bills of rights, especially those bills that are used to override democratically enacted legislation, but who are, nevertheless, fully committed to human rights objectives, human rights legislation takes on even greater significance, for it becomes the state's core contribution to the protection and furtherance of human rights.

By 'human rights legislation' I do not mean legislated (or statutory) bills of rights, that is, statements of general moral principles enacted as for the purpose of guiding judicial interpretation,[1] or setting up a system of judicial review of other legislation.[2] By 'human rights legislation' I mean legislation which promotes human rights in a legislative manner, that is, by the enactment of a body of clear and specific rules that can be followed and applied without using broadly based moral reasoning.[3] This normative model of legislation and the virtues of rule-governance associated with it generally are derived from a democratic theory of prescriptive legal positivism.[4]

Assuming, for the purpose of this chapter, that there is good reason either to do without or to tightly constrain bills of rights, I explore the idea of giving special status to human rights legislation, a status that reflects the heightened priority that an interest acquires by being identified as a human right. The objective is to provide a quasi-constitutional role for human rights that goes some way towards meeting the rationale for having bills of rights, namely providing some constraint on the immoralities that occur when democratic procedures, which are intended to provide decision-making mechanisms that manifest and serve the wishes and interests of all citizens, are distorted in ways that promote the illegitimate self-preferences of statistical majorities or privileged and powerful minorities.

The sort of constitutional role for human rights legislation I have in mind includes the relatively mild device of giving human rights legislation interpretive

---

1 Such as the New Zealand Bill of Rights Act 1990.

2 Such as the UK Human Rights Act 1998.

3 An example would be the Australian Racial Discrimination Act 1975 and its various state equivalents. Interestingly, these have been put forward as a model for an Australian Bill of Rights: Justice Roslyn Atkinson, 'Are anti-discrimination statutes a model for a bill of rights?', public lecture, University of Queensland, 16 September 1999.

4 TD Campbell, *The Legal Theory of Ethical Positivism*, Aldershot: Dartmouth, 1996.

priority when it conflicts, or appears to conflict, with other pre-existing or later legislation, or with the common law. Thus, the presumption that a Parliament does not intend to legislate to the detriment of fundamental principles of the common law would be supplemented, or displaced, by the assumption that a Parliament does not intend to legislate in a way that diminishes the force and application of existing human rights legislation. Such a presumption would be rebutted only if the later legislation clearly and unequivocally displaces existing human rights legislation. In the case of human rights legislation, it might be appropriate to require that it can be repealed or amended only through the use of a particular form of words comparable to the 'notwithstanding' clause of the Canadian Charter of Rights and Freedoms.[5]

This form of constitutionalisation is equivalent to the suggestion of Laws LJ and the logic of *Factortame (No 2)*[6] that the UK European Communities Act 1972 is a 'constitutional statute' in that it cannot be 'impliedly repealed'. According to Laws:

> Ordinary statutes may be impliedly repealed. Constitutional statutes may not. For the repeal of a constitutional Act or the abrogation of a fundamental right to be effected by statute, the court would apply the test: is it shown that the legislature's actual – not imputed, constructive or presumed – intention was to effect the repeal or abrogation? I think the test could only be met by express words in the later statute, or by words so specific that the inference of an actual determination to effect the result contended was irresistible. The ordinary rule of implied repeal does not satisfy this test. Accordingly, it has no application to constitutional statutes.[7]

A similar approach may be taken to the UK Human Rights Act 1998,[8] and even to particular statutory rights in ordinary legislation that are held to be in some way fundamental.[9]

Going much further, we might give human rights legislation a procedurally distinctive constitutional status by having it enacted and repealed or amended only by special procedures comparable to constitutional amendment. Such special procedures could either make it more difficult or easier to change human rights legislation. The rationale for making it more difficult, for instance by requiring

5 Something like this is achieved through the idea that certain provisions of an act are 'dispositive', a term used in ACT legislation to identify a provision that can only be repealed explicitly or from necessity. A stronger mechanism is to require a specific 'manner and form' in the wording of an Act that is to amend the existing legislation, as is provided for in the Australia Act 1986 (Cth). See J Goldsworthy, 'Parliamentary sovereignty and statutory interpretation' (in press).

6 *R v Secretary of State for Transport ex p Factortame Ltd (No 2)* [1991] 1 AC 603.

7 Laws LJ: 'A constitutional statute can only be repealed, or amended in a way that significantly affects it provisions touching fundamental rights or otherwise the relation between citizen and State, by unambiguous words on the face of the later statute' (*Thoburn* [2002] 3 WLR 247, at 263).

8 See J Burrows, 'The changing approach to the interpretation of statutes', *VUWLR*, Vol 22, 2002, 981.

9 *R v Home Secretary ex p Leech* [1994] QB 198 and *R v Lord Chancellor ex p Whitham* [1998] QB 575. Note *Cullen v Chief Constable of the Royal Ulster Constabulary* on Thursday 10 July 2003 with respect to the right to consult a lawyer as contained in the Northern Ireland (Emergency Provisions) Act 1987.

more than a simple majority of votes cast, is that this protects rights from selfish or ignorant majorities. The rationale for making it easier to change human rights legislation is to make it possible for vulnerable minorities to have privileged control over human rights legislation. For instance, a second chamber, elected on the basis of proportional representation, might be empowered to pass human rights legislation without the consent of a first chamber elected on a first-past-the-post basis.

Another possibility is to require human rights legislation to be endorsed by referendum. It would depend on knowledge of many demographical, political and legal variables to know whether such a procedure would provide better protection against powerful minorities or selfish majorities, but this approach has the potential to give human rights legislation the sort of preferred constitutional status that would warrant using it to trump ordinary legislation even where there is a clear incompatibility between the constitutional statute and the later legislation.

In fact, there are many less dramatic procedural requirements that could be entrenched or 'constitutionalised' in such a way as to encourage majoritarian political processes to give less partial and more empathetic consideration to human rights and provide better protection to vulnerable minorities. Some of these can be adapted from the UK Human Rights Act 1998, such as a requirement for government ministers to provide statements in relation to the compatibility of proposed legislation with existing human rights legislation when presenting new legislation to Parliament.[10]

In particular, there are many variations on the institutionalised role of a human rights committee of a legislature whereby such a committee, perhaps composed in such a way as to give statistically disproportionate representation to vulnerable minorities, has powers to require governments not just to provide reasons for apparent threats to human rights in proposed legislation, but actually to bring forward specified types of human rights legislation or propose amendments to existing human rights legislation in order to meet a perceived human rights deficit or, less dramatically, to delay the enactment of legislation that they deem to be in potential violation of enacted human rights.

Such constitutional mechanisms may be viewed as extensions of the inquisitorial and *de facto* delaying powers of parliamentary committees, as exemplified by the Australian Senate Standing Committee for the Scrutiny of Bills whose terms of reference require it to draw to the attention of the relevant Minister and subsequently of the Senate, if any proposed legislation seems to them to be in conflict with 'personal rights and freedoms'. Thus, in its Second Report of 2003, committee records show that it drew the attention of the Minister for Immigration and Multicultural and Indigenous Affairs to the fact that, in the Migration Legislation Amendment Bill (No 1) 2002, no reason is given for certain retrospective clauses and that it sought 'the Minister's advice as to why these provisions apply retrospectively and whether they will disadvantage any person',

10 See also the Queensland Legislative Standards Act 1992.

adding that, 'pending the Minister's response, the Committee draws Senators' attention to these provisions as they may be considered to trespass unduly on personal rights and liberties, in breach of principle 1(a)(I) of the Committee's terms of reference'.[11]

In the same report, a similar process is recorded relating to the abrogation of the rules of natural justice in relation to another bill:

> The rules of natural justice have been developed over many years to ensure fairness in the application of law. It is unusual to see them cast aside simply to avoid 'operational difficulties'. The Committee, therefore, seeks the Minister's advice as to the deficiencies in the existing provision and why such an extreme amendment is seen as necessary to deal with them.[12]

Clearly not satisfied by the Minister's response:

> The Committee thanks the Minister for this response and accepts that there may be substantial reasons in this case to abrogate the rules of natural justice. However, those rules are central to personal rights and should be excluded only in exceptional circumstances. The absence of procedural fairness in these provisions is a breach of such rights, but the Committee leaves to the Senate to decide whether, in the circumstances, it is an undue breach.[13]

In another matter, the Committee takes up a concern over the extension of strict liability in criminal law. A proposed new subsection in a bill that 'makes it an offence for a person to make arrangements that make it look as if two people are *de facto* spouses for the purposes of the regulations where the person knows or reasonably believes that they are not *de facto* spouses' appeared to them to make a change to the law in a way that introduced strict liability in so far as it would not be necessary for the prosecution to prove knowledge of a difficult and technical piece of law in this respect.

Going beyond the function of commenting on the rights implications of particular bills, the Committee also sought to bring about changes in the form of presentation of legislation by inserting a requirement that all bills provide a full and clear explanation of proposed legislation, especially where this has a potential impact on personal rights and democratic procedures:

> The Committee emphasises that an Explanatory Memorandum should include a full explanation of the background of the bill and its intended effect. This is particularly the case where it includes provisions which may affect personal rights or parliamentary propriety. An Explanatory Memorandum should be more than a brief introduction followed by notes on clauses that largely reproduce the clauses themselves. The purpose of the Explanatory Memorandum is to assist parliamentarians during the passage of the bill and to be a guide for all those affected by it proposed provisions. This would usually include a substantial discussion of these issues in addition to the notes on clauses.

---

11 Concerning the Migration Legislation Amendment Bill (No 1) 2002. *Alert Digest No 3 of 2002 to the Minister for Immigration and Multicultural and Indigenous Affairs*, 63.

12 *Ibid*, 64.

13 *Ibid*, 66.

This matter was taken up by the Committee with the Acting Parliamentary Secretary to the Prime Minister and to the First Parliamentary Counsel.

Such devices, actual and imagined, have a variety of objectives, particularly: (a) to improve the quality and direction of debate so as to reduce the impact of partisan and ill-informed majoritarianism and the capture of Parliaments by privileged minorities; (b) to protect the interests of identified vulnerable minorities and individuals by providing mechanisms for questioning or delaying legislation that, perhaps inadvertently, threatens important rights or to promote the passage of human rights legislation designed to further such interests; and (c) to provide an institutionalised way of justifying the prioritisation of human rights legislation.

Such mechanisms do not displace the need for a political culture which is deliberative in that a sincere and good faith commitment is made by the majority of those involved as leaders, activists and voters in seeking to arrive at decisions that are believed to be either in the equal interests of all citizens or represent morally justifiable departures from that standard. However, they may be seen as helping in the promotion of such a culture without undermining democratic rights in the way that court-centred bills of rights tend to do.

In particular, the oversight role of legislative committees could be enhanced by the existence of comprehensive human rights legislation that could be taken as an authoritative and specific expression of what constitutes the 'personal rights and freedoms' that are left unspecified in the terms of reference of the Senate Standing Committee for the Scrutiny of Bills. Indeed, the terms of reference of such committees and the political force of their comments and recommendations could be strengthened by enacting a non-justiciable bill of rights that identifies in a brief and eloquent manner the rights that they are charged to protect and enhance. Where there is also in place provision for the judicial review and invalidation of ordinary legislation, such scrutiny becomes a matter of predicting what courts might say rather than an independent assessment of the best legislative instantiation of abstractly formulated rights, but the process is capable of adaptation to a less legalistic and more moral form of reasoning and debate as to what abstract human rights are to mean in practice. In this context, there is room for what might be called a 'Democratic Bill of Rights', that is, a non-justiciable abstract statement of fundamental rights that is deployed in various ways to affect the agenda and outcome of legislative process so as to achieve closer attention to human rights issues without having to empower judiciaries to use overrule or radically reinterpret enacted legislation.

## HUMAN RIGHTS LEGISLATION

With these thoughts in mind, we can explore further the idea of human rights legislation. What might human rights legislation be? What are its distinctive characteristics? What marks it out from other human rights instruments? How might the concept be institutionalised?

Such questions present us with a number of fluid concepts that require some stipulated clarification before the above questions can be made answerable. With respect to 'legislation' itself, we should note that the term can be taken as referring either to a type of law-making or to a type of law. As a type of law-making, legislation is a complex process whereby an authorised individual or collective, the legislator(s), produce a bundle of interconnected rules and principles according to a process whose outcome is recognised as creating authoritative law in the jurisdiction in question. Legislation typically involves a formally defined process whereby policy decisions and commitments are turned into justiciable rules in a constitutionally recognised way. In democracies (the only type of government in which the idea of human rights legislation has any resonance), this is the work of a large representative elected assembly, or assemblies.

As a type of law (as distinct from a type of law-making), legislation is a collection of written rules and principles that determine in advance and in general terms what is lawful and what is unlawful in a jurisdiction. Legislation, in this sense, is distinct from the decisions that are made when these rules and principles are followed or applied by those to whom they refer – including courts – in so far as this is how their responsibilities are defined.

These definitions are crafted so as to promote a clear distinction between legislation and adjudication, the making of law and the application of law. Such a distinction is particularly clear when we have the enactment of specific and clear rules that can be applied to particular fact situations without the need for any interpretation beyond the contextual understanding of members of that linguistic community.[14] It is much less clear when the process of law-making produces not clear rules but general principles that gain applicable meaning more from an evocation of values rather than a prescription of a descriptively clear form of conduct. In these circumstances, the application of laws that have been made may itself be a form of law-making because of the degree of creativity that enters into applying a principle to a particular factual circumstance. This adjudicative law-making is not in itself legislation, either in process or outcome, except in so far as the decision overtly or implicitly creates a rule, as is the case when a particular application of a principle sets a descriptively specific precedent for future applications, thereby turning the principle into a rule.

In such cases, we might talk not of judicial law-making but of judicial legislation. However, it is preferable that the practice of making rules in the process of applying principles is referred to as a process of law-making, but not legislation, and that 'legislation' be used to identify the creation of rules other than in the process of making decisions about the lawfulness of particular circumstances. Such rules or norms may be denied the label legislation just because they are not the product of a legislature, as defined as a law-making body that is not also authorised to apply the rules that it makes. While the concept of legislation could be used so as to cover bodies of rules that emanate from courts in this way, I think it is important to mark the constitutional significance of the separation of powers by declining to regard the law-making practices of courts as legislation, which has the same normative status as enacted law. This is not to

---

14 N Naffine, R Owens and J Williams (eds), *Intention in Law and Philosophy*, Aldershot: Dartmouth, 2001, 291–320.

deny that courts do sometimes make laws, but the distinction in terms serves to affirm the democratic principle that legislation (the product of legislatures) trumps any law-making powers that courts may have.

In fact, there is conceptual force as well as practical convenience in excluding judicial law-making from the category of legislation. First, if and when judicial law-making occurs it must be done in the process of adjudication, that is, the determination of the lawfulness of a particular circumstance. Secondly, judicial law-making is done in a quite different manner and form to the law-making of legislators, that is, those who make rules in abstraction for determining the lawfulness of particular circumstances.

Thus far, my conceptual apparatus would enable us to speak correctly of legislating bills of rights, as indeed we do when we contrast a legislative with a constitutional bill of rights. By definition, a legislative bill of rights is the outcome of normal legislative process and not special constitution-creating procedures or revolutionary historical events. Such 'legislative' bills of rights may be distinguished from ordinary legislation in part by content – the type of law that is made – and in part by function, that is, the role that a legislative bill of rights is ascribed within the legal and political system, such as a guide to interpretation.

With respect to content, a bill of rights is characteristically a statement of principles in abstract form, usually with predominantly moral content, in that the key concepts involved are value-laden, asserting the priority of certain interests and institutional mechanisms for their protection. Bills of rights are typically, in their substantive content, brief, forceful and inspirational. They concern liberty, equality, justice, privacy and life itself. In their procedural content, they lay down in abstract terms participation rights, such as the right to vote, speak and associate.

With respect to function, the increasing prevalence of the American model of judicial review raises the presumption that bills of rights function within constitutional judicial review of legislation. This is historically inaccurate. Bills of rights in general have no definitionally essential function.[15] In fact, in the case of statutory bills of rights, their role is normally limited to an interpretive one, requiring courts to take the requirements of such bills into account when interpreting ordinary legislation, perhaps in such a way as to render that legislation consistent with the legislated bill of rights. The New Zealand legislative bill of rights is a paradigm example. The UK Human Rights Act 1998 represents a more sophisticated version that enacts a wider range of functions to such a bill, including the power of courts to make 'declarations of incompatibility' if they consider that ordinary legislation cannot be interpreted in such a way as to render it consistent with the European Convention on Human Rights and Freedoms.

If legislatures can enact bills of rights, it seems natural to assume that, whatever human rights legislation is, it includes legislative bills of rights. Indeed,

---

15 M Tushnet, *Taking the Constitution Away from the Courts*, Princeton, NJ: Princeton University Press, 1999.

this would seem to be the paradigm example of human rights legislation. However, I do not go along with this assumption, not because bills of rights are not about human rights, but because bills of rights do not conform to my normative model of legislation. Evidently, legislative bills of rights are legislation in the sense that they are the products of legislatures, rather than special constitutional procedures or implied by courts in the process of constitutional interpretation. However, legislative bills of rights are not legislation as a type of law in terms of their content or form because of the predominance of statements of abstract moral principles as contrasted with specific legal rules. If we approach legislation as a type of law-making typically undertaken by legislatures, then undoubtedly legislatures enact bills of rights; bills of rights can be the product of legislative process. If, however, we approach legislation as a type of law, then legislatively processed bills of rights are not appropriately regarded as legislation.

There are at least two reasons to resist the classification of legislative bills of rights as a type of legislation. First, and less controversially, bills of rights differ in function from legislation in general. They are typically used either for courts to render legislation invalid and hence not legislation at all, or as an invitation to courts to make new law on the basis of moral principle. Even where they are ostensibly confined to an interpretive role, they tend to be utilised by courts to bring about *de facto* legislative review. This means that bills of rights are not only not ordinary legislation, they are, as a type of law, not legislation at all.

Of course, as I have indicated, bills of rights may be given other roles. Thus, a bill of rights may not be directly enforceable by courts but serve the function of guiding governments and legislatures. I have suggested, for instance, that a legislated bill of rights could be used as a benchmark for a Human Rights Scrutiny Committee without itself being legislation. Something like this exists with respect to the Joint Human Rights Committee in the UK, which operates in relation to the European Convention on Human Rights, which has been incorporated into the UK by the Human Rights Act 1998 for a limited range of purposes, such as this one. However, this even more clearly does not make it conceptually correct to regard such bills of rights as examples of legislation.

The second and main reason for not regarding legislated bills of rights as legislation is that they are generally so far removed from the ideal of good legislation as to be legitimately denied the description of legislation at all. This is conceptually controversial in so far as it is based on a notion of 'good' legislation (here, of course, we mean formally not substantively good legislation) rather than on an evaluatively neutral meaning of 'legislation'.

Particular evaluative considerations lie behind the conceptual propriety of excluding certain forms of political decision-making from the genre of legislation. Thus, a system of governance that gives authority to certain persons to make binding decisions with respect to particular circumstances and particular parties is not appropriately called a legal system because of the absence of rules of general application enabling people to know in advance of their conduct what is and what is not mandatory within that political system. 'Palm tree justice' is not, on this view, legal justice, for the rules that govern it are limited to procedural rules that establish who has the right to make decisions but not the limits of what those decisions may be in form or content. By extrapolation from this extreme constitutional circumstance, it may be argued, along lines drawn with delightful clarity by Lon Fuller[16] that law-making has certain internal norms that require conformity to such standards as clarity, publicity, consistency, practicality, generality and prospectivity. These standards are prescriptive, but they are in effect constitutive of what we regard as law and, in particular, as legislation.

This model of legislation is a crucial part of positivist theories of the rule of law and has been become associated with a theory of democracy that ascribes normative significance to the role of democratic decision-making in the process of legislation. Thus, Jeremy Waldron, in his 'jurisprudence of legislation',[17] argues that the dignity and integrity of legislation requires that we respect the compromises embodied in its substance as a result of democratic compromise and accommodation to the views of others through open and public debate addressed directly to the issues (rather than inherited texts). Legislative texts are to be respected as the outcome of reasonable procedures in a situation of deep social disagreement. Legislation is not something to be tidied up by court even when they are blatantly over and under inclusive. Waldron sees legislation as a text that embodies an 'agreed' policy decision arising out of a debate in which all affected parties are participants, the outcome of which is determined by a process that gives equal weight to the choices of all those involved.[18]

Some of the ideals of good legislation that serve to identify its conceptual essence are exemplified in such instruments as the Legislative Standards Act 1992 (Qld) which establishes certain 'fundamental legislative principles' to ensure that Queensland legislation is of the 'highest standard', principles which are to be promoted through the Office of the Queensland Parliamentary Counsel. These 'are the principles relating to legislation that underlie parliamentary democracy based on the rule of law', that 'legislation has sufficient regard to (a) rights and liberties of individuals; and (b) the institution of Parliament'.[19] Enumerated examples of such principles include avoiding undue dependence on administrative power only, ensuring natural justice, limiting delegation of administrative power, retaining the onus of proof in criminal cases, keeping tight restrictions on search warrants, avoiding self-incrimination, excluding retrospectivity, requiring justification for granting immunities, achieving fair compensation for compulsory acquisition, having sufficient regard for Aboriginal tradition, and, importantly, requiring that legislation 'is unambiguous and drafted in a sufficiently clear and precise way'.[20] The Act requires that bills must

---

16 L Fuller, *The Morality of Law*, New Haven, CT: Yale University Press, 1969.

17 J Waldron, *Law and Disagreement*, Oxford: OUP, 1999.

18 See also L Wintgens (ed), *Legisprudence: A New Theoretical Approach to Legislation*, Oxford: Hart, 2002, which deals with 'legisprudence', an approach to the study of law-making that concentrates more on exploring standards for 'rational legislation' which moves beyond criteria such as consistency, to the duties of legislators with respect to establishing facts, weighing up alternatives, calculation of consequences and their advantages and disadvantages, and preparedness to modify legislation in the light of later experience.

19 Legislative Standards Act 1992 (Qld), s 4.

20 *Ibid*, s (3)(k).

include a brief assessment of the consistency of the Bill with fundamental legislative principles and, if inconsistent with fundamental legislative principles, give reasons for the inconsistency.

Whatever standards of good legislation we adopt, and how far we write these standards into the concept of legislation, it is clear that some of these standards are not met by bills of rights. I have excluded such bills from the category of human rights legislation because they seek to promote human rights objectives in ways that contradict the principles of legislation, including respect for the democratic legislative process. This creates logical space for the development of the concept of human rights legislation as an alternative to (or perhaps for others a supplement to) bills of rights, legislated or not.

The political justifications for this position are the familiar difficulties with bills of rights as a form of law. In form, bills of rights are made up of vague moral assertions in a form that renders them unfit for the purpose of guiding conduct, settling disputes and facilitating co-operation. Other problems arise in connection with their anti-democratic role in enabling courts to override the legislation of elected law-making assemblies. The first difficulty is constitutionally neutral but fundamental to the fairness of formal justice and the efficiency of rule-governance, an efficiency that can be used to serve human rights objectives. A vague right is, in practice, no right at all.

The second difficulty is constitutionally committed in that it endorses a notion of democracy whereby individuals have a formally equal say as to what becomes law. On this latter approach, whether or not bills of rights are to count as legislation, it is certainly the case that an elected assembly enacting a bill of rights is thereby abrogating its future democratic responsibilities as well as corrupting the separation of powers. It follows that, considering both types of objection, there are human rights reasons to avoid bills of rights as being potentially formally unjust and actually undemocratic.

Such bills are potentially unjust (and inefficient) because it is possible for a bill of rights to be formally good law. Thus, a right not to be subjected to capital punishment under any circumstances is as clear, unambiguous, practicable and prospective as can reasonably be hoped for, but bills of rights tend not to be like that. They normally consist of highly abstract affirmations in basically moral language. Indeed, this may be considered essential to their functioning in enabling judges to override legislation to protect vulnerable minorities through a direct appeal to fundamental moral values, thus limiting the power of elite minorities and populist majorities. However, to the extent that bills of rights do conform to Fuller-style criteria of rule-governance, then they do indeed present an exemplar of human rights legislation.

The question that then arises is what the institutional function of human rights legislation might be. The first, and primary, answer must be that there is or could be a constitutional requirement that there be human rights legislation so that the human rights objectives are not ignored or relegated to a subordinate place in that jurisdiction. The demand that all states have bills of rights is thus replaced by the demand that all states have comprehensive human rights legislation. This has the potential to secure more effective, because more radical and specific, legislation than is likely to emerge from judicial 'interpretation' of fundamental moral values or rare examples of judicial override of legislation.

It is not in fact necessary for human rights legislation to be given any particular function beyond the realisation of the specific objectives of the legislation in question. If applying such law serves human rights, then this is in itself a sufficient justification for its enactment. Human rights legislation is directly applied to the conduct of those who bear the correlative duties contained therein, be it government departments, private organisations or individual citizens.

However, many of the arguments in favour of bills of rights make important points about the need to avoid certain negative human rights outcomes that are a natural consequence of the typical systematic failure of electoral systems of democracy. Even if the solution offered by bills of rights is unacceptable because it is incompatible with the very rights it seeks to protect, or because it is ultimately ineffective in curbing entrenched power, this does not weaken the force of the critiques of electoral democracy, but merely casts doubt on the proposed cure. It is therefore an appropriate human rights objective to see whether this democratic deficit can be corrected through mechanisms that give a measure of entrenched priority to human rights legislation that is not vulnerable to the objections that are directed at bills of rights.

This takes us back to the constitutional devices indicated in the introduction to this essay, namely the idea that human rights legislation trumps ordinary legislation, that human rights legislation affects the interpretation of ordinary legislation and, perhaps, that such legislation is enacted or protected in distinctive ways that are designed to give it a measure of entrenchment without blocking its progressive development.

## SUPER-STATUTES

The proposal to recognise a specific type of legislation – human rights legislation – as having a special, quasi-constitutional status, to some extent echoes the idea of 'super-statutes' put forward by Eskridge and Ferejohn.

According to Eskridge and Ferejohn:

> [a] super-statue is a law or series of laws that (1) seeks to establish a new normative or institutional framework for state policy and (2) over time does 'stick' in the public culture such that (3) the super-statute and its institutional normative principles have a broad effect on the law – including an effect beyond the four corners of the statute. Super-statues are typically enacted only after a lengthy normative debate about a vexing social or economic problem, but a lengthy struggle does not assure a law super-statute status. The law must also prove robust as a solution, a standard or a norm over time, such that its earlier critics are discredited and its policy and principles become axiomatic for the public culture.[21]

---

21 WN Eskridge and J Ferejohn, 'Super-statutes', *Duke Law Journal*, Vol 50, 2001, 1215–76, at 1215.

Examples of super-statutes provided by Eskridge and Ferejohn include the Sherman Antitrust Act of 1890, the Civil Rights Act of 1964 and the Endangered Species Act of 1973. Each in their own way, they say:

> occupy the legal terrain once called 'fundamental law', foundational principles against which people presume their obligations and rights are set, and through which interpreters apply ordinary law. Today, this kind of law might be considered 'quasi-constitutional' – fundamental and trumping like constitutional law, but more tentative and susceptible to override or alteration by the legislature or determined judges and administrators.[22]

In some respect, the idea of super-statutes provides a model for my concept of human rights legislation. Super-statutes have a higher constitutional status than ordinary, more humdrum, legislation that makes it difficult to change a super-statute and carries interpretive significance for other legislation. In particular, the idea that such legislation cannot be overridden by subsequent legislation unless this is done explicitly accords with a central aspect of the status I would assign to human rights legislation.[23] Human rights legislation, like super-statutes, is not vulnerable to implied repeal.

However, in other respects super-statutes are different from human rights legislation. Super-statutes achieve their status through broad political support garnered over time.[24] Human rights legislation gains its status from being formally identified as such. No doubt human rights legislation aspires to achieve broad and lasting recognition, but legislation which, for instance, is designed to protect minorities may function legally as human rights legislation without broad and deep political support of the sort that applies by definition to super-statutes.

Nor is there a requirement that the enactment of human rights legislation always represents a major shift in national policy or norms.[25] In fact, much human rights legislation may be designed to consolidate and refine existing human rights protections, as they exist, for instance, in the common law. No paradigmatic shift of emphasis is required of human rights legislation.

Again, for Estridge and Ferejohn, it is a feature of super-statutes that they are liberally interpreted on a progressive understanding of their basic principles and the goals of the legislation in question, such as free trade, racial equality or the protection of endangered species. Thus, we are told, the Civil Rights Acts of 1866 were 'narrowly construed by the post-Reconstruction judiciary afraid to disturb the political consensus in favor of segregation' and only became super-statutes when 'the post-World War II civil rights movement revived interest in those laws

---

22 *Ibid*, 1216–17.

23 *Ibid*, 1235: 'the Court has repeatedly held that "repeals of the antitrust laws by implication from a regulatory statute are strongly disfavoured", and have found only two cases of plain repugnancy between antitrust and regulatory provisions', quoting *United States v Philadelphia National Bank* 374 US 321, 350–51 1962.

24 *Ibid*, 1230: 'The key to super-statutedom is acceptance in public culture. This cannot be mandated, nor is it earned exactly. It is a trial-and-error process which, when successful, creates its own gravitational field.'

25 *Ibid*, 1230: 'Our first criterion for super-statutes is that they alter substantially the then-existing regulatory baselines with a new principle or policy.'

and the Warren Court breathed new life into them in the 1960s with liberal interpretations'.[26] So called 'dynamic readings'[27] are in fact a common feature of many judicial approaches to bills of rights, but they are antithetical to the democratic basis of human rights legislation through which legislative assemblies seek to determine the scope and boundaries of rights with some precision.

This does not mean that human rights legislation is to be interpreted 'stingily',[28] or that where judges do have good reason to resort to broad-based judicial reasoning they should not resort to principles drawn from legislation as well as principles drawn from common law. Where gaps in the law need to be filled, there is no reason to exclude principles embodied in legislation from the relevant judicial reasoning. It is not the role of human rights legislation, however, to provide the basis for a new source of judicial creativity. That is to go down the bill of rights path.[29] Human rights legislation is not characterised principally by broad statements of principle that invite judicial law-making. The principles involved in human rights legislation are there to provide the context that helps to give meaning to the rules established in the legislation, not to give the courts a basis for delegated law-making. Formally good legislation not only identifies goals but lays down how and to what extent those goals be pursued, by establishing clear rules that are designed to capture the parameters of the right that the legislature intended to enact. The high priority given to such legislation is operationalised in terms of the superiority of its rules when they come into conflict with other enactments or common law decisions.

Three issues remain to be resolved in order to render the strategy of protecting human rights by human rights legislation feasible: (a) Can human rights legislation be distinguished from ordinary legislation? (b) Can human rights be reduced to specific rules that can be applied without recourse to moral and other disputable judgments? (c) Can human rights legislation be privileged without engendering new anti-democratic objections?

## CAN HUMAN RIGHTS LEGISLATION BE DISTINGUISHED FROM ORDINARY LEGISLATION?

Human rights legislation could be distinguished simply by the constitutional priority that is given to it, but this does not help us determine which legislation ought to be given such priority. That could readily be settled by identifying human rights legislation as legislation that is designed to and explicitly does seek

---

26 *Ibid*, 1225–26.

27 *Ibid*, 1247. Here this term is used to identify purposive, developmental, progressive and liberal methods of judicial interpretation: 'Super-statutes should be construed liberally and in a common law way, but in light of the statutory purpose and principle as well as compromises suggested by statutory texts.'

28 *Ibid*, 1226.

29 *Ibid*, 1265: the authors cite the UK Human Rights Act 1998 as an example of a super-statute that has quasi-constitutional status, and note that the judiciary assumes that such a statute should be interpreted 'liberally and imperially'.

to implement international treaty obligations with respect to international human rights law. This would identify human rights legislation through its origins in international law. A paradigm Australian example would be the Racial Discrimination Act 1975, a type of legislation that has been enacted in many jurisdictions in order to implement the Covenant Against All Forms of Racial Discrimination. For one selection of what might count as human rights legislation, see David Kinley.[30]

This approach, neat as it is, cannot purport to define human rights legislation exclusively. Not every article of the Universal Declaration on Human Rights (UDHR) or the two covenants (the International Covenant on Civil and Political Rights and the International Covenant on Economic, Social and Cultural Rights) has given rise to a convention, and many conventions, such as the Convention Against All Forms of Discrimination Against Women, are designed to supplement rather than explicate the UDHR and the Covenants.

However, if we take a broad view and include in human rights legislation any statutes that promote ends identified as human rights in the UDHR, for instance, then this has the potential to include all statutory provisions relating to the protection of life, physical integrity, property and basic welfare. On this approach, almost any legislation might count, at least in part, as human rights legislation.[31] Certainly, any government seeking to respect the UDHR could treat the basic provisions of its Crimes Act as human rights legislation. The right to life requires at least the prohibition and punishment of murder, and on a broad reading of the UDHR it would be possible to regard criminal law as an extended exercise in rendering certain human rights more specific and better protected. A similar approach to any area of law may be taken, rendering the boundary between human rights and ordinary legislation nugatory, especially if we give equal status to social, economic and cultural rights, along with the more traditional and generally prioritised civil and political rights.

However, in addition to identifying whole Acts as human rights legislation it would be possible to specify certain sections or clauses of Acts as dealing with human rights matters, thereby signalling its special status as human rights legislation. Thus, in relation to criminal law, human rights legislation could be identified as that part dealing with due process safeguards as are identified in the International Covenant on Civil and Political Rights, such as the minimum safeguards for accused persons listed in Art 14(3), which are required as part of the right to a fair trial.

Such a process of picking and choosing is dauntingly complex and controversial and would not be worth undertaking unless the benefits were evident and significant. This suggests it would be wise to retreat to a positivist bedrock for which the process of selection could be the international agreements entered into by the government concerned that are uncontroversially identifiable as dealing with human rights. This does not entail accepting as definitive of human rights all rights-oriented international legal sources, such as the case law

---

30 D Kinley (ed), *Human Rights in Australian Law*, Sydney: Federation Press, 1998.
31 *Ibid*.

emanating from the application of bills of rights in different jurisdictions, although such material could be relevant to the moral and political choices involved in identifying human rights legislation that is not treaty based.

On the other hand, it seems inadequate simply to accept the external authority of international human rights treaties or judicial views as to what counts as a human right, as exhaustive of what can be counted as human rights legislation. The content and boundaries of human rights are questions of moral and political substance on which there is reasonable disagreement of a sort that, according to human rights principles, ought to be settled by democratic process. Each jurisdiction must determine for itself what it counts as a human right, and what it means to identify something as a human right. It is an integral part of the idea of having human rights legislation rather than bills of rights that this gives the opportunity to determine the operative content of these categories through the democratic deliberative and decision-making processes of each self-determining jurisdiction. The fact that there can be reasonable disagreement as to what counts as a human right does not disable polities for developing and changing their own views on such matters and making clear legal determinations on what is and what is not to count as human right legislation through explicit textual determinations. Giving human rights responsibility to individual nation states is undermined by external determinations of what counts as a human right.

## CAN HUMAN RIGHTS BE REDUCED TO SPECIFIC RULES THAT CAN BE APPLIED WITHOUT RECOURSE TO MORAL JUDGMENTS?

If human rights are affirmations of fundamental interests that ought to have priority protection in all jurisdictions, then they would appear to be, at base value, affirmations. There are a number of problems this raises for the concept of human rights legislation, principally (a) questions about the moral status of human rights, (b) the abstract formulation of most statements of human rights, and (c) the particular lack of specificity of human rights with respect to the correlative duties implied by rights discourse.[32]

### The moral status of human rights

It may be argued that human rights are moral affirmations that cannot be captured in a body of specific and clear rules, particularly if they are to be applicable without the exercise of moral judgment as to their content. The right to a decent standard of living, for instance, incorporates a moral term ('decent') that is empirically imprecise and depends on judgments as to what are morally acceptable living conditions for any human being in different types of economies. On this view, the whole enterprise of human rights legislation is misguided. Human rights are broad moral principles, not empirically applicable rules.

---

32 TD Campbell, *op cit* fn 4.

One response to this line of argument is to point out that some human rights are given precise descriptive content. That there shall be no capital punishment is an example already mentioned. That there shall be two weeks holiday with pay is another precise requirement laid down in the UDHR. However, with respect to human rights, such precision is relatively uncommon, and such provisions as a requirement for two weeks holiday with pay have been strongly criticised as inappropriate precisely because of their specificity, which undermines the universality, and in this case also the fundamental importance, of human rights.[33]

However, the counter-examples given do suggest that there is no intrinsic problem in rendering human rights not only specific but morally neutral with respect to the content of the criteria used to identify the prescribed right. There is little descriptive dispute as to what is and what is not capital punishment. There is a lack of descriptive clarity as to what counts as leisure for the purpose of a right to leisure, but not as to what counts as two weeks holiday per year. Further, the development of human rights from the UDHR onwards can be seen as a process of increasing empirical specificity through the adoption of more specialised international instruments and a developing case law.

Of course, this move to specification in non-moral categories can itself be criticised as an unwarranted positivising of human rights. Certainly, there are reasons for disquiet if human rights are simply identified with positive law, even positive international human rights law, especially if it is evolving in the direction of codes of rules.[34] There will always be a need to use human rights morally to criticise such positive concretised human rights law as failing to meet proper human rights standards.

We have here a dilemma for human rights discourse. When states accept the broad principles of human rights, such as the right to life or the right to equality before the law, but deny that they are violating such rights by, for instance, having capital punishment or failing to provide legal aid to accused persons, it becomes necessary to spell out in more detail what it is that these rights require of us, hence the drive to specificity. However, to identify a human right with very particular matters, such as a particular abortion regime, seems to undermine the critical role of human rights discourse.

The way forward here is to combine affirmations of human rights values, such as equal worth, respect for persons, human dignity and autonomy (and perhaps embody them in a non-justiciable democratic bill of rights for the guidance of legislatures and governments), with specifications of what these values require in terms of empirically identifiable outcomes in the specific conditions of the societies to which they apply, while keeping such formulations open to constant revision and development. This requires the development of human rights rules,

---

33 M Cranston, *Human Rights Today*, London: Ampersand, 1962, 42.

34 For recent qualms about the legalisation of human rights, see the papers presented at a recent Conference on the Legalisation of Human Rights at University College, London, particularly David Chandler, 'The bureaucratic gaze of international human rights law: a case study of Bosnia', and Anthony Carty, 'Legalisation of human rights discourse in a coercive international legal order'.

rules that have in common their justification by human rights values. This recognises that human rights include but go beyond calls for certain interests to be protected by law and recognises that one means for protecting and furthering such rights is through legal mechanisms. It is these mechanisms, rather than human rights as such, that are to be identified as human rights legislation. At the same time, the basis of all human rights discourse remains a set of moral and political values.

This approach has many advantages. One is that it retains the discourse of rights as a basis for the critique of all law, including constitutional law. Further, it serves to mitigate one of the perennial problems about the concept of human rights, namely the alleged universality of such rights versus the evidently relevant differences between cultures and social systems: the human rights values are universal, while the human rights rules are relative to the type of society, be this defined in terms of its economic system or some broader way.

However, it is clear that the substance of human rights discourse goes beyond universality of values and claims a universality with respect to at least some human rights rules. The right to life does require a general prohibition on killing. Equal worth does require a general prohibition on the use of racial criteria in positive law. Respect for persons is inconsistent with the denial of freedom of expression. Human dignity does require the outlawing of slavery. Autonomy is inseparable from some quite precise democratic rights with respect to freedom of association and the opportunity to vote in elections.

That there is disagreement about human rights rules is undeniable, but it is equally undeniable that the discourse of human rights seeks to go beyond assertions of abstract value to the concretisation of these values in specific demands relating to social, economic and political arrangements in all societies. The moral role of human rights is to support morally irresistible demands for securing concrete protections for certain fundamental human interests. Providing specific rules, compliance with which is determined in an empirically objective manner, is an essential part of a human rights programme. Human rights legislation is, therefore, something human beings have a right to expect, but even this stronger position does not require that human rights are constituted by human rights legislation.

## The abstraction of human rights

The assumption that human rights are essentially abstract, along with the claim that they are moral abstractions, derives in part from the natural rights origins of human rights in political manifestos associated with revolutionary movements to curb or overthrow existing political authorities. To the extent that human rights still have this role, there is reason to focus on abstract moral claims, although these may usefully be combined with more specific demands, such as 'no taxation without representation'. However, the continuing assumption that human rights are essentially abstract moral claims gives support to the belief that the chief function of human rights is to provide courts with moral principles that they can use to correct legislation which they deem to conflict with these values. That is why it is so often assumed that we need bills of rights that are broad value assertions and hesitate to identify human rights with any set of specific rules.

Once we drop this assumption, the way is open for us to seek more precise formulations of human rights as part of what is involved in rendering human rights protectable. Nevertheless, there is danger in identifying human rights with these specific formulations when we use the discourse of rights to critique existing and proposed legislation. This suggests that we need to sustain a constant dialectic between human rights abstractions and more concrete articulations of these values in relation to specific sets of circumstances.

## Open-ended correlative duties

The third reason put forward as to why human rights rules cannot encompass human rights is the openness of rights to the discovery or imposition of new correlative duties. Here we come to a feature of legal norms that cuts across the boundary between legislation and common law. Anglo-American common law is a system that emphasises remedies and causes of action, so that legal rights depend on identifying a prior legal duty, neglect or violation of which has led to a wrong on the basis of which a legal claim may be made for compensation, or legal punishment be administered as the result of a criminal act.

In contrast, what has come to be called a right-based morality starts with the foundational claim that individuals or persons have certain rights, that is, interests, that are or ought to be protected, by law in the case of legal rights. This leaves it an open ended matter as to who has the duties and precisely what these duties might be that are required to protect and further the right in question.[35]

In the case of human rights, it has usually been taken that states are the main bearers of human rights duties, that is, the duties that correlate with human rights, although there is an equally strong assumption that such duties apply to all human beings and human collectives. Nevertheless, states are assumed to have the primary obligation of seeing to it that such universal human rights duties as there may be are respected. This now needs to be supplemented by obligations of non-state actors, such as multinational corporations. Even where there is a fair measure of clarity as to the rights-bearers, there is little that can be assumed about the nature and scope of the duties involved. Thus, governments may accept that they have duties in relation to the right to development, but have very different views about whether these duties are negative or positive, and in either case what these duties might be. The logic of a rights approach is that the right is established before we work out how to go about securing that right.

On this view, human rights legislation could involve the ascription of specific rights, that is, rights to quite specific things and conditions, but would leave it open what this involves by way of correlative duties. Since, by norms of 'good legislation', such legislation would be deficient through its failure to provide a

---

35 DN MacCormick, 'Rights in legislation', in P Hacker and J Raz (eds), *Law, Morality and Society*, Oxford: Clarendon Press, 1977.

basis for regulating human interaction in foreseeable ways, it can be argued that there is an incoherence in the idea of human rights legislation.

It is feasible to rebut this claim by arguing that we have moved beyond this historical stage in the development of human rights and come to realise that their effective protection depends on specifying correlative duties in such a way as to ensure the protection of the relevant interests. If human rights are to be more than pleasing rhetoric, they must be concretised in legislation that is up front on the matter of correlative duties, particularly as governments are by no means the sole source of human rights violations. Any resistance to this development could be put down to a desire to reserve for judiciaries decisions as to what these duties are to be.

However, some concession can be made to the idea of a relatively duty-free rights approach to morals and law by accepting that the concept of rights can usefully be deployed to identify core interests that are protected in a variety of duty-specified ways. Moreover, it is to be expected that the content of these duties must be open to constant revision as these interests are threatened in new ways or new sources of remedial action become available. This, however, argues only for constant and ongoing revision of human rights legislation, particularly with respect to the locus and other details of the correlative rights, and does not involve a rejection of the concept of human rights legislation. Indeed, it strengthens the case for developing human rights legislation to articulate who, in the circumstances of the time, bears the specific correlative obligations.

## CAN HUMAN RIGHTS LEGISLATION BE PRIVILEGED WITHOUT ENGENDERING ANTI-DEMOCRATIC OBJECTIONS?

A third problem that complicates the passage to acceptance of the idea of human rights legislation is that any special status given to such legislation undermines the democracy it is meant to protect and is therefore itself a violation of human rights in much the same way as court-centred bills of rights. The preference for human rights legislation over court-administered bills of rights is based in part on the idea of effective democracy. This in itself is enough to raise questions about the idea of human rights legislation because much human rights discourse is based on a critique of democracy, and this includes a disparagement of legislation in so far as it emanates from the wheelings and dealings of democratic politics.

This is one of the topics explored by Jeremy Waldron in his 'jurisprudence of legislation'.[36] Waldron seeks to re-establish what he calls 'the dignity of legislation' by showing that elected representative legislatures are entitled to respect simply because they are the product of a process that institutionalises the belief that each human being's opinion has equal value and ought to be respected. Standard arguments for court-administered bills of rights systematically disparage democracy by arguing that such bills of rights are necessary for the

---

36 J Waldron, *The Dignity of Legislation*, Cambridge: CUP, 2000.

protection of democracy,[37] thus exhibiting a double standard in both extolling and diminishing democracy. It is not difficult to show, as Waldron does, that there are models of democracy totally different from the caricatures of majoritarian self-interest that are taken for granted in court-administered bills of rights.[38]

Nevertheless, I have argued that there is a need to prevent actual democracies tending towards such aberrant models in which people whose interests are not compatible with those of majorities have those interests discounted simply because of the accidental fact that they are in a minority. The problem is how to counter this tendency without privileging a minority as is the case with a court-administered bill of rights.

One essential ingredient in the strategy for making and keeping democracies more democratic is to foster a culture in which it is accepted that voting ought to be based on opinions as to the common good and impartial social justice and not on calculations of individual or group self-interest. This is not incompatible with using the vote as a source of power to protect certain interests, but these interests must be selected on the basis of their justified importance and not because they just happen to be the interests of the voter. That culture can be fostered in many institutionalised ways. Some of these relate to sustaining such civil and political rights as freedom of speech; others relate to social and economic rights such as education.

Beyond these broad societal prerequisites of an effective democracy, there are many specific constitutional devices that can be deployed to bring systematic institutional pressure to bear on those who neglect the common good by steering the decision-making agenda and its procedures in a certain sort of democratic direction. Some of these devices have presented bills of rights as justified only in so far as it is their function to maintain the conditions of democracy. In the attempt to deal with anti-democratic objections to bills of rights, mechanisms have been suggested and adopted to make legislatures more responsive to human rights and less responsive to sectional interests. These, as we have seen, include scrutiny of bills committees and delaying powers of second chambers.

In the case of court-centred bills of rights, the cure is in general worse than the curse, but it may well be that the less radical devices for discouraging the tendency of majorities towards illegitimate self-interest are not, on balance, anti-democratic devices, if democracy is seen as a model of government that is designed to instantiate equal political power in a system that is committed to justice and human rights. In that context, a constitution that gives power to vulnerable minorities so that they can play a more effective role in determining agendas and debating and delaying certain matters that threaten their wellbeing need not be viewed as a democratic deficiency. Indeed, such procedures can be viewed as ways of enhancing the dignity of legislation and respect for the rule of law.

---

37 JH Ely, *Democracy and Distrust: A Theory of Judicial Review*, Cambridge, MA: Harvard University Press, 1980.

38 TD Campbell, 'Legal positivism and deliberative democracy', *Current Legal Problems*, Vol 15, 1998, 68–92 and J Waldron, *op cit* fn 17.

Perhaps the crucial factor here is how far these devices are imposed through a constitution or common law convention that it is beyond the power of a democratic legislature to change, and how far it is the outcome of self-denying ordinances by the legislatures themselves. Clearly, the latter is democratically preferable, although it may only be feasible in a jurisdiction imbued with a significant human rights culture. The challenge is to promote that culture without weakening those human rights that are enshrined in the democratic rights of citizens. To this end, it is better to give quasi-constitutional status to human rights legislation than to subordinate human rights to judicial power.

# APPENDIX

## PUBLICATIONS BY TOM CAMPBELL

### Books

*Adam Smith's Science of Morals*, London: Allen & Unwin, 1971.
*Seven Theories of Human Society*, Oxford: OUP, 1981 (reprinted 1985, 1989). Spanish edn 1985, Japanese edn 1992.
*The Left and Rights: A Conceptual Analysis of the Idea of Socialist Rights*, London: Routledge and Kegan Paul, 1983.
*Justice*, 2nd edn, London: Macmillan, 1988, 2001.
*Mental Illness: Prejudice, Discrimination and The Law* (with C Heginbotham), Aldershot: Dartmouth, 1991.
*The Legal Theory of Ethical Positivism*, Aldershot: Dartmouth, 1996.

### Edited books

*Human Rights: From Rhetoric to Reality*, London: Blackwell, 1986, co-editors D Goldberg, SAM McLean and T Mullen.
*Law and Enlightenment in Britain*, Aberdeen: Aberdeen University Press, 1991.
*Freedom of Communication*, Aldershot: Dartmouth, 1994, co-editor W Sadurski.
*Legal Positivism*, Aldershot: Dartmouth, 1999.
*Judicial Power, Democracy and Legal Positivism*, Aldershot: Dartmouth, 2000, co-editor J Goldsworthy.
*Human Rights in Philosophy and Practice*, Aldershot: Dartmouth, 2001, co-editor B Leiser.
*Sceptical Essays on Human Rights*, Oxford: OUP, 2001, co-editors KD Ewing and A Tomkins.
*Law and Democracy*, Aldershot: Dartmouth, 2001, co-editor A Stone.
*Legal Interpretation in Democratic States*, Aldershot: Dartmouth, 2001, co-editor J Goldsworthy.
*Protecting Human Rights: Instruments and Institutions*, Oxford: OUP, 2003, co-editors J Goldsworthy and A Stone.
*Human Rights and the Moral Obligations of Corporate and Public Sector Organisations*, Dordrecht: Kluwer, 2004, co-editor S Miller.

### Articles and essays

**1970** 'The normative fallacy', *Philosophical Quarterly*, Vol 20, 1970, 368–77.
**1971** 'John Stuart Mill and freedom of speech', *Il Pensiero Politico*, Vol 4, 1971, 443–50.
**1972** 'On philosophy and relevance', *The Philosophical Journal*, Vol 9, 1972, 130–39.

**1973** 'Formal justice and rule-change', *Analysis*, Vol 33, 1973, 113–18.

**1974** 'Humanity before justice', *British Journal of Political Science*, Vol 4, 1974, 1–16.

'Formal justice and rule-change: a reply', *Analysis*, Vol 35, 1974, 19–21.

'Rights without justice', *Mind*, Vol 83, 1974, 445–48.

'Equality of opportunity', *Proc Aristotelian Society*, Vol 75, 1974, 51–63.

**1975** 'Perfect and imperfect obligation', *Modern Schoolman*, 1975, 285–301.

'Scientific explanation and ethical justification in the moral sentiments', in AS Skinner and T Wilson (eds), *Essays on Adam Smith*, Oxford: Clarendon Press, 1975, 68–82.

**1977** 'Oswald Spengler and the approaching death of western civilisation', *Futures*, Vol 8, 1977, 438–43.

'Punishment in juvenile justice', *Journal of Law and Society*, Vol 4, 1977, 77–86.

'Discretion and rights within the children's hearing system', *Philosophical Journal*, Vol 4, 1977, 1–21.

'Adam Smith and natural liberty', *Political Studies*, Vol 25, 1977, 523–34.

**1978** 'Discretionary rights', in N Timms and D Watson (eds), *Philosophy and Social Work*, London: Routledge and Kegan Paul, 1978, 50–77.

'Antenatal injury and the rights of the foetus', with AJM McKay, *Philosophical Quarterly*, Vol 28, 1978, 17–30.

**1981** 'Counter-productive welfare law', *British Journal of Political Science*, Vol 11, 1981, 331–50.

'The utilitarianism of Adam Smith's policy advice', with IS Ross, *Journal of the History of Ideas*, Vol 42, 1981, 73–92.

'Sterilisation', with SAM McLean, in SAM McLean (ed), *Legal Issues in Medicine*, Aldershot: Gower Press, 1981, 176–90.

**1982** 'The socialist concepts of rights', *Bulletin of the Australian Society of Legal Philosophy*, Vol 23, 1982, 72–104.

'The theory and practice of the wise and virtuous man', with IS Ross, *Studies in Eighteenth-Century Culture*, Vol 11, 1982, 65–74.

'Frances Hutcheson: father of the Scottish Enlightenment', in RH Campbell and AS Skinner (eds), *The Origins and Nature of the Scottish Enlightenment*, Edinburgh: John Donald, 1982, 167–85.

**1984** 'Adam Smith and the economic analysis of law', in V Hope (ed), *Philosophers of the Scottish Enlightenment*, Edinburgh: Edinburgh University Press, 1984, 133–56.

'Compensation as punishment', *University of New South Wales Law Journal*, Vol 7, 1984, 338–61.

**1985** 'The rights' approach to mental health', in A Phillips Griffiths (ed), *Philosophy and Practice*, Cambridge: CUP, 1985, 221–54.

'Is special legislation for the mentally ill ethically defensible?', in K Jensen and B Pedersen (eds), *Commitment and Civil Rights of the Mentally Ill*, Copenhagen: Sind, 1985, 84–93.

'Philosophy, ideology and rights', *Legal Studies*, Vol 5, 1985, 10–19.

'Ethical positivism', *Archives for Philosophy of Law and Social Philosophy*, 1985, 67–70.

**1986** 'Realizing human rights', in TD Campbell, D Goldberg, SAM McLean and T Mullen (eds), *Human Rights, from Rhetoric to Reality*, London: Blackwell, 1986, 2–13.

'The rights of the mentally ill', in TD Campbell *et al* (eds), *Human Rights from Rhetoric to Reality*, London: Blackwell, 1986, 124–47.

'Can law control force?', in J Dewar, A Paliwala, S Picciotto and M Ruete (eds), *Nuclear Weapons, the Peace Movement and the Law*, London: Macmillan, 1986, 72–88.

'Power and resistance: a legal perspective', *Societas Ethica Jahresbericht*, 1986, 29–51.

**1988** 'Mistaking the relevance of gender', in N Burrows and SAM McLean (eds), *The Legal Relevance of Gender*, Basingstoke: Macmillan, 1988, 16–39.

**1990** 'Obligation: societal, political and legal', in P Harris (ed), *On Political Obligation*, London: Routledge, 1990, 120–50.

'Liberalism and the law of contract', in A Gamble (ed), *Obligations in Context*, Edinburgh: W Green, 1990, 111–25.

**1991** 'Markets and justice', in *Justice and the Market*, Centre for Theology and Public Issues, Edinburgh: University of Edinburgh, 1991, 18–27.

**1992** 'Discrimination', in W Sadurski (ed), *Moral Values and Legal Theory*, Amsterdam: Rodolpi, 1992, 153–70.

'The rights of the minor: as person, as child, as adolescent and as future adult', *International Journal of Law and the Family*, 1992, 1–23.

'Collecting legal theories', *Current Legal Theory*, 1992, 17–32.

'Ethical markets', *Archives for Philosophy of Law and Social Philosophy*, 1992, 201–07.

**1993** 'Legal studies', in R Goodin and P Pettit (eds), *A Companion to Contemporary Political Philosophy*, London: Blackwell, 1993, 183–211.

**1994** 'Legal change and legal theory', in W Krawietz *et al* (eds), *Prescriptive Formality and Normative Rationality in Modern Legal Systems*, Berlin: Dunker and Humbolt, 1994, 605–30.

'Democracy, human rights and positive law', *Sydney Law Review*, Vol 16, 1994, 195–212.

'Free speech rationales', in TD Campbell and W Sadurski (eds), *Freedom of Communication*, Aldershot: Dartmouth, 1994, 17–44.

'Real rights for children', *International Journal of Children's Rights*, Vol 2, 1994, 259–63.

'Mental health law: institutionalised discrimination', *Australian and New Zealand Journal of Psychiatry*, 1994, 1–6.

'Communication rights: defaming free speech', in R Martin and G Sprengher (eds), *Rights*, Stuttgart: Franz Steiner, 18–25.

**1996** 'Conceptions of equality and the functions of quotas', in *Quoten und Gleichstellung von Frau und Mann*, Zurich: Helbing & Lichtenhahn, 1996, 55–70.

**1997** 'Judicial powers', in A Vincent (ed), *Political Theory: Tradition, Diversity and Ideology*, Cambridge: CUP, 1997, 172–91.

'Human rights, humane values and positive law', in J Tasioulas (ed), *Law, Values and Social Practices*, Aldershot: Dartmouth, 1997, 99–128.

**1998** 'The point of legal positivism', *King's College Law Review*, Vol 9, 1998, 63–87.

'Moral autonomy for lawyers', *Legal Ethics*, Vol 1, 1998, 201–12.

'Legal positivism and deliberative democracy', *Current Legal Problems*, Vol 15, 1998, 68–92.

'Consensus and pluralism in law', in AJ Armaud and P Koller (eds), *Justice and Culture*, Stuttgart: Franz Steiner, 1998, 19–23.

**1999** 'Human rights: a culture of controversy', *Journal of Law and Society*, Vol 26, 1999, 6–22.

'The ethical costs of health care', *Australian Journal of Law and Medicine*, Vol 8, 1999, 191–92.

**2000** 'Democratic aspects of legal positivism', in TD Campbell and J Goldsworthy (eds), *Judicial Power, Democracy and Legal Positivism*, Aldershot: Dartmouth, 2000, 3–36.

'Foreclosures', *Australian Journal of Legal Philosophy*, Vol 25, 2000, 235–42.

**2001** 'Democracy in a world of global markets', in C Sampford and T Round (eds), *Beyond the Republic*, Sydney: Federation Press, 2001.

'Law and morality', in NJ Smelser and PB Bates (eds), *International Encyclopedia of the Social and Behavioral Sciences*, Amsterdam: Elsevier, 2001.

'Democratising human rights', in TD Campbell and B Leiser (eds), *Human Rights in Philosophy and Practice*, Aldershot: Dartmouth, 2001.

'Legislative intent and democratic decision-making', in N Naffine, R Owens and J Williams (eds), *Intention in Law and Philosophy*, Aldershot: Dartmouth, 2001.

'Incorporation through interpretation', in TD Campbell, KD Ewing and A Tomkins (eds), *Sceptical Essays on Human Rights*, Oxford: OUP, 2001, 79–102.

'Human rights and the partial eclipse of justice', in A Soeteman (ed), *Pluralism and Law*, Dordrecht: Kluwer, 2001.

**2002** 'Grounding theories of interpretation', in J Goldsworthy and TD Campbell (eds), *Legal Interpretation in Democratic States*, Aldershot: Dartmouth, 2002, 29–44.

**2003** 'Judicial activism: justice or treason?', *University of Otago Law Journal*, Vol 10, 2003, 307–26.

'Human rights: the shifting boundaries', in TD Campbell, J Goldsworthy and A Stone (eds), *Protecting Human Rights: Institutions and Boundaries*, Oxford: OUP, 17–38.

'Blaming legal positivism', *Australian Journal of Legal Philosophy*, Vol 28, 2003, 31–38.

**2004** 'The equal worth project', in K Horton and H Patapan (eds), *Globalisation and Inequality*, London: Routledge, 2004.

'The rights factor in management', *Philosophy of Management*, 2004.

# Index